THE GOVERNANCE OF MACROPRUDENTIAL POLICY

This book critically examines the theoretical foundations and legal framework for macroprudential policy, its tools and governance in the UK, the US and the EU. It goes deeper into a normative discussion of the legitimacy of macroprudential policy in these jurisdictions, where the mandate for maintaining financial stability has been delegated to independent authorities.

The Global Financial Crisis of 2007–2008 reopened debates regarding legitimacy of the independent regulatory state, given its democratic deficit. The response to a perceived legitimacy gap has been to increase political oversight in financial policymaking and regulation. The book posits that the real problem is not a lack of democracy, but rather a lack of social justice. Across the globe, there is growing dissatisfaction with a financial system and regulatory process that appear depersonalised and perpetuate inequalities. Citizens are calling for more socially just systems of governance and the future success of financial policymakers and regulators will hinge on this. Given the marked distributional effects that have been noted in some macroprudential policy tools, the book questions whether macroprudential policy should be solely based on highly rationalised and strongly quantitative reasons.

By proposing that macroprudential policymakers should have a social justice mandate alongside their financial stability mandate, as well as legal mechanisms for operationalising the added authority, the book contributes to the growing discourse on the role of social justice in public policy.

Hart Studies in Commercial and Financial Law: Volume 12

Hart Studies in Commercial and Financial Law
Series Editors: John Linarelli and Teresa Rodríguez de las Heras Ballell

This series offers a venue for publishing works on commercial law as well as on the regulation of banking and finance and the law on insolvency and bankruptcy. It publishes works on the law on secured credit, the regulatory and transactional aspects of banking and finance, the transactional and regulatory institutions for financial markets, legal and policy aspects associated with access to commercial and consumer credit, new generation subjects having to do with the institutional architecture associated with innovation and the digital economy including works on blockchain technology, work on the relationship of law to economic growth, the harmonisation or unification of commercial law, transnational commercial law, and the global financial order. The series promotes interdisciplinary work. It publishes research on the law using the methods of empirical legal studies, behavioural economics, political economy, normative welfare economics, law and society inquiry, socio-legal studies, political theory, and historical methods. Its coverage includes international and comparative investigations of areas of law within its remit.

Volume 1: The Financialisation of the Citizen: Social and Financial Inclusion through European Private Law
Guido Comparato

Volume 2: MiFID II and Private Law: Enforcing EU Conduct of Business Rules
Federico Della Negra

Volume 3: Reforming Corporate Retail Investor Protection: Regulating to Avert Mis-Selling
Diane Bugeja

Volume 4: The Future of Commercial Law: Ways Forward for Change and Reform
Edited by Orkun Akseli and John Linarelli

Volume 5: The Cape Town Convention: A Documentary History
Anton Didenko

Volume 6: Regulating the Crypto Economy: Business Transformations and Financialisation
Iris H-Y Chiu

Volume 7: The Future of High-Cost Credit: Rethinking Payday Lending
Jodi Gardner

Volume 8: The Enforcement of EU Financial Law
Edited by Jan Crijns, Matthias Haentjens and Rijnhard Haentjens

Volume 9: International Bank Crisis Management: A Transatlantic Perspective
Marco Bodellini

Volume 10: Creditor Priority in European Bank Insolvency Law: Financial Stability and the Hierarchy of Claims
Sjur Swensen Ellingsæter

Volume 11: Chinese and Global Financial Integration through Stock Connect: A Legal Analysis
Flora Huang

Volume 12: The Governance of Macroprudential Policy: How to Build Regulatory Legitimacy Through a Social Justice Approach
Tracy C Maguze

The Governance of Macroprudential Policy

How to Build Regulatory Legitimacy Through a Social Justice Approach

Tracy C Maguze

•HART•

OXFORD • LONDON • NEW YORK • NEW DELHI • SYDNEY

HART PUBLISHING

Bloomsbury Publishing Plc

Kemp House, Chawley Park, Cumnor Hill, Oxford, OX2 9PH, UK

1385 Broadway, New York, NY 10018, USA

29 Earlsfort Terrace, Dublin 2, Ireland

First published in Great Britain 2024

A catalogue record for this book is available from the British Library.

A catalogue record for this book is available from the Library of Congress.

Library of Congress Control Number: 2023944891

ISBN: HB: 978-1-50996-839-8
ePDF: 978-1-50996-841-1
ePub: 978-1-50996-840-4

Typeset by Compuscript Ltd, Shannon

To Rosewitter and Douglas

CONTENTS

LIST OF ABBREVIATIONS

AFR	Americans for Financial Reform
ASC	Advisory Scientific Committee
ATC	Advisory Technical Committee
BCBS	Basel Committee on Banking Supervision
BHC	Bank Holding Company
BIS	Bank for International Settlements
BoE	Bank of England
CBA	Cost-Benefit Analysis
CCB	Capital Conservation Buffer
CCyB	Countercyclical Capital Buffer
CHIPS	Clearing House interbank Payment System
CPSS	Committee on Payment and Settlement Systems
CRD IV	Capital Requirements Directive
CRR	Capital Requirements Regulation
D-SIB	Domestic Systemically Important Bank
DNB	De Nederlandsche Bank
DSTI	Debt-Service-to-Income
DTI	Debt-to-Income
EBA	European Banking Authority
ECB	European Central Bank
EFFR	Europeans for Financial Reform
EIOPA	European Insurance and Occupational Pensions Authority
ESA	European Supervisory Authorities
ESCB	European System of Central Banks

ESFS	European System of Financial Supervision
ESMA	European Securities and Markets Authority
ESRB	European Systemic Risk Board
EU	European Union
EUMR	European Union Merger Regulations
Fannie Mae	Federal National Mortgage Association
FCA	Financial Conduct Authority
FDIC	Federal Deposit Insurance Corporation
Fed	Federal Reserve System
FMU	Financial Market Utility
FPC	Financial Policy Committee
Freddie Mac	Federal Home Loan Mortgage Corporation
FRTB	Fundamental Review of The Trading Book
FSA	Financial Services Authority
FSAP	Financial Sector Assessment Program
FSB	Financial Stability Board
FSOC	Financial Stability Oversight Council
FSR	Financial Stability Report
FX	Foreign Exchange
G-SIB	Global Systemically Important Bank
G-SII	Globally Systemically Important Institution
G10	Group of 10
G20	Group of 20
G30	Group of 30
G7	Group of 7
GDP	Gross Domestic Product
GFC	Global Financial Crisis
HMT	Her Majesty's Treasury

IAIS	International Association of Insurance Supervisors
ICAAP	Internal Capital Adequacy Assessment Process
ICR	Interest Coverage Ratio
IMF	International Monetary Fund
IOSCO	International Organisation of Securities Commissions
IRB	Internal Ratings-Based Approach
IRC	Incremental Risk Capital Charge
JST	Joint Supervisory Team
LCR	Liquidity Coverage Ratio
LGD	Loss Given Default
LTD	Loan-to-Deposit
LTI	Loan-to-Income
LTV	Loan-to-Value
MCA	Multi-criteria Analysis
MRA	Market Risk Amendment
NCA	National Competent Authority
NCB	National Central Bank
NSFR	Net Stable Funding Ratio
O-SII	Other Systemically Important Institution
OCC	Office of the Comptroller of the Currency
OECD	Organisation for Economic Co-operation and Development
OfCom	Office of Communications
OFR	Office of Financial Research
PRA	Prudential Regulation Authority
RBNZ	Reserve Bank of New Zealand
RTGS	Real Time Gross Settlement
RWCR	Risk-weighted Capital Requirements
SEC	Securities Exchange Commission
SIB	Systemically Important Bank

SIFI	Systemically Important Financial Institution
SRB	Systemic Risk Buffer
SREP	Supervisory Review and Examination Process
SSM	Single Supervisory Mechanism
SSMFR	Single Supervisory Mechanism Framework Regulation
SSMR	Single Supervisory Mechanism Regulation
Target	Trans-European Automated Real-time Gross Settlements Express Transfer
TBTF	Too-Big-to-Fail
TFEU	Treaty on the Functioning of the European Union
TSC	Treasury Select Committee
UK	United Kingdom
US	Unites States of America
VaR	Value at Risk

LIST OF FIGURES

LIST OF TABLES

TABLE OF LEGISLATION AND TREATIES

European Union Legislation

United Kingdom Legislation

Rules, Statutes, Decisions and Resolutions of International Organisations

1

Introduction

In the years leading up to the global financial crisis of 2007–2008, (GFC), most politicians and financial regulators from developed economies did not believe that the financial markets were heating up or that a collapse was imminent. Or even if they were aware of this, they chose not to believe that the financial system was taking on potentially dangerous levels of risk, that a credit and housing bubble was forming and the world should expect a 'nightmare hard-landing scenario' when the bubble burst.[1] In fact, they bravely encouraged competition to flourish in the markets, with little government intervention, since this was thought to undermine market efficiency, believing instead in the rationality of individuals.[2] Their claims were taken as legitimate, until they were not.

It all began unravelling in 2007, after a downturn in the US housing market generated widespread liquidity problems, which spread to other parts of the world through interlinkages in the global financial system. The crisis peaked in 2008 with the collapse, or near collapse, of numerous financial institutions, most notably Lehman Brothers.[3] The global financial crisis was a banking crisis, which became a sovereign debt crisis in 2010. Financial crises can be categorised as sovereign debt crises; banking crises; exchange rate crises; or crises marked by bouts of very high inflation.[4] A common characteristic in all these crises is that they are preceded by

[1] For instance, Raghuram Rajan's warnings that the financial system was taking on potentially dangerous levels of risk were largely dismissed, Robert Shiller cautioned a housing bubble in the US but also went unheeded, Nouriel Roubini was dubbed 'Dr Doom' by the media for his predictions that the bubble would eventually burst and its effect would spread to other areas of the financial system, the US economy and eventually the rest of the world. See P Krugman, 'How Did Economists Get It So Wrong?' *New York Times* (6 September 2009) Available at: www.nytimes.com/2009/09/06/magazine/06Economic-t.html.

[2] This is the essence of the neoliberal economic theory, which has dominated economic policy making since the 1980s, and has also been adopted as a political ideology in developed western economies. Broadly, neoliberal theories extol the virtues of allocation of goods and services by competitive markets, directed by rational individuals, and suppressed regulation of economic activity by the state. See A Saad-Filho and D Johnston (eds), *Neoliberalism: A Critical Reader* (Pluto Press, 2005) and S Springer, K Birch and J MacLeavy, *Handbook of Neoliberalism* (Routledge, 2016).

[3] For a chronological account of the global financial crisis see A Hausman and WJ Johnston, 'Timeline of a Financial Crisis: Introduction to the Special Issue' (2014) 67 *Journal of Business Research* 2667.

[4] C Reinhart and K Rogoff, *This Time Is Different: Eight Century of Financial Folly* (Princeton University Press, 2009).

a period where credit is more widely available in the system, usually funded by foreign capital inflows.[5] The episode brought financial stability into sharper focus.

In the aftermath of the GFC, numerous enquiries were launched, which pointed to equally numerous causes for this financial instability. It is beyond the scope of this work to detail all of the causes that have been put forward, suffice to say, they can be categorised as causes emanating from the macroeconomic environment; causes arising from the risk taking and borrowing trends of individuals, and banks; market reliance on credit rating agencies; failures in corporate governance; and regulatory failures.[6] Of all these causes, regulatory failures have received considerable attention.[7]

1.1. The Regulation of Financial Stability

1.1.1. The Not-so-prudent Microprudential Regulation

Regulation of financial stability in the pre-crisis era was framed in relation to the stability of individual financial institutions. Traditionally, such regulation was directed at banks and was managed using the microprudential regulatory templates developed under the Basel Capital Accords. Broadly, the microprudential approach requires individual banks to calculate and set aside additional equity capital to cover their credit, liquidity, market and operational risks, which may build up over time. Pre-crisis microprudential regulation, however, suffered from major flaws, which had to do with either what it did or neglected to do. Its most fundamental flaw was its square focus on the safety and soundness of individual banks to ensure stability of the whole system, the composition fallacy as articulated by Brunnermeir et al.[8]

[5] C Kindleberger and R Aliber, *Manias, Panics and Crashes: A History of Financial Crises* 6th edn (Palgrave McMillan, 2011), Chapter 2.

[6] For more detailed exploration of the causes see O Merrouche and E Nier 'What Caused the Global Financial Crisis: Evidence on the Drivers of Financial Imbalances 1999–2007' (December 2010) IMF Working Papers WP/10/265. Available at: www.imf.org/en/Publications/WP/Issues/2016/12/31/What-Caused-the-Global-Financial-Crisis-Evidence-on-the-Drivers-of-Financial-Imbalances-1999-24370; United States Financial Crisis Inquiry Committee, *The Financial Crisis Inquiry Report* (U.S. Government Printing Office, 2011); European Parliament Special Committee on the Financial, Economic and Social Crisis, *Documentation Relating to the Committee's Work from October 2009 to July 2011* (European Parliament, 2011). See also series of reports of the House of Commons Treasury Committee Inquiry into the Banking Crisis published during 2009. Available at: www.parliament.uk/business/committees/committees-a-z/commons-select/treasury-committee/inquiries1/parliament-2005/banking-crisis/.

[7] House of Representatives Committee on Oversight and Government Reform, 'The Financial Crisis and The Role of Federal Regulator' (Serial No 110–209, US Government Printing Office 23 October 2008); Treasury Committee, *Banking Crisis: Regulation and Supervision* (HC 2008-09 767).

[8] MK Brunnermeier et al, *The Fundamental Principles of Financial Regulation* (International Centre for Monetary and Banking Studies/Centre for Economic Policy Research, 2009).

Microprudential regulation assumed that the rational actions of one market actor were indicative of the prudent behaviour of the rest of the market, but this ignored the fact that even seemingly rational behaviour in managing risk can have a negative impact on the rest of the system. For instance, if a systemically important bank reduces lending in response to loan losses, this can have a negative downstream effect on all other banks in the system that either borrowed from it or lent it funds. Following the fortunes of individual institutions also made micro regulation procyclical, it tightened requirements at the bottom of the credit cycle when banks' activities were considered risky, and loosened them in good times, feeding into the euphoria that creates a credit boom and amplifies the risks attendant to banking over time.

Even if it could be assumed that focusing on individual banks may be enough to ensure financial stability, the models used to calculate minimum capital requirements were flawed. The models calculated asset prices based on data from too short a period, which also happened to be a period of exuberance; they did not capture correlations among assets, neither did they capture tail risk (so called fat tails or black swans); they focused on credit risk and did not pay enough attention to market risk, even though asset price changes can be dangerous since bank assets are marked to market; they completely ignored liquidity risk; and, lastly, they did not measure endogenous risk, namely the impact of individual actions on other institutions and the market.[9]

All these flaws were compounded by the knowledge gaps suffered by regulators, either because they lacked the proper analytical tools or simply, as Avgouleas charges, they lacked the intellectual curiosity to delve deeper into the emerging complex system. This meant they could not spot risks on trading book, off-balance sheet exposures, complex structured products, over-the-counter instruments, and systemically important non-bank financial institutions.[10]

Changes to microprudential regulation were introduced via Basel III, which increased capital buffers, introduced liquidity requirements, and placed caps on leverage. There was a consensus after the crisis that a policy and regulatory framework dedicated to financial stability was required, which hitherto had been directed by a combination of monetary policy and microprudential regulation.[11] This is

[9] See J Danielson, 'The Emperor has no Clothes: Limits to Risk Modelling' (2002) 26 *Journal of Banking and Finance* 1252; MK Brunnermeier and LH Pedersen 'Market Liquidity and Funding Liquidity' (2009) 22 *Review of Financial Studies* 2201; M Hellwig, 'Capital Regulation after the Crisis: Business as Usual?' (2010) 2010/31 *Preprints of the Max Planck Institute for Research on Collective Goods Bonn*; E Avgouleas, *Governance of Global Financial Markets: The Law the Economics the Politics* (Cambridge University Press, 2012).

[10] Avgouleas, *Governance of Global Financial Markets* 138–42.

[11] Financial Services Authority, *The Turner Review: A Regulatory Response to the Global Banking Crisis* (FSA, 2009); Group of 20, 'The Global Plan for Recovery and Reform' (Final communiqué of meeting of G20 Leaders in London, 2 April 2009); De Larosière Group, *Report of the High-Level Group on Financial Supervision in the EU* (European Commission, 2009); S Claessens and L Kodres, 'The Regulatory Responses to the Global Financial Crisis: Some Uncomfortable Questions' (March 2014) IMF Working Paper WP/14/46. Available at: www.imf.org/external/pubs/ft/wp/2014/wp1446.pdf.

not to say that financial stability was not a concern in the pre-crisis era. Financial stability began to receive more attention from policy makers in the early 2000s and Crockett attributes this evolution to financial liberalisation and technological innovation.[12] Liberalisation and innovation increased liquidity, and therefore the potential for leveraging by financial intermediaries; as well as competitive pressures, and the temptation to improve returns by taking on added risk. As financial institutions grew bigger, the value of the implicit safety net provided by government also increased, leading to mispricing of risk. Finally, increased movement of capital also extended and tightened financial linkages across institutions, markets and countries.[13]

Policy makers have long since recognised the usefulness of broad oversight structures to track emerging vulnerabilities in the financial system. Starting at international level, the G7 Finance Ministers and Central Bank governors established the Financial Stability Forum (now renamed the Financial Stability Board), whose role was to enhance cooperation among national and international supervisors and promote financial stability.[14] At national level, many central banks also began to track vulnerabilities in the financial system, as evidenced by an increase in the number of financial stability reports. In 1995 not one central bank had issued such a report; by the end of 2005, 50 central banks had published reports detailing their assessment of financial stability.[15] Unfortunately, simply tracking vulnerabilities in the financial system did not go far enough. Policy makers have now turned to macroprudential policy, to identify and act upon imbalances and risk concentrations that may threaten financial stability; new authorities have been created to craft and implement macroprudential policy.

1.1.2. Macroprudential Policy to the Rescue

The term 'macroprudential' is by no means a new concept; it predates the 2008 financial crisis and can be traced as far back as the 1970s, when it was used to define financial system stability in relation to the broader macroeconomy.[16] Clement provides a concise history of the term's usage at the international level and notes

[12] A Crockett, 'International Standard Setting in Financial Supervision' (Lecture at Cass Business School, City University, London, 5 February 2003). Available at: www.bis.org/speeches/sp030205.htm.

[13] ibid.

[14] See www.fsb.org/about/history/.

[15] M Čihák, 'How Do Central Banks Write on Financial Stability?' (June 2006) IMF Working Paper WP/06/163. Available at: www.imf.org/external/pubs/ft/wp/2006/wp06163.pdf. For instance, the Bank of England began issuing Financial Stability Reviews in 2000, while the ECB published their Financial Stability Reports in 2004. Surprisingly, the US, one of the world's biggest economies, only joined the stability report trend much later in the game in 2011. See M Čihák, S Muñoz, S Teh Sharifuddin, and K Tintchev, 'Financial Stability Reports: What Are They Good For? (January 2012) IMF Working Paper WP/12. Available at: www.imf.org/external/pubs/ft/wp/2012/wp1201.pdf.

[16] P Clement, 'The Term 'Macroprudential': Origins and Evolution' (March 2010) *BIS Quarterly Review* 59. Available at: www.bis.org/publ/qtrpdf/r_qt1003h.pdf.

that, when the term made its first public appearance at a meeting of the Cooke Committee, it was related to the rapid rate of lending to developing countries. In subsequent appearances, the term macroprudential emerged in discussions relating to the use of prudential measures to constrain lending,[17] the impact of financial innovation on capital markets,[18] how banks were functioning in sectors beyond banking and the relationships between the various interbank markets,[19] the derivatives markets[20] and effective bank supervision.[21] At the beginning of the decade that saw the crisis, the macroprudential approach received new impetus from Andrew Crockett at an International Conference of Banking Supervisors in 2000, when he called for a strengthening of the macroprudential perspective in order to achieve financial stability.[22]

The precise definition of macroprudential policy, as utilised in the post-GFC era, tends to vary with the context. It is most commonly defined as the use of primarily prudential tools to limit system-wide financial risk to prevent disruption to key financial services and the economy.[23] It represents a departure from micro-prudential regulation in that its aim is to limit system-wide risk, as opposed to risk in individual institutions, and it covers the whole financial system, including how the system affects and is affected by the real economy. However, like micro-prudential supervision, it primarily relies on prudential regulatory tools, typically (countercyclical) capital and reserve requirements, but also, inter alia, caps on loan-to-value ratios and sectorial loan limits, which target the asset side of banks' balance sheets.[24]

As Dalhuisen first pointed out, macroprudential policy is properly classified as a macroeconomic policy, at par with monetary policy and fiscal policy,

[17] A Lamfalussy, 'The Use of Prudential Measures in the International Banking Markets' (24 October 1979) BISA 7.18(15) – Papers Lamfalussy, LAM25/F67.

[18] Bank for International Settlements, *Recent Innovations in International Banking* (Cross Report) (BIS, 1986).

[19] Bank for International Settlements, *Recent Developments in International Bank Relation* (Promisel Report) (BIS, 1992).

[20] Bank for International Settlements, *Issues Related to The Measurement of Market Size and Macroprudential Risks in Derivatives Markets* (Brockmeijer Report) (BIS, 1995).

[21] C Lindgren and D Folkerts-Landau, *Toward a Framework for a Sound Financial System* (International Monetary Fund, 1998).

[22] A Crockett, 'Marrying the Micro- and Macroprudential Dimensions of Financial Stability' (Remarks before the Eleventh International Conference of Banking Supervisors, Basel, 21 September 2000). Available at: www.bis.org/speeches/sp000921.htm.

[23] J Caruana, 'Monetary Policy in a World with Macroprudential Policy' (Speech at the SAARCFINANCE Governors' Symposium, Kerala, 11 June 2011). Available at: www.bis.org/speeches/sp110610.htm. See also C Borio, 'Towards a Macroprudential Framework for Supervision and Regulation?' (February 2003) BIS Working Paper No 128.

[24] CH Lim et al, 'Macroprudential Policy: What Instruments and How to Use Them? Lessons from Country Experiences' (October 2011) IMF Working Paper No 11/238. Available at: www.imf.org/external/pubs/ft/wp/2011/wp11238.pdf; AK Kashyap, R Berner, and CAE Goodhart, 'The Macroprudential Toolkit' (2011) 59(2) *IMF Economic Review* 145; E Cerutti, R Correa, E Fiorentino and E Segalla, 'Changes in Prudential Policy Instruments – A New Cross-Country Database' (June 2016) IMF Working Paper WP/16/110. Available at: www.imf.org/external/pubs/ft/wp/2016/wp16110.pdf.

which aim at *stabilising* the wider economy.[25] While not all fluctuations in the economy are driven by the financial system, there is growing empirical evidence that financial and business cycles tend to co-move, and the most severe fluctuations in the business cycle are associated with the boom-and-bust cycle of the financial system.[26] It follows, therefore, that financial regulation would acquire a macroeconomic dimension. It is more than just additional support to internal risk management by bank management because it does not focus on how risk is accumulating within individual firms. It is cognisant of the effects of the risk from the collective financial system and the broader economy. The macroprudential approach puts the interaction between the financial system and the economy front and centre.[27]

Like other macroeconomic policies, macroprudential policy also applies prudential tools in a countercyclical manner to actively limit the build-up of financial imbalances and build resilience of the overall financial system to shocks during downturns.[28] Targeting the size and inter-connections amongst financial institutions also bolsters resilience, as these are the channels through which financial imbalances spread. Thus, the macroprudential approach has a structural dimension to it and, like all structural policy, it aims to change the (financial)

[25] See JH Dalhuisen, *Dalhuisen on Transnational Comparative, Commercial, Financial and Economic Law* Vol 3, 6th edn (Hart Publishing, 2016), 492, 513–14. See also D Schoenmaker and P Wierts, 'Macroprudential Policy: The Need for a Coherent Policy Framework' (July 2011) *Duisenburg School of Finance Policy Paper No 13* ssrn.com/abstract=1876595 and O Blanchard, G Dell'Ariccia, and P Mauro, 'Rethinking Macroeconomic Policy' (12 February 2012) IMF SPN/10/03. Available at: www.imf.org/en/Publications/IMF-Staff-Position-Notes/Issues/2016/12/31/Rethinking-Macroeconomic-Policy-23513. Some have argued that the macroprudential approach is merely an extension of microprudential regulation.

[26] See, for instance, C Borio, 'The Financial Cycle and Macroeconomics: What Have We Learnt?' (December 2012) BIS Working Papers No 395. Available at: www.bis.org/publ/work395.pdf and Ò Jordà, M Schularick and AM Taylor, 'Macrofinancial History and the New Business Cycle Facts' in M Eichenbaum and JA Parker (eds), *NBER Macroeconomics Annual 2016* Vol 31 (NBER, 2017) 213.

[27] Some have suggested that it is merely a supplement to microprudential regulation because it is not intended to deal with a crisis once it sets in, that in any case the last crisis was caused by a failure of microprudential regulation and the policy is, in fact, implemented using tools traditionally associated with microprudential regulators anyway. See L Ellis, 'Macroprudential Policy: A Suite of Tools or a State of Mind?' (Speech delivered at Paul Woolley Centre for Capital Market Dysfunctionality Annual Conference, Sydney, 11 October 2012). Available at: www.rba.gov.au/speeches/2012/sp-so-111012.html, as cited in A Godwin, S Kourabas and I Ramsay, 'Financial Stability Authorities and Macroprudential Regulation' (2017) 32 *Banking & Finance Law Review* 223.

[28] Monetary policy uses time varying conventional instruments (interest rate controls, credit controls, discount policies, open market operations and reserve requirements) and non-conventional instruments (recently quantitative easing and negative interest rates) to maintain price stability and support economic growth. See K Mathai, 'Monetary Policy: Stabilizing Prices and Output' *Finance & Development* (29 July 2017). Available at: www.imf.org/external/pubs/ft/fandd/basics/monpol.htm. Similarly, fiscal policy uses time-varying instruments to promote growth and reduce poverty, for instance increasing government spending or lowering taxes to increase aggregate demand and close a negative output gap or adopting contractionary or 'tight' fiscal policy to reduce demand and combat a positive output gap. See M Horton and A El-Ganainy 'Fiscal Policy: Taking and Giving Away' *Finance & Development*, (29 July 2017). Available at: www.imf.org/external/pubs/ft/fandd/basics/fiscpol.htm.

institutions of the economy and ultimately improve the economy's *long-term growth* potential.[29]

In the ten years after the crisis, literature on macroprudential policy has grown, as Galati and Moessner demonstrate.[30] The literature elaborates the analytical underpinnings of macroprudential policy (namely financial instability and systemic risk), the mandate and objectives of macroprudential policy, policy instruments, interactions with other policies and its links to the macro economy.[31] The IMF, FSB and BIS took the lead in synthesising these various lines of research and suggesting frameworks for operationalising macroprudential policy.[32] A key operating principle for macroprudential policy is the design of suitable governance frameworks, which identify the agency responsible for the policy, how the agency functions and how it is held to account for it decisions. According to the literature, the design of the governance framework should be guided by the notion that it needs to be geared towards countering inaction and reflect the system-wide nature of macroprudential policy.[33]

In light of the guiding principles elucidated by the IMF-FSB-BIS, most commentators have advanced arguments in favour of depoliticisation of macroprudential policy, akin to that observed in monetary policy.[34] Depoliticisation, creates a barrier between government and special interests which may seek to influence policy, negatively or positively, by shifting responsibility and control of policy to technocratic bodies, while retaining power over policy goals. As a corollary, the independent agencies cannot make policy decisions with a distributional effect.

[29] Schoenmaker and Wierts, 'Macroprudential Policy' (n 25).

[30] G Galati and R Moessner, 'Macroprudential Policy – A Literature Review' (February 2011) BIS Working Papers No 337.

[31] ibid.

[32] FSB-IMF-BIS, 'Macroprudential Tools and Frameworks: Update to G20 Finance Ministers and Central Bank Governors' (February 2011). Available at: www.fsb.org/wp-content/uploads/r_111027b.pdf?page_moved=1; International Monetary Fund, 'Macroprudential Policy: An Organising Framework' (March 2011) *IMF Policy Papers* Available at: www.imf.org/external/np/pp/eng/2011/031411.pdf; EW Nier, J Osiński, LI Jácome, and P Madrid, 'Institutional Models for Macroprudential Policy' (November 2011) IMF Staff Discussion Note SDN/11/18. Available at: www.imf.org/external/pubs/ft/sdn/2011/sdn1118.pdf; International Monetary Fund, 'Key Aspects of Macroprudential Policy' (10 June 2013) IMF Policy Papers. Available at: www.imf.org/en/Publications/Policy-Papers/Issues/2016/12/31/Key-Aspects-of-Macroprudential-Policy-PP4803; IMF-FSB-BIS, 'Elements of Effective Macroprudential Policies Lessons from International Experience' (31 August 2016). Available at: www.bis.org/publ/othp26.pdf.

[33] Caruana, 'A World with Macroprudential Policy' (n 23); European Systemic Risk Board, 'Allocating Macroprudential Powers' (2011) Reports of the Advisory Scientific Committee No 5/November 2011. Available at: www.esrb.europa.eu/pub/pdf/asc/Reports_ASC_5_1411.pdf; A Cukierman, 'Regulatory Reforms and the Independence of Central Banks and Financial Supervisors' in EG Morten Balling, *States, Banks and the Financing of the Economy: Monetary Policy and Regulatory Regimes* (SUERF, 2013) 121; K Knot, 'Governance of Macroprudential Policy' (2014) 18 *Banque de France Financial Stability Review* 25.

[34] See, for instance, V Acharya, 'Financial Stability in The Broader Mandate for Central Banks: A Political Economy Perspective' (14 April 2015) Hutchins Center Working Paper #11.

Naturally, central banks were often touted as the most ideal institutions to formulate and execute macroprudential policy, citing their independence, the effect of central banks on the macroeconomic environment, their status as lender of last resort, and their macroeconomic focus, which gives them an understanding of financial markets, institutions and infrastructures.[35] Studies on the effectiveness of various types of governance arrangements give credence to these assertions, as they report more timely use of macroprudential policy instruments in countries where the central bank is in charge of macroprudential policy.[36] More importantly, the same studies note a lower likelihood of financial instability if the central bank in charge of macroprudential policy enjoys operational independence.[37] The literature underscores, however, that independence in the financial stability framework needs to be complemented with increased transparency and accountability.[38] While the bulk of the research into appropriate institutional and governance structures revolves around central banks, the key issue emerging here is that independence correlates to a higher probability of macroprudential functions being delegated to an institution.

Following from the economic studies, much work went into recommending and designing legal reforms to underpin the macroprudential policy framework.[39] Three models have emerged, which build on existing institutional and governance frameworks by assigning the macroprudential mandate to either a central bank, a committee within the central bank, or an interagency body.[40] Just as the

[35] EW Nier, 'Financial Stability Frameworks and the Role of Central Banks: Lessons from the Crisis' (April 2009) IMF Working Paper 09/70. Available at: www.imf.org/external/pubs/ft/wp/2009/wp0970.pdf; Bank for International Settlements, *Central Bank Governance and Financial Stability* (Ingves Report) (BIS, 2011).

[36] C-H Lim et al, 'The Macroprudential Framework; Policy Responsiveness, and Institutional Arrangements' (July 2013) IMF Working Papers 13/166. Available at: www.imf.org/external/pubs/ft/wp/2013/wp13166.pdf.

[37] E Balls, J Howat, A Stansbury, 'Central Bank Independence Revisited: After the Financial Crisis, What Should a Model Central Bank Look Like?' (April 2018) *M-RCBG* Associate Working Paper Series No 87. Available at: www.hks.harvard.edu/sites/default/files/centers/mrcbg/working.papers/x87_final.pdf; D Masciandaro and A Volpicella, 'Macro Prudential Governance and Central Banks: Facts and Drivers' (2016) 61 *Journal of International Money and Finance* 101; A Khan, H Khan and H Dewan, 'Central Bank Autonomy, Legal Institutions and Banking Crisis Incidence' (2013) 18(1) *International Journal of Finance and Economics* 51; M Čihák, 'Price Stability, Financial Stability, and Central Bank Independence' [2010] *Oesterreichische Nationalbank 38th Economic Conference* 45; J Klomp and J de Haan, 'Central Bank Independence and Financial Instability' (2005) 5 *Journal of Financial Stability* 321.

[38] AWS Duff, 'Central Bank Independence and Macroprudential Policy: A Critical Look at the US Financial Stability Framework' (2014) 11(1) *Berkeley Business Law Journal* 183.

[39] International Monetary Fund, 'Implementing Macroprudential Policy – Selected Legal Issues' (17 June 2013) IMF Policy Papers. Available at: www.imf.org/external/np/pp/eng/2013/061713.pdf; RM Lastra, 'Systemic Risk and Macro-prudential Supervision' in N Moloney, E Ferran, and J Payne (eds), *Oxford Handbook of Financial Regulation* (Oxford University Press, 2015).

[40] R Edge and N Liang, 'New Financial Stability Governance Structures and Central Banks' (August 2017) Hutchins Center Working Paper No 32. Available at: www.brookings.edu/wp-content/

institutional arrangements vary, the objectives, functions, powers and instruments assigned to each also vary widely across jurisdictions.[41] However, one thing remains common – all of these institutions are independent.

The scholarship on the political economy of macroprudential policy usually justifies this delegation of powers to independent macroprudential institutions on the grounds of functionalist and ideational arguments.[42] Although some have argued instead that the delegation of powers by politicians was more symbolic than anything else – they had to be to be seen to be doing something in the wake of the crisis, by creating more accountable regulators.[43]

Whatever the motivation, the depoliticisation of macroprudential policy has reopened debates about the legitimacy of independent regulatory agencies. There is unease about governments in advanced economies' ever-growing reliance on unelected technocrats, these technocrats' increasing power over financial regulation and monetary policy[44] and fears that the creation of additional independent agencies removed from electoral sanction, or repurposing existing ones, will eventually lead to a crisis of legitimacy.[45] The depoliticisation has only increased political contestation and scrutiny. The portrayal of macroprudential authorities as technically adept experts, free from the influence of the electoral cycle, has resulted in a legitimacy paradox.[46]

At this point the reader may well ask, 'Does legitimacy really matter?' To paraphrase Peter Conti-Brown, legitimacy isn't a side show to the real questions; it may, in fact, be the whole show.[47]

uploads/2017/08/es_20170808_liang_newfinancialstabilitygovernancestructures.pdf. In some jurisdictions, the responsibility is shared amongst all the financial regulators, or it is placed with the microprudential regulator, however the number of such jurisdictions is negligible.

[41] A Khan, 'Central Bank Legal Frameworks in the Aftermath of the Global Financial Crisis' (May 2017) IMF WP/17/. Available at: www.imf.org/en/Publications/WP/Issues/2017/05/01/Central-Bank-Legal-Frameworks-in-the-Aftermath-of-the-Global-Financial-Crisis-44858; M Lee, R Gaspar, and ML Villaruel, 'Macroprudential Policy Frameworks in Developing Asian Economies' (March 2017) ADB Economics Working Paper No 510 Available at: www.adb.org/publications/macroprudential-policy-asian-economies.

[42] See, for instance, A Baker, 'The Bankers' Paradox: The Political Economy of Macroprudential Regulation' (April 2015) SRC Discussion Paper No 37. Available at: http://eprints.lse.ac.uk/61998/1/dp-37.pdf.

[43] See, for instance, D Lombardia and M Moschellaa, 'The Symbolic Politics of Delegation: Macroprudential Policy and Independent Regulatory Authorities' (2017) 22(1) *New Political Economy* 92.

[44] P Tucker, *Unelected Power: The Quest for Legitimacy in Central Banking and the Regulatory State* (Princeton University Press 2018).

[45] See, for instance, D Archer, a specialist in the institutional design of central banks with the BIS, David Archer, 'A Coming Crisis of Legitimacy' (2016) 3 *Sveriges Riksbank Economic Review* 86 Available at: archive.riksbank.se/Documents/Rapporter/POV/2016/2016_3/er_2016_3%20A%20coming%20crisis%20of%20legitimacy%20by%20David%20J.%20Archer.pdf.

[46] Baker, 'Bankers' Paradox' (n 42).

[47] P Conti-Brown, *The Power and Independence of the Federal Reserve* (Princeton University Press, 2016), 26.

1.2. What is Legitimacy and Why Does it Matter for Financial Regulation?

Legitimacy is a 'reservoir of good-will' that allows the institutions of government to exercise authority over citizens. Legitimacy inspires acceptance and compliance with the orders issued by those in authority. It is, therefore, central to the success of regulatory endeavours, because if an independent regulatory authority's actions are perceived as lacking legitimacy the constituents whom it seeks to direct will ignore its orders. Often, however, it is sidelined over seemingly more pressing questions about the nature of policies adopted by government and how effective these are. Many equate political legitimacy to policy efficacy and see no reason to separate the two.[48] The two concepts are, however, different although complimentary. You cannot have one without the other, legitimacy, begets efficacy, begets legitimacy, and so it goes on.[49]

Usually, those who are subject to the authority will comply because they believe the person issuing rules was properly appointed in accordance with generally accepted principles of due process.[50] This is the formal aspect of legitimacy, in order for an institution to be recognised, it must be constituted and operate in the accepted manner, or within accepted principles. But what are these so-called accepted principles? This leads us to the second aspect of legitimacy, the evaluative aspect, because it is these underlying values that motivate the acceptance of an institution.[51]

In most western states acceptance of the exercise of authority by the government is motivated by the values of democracy.[52] These values are embodied in the democratic processes, the most prevalent form of which being the election of leaders by those who support the broad values on which the state is based – representative democracy.[53] Democracy-based authority utilises the electoral process not as a method to arrive at the optimal substantive solution, but as a mechanism that aggregates opinions of all citizens in a way that achieves the freedom and equality which democracy demands. The electoral process respects the individual differences in opinion and enables ownership in the final decision.[54] As a result of electoral accountability, politicians' choices command respect from all voters.

[48] This was certainly the view advanced by some politicians in the post crisis era, such as former US Treasury Secretary Timothy Geitner. See Philip A Wallach, *To the Edge: Legality, Legitimacy, and the Responses to the 2008 Financial Crisis* (Brookings Institution Press, 2015).

[49] ibid.

[50] T Franck, *The Power of Legitimacy Among Nations* (Oxford University Press, 1990), p. 24.

[51] G De Búrca, 'The Quest for Legitimacy in the European Union' (1996) 59(3) *Modern Law Review* 349.

[52] See V Bekker et al (eds), *Governance and Democratic Deficit: Assessing the Democratic Legitimacy of Governance Practices* (Ashgate Publishing, 2007). Bekker et al provide a taxonomy of models of democracy which include representative, Direct, Pluralist, Deliberative, Associative, Client/Consumer.

[53] De Búrca, 'The Quest for Legitimacy' (n 51).

[54] J Waldron, 'Legislation, Authority and Voting' (1996) 84 *Georgetown Law Journal* 2185, 2204.

Independent policy makers like the new macroprudential authorities are, however, neither directly elected nor are they managed by elected officials on a day-to-day basis. Instead, they have powers delegated to them by the legislature. The chief criticism against appointing independent policy makers is that they are not subject to the direct effect of political control like elected officials – therefore they lack democratic legitimacy.[55] Despite this 'democratic deficit', independent regulators continue to exert power and influence, which suggests that there is an alternative source of legitimacy.

The answer lies instead in currently dominant theories of economics; specifically neoliberal economic theories that believe efficient and rational markets are better able to achieve allocative efficiency. The neoliberal argument is that, ordinarily, government intervention distorts allocative efficiency, but markets produce more efficient and stable outcomes, and can absorb shocks better.[56] Markets should therefore be left to their own devices. However, there are instances where the self-correcting mechanism of markets fails, and government intervenes to correct those market failures. Unfortunately, government cannot be relied on to commit to always correcting these failures, as it may be unpopular with part of their constituencies, and, in any case, they may lack the level of expertise required to carry out the correction.

These two features make independent policy makers attractive, as they are technically adept and not beholden to the political cycle. Allocative efficiency thus provides an alternative framing of the normative propositions that are preconditions for legitimacy. Independent agencies enjoy functional legitimacy. The force of allocative efficiency as a value that can legitimate the exercise of authority was given further impetus by empirical scholarship on central bank independence, which concluded that majoritarian government was not a prerequisite to regulatory legitimacy.

1.3. Is it time for a Social Justice Approach to Financial Regulation?

In the wake of the crisis, it appears not all were enamoured of independent policy makers. The Turner Review suggests that the crisis raised important questions about whether regulatory approaches based on theories of efficient and rational

[55] RM Lastra, 'The Independence of the European System of Central Banks' (1992) 33(2) *Harvard International Law Journal* 475, 478.

[56] It is beyond the scope of this work to delve into an analysis of the propriety of this theory, suffice it to say that the global financial crisis brought the weaknesses of this theory into sharp relief. The crisis exposed the tendency of markets to misprice goods and services due to irrational exuberance and cognitive biases, leading to allocative inefficiencies. See Avgouleas (n 9) 110–11.

markets are optimum.[57] The challenges to these foundational assumptions have implications not only for the design of regulation, but those who govern it.

What is most interesting is that the assumptions are being challenged not just by academics and policy makers, but by the public as well. The world of finance and its regulation is no longer an impenetrable jungle of jargon but has become a fundamental theme of today's public debate, as reflected in the emergence of civil society groups which regularly criticise financial regulators; such as the Occupy Movements, the Americans for Financial Reform, (AFR), and their European counterparts, the Europeans for Financial Reform, (EFFR), or the Transforming Finance Network in the UK.[58]

While academic discourse has focused on financial stability and market efficiency, in public discourse, concerns range from protecting the public from deception;[59] to providing housing; to democracy; to curbing the greed of financiers and promoting fairness;[60] to equality; to supporting economic growth and providing broad access to financial services and products.[61]

These are issues of social justice that go to the identity, security, or values of a nation. In a financial system where the upside of risk is enjoyed by a few, but downside is shared with taxpayers, households and firms, financial regulation is no longer just about allocative efficiency and preventing crises, it has also become a matter of social justice.[62] Consequently those who regulate finance must also earn and maintain their legitimacy not just in the context of allocative efficiency, but also social justice.

[57] Financial Services Authority, 'Turner Review' (n 11) 39.

[58] Membership of these groups is wide ranging, and includes coalitions of community-based, consumer, small businesses, investors, faith-based groups, civic groups, political parties, NGOs, trade unions and individual experts. But their underlying message is the same despite being separated by oceans – they are fighting for changes to the financial system to make it fairer, just, democratic, and responsible.

[59] The Cato Institute's 2017 Financial Regulation Survey, which revealed that, in the US, 65% of the public believe that regulation should protect consumers from fraud, while 56% believe it should ensure that banks fulfil their obligations. See E Ekins, 'Wall Street vs The Regulators: Public Attitudes on Banks, Financial Regulation, Consumer Finance, and the Federal Reserve' (Cato Institute Survey Reports, Cato Institute 2017). Available at: object.cato.org/sites/cato.org/files/survey-reports/pdf/financial_regulation_survey_report_updated.pdf.

[60] See L Kastner, *Civil Society and Financial Regulation* (Routledge, 2017).

[61] See World Economic Forum, 'The Role of Financial Services in Society A Multistakeholder Compact' (August 2013). Available at: www3.weforum.org/docs/WEF_FS_RoleFinancialServicesSociety_Report_2013.pdf. But even academics have jumped on this bandwagon of advocating for finance which serves a social purpose. See, for instance, R Shiller, *Finance and the Good Society* (Princeton University Press, 2012), where he suggests 10 ways for making finance work towards a society that is both comfortable for all of us, while also stimulating and forward moving.

[62] See P Tucker, 'The Debate on Financial System Resilience: Macroprudential Instruments' (Speech at Barclays Annual Lecture, London, 22 October 2009). Available at: www.bankofengland.co.uk/-/media/boe/files/speech/2009/the-debate-on-financial-system-resiliance.pdf and CAE Goodhart and RM Lastra, 'Populism and Central Bank Independence' (2018) 29(1) *Open Economies Review* 49.

However misguided or not these expectations may be, the call for social justice is not a passing phase. While memories of the crisis will eventually fade, the human desire for justice, however that may be defined, is a part of the human condition.[63] There needs, therefore, to be a more concerted effort to extend the underlying premise of financial regulation, to include a social justice dimension. This is not to discredit those post-crisis regulatory reforms that were conducted along the conventional economic rationale for regulation. After all, the neoliberal approach is cognisant of the social costs of financial activity in the form of negative externalities and attempts to mitigate these, for instance through the theories of Pigou, who suggested tax and subsidy remedies to protect public welfare;[64] or Coase, who suggested the assignment of strong property rights and private contracts as the best means to protect the equal freedom and dignity of individuals and increase overall welfare.[65]

Firstly, however, as the word 'costs' suggests, these theories focus more on allocating losses rather than the gains from the financial system, which does not adequately capture the numerous dimensions of social justice. Secondly, and more importantly, by their very nature they have a restricted sense of the collective because they reduce the social world into individual self-centred decisions.

Financial regulators cannot continue to ignore the murmurings of social justice.[66] I say 'murmurings' because the new direction has not been clearly articulated. As already stated, the calls range from the lofty, like equality, fairness, and democracy, to more practical ones, like housing, jobs, and growth – all of which have so far been presumably achieved by opening up the liquidity supply tap. Can one idea have so many meanings you ask? The real question is, to quote Humpty Dumpty, 'which is to be master – that's all'.[67] At the moment it appears that growth, driven by a steady and plentiful supply of credit to all, is the preferred definition of social justice.[68]

The danger, however, is that this may be the wrong master and opening up the liquidity tap to serve that master may end up achieving the opposite. A case in point is the subprime mortgage crisis in the US. After the crisis, it was easy to blame the greedy bankers who took senseless risks, but the unpleasant truth, is that society, through elected government, also encouraged banks to provide credit on

[63] J Habermas, 'Life Forms, Morality and the Task of the Philosopher' in Peter Dews (ed), *Autonomy and Solidarity: Interviews with Jurgen Habermas* (Verso, 1986) 187.

[64] AC Pigou, *The Economics of Welfare* 4th edn (Macmillan, 1932).

[65] RH Coase, 'The Problem of Social Cost' (1960) 3 *Journal of Law and Economics* 1.

[66] Even a supranational financial regulator, of the kind suggested by Dalhuisen, Garricano and Lastra or Avgouleas, would not escape this expectation. To do so would risk resistance or eventual rejection of the 'Super Regulator'.

[67] L Carroll, *Through the Looking Glass* (1934), 205.

[68] Dalhuisen, *Transnational Law* 6th edn, 543–44, 547–54.

demand, in the name of providing affordable housing for all – leading to a housing boom and large losses when the bubble burst.[69]

What is clear though is that an unfettered supply of credit, in the name of equality, financial inclusion, growth, or whatever else, cannot lead to social justice, because eventually it leads to collapse of the whole system.[70] At some point, society will have to give greater attention to the true definition of social justice, because any institution that purports to regulate finance must ultimately stand or fall by this definition. It is, as Dalhuisen remarks, that the financial system reflects society and is not some dark invention of evil spirits.[71] That is the crux of this book.

Macroprudential policy and its governance structures provide the perfect opportunity to introduce a social justice dimension to financial regulation, for which the public has been clamouring.[72] Andrew Baker identifies a 'macrosocial ontology' in the underlying premise for macroprudential policy, in that the macroprudential approach encourages regulators to conduct holistic assessments of the financial system, as opposed to confining analysis to sectors; how individual private decisions can threaten the system; the interlinkages within the system and how collective optimism or pessimism about future earnings leads to booms and busts.[73] In short, the systemic approach underlying macroprudential policy forces financial regulators to take into account the collective functioning and effect of finance in society, and is an avenue for strengthening their legitimacy.

[69] During the era of the Bush and Clinton administrations, the government made a concerted effort to provide housing for all citizens, by subsidising mortgages offered by financial institutions, often to individuals with weak credit. The government guaranteed mortgage loans through the government sponsored enterprises, the Federal National Mortgage Association (Fannie Mae) and the Federal Home Loan Mortgage Corporation (Freddie Mac), which in turn encouraged banks to lend more. See the empirical studies, supporting the notion that populist pressures on the government led policies which encouraged banks to create low-quality housing loans, detailed in CW Calomiris and SH Haber, *Fragile by Design* (Princeton University Press, 2014).

[70] HP Minsky, 'The Financial Instability Hypothesis' (May 1992) Levy Economics Institute Working Paper No. 74.

[71] JH Dalhuisen, *Dalhuisen on Transnational Comparative, Commercial, Financial and Trade Law: Financial Products, Financial Services and Financial Regulation* Vol 3, 7th edn (Hart Publishing 2019), 870.

[72] A view shared by others like Baker and Andenas and Chiu. See A Baker, 'Macroprudential Regimes and the Politics of Social Purpose' (2018) 25(3) *Review of International Political Economy* 293; M Andenas and IHY Chiu, *The Foundations and Future of Financial Regulation: Governance for Responsibility* (Routledge, 2013).

[73] Baker, 'Macroprudential Regimes and Politics'. Baker analyses papers from two groups of forerunners in macroprudential thought, the BIS staff and academic economist responsible for the 11th of the Geneva Reports on the World Economy – Markus Brunnermeier, Andrew Crockett, Charles Goodhart, Avinash D Persaud and Hyun Song Shin. He contends that these early discussions which formed the basis of macroprudential policy drew heavily, although implicitly, from the work of Keynes, Minsky and Kindleberger who argued for streamlining the process of social distribution of wealth, equality and democracy in economic planning.

1.4. Conclusion

This book proposes a framework for increasing legitimacy by giving macroprudential authorities explicit goals that account for both economic and non-economic values of society. Using a comparative empirical analysis of legislation, the book explores the drivers of legitimacy for independent policy makers and juxtaposes these against three case studies from the United States, (US); the United Kingdom, (UK); and the European Union, (EU). An understanding of macroprudential policy as conducted in these three jurisdictions is important because they are home to the largest and most sophisticated financial markets in the world, with well-developed complex institutions and have a significant influence on the world economy. Thus, they have the potential to affect global practices.

Chapter 2 lays the foundation for the discussion by providing a theoretical framework for legitimacy. It expands on the concept of value driven acceptance of authority. I lay out three sets of values – political, economic and social values – that may form the basis of legitimacy for policy makers, and the type of governance arrangements each set of values may call for.

Chapter 3 describes the financial system, why it matters in the achievement of the economic values identified in Chapter 2, and how it can be destabilised. The system shall be explained from the point of view of commercial banks, which are now active in both capital and banking sectors. This will allow a more streamlined discussion. The last point, 'How can the financial system be destabilised?' will, in turn, inform the discussion on the scope of financial regulation. The chapter will focus on how financial regulation maintains financial stability, as this directly relates to the mandate of macroprudential authorities that are the subjects of this study. It begins with a description of the traditional microprudential approach and demonstrates that, even after the changes introduced by Basel III, microprudential regulation cannot guarantee financial stability.

Chapter 4 discusses the second, and contemporary, method of addressing financial stability – the macroprudential approach. Using examples from the US, UK, and the EU, an account is provided of present iterations of macroprudential policy including its definition, objectives, and tools. This chapter seeks to highlight the differences between the micro and macroprudential approach and why the macroprudential approach is more suited to pursue financial stability because it dampens the build-up of credit over time, making the system more resilient in downswings, and tries to reduce the channels through which risk spreads in the first place, thus limiting, and containing the fallout from systemic risk.

The chapter also highlights that while macroprudential policy is a better agent of financial stability, than microprudential regulation, it can prove unpopular, and, therefore, is susceptible to time-inconsistency. The governance of macroprudential policy becomes a decisive factor in its success and there is a strong case for assigning the macroprudential mandate to an independent policy maker, who can demonstrate credible commitment and technical expertise. This functional independence then becomes the source of their legitimacy.

Chapter 5 evaluates the independence and accountability, through an analysis of the legal frameworks establishing macroprudential policy authorities, in the three jurisdictions. Some significant differences are found in the articulation of independence of macroprudential policy authorities, when compared to other independent macroeconomic policy makers. Firstly, their independence is reduced as there is subtle, but significant, political interference and secondly, policy makers are not required to account for the distributional impacts of macroprudential policy – in other words, society's other social justice values are not explicitly considered. The findings of the evaluation raise serious questions regarding macroprudential policy makers legitimacy.

Chapter 6 proposes that the policy legal framework includes a social justice objective to be considered alongside the main financial stability objective. I argue that while conventional wisdom argues that independent regulatory agencies should not be making distributional choices, macroprudential policy has unavoidable distributional effects and the decision to activate macroprudential policy, what Dalhuisen refers to as 'calling the moment', should not be solely based on highly rationalised and strongly quantitative reasons, because this risks real social concerns becoming de-personalised. The two need to be balanced or, at the very least, social concerns should be acknowledged in the policy-making process. The chapter offers devises for introducing social justice concerns to policy decisions, which can be embedded in the legal framework.

Chapter 7 offers a general conclusion, drawing together the main themes in the preceding chapters. Overall, I hope to convince the reader that macroprudential policy provides an opportunity to promote an additional narrative to the rationale for financial regulation, namely a social justice rationale, and thus complete its legitimacy.

2

Legitimacy: A Theoretical Framework

Establishing the legitimacy of independent macroprudential authorities is central to their acceptance and ultimately the success of macroprudential policy. To do so, a definition is needed of what legitimacy represents in theoretical terms, and how legitimacy in financial regulation is to be distinguished from other kinds of legitimacy analyses.

So, why is it that the government can intervene to correct market failures and financial market participants follow the laws and regulations they issue? The short answer, according to the positivists, is that it is because the government, as the authority, said so. But why should this preclude any deliberation of the subject by individuals? As Hart points out, although a directive may be law according to the positivist criteria because a duly appointed authority posited it, this does not provide any reason for it to actually be respected.[1] The fact that a directive has been issued by a government is, on its own, no reason for citizens to forgo deliberating the substance of an issue.[2] In the case of the financial sector it should not provide a reason for participants to order their transactions and firms as directed by the legislature, who are, in any case, not experts in financial markets. Indeed, the theories of autonomy and rationality argue against this.[3]

One may argue that governments exercise authority by virtue of their ability to punish non-compliance, but coercive power is not sustainable and at some point, compliance must become voluntary. In any case, the argument based on power and force ignores the reality that rules and laws, for instance financial regulations, are not just about prohibiting particular behaviour under threat of punishment, but also permitting action and delineating the boundaries of the permitted action. As Wolff highlights, power is merely the ability to compel

[1] HLA Hart, *The Concept of Law* 3rd edn (Oxford University Press, 2012), 203.

[2] J Waldron, 'Legislation, Authority and Voting' 1996 (84) *Georgetown Law Journal* 2185–2214, 2190.

[3] See S Shapiro, 'Authority' in JL Coleman et al (eds), *The Oxford Handbook of Jurisprudence and Philosophy of Law* (Oxford University Press 2004) 391. Autonomous agents cannot act on reasons simply because they are peremptory and without assessing their content. Additionally, authoritative directives can never be reasons for action if they are unreasonable and, if they are reasonable, then the reasonable agent was going to act in that way anyway and the directive is irrelevant.

compliance through force, but authority imposes a moral obligation on the subject of the directive to obey.[4] Those who claim that obedience is engendered by more non-coercive factors generally use the term legitimacy to denote these alternative non-coercive drivers of obedience.[5]

Tyler speaks of legitimacy as a reservoir of loyalty that leaders continually draw on to effectively govern.[6] Legitimacy is critical, therefore, because it justifies the exercise of authority which, in turn, motivates behavioural responses to that authority.[7] The desired behaviour is acceptance of the leader's authority and a change in conduct in response to their commands, indicated by compliance with the said commands. Compliance is a necessary condition for effective governance.[8] The type of desired behaviour will, of course, differ according to the addressee of the authority. There are, as Black refers to them, multiple legitimacy communities.[9] In the context of financial policy makers they must not only be accepted by those to whom their regulations directly apply, the financial institutions, but also by the public who ultimately bear the costs and benefits of policy actions.

Numerous descriptive and normative approaches exist in the literature to describe the legitimacy of political authority in general, and independent financial regulators in particular. The first section of this chapter describes the difference between descriptive and normative conceptions of legitimacy, and the sources of legitimacy under each type of concept. The descriptive conception of legitimacy does not give a satisfactory answer to the question of source; therefore, we must turn to the normative sources of legitimacy, which are derived from the value system of those who are subject to authority and whose compliance is sought. Among the values which form the basis of normative legitimacy, democracy is identified as the most compelling, but it is not enough to explain all forms of authority, particularly that of independent regulatory agencies. The second section of this chapter explores two alternative sources of legitimacy for independent regulatory agencies, namely economic and social justice values, and explains how these values shape the exercise of authority.

[4] RP Wolff, 'The Conflict Between Authority and Autonomy', in Joseph Raz (ed), *Authority* (New York University Press 1990) 20.

[5] T Franck, *The Power of Legitimacy Among Nations* (Oxford University Press, 1990).

[6] TR Tyler, *Why People Obey the Law* (Yale University Press 1990) 26. (*Why Obey the Law*).

[7] MC Suchman, 'Managing Legitimacy: Strategic and Institutional Approaches' (1995) 20(3) *Academy of Management Review* 571; LG Zucker, 'Institutional Theory of Organizations' (1987) 13 *Annual Review of Sociology* 443. A fourth form of legitimacy, charismatic legitimacy, is also noted by these writers.

[8] Organisation for Economic Co-operation and Development, *Reducing the Risk of Policy Failure: Challenges for Regulatory Compliance* (OECD, 2000); TR Tyler, 'The Psychology of Legitimacy: A Relational Perspective on Voluntary Deference to Authorities' (1997) 1 *Personality and Social Psychology Review* 323–45, Tyler, *Why Obey the Law* (n 6).

[9] J Black, 'Legitimacy and the Competition for Regulatory Share' LSE Law, Society and Economy Working Papers 14/2009.

2.1. Sociological/Descriptive Legitimacy

The concept of legitimacy is closely related to, and often used as, the basis for justification and acceptance of authority. In order to decide whether an institution and/or its rules are legitimate it is necessary to define the concept of 'legitimacy'. While it is a familiar concept in legal theory, it has several varying interpretations, which is a sign of its complexity.

The philosophers of legitimacy teleology fall into two categories. The first group defines legitimacy in terms of specific processes set out in a constitution which sets out the processes for appointing leaders, legislating, governing and adjudication.[10] In this view, a financial regulator, and any rules they issue, acquire validity because of their legality, for example, they were honestly elected, the regulations were duly passed by a majority with a quorum present, and they respect the rule of law. A leading exponent of this view is Max Weber, whose analysis of the legitimacy of political authority provides a starting point for many modern studies of legitimacy.

Following Weber, compliance with an authority's commands may be driven either by emotions and a sense of community or, for practical reasons, such as personal gain, or simply because it is tradition. However, these are usually not a sufficiently reliable basis for the exercise of authority. Weber famously posited that the determining element is a belief in the legitimacy of the authority, based on a conviction that they were elevated via laws that were made in formally correct procedures, regardless of their content.

While he does not deny that those subject to authority and its commands hold opinions about the content of the law, Weber claimed there were inherent obstacles to ascribing value judgments to others. Weber argued that values, as a source of legitimacy, were too vague, variable, uncertain, and scientifically impenetrable to be recognised as a basis of legitimacy.[11] There was, for Weber, no possibility of addressing the 'truth' of those beliefs or values because the world is characterised by a plurality of values and beliefs, which, by the way, are constantly in flux.

Regardless, one could deduce from the fact that citizens are actually complying with the law that it somehow accords with the values they might hold. In other words, 'an order (will) be called "valid" if it's in some *appreciable* way regarded by the actor as in some way obligatory or exemplary for him'.[12] The ability to assert authority does not, therefore, depend on whether the leader and their commands reflect values held by those who accept their legitimacy, as long as both conform to legal requirements. The law becomes a tool for founding

[10] Franck, *The Power of Legitimacy* (n 5).
[11] ibid.
[12] M Weber, *Economy and Society: An Outline of Interpretive Sociology* (University of California Press, 1979) 31.

authority and exercising it.[13] Weber's treatment of the relationship between legality and legitimacy provides a sociological or descriptive definition of legitimacy.

2.2. Normative Legitimacy

This Weberian conception of legitimacy has been criticised for being merely descriptive and not a sufficient explanation of legitimacy as it ignores the reasons or values behind the norm that make a regulatory regime obligatory or exemplary. This leads us to the second group of legitimacy philosophers, those who contend, like Habermas, that legitimacy is based upon 'good reasons'.[14] In other words, there are underlying values which support the acceptance of authority. Legitimacy, therefore, also has a normative dimension, that is, it is based on the belief that certain institutions are the most appropriate ones for society and therefore ought to be in charge because they accord with the values held by society – which is, in any event, the final arbiter of legitimacy. To put a fine point on it, a particular authority is legitimate if it can be justified in terms of the beliefs of the people it governs.[15]

This approach provides a more normative definition of legitimacy or, in other words, the justification of authority. Insofar as legitimacy is understood normatively, there is the question of what grounds this normativity. As already pointed out, however, there are numerous competing value systems and beliefs. Accounts of sources of legitimate authority range from those based on a sort of contractual agreement by individuals, in the tradition of Locke, Hobbes, and Kant; to accounts which flow from these three traditions and posit that the agreement is based on some beneficial consequence to obeying the commands of authority, in the view of Bentham and Mill; public reason grounded in the values of justice, as conceived by Rawls, or democratic approval in the style of Rousseau.

2.2.1. Consent

Some political philosophers argue that the exercise of authority must arise from the actual or implied consent of the governed. Why citizens grant this consent

[13] R Cottrell, *Law's Community Legal Theory in Sociological Perspective* (Oxford University Press, 1997) 137.

[14] J Habermas, *Communication and the Evolution of Society* (T McCarthy trs, Beacon Press, 1979) 200. See also SM Lipset, 'Some Social Requisites of Democracy: Economic Development and Political Legitimacy' (1959) 53(1) *The American Political Science Review* 69, 86–87.

[15] D Beetham, *Legitimation of Power* (Palgrave, 1991) 11. Tucker illustrates the importance of values through the example of the Bank of England which went from simply relying on authority born of tradition and belief in its aptness, to having to demonstrate, via accountability and increased transparency, that it squared off with people's deep values. P Tucker, *Unelected Power: The Quest for Legitimacy in Central Banking and the Regulatory State* (Princeton University Press, 2018).

differs. For Locke, each person has an equal natural right to freedom and therefore cannot be subordinated to anyone else's commands by nature. We would have to *voluntarily consent* to an obligation to obey a political authority. This account of legitimacy falters, however, on the fact that citizens hardly ever give explicit consent, the account relies on the more tenuous tacit consent, which is signalled by voting (at least in democratic states). In contrast, while Hobbes proposes that individuals enter a social contract, they do so to pursue their rational interests such as peace and security. Kant also believes in public reason leading to agreement, in so far as this hypothetical agreement reflects everyone's inalienable right to freedom. Like Kant, Rousseau begins from the position that all citizens are endowed with freedom and equality by nature. Through agreement, we maintain this freedom *and* live with others by submitting our individual will to the general will.

2.2.2. Utilitarian Values

The utilitarian view, which grew out of the Hobbesian tradition, rejects voluntarism, and instead advocates for legitimacy based on utility to the citizens subject to the authority. Utility can mean contributing to the happiness of individuals;[16] being instrumental in arriving at good law and policy or improving the characters of participants in a democratic process;[17] providing a reason for action, at the exclusion of all other reasons;[18] or enabling citizens to fulfil their Samaritan duty to each other.[19]

2.2.3. Public Reason Grounded in Social Justice

Public reason accounts of legitimacy justify the exercise of authority when it is supported by motives all reasonable persons endorse. The idea was more fully developed in Rawls's liberal principle of legitimacy, which dictates that the exercise of authority is only justified if it is done in accordance with a constitution which all reasonable and rational citizens would support.[20] This human reason is, however, restricted to political conceptions of justice and avoids the controversial moral and religious beliefs held by the public on what is good. The restriction on

[16] J Bentham, *An Introduction to the Principles of Morals and Legislation* (Clarendon Press, 1907).

[17] JS Mill, *Considerations on Representative Government* (First published 1861, Prometheus Books, 1991), Chapter 3.

[18] The so-called 'normal justification thesis' developed by J Raz, *The Authority of Law: Essays on Law and Morality* 2nd edn (Oxford University Press, 2009).

[19] C Wellman, 'Liberalism, Samaritanism, and Political Legitimacy' (1996) 25(3) *Philosophy and Public Affairs* 211.

[20] J Rawls, *Justice as Fairness: A Restatement* (Harvard University Press, 2001), 41.

the content of public reason also means that its scope of application should be limited, and Rawls suggests that public reason be applied to constitutional issues and basic justice.

Social justice is an ambiguous concept, which has inspired great disagreement about the true meaning of justice, so translating it into practice is even harder. The principles of justice guide how society assigns rights and duties, as well as how it distributes resources and opportunities.[21] The distribution, according to scholarship on social justice, is based on either (i) deserts, which is the idea that if someone has performed a valuable activity, they should be suitably rewarded,[22] or (ii) entitlement, which is the idea that those who own goods are entitled to do what they want with them,[23] or (iii) fairness, which is the idea that the state should intervene in the distribution of resources to ensure the least advantaged are made better off.

The first approach believes that people make choices for which they are responsible and can deserve a greater or lesser reward based on those choices. This approach, however, ignores the fact that there are factors that are beyond the control of individuals, such as their level of health or intelligence, which affect their ability to acquire resources – they do not necessarily deserve what they end up with. Under the second approach, justice means respecting people's property rights and using the state power to protect those rights and not to coerce them to share. However, the theory does not satisfactorily account for how individuals come to own the property in the first place, such that it cannot sustain the protection of individual property rights whatever the distribution results. The third approach, though it too has its failings, is, for this writer, the most appealing, as will be explained in the following paragraphs.

Rawls's theory of justice as fairness is a good place to begin exploring the notion of distributive justice. Rawls theorised that the principles of justice emerge as a hypothetical contract amongst members of society, but fair conditions are a prerequisite for this agreement. Fair conditions here mean the individuals deciding that they must have no knowledge of particular facts about themselves and their beliefs – a veil of ignorance must cover them. The logic is that if individuals do not know who they are going to be, then they are likely to choose fair principles to ensure they are not left worse off in future.

Parties to this hypothetical contract thus exist in their original state – which is a state of freedom and equality. Firstly, individuals are treated equally because the social standing or natural talents of those deciding, which would bias distributive outcomes, do not factor in the decision. Of course, in reality, people are born into different families and have different talents, but Rawls argues that these factors

[21] J Rawls, *A Theory of Justice* (Harvard University Press, 1971), 61.
[22] See, for instance, D Miller, *Principles of Social Justice* (Harvard University Press, 2001).
[23] See R Nozick, *Anarchy, State and Utopia* (Basic Books, 1974).

should not matter in the distribution of benefits and burdens because they are completely arbitrary from a moral standpoint. Secondly, individual conceptions of what is 'good' should also not factor into the agreement of principles because these are obviously varied and change over time amongst individuals. Instead, what matters is that individuals have the *freedom* to decide what beliefs to hold, and the freedom to act upon these beliefs or change them. According to Rawls, under the conditions just outlined above, two principles would emerge – (i) each person should have the equal right to engage in activities, as long as they do not infringe the rights of others; and (ii) social and economic inequalities should only be allowed if (a) it is going to maximise the improvement of the least-advantaged members of society (the Difference Principle), and (b) there is equal access to opportunities (offices and positions) for all.[24]

The first principle is the result of individuals being ignorant of their beliefs, and therefore being concerned with creating a system that allows them to choose, act upon and change beliefs. Therefore, they are granted basic liberties or rights such as protection from discrimination, freedom of thought, expression, assembly, movement and so on. The second principle is a result of individuals having no knowledge of their position in society. Therefore, all citizens should have an equal opportunity to achieve their positions in life. However, if there are social and economic inequalities, such inequalities are only justified if, in the long run, they benefit the least advantaged members of society. This is also known as the difference principle. For Rawls, the first principle would take priority because it creates the framework of fairness.

Translating these principles into practice is equally fraught with challenges. A common approach to securing justice in the system of government is by enshrining the fundamentals of social justice within the constitution in the form of socio-economic and civil rights. Typically, constitutional rights protect basic needs such as education, housing or health; and liberties such as freedom of movement, the right to vote or protection from discrimination.[25]

2.2.4. Democratic Approval

Accounts of legitimacy based on democratic approval value the equal participation of citizens in the political process. For Rousseau, tacit consent cannot suffice for legitimacy, as one cannot transfer their will. This would distort the general will. Rousseau advocates a more direct form of participation. Democratic systems have

[24] Rawls, *Theory of Justice* (n 21) 302.

[25] L Valentini, 'Justice and Democracy' (November 2010) CSSJ Working Paper SJ012. Available at: www.politics.ox.ac.uk/materials/centres/social-justice/working-papers/SJ012_Valentini_Justice&Democracy.pdf.

evolved in ways which differ significantly from this direct approach; however, in most western states, acceptance of the exercise of authority by the government is motivated by the values of democracy.[26]

2.3. The Only Game in Town: Democracy as a Source of Legitimacy

The concept of democracy has acquired 'catchphrase' status; making it difficult to lock down a definitive meaning. While it is often defined as 'government for the people by the people', this says nothing about the values that would make this type of government desirable. Amongst democratic states, there are wide-ranging differences as to how such values are recognised and protected within their legal systems. Majone, for instance, highlights variances in approaches to public services in the UK and other EU democracies, and in the transatlantic approaches of the UK and US, despite their shared common law tradition.[27]

Even within the same states considerable differences exist depending on the political ideology of the individual defining democracy.[28] For instance, *classical liberalism* emphasises property rights, rule of law and freedom from interference, while *ordoliberalism* prioritises clear rules for economic life and government intervention to protect the interests of a healthy society and social justice. In contrast, shared values, deliberation, collective self-government, and public interests over individual interests are identified as *civic republican* commitments. *Neorepublicanism* prioritises liberty, the importance of people as individuals and the ability to participate in political life and challenge policy, although unanimous agreement is not a requirement. *Conservatism* represents tradition, but is not opposed to change, as long as it occurs gradually through the passage of time. Lastly, in the concept of *social democracy*, the state's role is to enhance the people's ability to realise their capabilities and entitlements, and to fulfil a substantive conception of justice. In contrast to socialism and communism, it values the individual. Despite their differences, common themes run across all these ideologies – namely freedom and equality. Therefore, it is possible to form a definition of democracy as a political system in which freedom and equality of individuals are prioritised.

Often, however, individual preferences may be at a variance since individuals place different weight on society's values. That means that there are

[26] K Stapelbroek, 'The Idea of Democracy and The Eighteenth Century' in V Bekker et al (eds) *Governance and Democratic Deficit: Assessing the Democratic Legitimacy of Governance Practices* (Ashgate Publishing, 2007) 61.

[27] G Majone (ed), *Regulating Europe* (Routledge, 1996).

[28] Tucker, *Unelected Power* (n 15) 163–68.

numerous *legitimacy communities* as Black refers to them, or, per Tucker, *legitimacy audiences*, that must be satisfied.[29]

It is necessary, therefore, to have a procedure for counting and assessing the multitude of individual opinions.[30] Bekker and Edwards provide a taxonomy of models of democracy, which include direct, representative, pluralist, deliberative, associative and client/consumer.[31] These models, or procedures for aggregating opinions, are designed to espouse the values of democracy. The first two are based on aggregating the various opinions through voting, either by directly voting on policies and laws, or by appointing a representative to make those policy and legislative decisions. Direct majority decision making achieves the equality which democracy demands because it respects the individual differences in opinion and enables ownership in the final decision. While everyone is entitled to their own opinion, it is only counted at its worth and no more.[32]

This means that different opinions carry different weight, based on criteria such as the level of reason, wisdom, and experience – often embodied in the form of age limits or mental capacity laws. This justifies the discounting of certain individuals from participating in voting processes or the use of a plural voting system at national level. Nevertheless, for practical reasons, individuals cannot always directly participate in the decision making. The alternative lies in appointing representatives, through the same process of voting, who then make decisions on behalf of the electorate.

Representation does not remove the element of participation that engenders equal respect, but merely reduces deliberation and voting to a manageable scale. Thus, governments have democratic legitimacy through representative democracy; and the financial regulations that they enact deserve the compliance of market participants because they are achieved in a way which accords equal respect and participation by all. If voters lose confidence in the representatives and their ability to represent their interests, they can withdraw their support via the same electoral process. Thus, the electoral process also acts as a method of holding representatives accountable.[33]

Two problems should be noted with purely majoritarian forms of government. Firstly, they give rise to normative problems of 'tyranny of the majority', in which the views of the minority are disregarded, no different to a state governed

[29] Tucker, (n 15) 161. Tucker therefore encourages central banks to become self-conscious legitimacy seekers among multiple audiences because losing just one significant audience can be problematic.

[30] Waldron, 'Legislation, Authority and Voting' (n 2) 2205.

[31] V Bekkers and A Edwards, 'Legitimacy and Democracy: A Conceptual Framework for Assessing Governance Practices' in V Bekker et al, eds *Governance and Democratic Deficit: Assessing the Democratic Legitimacy of Governance Practices* (Ashgate Publishing, 2007) 35, 48–54.

[32] Mill, *Considerations on Representative Government* (n 17).

[33] F Amtenbrink and RM Lastra, 'Securing Democratic Accountability of Financial Regulatory Agencies – A Theoretical Framework' in RV de Mulder (ed), *Mitigating Risk in the Context of Safety and Security. How Relevant is a Rational Approach?* (Erasmus School of Law and Research School for Safety and Security (OMV), 2008) 115.

by a despot. This reveals a second problem, that the approach is dismissive of the effects of majoritarian acts. To be sure, the concept of democracy embodies not only beliefs about how decisions are reached, but also the impact of the decisions on individuals. The inference that equal respect and freedom can only be achieved through majoritarian decision making implies a narrow understanding of the concept of equality and fairness as being merely procedural and excludes concerns with the substantive content or outcome of rulemaking.[34]

Alternatively, therefore, democratic processes may be deemed valuable not only because they embody the values of equality, freedom and self-realisation, but also because governance structures created via democratic processes are effective. Such effectiveness could be in the form of good or correct decisions or the intellectual and moral development of citizens.[35] This is a more instrumentalist definition of democracy, which accords with Scharpf's distinction between input-based legitimacy achieved via the democratic process for appointment of those in authority and the creation of laws and regulations; and output-based legitimacy, concerned with the efficacy of the laws and rules promulgated by those in authority.[36] For Scharpf, who developed the concept in the context of the EU, both elements are necessary for democratic legitimation.[37] Schmidt further developed Scharpf's views on political legitimacy. For Schmidt, output legitimacy requires policies to resonate with citizens' values and identity, not just to be effective.[38] This contrasts with input legitimacy, which only requires that the procedure be followed by citizens expressing their demands, through representative politics.[39]

One may be tempted to think that democracy equates to justice. However, there is a difference between the two concepts and, in fact, justice and democracy are often at variance. Justice is concerned with egalitarian redistribution of burdens and benefits, while democracy is concerned with egalitarian procedures. Thus, rules made by democratically elected governments may fail to meet the standard of social justice, but still be regarded as legitimate, because they were arrived at in a manner that accorded equality to all. A common response to the problems posed by democratic decision making is to enshrine the fundamental requirements of justice in the constitution, thus removing them from the whims of the democratic process.[40] This is not to say that democracy serves no purpose for justice. As highlighted above, democratic procedures may serve an instrumentalist function; in

[34] CR Beitz, *Political Equality: Essay in Democratic Theory* (Princeton University Press, 1992) 58–67.
[35] Mill (n 17).
[36] F Scharpf, *Governing in Europe: Effective and Democratic?* (Oxford University Press, 1999).
[37] ibid 11–13.
[38] VA Schmidt, 'Democracy and Legitimacy in the European Union Revisited: Input, Output and "Throughput"' (2013) 61(1) *Political Studies* 2.
[39] ibid.
[40] Valentini, 'Justice and Democracy' (n 25).

other words, they serve as a means of distributing resources and opportunities in a just manner.

Today, representative democracy has no credible rival in the western world.[41] It is almost taken for granted that democracies are the legitimate way to organise collective decision making.[42] On the face of it, values of democracy now appear to be globally endorsed. Kriesi demonstrates, however, through a review of surveys on attitudes towards democracy, that support of the principle is rather shallow, particularly beyond the western world, in developing countries and what are considered non-democratic countries.[43]

Nowhere is it more apparent that democratic values fail to provide a complete answer to the question of legitimacy than in the case of the regulatory state, a model of governance in which an unelected body, that has power delegated to it by public or elected officials, regulates markets.[44] Independent regulatory agencies, like macroprudential authorities, are appointed and have authority delegated to them. They are not democratically elected, yet they still exercise authority. This presents a serious challenge to legitimacy. According to the purely proceduralist conception of democratic legitimacy, which ties it to collective decision-making procedures, the authority of independent regulatory agencies cannot be justified. The logical conclusion would therefore be that the independent agencies and their commands need not be accepted and cannot induce compliance. However, the reality is that they do exert influence. This means that either the concept of democratic legitimacy extends beyond majoritarian decision making; or democratic legitimacy is not a prerequisite for the authority of independent regulatory agencies.

2.4. Legitimacy and Independent Regulatory Authorities

2.4.1. The Democratic Deficit

It is obvious that the conditions for the legitimacy of the state and government do not carry over to unelected independent agencies. In fact, independence moves governance two steps away from the citizens who are the subjects of governance,

[41] G De Búrca, 'The Quest for Legitimacy in the European Union' (1996) 59(3) *Modern Law Review* 349–76, 352.

[42] M Maggetti, 'Legitimacy and Accountability of Independent Regulatory Agencies: A Critical Review' (2010) 2 *Living Reviews in Democracy* 1.

[43] H Kriesi, 'Democratic Legitimacy: Is There a Legitimacy Crisis in Contemporary Politics?' (2013) 54(4) *Politische Vierteljahresschrift* 609.

[44] DC and M Thatcher, 'The New Governance of Markets and Non-Majoritarian Regulators' (2005) 18(3) *Governance – An International Journal of Policy and Administration* 329.

without their consent, which would be granted via the ballot, and denies them the ability to express their displeasure with independent agencies, which again would be achieved via the ballot.[45]

Therefore, for agencies like macroprudential authorities, who do not have the benefit of being direct representatives of the people's will, establishing legitimacy is not only necessary for their authority to be accepted, but it also ensures their continued survival as a regulatory body. Some authors attempt to reconcile independent regulatory agencies with the theory of democracy either by extending the democratic legitimacy enjoyed by the government to the agency itself, an indirect legitimacy,[46] or by locating it as a fourth branch of government which limits and controls power, thus preventing abuse, as envisaged in the original *trias politica*.[47]

2.4.2. Economic Values as a Foundation for Legitimacy

Confidence in independent regulators is better attributed to the influence of neoliberal economic theories in shaping the regulatory state.[48] According to neoliberal theorists, unfettered, competitive markets are most likely to produce efficient outcomes, and interference by governments will almost always unbalance the finely tuned logic of the marketplace.[49]

The 1980s ushered in a shift in ideology as the concept of free markets took over. The idea that the economy needed to be managed by the state gave way to management by the markets, leading to the privatisation of industries, tax cuts, cuts in government spending, and, more importantly, the deregulation

[45] Although, as Tucker points out, the rise in economic might of states such as China and the United Arab Emirates supports the idea that democratic legitimacy is not a prerequisite for a flourishing financial system, therefore having independent financial regulators is perfectly fine.

[46] For instance, a popular example of this theory is the EU and its institutions. See, for instance, A Moravcsik, 'Reassessing Legitimacy in the European Union' (2002) 40(4) *Journal of Common Market Studies* 603.

[47] Lastra and Miller, for instance, appear to do this when they liken independent central banks to an independent judiciary. The judiciary in most liberal democracies, like central banks, are non-majoritarian institutions. An independent judiciary can provide an effective check to executive and legislative power for three reasons – (i) the special expertise that courts possess in interpreting the law; (ii) their insulation from political pressures and private interests; and (iii) the lack of powers that other government agencies possess. The same set of reasons can be used to justify independent central banks. They have proved to be the best at managing the money supply and price levels, they are insulated from special interests which may tempt them to manipulate policy for short-term gains and they generally do not enjoy wide ranging authority. See RM Lastra and G Miller, 'Central Bank Independence in Ordinary and Extraordinary Times' in J Kleinman (eds) *Central Bank Independence. The Economic Foundations, the Constitutional Implications and Democratic Accountability* (Kluwer Law International, 2001) 31.

[48] A Saad-Filho and D Johnston, *Neoliberalism – A Critical Reader* (Pluto Press, 2005).

[49] DE Thorsen and A Lie, 'What is Neo-Liberalism' (2006) Department of Political Science University of Oslo. Available at: ww.2006folk.uio.no/daget/What%20is%20Neo-Liberalism%2010-11-06.pdf.

of industries. The banking and financial industries were at the centre of this deregulation because they were the vehicle for the efficient allocation of resources in the free market. As a result, in most states, interest-rate caps were abolished, central banks ceased trying to control the growth of credit directly through reserve ratios, and the restrictions on banks owning non-bank financial institutions were gradually removed.

Markets, however, often fail to conform to this idealised model, and require government intervention, in the form of regulation, to produce optimal outcomes. The theory of 'market failure' is the starting point for devising financial regulation in the neoliberal framework. Neoliberal economic theory recognises three fundamental market failures that justify regulation:

(i) ***Negative Externalities***, which arise where economic activity generates costs to others for which they are not compensated.
(ii) ***The Agency Problem***, which occurs when the interests of the agent and those of the principle diverge.
(iii) ***Information Asymmetries***, a situation in which the parties to a contract do not hold the same information regarding the transaction, and one has less accurate or comprehensive information.

It is assumed that in some policy areas, particularly those that are economic, independent regulatory agencies are better placed to promote allocative efficiency and reduce market failures because they are manned by technical experts with a unique acquaintance with the regulated sector, are faster and can produce better policies than elected officials. One may well argue that governments are free to hire experts, but there is a second reason why even those experts working under direct control of government cannot be trusted – namely credibility.

Unlike politicians, independent regulators are not subject to the influence of the political cycle and are therefore unlikely to constantly change policies to garner votes from the electorate. They can offer credible commitment to a policy. Consistency, therefore, is an important feature of efficiency, alongside technical efficacy. This leads to two conclusions. Firstly, in economic policy, efficacy and efficiency are more important than democratic deliberative or representative procedures. Secondly, the delegation of authority to independent regulatory agencies is best understood in functional terms – authority is justified by the functions performed by the agency. Therefore, they enjoy a different kind of legitimacy – *functional legitimacy*.

Independent central banks provide here a useful analogy of the influence of these economic values, as opposed to democratic values, and how these shape governance structures. Since the 1990s, most jurisdictions have converged on an independent central bank model. Central bankers are appointed and operate independently of the government in the making of monetary policy and, in some jurisdictions, bank supervision. The chief criticism against granting an independent central bank power over policy and regulation is that it is not subject to the direct effect of political control, like elected officials – therefore it suffers from a democratic deficit.[50] Despite this 'democratic deficit' central banks continue to exert power and influence, which suggests that there is an alternative source of legitimacy. In the following section, insights from selected literature on governance of independent monetary policy institutions will be used to develop a framework for justifying the authority of independent regulatory agencies.

2.4.3. Central Bank Independence and Monetary Policy

2.4.3.1. Objectives and Conduct of Monetary Policy

Monetary policy consists of actions taken by the monetary authorities to manage the supply and the cost of money. There are six objectives usually mentioned in central bank statutes, in combination or individually, namely: (1) high employment; (2) economic growth; (3) price stability; (4) interest-rate stability; (5) financial stability; and (6) exchange-rate stability.[51] The central bank achieves these objectives through a set of tools that can affect the goals indirectly during protracted periods.[52] However, the bank needs a way to judge more quickly whether its policies are on track to reach the objectives, before irreversible mistakes are made. Consequently, the central bank aims at variables that lie between the ultimate objective and the tool.[53] These are intermediate targets, such as monetary aggregates, exchange rates and inflation levels. Goodhart traces four epochs of monetary policy after World War II, in which different targets were pursued to achieve the objectives of monetary policy. The period of the Bretton Woods Consensus, when the focus was on exchange rate targets; the Disturbed Decades, when policy shifted to monetary targets; the Great Moderation, when inflation targeting moved to the forefront; and the Great Financial Crisis, which retained the inflation target.[54]

Price stability, achieved via inflation targeting, now takes paramount importance amongst monetary policy objectives. This grew out of the recognition that rising price levels – inflation – generate significant uncertainty and costs to society's welfare. If households and businesses are unsure about the future level of prices, and hence the outcome of business decisions and profitability, they will make suboptimal decisions about savings and investments. There are also negative effects on the cost of capital due to the interaction between inflation and the tax system, conflicts in industrial relations and there may be a sudden redistribution of

[50] RM Lastra, 'The Independence of the European System of Central Banks' (1992) 33(2) *Harvard International Law Journal* 475, 478.

[51] FS Mishkin, *The Economics of Money, Banking and Financial Markets* 7th edn (Pearson, 2004) 411.

[52] ibid 414.

[53] ibid 415.

[54] CAE Goodhart, 'The Changing Fortunes of Central Banking' (Lecture delivered at Queen Mary, University of London LLM Seminar in Regulation of Financial Markets, 23 November 2016).

wealth. All these costs combine to ultimately lower economic growth.[55] It should be noted that although price stability is typically the primary objective of monetary policy, it is not pursued at the expense of growth. As such, in most countries, policy makers are required to place some weight on both inflation and output.

Within the policy framework of inflation targeting, short-term interest rates and forward guidance have been the preferred tools of central banks. When central banks adjust the rate that they charge to banks for short-term loans, the movements in interest rates are passed on to firms and households.[56] Things changed, however, when policy rates hit the perceived lower bound. When interest rates fall to zero due to powerful economic shocks, it is impossible to cut policy rates further to stimulate spending and thus raise inflation towards the target.[57] This led central banks to consider other forms of intervention.

Unconventional monetary policy takes many forms; in some cases, it involves the use of negative interest rates, while some commentators advocate suspension or changes to inflation targets.[58] Typically, however, unconventional monetary policy targets the central bank's balance sheet to influence financial conditions beyond the short-term interest rate. Examples of balance sheet policy include large-scale asset purchases and the supply of liquidity at non-standard terms and conditions, for instance at long maturities and for specific lending purposes. The central bank may also wish to use forward guidance to steer expectations about future balance sheet adjustments.[59]

[55] HM Treasury, *Review of the Monetary Policy Framework* (Cm 8588, 2012). See also RM Lastra, *Central Banking and Bank Regulation* (LSE Financial Markets Group, 1996) 14.

[56] When commercial banks can borrow from the central bank at low rates, they are able to lend more and cheaper to households and firms, who are the final consumers of financial products. In turn, consumers have more to spend on goods and services, which boosts demand and consequently employment to meet increased production needs. The greater the demand for workers, the further wages and other costs rise. Movements in short-term interest rates also influence the interest rates of long-term assets, such as residential mortgages, because their interest rates are partly a function of short-term rates. In addition, shifts in long-term interest rates affect other asset prices, most notably equity prices and foreign exchange. The effectiveness of monetary policy depends as much on the public's expectations about how interest rates, inflation, and income are likely to evolve, as it does upon the bank's actual actions regarding interest rates. Therefore, forward guidance is another important tool in monetary policy. Alan S. Blinder et al, 'Central Bank Communication and Monetary Policy: A Survey of Theory and Evidence' (May 2008) ECB Working Paper Series No 898. Available at: www.ecb.europa.eu/pub/pdf/scpwps/ecbwp898.pdf.

[57] Y Korniyenko and E Loukoianova, 'The Impact of Unconventional Monetary Policy Measures by the Systemic Four on Global Liquidity and Monetary Conditions' (2015) IMF Working Paper WP/15/287 7. Available at: www.imf.org/external/pubs/ft/wp/2015/wp15287.pdf.

[58] C Borio and A Zabai 'Unconventional Monetary Policies: A Re-Appraisal' (July 2016) BIS Working Papers No 570. Available at: www.bis.org/publ/work570.pdf.

[59] The most popular form of unconventional monetary policy has been Quantitative Easing (QE). The phrase was first applied to Japan as it dealt with the bursting of a real estate bubble in the 1990s and the deflationary pressures that followed. Through QE, the central bank expands its balance sheet by purchasing assets issued by either the government or the private sector. The central bank can make such a large number of purchases because of its ability to create acceptable means of payment in unlimited quantity – namely to print money. By selling assets to the central bank, the private sector is left with claims against the central bank, which is a more liquid asset. Eventually the greater liquidity

2.4.3.2. Economic Rationale for Central Bank Independence in Monetary Policy

Empirical studies appear to be unanimous in the conclusion that central bank independence will deliver lower inflation than any other central bank constitution.[60] Such conclusions derive from the pioneering work of Barro and Gordon; and Kydland and Prescott, who concluded that political authorities are prone to 'time-inconsistency'.[61] As welfare maximisers, political authorities have an incentive to let the rate of inflation rise above the expected rate, to create more output and employment. They have an inflationary bias. However, rational expectations wage setters anticipate this incentive and incorporate the expected increases into their nominal wage demands.

In the end, there is no monetary surprise and no employment gain, but a positive rate of inflation which undercuts real wages. The cost of inflation thus exceeds the benefit. Furthermore, short political cycles provide an incentive to manipulate monetary policy for political mileage, while at the same time there is pressure from private lobbyists. To avoid the inflationary bias Rogoff suggested the appointment of an authority whose preferences are known to diverge from those of the welfare maximising authority.[62] An independent, but conservative, central bank is thought to place more weight on avoiding inflation than unemployment.[63]

translates into lending into the broader economy, helping drive prices up and remove deflationary forces. The purchase of assets has implications for interest rates as well. Removing particular assets from the market, thus leaving less for other buyers, pushes their prices up; the higher the price, the lower the interest rate charged and, hopefully, the reduction in yields will filter through to the rest of the economy.

Since the Global Financial Crisis of 2007–2008, QE has most notably been used by the central banks of the US, the Euro area and the UK; variously named as Large Scale Asset Purchases (LSAPs), Maturity Extension Programme (MEP), Securities Markets Programme (SMP); Outright Monetary Transactions (OMT); Asset Purchase Programme (APP); Asset-Backed Securities Purchase Programme (ABSPP); Covered Bond Purchase Programme 3 (CBPP3); Public Sector Purchase Programme (PSPP); and Asset Purchase Facility (APF). Assets targeted have been from both the public and private sector; and the asset purchase programmes have been supported by calendar-based guidance and state-contingent guidance about the central bank's inflation predictions. See M Joyce et al, 'Quantitative Easing and Unconventional Monetary Policy – An Introduction' (2012) 122(564) *The Economic Journal* 271; and Borio and Zabai 'Unconventional Monetary Policies'.

[60] See, for instance, R Bade and M Parkin, 'Central Bank Laws and Monetary Policy' (1987) *University of Ontario, Department of Economics Discussion Paper*; A Cukierman et al, 'The Measurement of Central Bank Independence and Its Effect on Policy Outcomes' (1992) 6 *The World Bank Economic Review* 353; G Debelle and S Fisher, 'How Independent Should a Central Bank Be?' (1994) Working Papers in Applied Economic Theory; E Balls, J Howat & A Stansbury 'Central Bank Independence Revisited: After the Financial Crisis, What Should a Model Central Bank Look Like?' (April 2018) M-RCBG Associate Working Paper Series | No 67 Series No 87. Available at: www.hks.harvard.edu/sites/default/files/centers/mrcbg/working.papers/x87_final.pdf.

[61] See FE Kydland and EC Prescott, 'Rules Rather than Discretion: The Inconsistency of Optimal Plans' (1977) 85 *Journal of Political Economy* 473; and R Barro and DM Gordon, 'Rules, Discretion and Reputation in a Model of Monetary Policy' (1983) NBER Working Paper No 1079.

[62] KS Rogoff, 'The Optimal Degree of Commitment to an Intermediate' (1985) 100 *Quarterly Journal of Economics* 1169.

[63] Adolph proposes that the preferences of independent central bankers are observable through their career paths. He devised an index of Central Banker Career Conservatism, which depends on how

Of course, political authorities could always promise not to increase inflation, however such promises are not credible because the welfare maximising government has an incentive to renege on this promise once wage contracts have been signed. There is, therefore, a second distinguishing element, commitment to policy rule. Technical skills and the discretion to exercise said skills are meaningless if policy makers are erratic in their decision making.[64]

A rule to which the monetary authority is bound would signal a commitment to maintaining the expected inflation rate.[65] Rules also prevent political pressures that distort the market and incentives and limit the monetary authority's ability to placate special interests. Given that the preferences of this authority are known by the public to be conservative, both the expected and actual rate of inflation would fall.[66] This is not to say that discretionary policy is never desirable. Goodhart cautions against giving complete priority to medium-term objectives.[67] The effects of monetary policy on the short run, on output and employment, matters and policy makers should be able to react to shock events like political turmoil, civil unrest, and wars.

A possible compromise between rules and discretion is the use of flexible inflation targeting. In most countries, the policy objective of price stability is specified in statute governing the central bank, in addition there is a fixed inflation target, typically at 2 per cent, which is set by either the government, the central bank or is agreed bilaterally.[68] Despite the explicit target, the central bank is given leeway to set the horizon for monetary policy and deviations from the target due to unexpected events. An implicit factor in granting independent central banks some discretion is a belief that the skills, expertise, and superior qualifications of central bankers, compared to politicians, results in a more neutral; objective and faster decision-making process.[69]

Credible commitment is the true driver of delegation of power. Otherwise, experts could simply advise the government. Having established the most efficient entity, namely an independent entity, the next question is about how the freedom

long a central banker has held a conservative job. He found an increase in conservatism led to a correlated decline in inflation. See C Adolph, *Bankers, Bureaucrats and Central Bank Politics: The Myth of Neutrality* (Cambridge University Press, 2013).

[64] M Woodford, *Interest and Prices: Foundations of a Theory of Monetary Policy* (Princeton University Press, 2013), 14.

[65] See for example, the Taylor Rule, JB Taylor, 'Discretion versus Policy Rules in Practice' (1991) 39 *Carnegie Rochester Conference Series on Public Policy* 195.

[66] Rogoff, 'The Optimal Degree of Commitment' (n 62) 1177.

[67] CAE Goodhart, 'Central Bank Independence' in CAE Goodhart, *The Central Bank and the Financial System* (Cambridge MA, MIT Press, 1995).

[68] HM Treasury, *Review of the Monetary Policy*. The 2% inflation target is considered as the optimal level at which the costs of inflation are minimised while avoiding falling into a liquidity trap at the zero lower bound. In the wake of the GFC, some economists now advocate a higher inflation target that is further away from the zero lower bound.

[69] L Goodhart, 'Brave New World? Macro-prudential Policy and the New Political Economy of The Federal Reserve' (2015) 22(2) *Review of International Political Economy* 280.

of the independent entity is to be construed. This is essentially a question about the meaning of 'independence'.

2.4.3.3. *Articulation of Independence in Monetary Policy*

Friedman distinguishes between a trivial meaning and a more basic meaning of independence in the context of central banks. The trivial meaning relates to separate administrative organisations, outside the regular government departments, but which are still subordinate to the chief executive or officer of the government department.[70] A more basic meaning of independence situates the central bank as a fourth branch of government, which operates alongside, and whose power is checked by, the legislative, executive and judicial branches of government.[71] This is the form of most independent central banks around the world. This second form of independence requires the establishment of a central bank through constitutional provision, subject to change only by constitutional amendment.[72] However, unlike the legislature, executive and judiciary, the independence of central banks is not absolute because it is not a constitutive part of the rule of law.[73] Therefore, in most jurisdictions, the central bank is established via statute passed by the legislature. What we find instead is that central bank independence is a qualified independence.[74] As highlighted above, political authorities set the objective of monetary policy, price stability, which is achieved via a fixed strategy, inflation targeting. Policy makers are, however, free to decide how the target is to be achieved.

What does it matter for inflation targeting to grant instrumental independence and not independence in setting goals? Numerous empirical studies have been dedicated to determining the nature of independence that is conducive to lowering inflation. In their seminal article, Bade and Parkin distinguished between financial independence and policy independence.[75] They found that financial independence, meaning independence from government influence in selecting board members and setting their salaries and determining the bank's budget and profit sharing had little effect in lowering inflation.[76] However, banks that had comparative policy independence, meaning freedom from government influence in policy deciding meetings and final say on policy, produced significantly lower inflation.[77]

[70] M Friedman, *Dollars and Deficits* (Prentice-Hall, 1968), reprinted from LB Yeager (ed), *In Search of a Monetary Constitution* (Harvard University Press, 1962) 179.

[71] ibid.

[72] ibid.

[73] Lastra, *Central Banking* (n 55) 11.

[74] ibid 18.

[75] Bade and Parkin, 'Central Bank Laws' (n 60).

[76] ibid.

[77] ibid.

Subsequent studies also attempted to either rank independence based on the formal arrangements provided for in the law[78] or on informal arrangements that determine the level of independence and consequently inflation.[79] Different authors use different delineations when describing the arrangements for independence, however, these can be broadly summarised as political independence, which is the ability of the central bank to set its goal; and operational independence, which denotes the freedom to pick and choose policy instruments, as well as how and when to use them. A third category of independence is de facto professional independence, which manifests in the personalities and circumstances which influence or surround the central bank's functions, such as the central bank governor and minister of finance, the historical, political and economic context, and the national priorities of a country.[80] However, given the difficulty of measuring these variables, de facto professional independence remained largely ignored in studies measuring the impact of independence on inflation.

The consensus from studies is that operational independence is more important for lowering inflation. Thus, central banks are significantly operationally independent. Political independence, on the other hand, does not appear to have a significant effect on the success of monetary policy.[81] That is not to say that central banks are subject to absolute political control since that would defeat the whole purpose of making them independent. Rather it reflects the fact that there is a need for central banks to remain politically accountable for implementing a public policy.

Efficacy in monetary policy can only be used as an evaluative benchmark of regulatory legitimacy in so far as it is independent of distributional considerations, in other words it does not influence the state of equity or fairness in society. A corollary to the idea that economic policy decisions are value free is that discretion should only be delegated where the decisions of independent regulators have no distributive consequences, and financial regulation would have to become

[78] Bade and Parkin (n 60). See also D Masciandero and GE Tabellini, 'Monetary Regimes and Fiscal Deficits: A Comparative Analysis' in H-S Cheng, *Monetary Policy in Pacific Basin Countries* (Kluwer Academic Publishers, 1988); Cukierman et al, 'Measurement of Central Bank Independence' (n 60); Debelle and Fisher, 'How Independent Should a Central Bank Be' (n 60); Balls et al, 'Central Bank Independence Revisited' (n 60).

[79] Cukierman et al (n 60); J De Haan and W Kooi, 'What Really Matters: Conservativeness or Independence?' (1997) 50 *Banca Nazionale del Lavoro Quarterly Review* 23; C Crowe and E Meade, 'Central Bank Independence and Transparency: Evolution and Effectiveness' (May 2008) IMF Working Paper WP/08/119. Available at: www.imf.org/external/pubs/ft/wp/2008/wp08119.pdf.

[80] Lastra, *Central Banking*, (n 55) 12. De jure professional independence can be considered an element of organic independence.

[81] Balls et al find, however, that in emerging or developing economies the objectives of politicians and central bankers often come into conflict, and elected officials interfere in monetary policy. In such cases, mere operational independence may not be enough and greater political independence is required. See Balls et al (n 69).

value-neutral[82] – a feat next to impossible as we shall see in Chapter 4 when macroprudential policy tools are described.

The fact that independent regulators are insulated from political pressures which helps them to make more focused decisions, does not mean that those decisions will not have distributional effects, which is normally the preserve of elected representatives.[83] Even where the standard for effectiveness is explicitly articulated, 'effective output' may conflict with democratic values. The impossibility of avoiding distributional consequences means that independent financial regulators will always require political oversight. Oversight, quite simply, translates to the regulatory agency being made accountable.

Accountability is the process of explaining and justifying policy decisions or providing redress to those harmed by policy. Accountability is administered either by the executive, legislature and judiciary, which constitute political forms of accountability, or through performance reviews.[84] It should not, however, compromise the independence of the regulators. The object is to ensure that the agency is free to act, but is not beyond control.[85] Some, like Schmidt, view accountability as adding an extra layer of legitimacy, which he refers to as throughput legitimacy. For Schmidt, political legitimacy is measured by how far citizens accept the elements of input, throughput and output legitimacy (ie the voting/decision making, accountability and policy outcomes), and therefore are willing to comply with government directives even if they go against their own interests.[86] We will return to this argument later, for now it will suffice to say, for this writer, it is difficult to see accountability as a standalone form of legitimacy as it always relates to either increasing input or securing the desired output. Accountability facilitates the other forms of legitimacy.

[82] G Majone, 'Independence v Accountability: European Non-majoritarian Institutions and Democratic Government in Europe' (1994) EUI Working Papers (SPS) 1993/09.

[83] Sceptics of value-free economic justifications of authority include Scharpf.

[84] RM Lastra, *International Financial Law* (Oxford University Press, 2015), 90. There is a strong desire to constrain independent agencies. Nowhere is this more apparent than in the US where a swathe of legislation exists which attempts to constrain the power of regulatory agencies, such as the Administrative Procedures Act (APA), which essentially binds the adjudication and policy-making processes of regulators; the Congressional Review Act, which allows Congress to review new federal regulations from government agencies; and, more recently, the proposed REINS Act, which would require material regulation to be formally approved by the House of Representatives and Senate; the Regulatory Accountability Act which would require adversarial style hearings on proposed rules and empower the courts to interpret rules; and the Financial CHOICE Act, which would oblige the Fed to seek annual approval of its budget from Congress. See Tucker (n 15) 10 & 33.

[85] TM Moe, 'Interests, Institutions, and Positive Theory: The Politics of NLBR' (1987) 2 *Studies in American Political Development* 236.

[86] Schmidt, 'Democracy and Legitimacy in the European Union' (n 38) 9–10. Scharpf divided democratic legitimation into output, judged in terms of the effectiveness of the EU's policy outcomes for the people, and input, judged in terms of the EU's responsiveness to citizen concerns because of participation by the people.

Two conclusions can be drawn from the example of independent central banks. Firstly, the exercise of authority over the monetary regime (or in economic issues more generally) is legitimated by a different set of values to the traditional reasons given for acceptance of authority. Secondly, the different set of values require a different input and output to achieve legitimacy. It can be illustrated as follows:

Table 2.1 Values and Legitimacy

Values	**Input**	**Output**
Political	Voting (Equity & Freedom)	Effectiveness (eg good or correct decisions or the intellectual and moral development of citizens) + Equity & Freedom
Economic	Independence (Credible Commitment)	Effectiveness (eg price stability) + Allocative Efficiency

Some authors contend, however, that in achieving economic values of allocative efficiency, society's democratic needs, in other words the need for equity and freedom, will also be satisfied. The free market is presented as the ultimate conduit for individual representation and participation in socio-political processes.[87] The economic democracy line of reasoning is arguable. If anything, the neo-liberal ideology undoes democratic institutions, as we know them, by replacing public deliberation and voting with the price mechanism and individual negotiation. Furthermore, the idea of free choice in markets is deceptive because, in reality, the individual's negotiating power is determined by the money they have, the availability of alternatives in the market and general widespread inequality.[88] The result of this market primacy is that rather than democratic values shaping the economy, we live in a *Marktkonforme Demokratie*, 'market-conforming democracy', as the former German Chancellor Angela Merkel called it. More importantly, neither approach satisfies the growing calls for a more socially just financial system highlighted in the previous chapter.

2.5. Social Justice as an Alternative for Regulatory Legitimacy

Allocative efficiency and democracy are not the only values held by society. As demonstrated in Chapter 1, in the wake of the global financial crisis the list of

[87] C Crouch, D della Porta and W Streeck, 'Democracy in Neoliberalism?' (2016) 16(4) *Anthropological Theory* 497.
[88] ibid.

concerns is as long as Jefferson's list of 27 grievances to King George III. Numerous civil society organisations have raised concerns which range from protecting the public from deception; to providing housing; to curbing the greed of financiers and promoting fairness; to equality; to supporting economic growth and providing broad access to financial services and products. All these demands actually fall under the rubric of social justice, which is to be distinguished from democracy. Meeting social justice demands, in addition to democratic and/or functional demands, is a requirement for achieving legitimacy.

Again, some may argue that in achieving economic values of allocative efficiency, society's needs for social justice (as well as freedom and equality) would also be satisfied. After all, profitable banks or liquid capital markets are able to provide more credit to the economy, which ordinary citizens can use to fulfil their aspirations. However, society's socio-political aspirations are different from its economic aspirations. *Homo economicus*, who inhabits the ordinary marketplace, does not behave the same way when inhabiting the socio-political arena, because economic approaches can tend to understate individual rights and freedoms; are not politically neutral; and rely on simplistic majoritarianism which fails to take into account existing power inequalities.[89]

What does it mean for policy makers to be socially just? The social justice credentials of policy need to be articulated and emphasised; however, identifying the general content of a social justice goal is no easy task, given society's plurality of definitions and pervasive disagreement over which to prioritise.

Rawls' approach of justice as fairness may be the most ideal. Unlike distribution of resources based on just deserts, it does not ignore that there are numerous factors outside the control of an individual that affect their ability to 'work hard' such as level of health or intelligence. Nor does it discourage production of primary goods, which would be the result under a purely egalitarian approach, when individuals are aware that no matter how much they contribute to the economy they will get the same amount as everybody else.

But this still leaves us with the question of which individual or entity is best placed to execute any policy or make rules with an underlying value of social justice. As highlighted in the discussion on central banks, conventional wisdom has always said that decisions in the socio-political realm must be left solely to elected officials, or at least agencies that report directly to them. Independent agencies cannot, and should not, determine the scope of distributional adjustments to policy, and should only step in when technocratic ability and credible commitment are required for success. However, as we shall see in the discussion of macroprudential policy in Chapter 4, in some cases, it may be virtually

[89] See M Kelman, 'Legal Economists and Normative Social Theory', in A Wiener Katz (ed), *Foundations of the Economic Approach to Law* (Oxford University Press, 1998) and AA Leff, 'Economic Analysis of Law: Some Realism About Nominalism' in A Wiener Katz (ed), *Foundations of the Economic Approach to Law* (Oxford University Press, 1998).

impossible to draw a clean line between technical efficiency and distributional effects. Macroprudential policy straddles the line and cannot be exclusively measured in purely economic terms. Therefore, it is entirely possible that independence may be necessary for a system of governance that also pursues social justice. In any case, requiring independent regulators to pursue social justice concerns is nothing new. Provisions requiring policy makers to either promote previously disadvantaged groups or prohibit discrimination based on race, gender, sexual orientation or religion are woven into many economic laws and policies around the world.

In short, it may not matter if the decision maker is an elected official (pursuing equity and freedom) or if it is an independent policy maker (pursuing allocative efficiency), in either case for them to be fully legitimate (either democratic legitimacy or functional legitimacy), they must also be seen to prioritise social justice (pursuing equal rights and liberties, equal access to opportunities and the greatest benefits to the least advantaged of society).

The extended set of values underlying legitimacy may be illustrated thus:

Table 2.2 Extended Values and Legitimacy

Values	Input	Output
Political	Voting (Equity & Freedom)	Effectiveness (eg good or correct decisions or the intellectual and moral development of citizens) Equity & freedom
		+
Social		Equal rights and liberties + Equal access to opportunities + Greatest benefits to the least advantaged of society
Economic	Independence (Credible Commitment)	Effectiveness (eg price stability) + Allocative efficiency
		+
Social		Equal rights and liberties + Equal access to opportunities + Greatest benefits to the least advantaged of society

2.6. Conclusion

Maintaining legitimacy in the eyes of the public is central to motivating the acceptance of authority and consequently compliance with the orders of those in authority.[90] Traditional conceptions of legitimacy would require the financial regulator or policy maker to be democratically elected. However, as we saw in the case of central banks, elected decision makers may be susceptible to the time-inconsistency problem and struggle with credible commitment in certain policy spheres, leading to negative policy outcomes. Thus, it is not enough that they meet the requirements of procedural democracy. More importantly, this indicates that democracy does not exhaust society's values.

Economic efficiency is also an important value, and it is espoused by the independence of those in charge of policy decisions, which gives policy makers the ability to operate efficiently, that is consistently over time and with credible commitment. In this way, economic justification for authority, like democratic legitimacy, is based on the procedural (independence) and instrumental (effectiveness + allocative efficiency) value of that particular method of organising governance.

However, as we have seen from the public's growing discontent with policy outcomes, it is no longer enough that independent agencies rest their credibility and claims to authority on their expertise and mastery of mathematical models, data, and formal analysis. While delegation of authority was intended to insulate technical decision making from the disruptive realm of politics and social engineering, policy decisions are influencing social outcomes and if legitimacy is to be retained policy makers must somehow be aligned with all of society's values, or at the very least, must be seen not to run contrary to them.

[90] That being said, ensuring acceptance and compliance does not guarantee achievement of the intended goals of those exerting authority. The achievement of policy objectives will depend not only on the legitimacy of the policy maker but requires that the policy maker identifies the correct problem and its drivers, as well as the most appropriate tools and methodology to remedy the problem. See OECD, *Reducing Risk of Policy Failure* (OECD, 2000).

3

The Objectives and Conduct of Modern Financial Regulation

The financial sector has permeated every facet of modern existence and is now part of the very fabric of society; its attraction goes beyond the reduction of costs, resource mobilisation and risk management. Financial systems that are more effective at allocation of resources to their most productive use can have a profound impact on productivity and economic development and, in turn, social justice. This essential role of financial systems has been forcefully brought to the fore by the body of research showing the link between finance and economic growth and the succession of financial crises over the last two decades.[1]

The link between a developed financial sector and economic growth has been the subject of numerous studies since the seminal work of King and Levine.[2] The research has shown that a broad, deep and liquid financial system is a key determinant of economic and social development;[3] can be used to manage the risk of all consumers of financial products, whether they shop on Wall Street or at Wal-Mart;[4] and can aid the poorest 40 per cent of households to transact more efficiently and safely.[5]

The next sections of this chapter will go through how the financial system contributes to allocative efficiency which was identified as the value motivating acceptance of economic regulators' authority; why financial markets fail and the effects of such failure; and how the state intervenes to correct the market failures in order to restore efficiency. While there have been a number of market failures and consequently effects, this book will focus on failures in the form of negative externalities and the resultant financial instability.

[1] D Arner, *Financial Stability, Economic Growth, and the Role of Law* (Cambridge University Press, 2007) 36.

[2] RG King and R Levine, 'Finance, Entrepreneurship, and Growth' (1993) 32 *Journal of Monetary Economics* 513.

[3] RG Rajan and L Zingales, *Saving Capitalism from the Capitalists: Unleashing the Power of Financial Markets to Create Wealth and Spread Opportunity* (Crown Business, 2003), 1.

[4] R Shiller, *The New Financial Order. Risk in the 21st Century* (Princeton University Press, 2003), 1–2.

[5] A Demirguc-Kunt, L Klapper and D Singer, 'Financial Inclusion and Inclusive Growth: A Review of Recent Empirical Evidence' (April 2017) World Bank Policy Research Working Paper No 8040, 18. Available at: documents.worldbank.org/curated/en/403611493134249446/pdf/WPS8040.pdf. For an overview of finance and development see CAE Goodhart (ed), *Financial Development and Economic Growth: Explaining the Links* (Palgrave, 2004).

3.1. The Financial System and Allocative Efficiency

The financial system enables a more efficient allocation of resources to their most productive use, which means moving funding from underperforming or ageing sectors and directing it into newer or more promising ones.[6] This function is fulfilled through five channels:

(i) pooling of resources;
(ii) maturity and liquidity transformation;
(iii) producing *ex ante* information on investments;
(iv) risk management and mitigation; and
(v) facilitating corporate governance.

Of the five channels listed above, the maturity and liquidity transformation channel is, perhaps, the most important. Often, investments offering a high return require long-term funding. Conversely, however, savers and investors are generally reluctant to lock in their savings for long periods that would leave them in an illiquid position. Thus, resources are less likely to be directed to their most efficient use. Financial intermediaries provide a service that allows savers and investors to continue to hold their savings in liquid assets, such as demand deposits, shares or bonds, which can easily and quickly be sold. Simultaneously, the funds collected from savers and investors are converted into long-term loans and capital investments, for individual borrowers and firms alike. This is maturity transformation – the financing of long-term assets with liabilities that are either callable or short term. In essence, the reduction of savers and investors' liquidity risk encourages more investment to be channelled to the economy.

Of course, suppliers of funds could simply provide direct finance to those who require it, in exchange for the same liquid instruments. However, the wide range of costs associated with maturity and liquidity transformation make this a less attractive option. Firstly, the pooling of funding from disparate sources would be a costly process if savers and investors had to enter into multitudes of individual bi-lateral contracts with borrowers and issuers of securities. Financial intermediaries lower the cost of contracting by centralising the process, mobilising funds from savers who have surplus funds, permitting them to earn a return on their capital and thereby enjoy greater consumption in the future, and allocating these funds to individuals and institutions that need them.[7]

Secondly, financial intermediaries overcome information asymmetries, which would make savers and investors reluctant to place their funds outside of their control. In order to make investment decisions, savers and investors would require good information about firms, managers and market conditions. However, the

[6] J Wurgler, 'Financial Markets and the Allocation of Capital' (2000) 58 *Journal of Financial Economics* 187.
[7] J Armour et al, *Principles of Financial Regulation* (Oxford University Press, 2016) 24.

costs associated with collecting such information are rather large, and, in any case, individual savers may not have the ability to process such information to identify the best technologies or products. Coupled with entrepreneurs who are themselves unable, or lack the skills, to communicate the value of their business proposition, the high cost of producing information can keep capital from reaching the highest value-uses.

Financial intermediaries reduce the costs for savers by acquiring, processing and evaluating the information, thus identifying entrepreneurs, products and processes most likely to succeed.[8] A corollary to lower information costs is that it allows the production of information on more firms, thus increasing the pool which savers and investors can choose from, allowing them to diversify their risk. While savers and investors are generally risk averse, they are faced with the paradox that high-risk projects tend to produce higher returns, compared to those with lower risk. The ability to hold a diversified portfolio reduces that risk and promotes investment in growth enhancing innovative projects.[9]

Lastly, financial intermediaries may be good agents of strong corporate governance. The extent to which shareholders monitor firms and induce managers to maximise firm value improves the efficiency with which firms allocate resources; and make savers and investors more willing to finance production and innovation. However, the high costs may deter shareholders from closely monitoring management, leaving management to engage in rent-seeking behaviour. Financial intermediaries overcome the high agency costs, associated with maturity and liquidity transformation, through creditor monitoring, under commercial banking, as well as stock pricing and the market for corporate control, which are disciplining mechanisms created by the capital markets.[10] A developed financial sector is, therefore, one that fosters maturity transformation at lower information, transaction and agency costs, while mitigating risk.

Markets do not always function as they should though. As we saw in Chapter 2, there are three fundamental market failures that justify regulation:

(i) *Negative Externalities* – A typical example in financial markets, is that failure of one bank may throw doubt on the solvency of others thus creating a contagious panic of deposit withdrawals, which may actually lead to insolvency of a group of firms or, in the worst case scenario, lead to the collapse of the whole system.

(ii) *The Agency Problem* – In financial markets, investors are willing to hand over their excess funds to financial intermediaries because they provide an invaluable service of gathering information that is not directly available to investors

[8] DW Diamond and PH Dybvig, 'Bank Runs, Deposit Insurance, and Liquidity' (1983) 91 *Journal of Political Economy* 401.

[9] E Avgouleas, *Governance of Global Financial Markets* (Cambridge University Press, 2012).

[10] F Easterbrook and DR Fischel, *The Economic Structure of Corporate Law* (Harvard University Press, 1991).

and monitoring investments. However, if left unchecked, owners and managers of intermediaries can misdirect the funds to benefit themselves at the expense of both the firm and investors' safety.

(iii) *Information Asymmetries* – In financial markets it arises because borrowers usually have more information on the projects they wish to undertake than the investors providing funding. The result of such information asymmetries is *adverse selection*, meaning that investors are more likely to fund parties who will produce an adverse outcome.[11] Additionally, information asymmetries can result in *moral hazard*, meaning borrowers will take on more risk than the lender would otherwise be comfortable with, because the borrower will enjoy the rewards that come with the high risk, but the lender bears the losses if the venture fails. Information asymmetries perpetuate moral hazard because the lender has no way of monitoring the borrower's activities or it is simply too costly.

These market failures can result in an erosion of the market integrity or the abuse of consumers of financial products and services. The most devastating effects, though, are those resulting from negative externalities, which manifest as financial instability. For example, the Global Financial Crisis of 2007–08 was associated with a huge loss of economic output and financial wealth, unemployment as well as the skill atrophy and psychological damage that come with job losses.[12]

The costs of the financial crisis went beyond statistics on economic output, wealth, government aid and unemployment. As Janet Yellen noted, commenting on the unemployment that resulted from the financial crisis, long-term unemployment had devastating effects on the physical and mental health of workers and their families. Extended periods of unemployment increased the likelihood they would be unable to pay their mortgages and they risked becoming homeless or decreased their chances of qualifying for a rented property, let alone being able to relocate to places where jobs are available.[13]

The GFC renewed interest in research on the causes of financial crises, their resolution and prevention of future crises. If financial instability only affected the

[11] This is because those borrowers pursuing high-risk activities, which have the potential for high returns, are more active in seeking out funding, but investors cannot tell the difference between those borrowers with good or bad credit risk. As a result, investors may decide to simply withhold funding altogether. This is an example of the classic *lemons problem* first described by economist George Akerlof. See G Akerlof, 'The Market for "Lemons': Quality Uncertainty and the Market Mechanism' (1970) 84(3) *The Quarterly Journal of Economics* 488.

[12] T Atkinson, D Luttrell and H Rosenblum, 'How Bad Was It? The Costs and Consequences of the 2007–09 Financial Crisis' (July 2013) *Dallas Fed Staff Papers No 20*. Available at: www.dallasfed.org/~/media/documents/research/staff/staff1301.pdf.

[13] JL Yellen, 'A Painfully Slow Recovery for America's Workers: Causes, Implications, and the Federal Reserve's Response' (Address at the 'A Trans-Atlantic Agenda for Shared Prosperity' Conference, Washington, DC, 11 February 2013). Available at: www.federalreserve.gov/newsevents/speech/yellen20130211a.htm as cited in HJ Allen, 'What Is "Financial Stability"? The Need for Some Common Language in International Financial Regulation' (2014) 45 *Georgetown Journal of International Law* 929, 946.

profitability and solvency of institutions and markets within the financial system, then there would be less need to target financial stability as a policy goal or intervene when financial institutions or markets fail.

3.2. Financial Stability

3.2.1. What is Financial Stability?

Financial stability is one of the core objectives of financial regulation, however, the term itself has so far eluded precise definition. In taking on its intermediary role, the financial sector becomes a clearing house for risk.[14] In order to enjoy the benefits of a financialised economy we are forced therefore to live with vulnerabilities and the potential for meltdowns. Hence, there is never a totally risk-free moment in the financial sector; instead, we live on a continuum between financial stability and instability. The question then becomes, at which point along the continuum we consider the system to be sufficiently stable. This will depend on who is making the call: the banks, the government, regulators or the public.[15]

This is why financial stability is such a protean concept, with various manifestations and different understandings of its basic facets. Unlike its counterpart, price stability, financial stability is a more nebulous concept and, when trying to define it, the temptation all too often is to simply declare that it is more identifiable in its negative form as the absence of instability.[16] Other scholars have then gone on to describe this state of instability as being when there are fears that means of payment may be unavailable at any price,[17] there is inefficient allocation of savings to investment opportunities,[18] financial institutions, and only them, are unstable or fail,[19]

[14] GJ Schinasi, 'Defining Financial Stability' (October 2004) IMF Working Paper WP/04/187. Available at: www.imf.org/external/pubs/ft/wp/2004/wp04187.pdf.

[15] N Luhmann, *Risk: A Sociological Theory* (Walter de Gruyter, 1993) 3, as cited in M Andenas and IH-Y Chiu, *The Foundations and Future of Financial Regulation: Governance for Responsibility* (Routledge, 2014).

[16] Allen and Wood provide a succinct review of the literature defining financial instability. See WA Allen, and G Wood, 'Defining and Achieving Financial Stability' (2006) 2(2) *Journal of Financial Stability* 152. See also CAE Goodhart, 'A Framework for Assessing Financial Stability?' (2006) 30 *Journal of Banking and Finance* 3415.

[17] AJ Schwartz, 'Real and Pseudo Financial Crises' in F Capie and G Wood, (eds), *Financial Crises and the World Banking System* (Macmillan, 1986), 11.

[18] F Mishkin, 'Anatomy of Financial Crisis' (1991) NBER Working Paper No 3934; European Central Bank, 'Assessing Financial Stability: Conceptual Boundaries and Challenges' (2005) *June Financial Stability Review* 117; O Issing, 'Monetary and Financial Stability: Is There a Trade-Off?' (Paper Delivered to Conference on 'Monetary Stability, Financial Stability and the Business Cycle', Basel, 28–29 March 2003). Available at: www.ecb.europa.eu/press/key/date/2003/html/sp030329.en.html.

[19] Issing, 'Monetary and Financial Stability' (n 18), O De Bandt and P Hartmann, 'Systemic Risk: A Survey' (2000) European Central Bank Working Paper No 35; T Padoa-Schioppa, 'Central Banks and Financial Stability: Exploring a Land in Between' (Paper Delivered at the Second ECB Central Banking Conference 'The Transformation of the European Financial System', Frankfurt, October 2002).

financial market bubbles grow,[20] the savings–investment balance in the economy is less than optimal.[21]

There is, however, literature framing financial stability in the positive, as a state in which the financial system can withstand unforeseeable events or shocks without major disruption and continue providing its services to the real economy.[22] Alternatively, it is a situation in which the financial system can efficiently and smoothly facilitate the allocation of resources, accurately assess and price forward-looking financial risks, and absorb financial and real economic surprises and shocks.[23] Allen considers it important that the definition of "financial stability" reflects that a stable financial system is not an end in itself, but is rather a means to achieving a healthy real economy and its social benefits, which is the ultimate goal.[24] Allen hints that there are other societal values, besides efficiency, which financial regulators consider, in the form of social benefits of regulation. However, social benefits here are treated as a corollary of a healthy economy and not as standalone values.

Despite the different iterations of financial stability, there are some common elements to be drawn. There is (i) the appearance of shocks, which (ii) cause the failure of financial intermediaries, leading to (iii) a disruption of financial services, and (iv) which has an adverse effect on the real economy. But what is the source of the initial shocks that precipitate failure?

3.2.2. The Concept of Systemic Risk

Literature in the wake of the financial crisis generally defines financial stability in terms of the concept of systemic risk and its sources.[25] As with financial stability, there is no one definition of systemic risk. One approach is that of the Group of Ten which defines systemic risk as the risk that an event triggers an economic loss

Available at: www.ecb.int/events/pdf/conferences/tps.pdf; GJ Schinasi, 'Responsibility of Central Banks for Stability in Financial Markets' (2003) IMF Working Paper WP/03/121, Available at: www.imf.org/external/pubs/ft/wp/2003/wp03121.pdf.

[20] Issing, (n 18).

[21] AG Haldane et al, 'Financial Stability and Macroeconomic Models' (2004) 16 *Bank of England Financial Stability Review*, 80.

[22] See, for instance, the ECB definition. Available at: www.ecb.europa.eu/ecb/tasks/stability/html/index.en.html.

[23] GJ Schinasi, *Safeguarding Financial Stability: Theory and Practice* (International Monetary Fund, 2006) 82.

[24] HJ Allen, 'What Is "Financial Stability"? The Need for Some Common Language in International Financial Regulation' (2014) 45 *Georgetown Journal of International Law* 929, 946.

[25] See G Galati and R Moessner, 'Macroprudential Policy – A Literature Review' (February 2011) Bank for International Settlements Working Papers No 337, 13. Available at: www.bis.org/publ/work337.pdf.

or loss of confidence in a large part of the financial system that is serious enough to adversely affect the economy.[26] In contrast, the IMF-FSB-BIS defined it as the risk of weaknesses in the financial system disrupting financial services and having very negative effects on the real economy.[27] This is also the definition favoured by the ECB.[28]

The effects on the financial system and the economy vary, from the drying up of liquidity and an increase in the cost of the capital that is available,[29] to extreme credit rationing in the real economy[30] to a reduction in the growth of the global GDP.[31] These various definitions contain all the same elements as the definition for financial stability – an event, causing disruption to the financial system which severely impairs the real economy.

3.2.3. Shocks, Disruptions and Impairment

The systemic event could be triggered by an exogenous shock, which means it emanates from outside the financial system, such as an economic downturn, which simultaneously affects all financial firms and the system.[32] Alternatively, the trigger could be endogenous, meaning from within the financial system. Literature in the decade after the crisis focused a great deal on endogenous risks. The endogenous triggers, as identified by economists and finance scholars, have two roots: (i) financial imbalance,[33] and (ii) contagion.[34] Therefore, the prevention of financial crises requires an understanding of the channels of contagion and triggers for financial booms and busts. Regulation for financial stability is organised around these two concepts.

[26] Group of Ten, *Report on Consolidation in the Financial Sector* (BIS-IMF-OECD, 2001), 126.

[27] IMF-BIS-FSB, 'Guidance to Assess the Systemic Importance of Financial Institutions, Markets and Instruments: Initial Considerations' (Report to the G-20 Finance Ministers and Central Bank Governors, October 2009). Available at: www.imf.org/external/np/g20/pdf/100109.pdf.

[28] European Central Bank, *Financial Stability Review* (December 2009).

[29] SL Schwarcz, 'Systemic Risk' (2008–2009) 97 *Georgetown Law Journal* 193.

[30] De Bandt and Hartmann, 'Systemic Risk' (n 19).

[31] JP Fouque and JA Langham (eds), *Handbook on Systemic Risk* (Cambridge University Press, 2013) xxi.

[32] ECB, *Financial Stability Review* (n 28) 135.

[33] F Allen and E Carletti, 'Systemic Risk from Real Estate and Macro-Prudential Regulation' (2013) 5(1/2) *International Journal of Banking, Accounting and Finance* 28; Franklin Allen and Douglas Gale, 'Financial Contagion' (2000) 108(1) *Journal of Political Economy* 1.

[34] X Freixas, BM Parigi and J Rochet, 'Systemic Risk, Interbank Relations and Liquidity Provision by the Central Bank' (2000) 32(3) *Journal of Money, Credit & Banking* 611. Schwarz, however, criticises how there has been little attempt to go further and identify the underlying market failures which cause contagion and financial imbalance. For Schwarz, this should be the first step in the regulatory process, given that regulation is justified as an attempt to correct market failures. He puts forward five such market failures and argues that regulation should ultimately be aimed at addressing those failures. SL Schwarcz, 'Systematic Regulation of Systemic Risk' (2019) 1(2019) *Wisconsin Law Review* 1.

3.2.3.1. Contagion via the Banking and Payment System

Contagion, strictly speaking, refers to the 'domino effect' that the failure of one bank has on other banks and financial intermediaries.[35] Failure of individual banks is a result of the unique combination of activities carried out by banks, which leave them vulnerable to insolvency. To understand how this failure is transmitted, this section will take the reader through the activities carried out by banks and the inherent risks that can lead to failure.

(a) What do Bankers Do?

(i) Payment Systems

The story of banks can be traced back to the evolution of trade from the barter system to one in which payments were made with coins made from precious metals. Since then, payment systems have evolved from bills of exchange to book entries on the accounts of the payer and payee in the bank's ledger; to checking accounts where account holders could simply draw a check instructing their bank to debit their account and credit the account of another individual. Now payments simply take the form of electronic instructions that are made through debit cards or internet banking platforms, to make electronic deductions direct from bank accounts. Virtually all modern payments involve the debit or credit of an account held with a bank, even with the advent of mobile money and cryptocurrencies.[36]

The payment system is a set of mechanisms for transferring ownership of a narrow set of claims to discharge obligations incurred by economic agents as they trade. These claims, by virtue of their wide acceptability, are known as money, and include claims on government or the central bank, in the form of coins, notes and bank reserves; and claims on other banks in the form of deposits.[37] The transfer of funds to settle payment instructions can be done individually on a continuous basis, a real time gross transfer; or through multilateral netting arrangements, a transfer at distinct intervals of the difference between the money owed to and by each bank in the payment system.[38] The multilateral netting arrangement is the traditional method of making payments; it was created to reduce the need for banks to hold large balances to meet individual payment requests as they occurred,

[35] X Freixas, L Laeven, and JL Peydró, *Systemic Risk, Crises, and Macroprudential Regulation* (MIT Press, 2015) 103.

[36] Armour et al, *Principles of Financial Regulation* (n 7) 25.

[37] C Borio and P Van den Bergh, 'The Nature and Management of Payment System Risks: An International Perspective' (13 February 1993) BIS Economic Papers No 36.

[38] In some countries payment systems operate in a tiered structure, where a small number of banks act as correspondent banks for the rest and only they do the final settlement on the clearing agent's books (eg CHIPS in the US and CHAPS in the UK). Banks involved in making cross-border payments are linked via a series of communication networks which carry payment instructions to various domestic payment systems, such as the Society for Worldwide Interbank Financial Telecommunication (SWIFT). Borio and Van den Bergh, 'Nature and Management of Payment System Risks', ibid.

and to make numerous adjustments to their balance sheets throughout the day. Instead, payment requests are sent via a central clearing agent, traditionally the central bank, and, at the end of the day, the clearing agent calculates net balances to be transferred.

(ii) Deposit Taking and Loan Origination

Apart from facilitating payments, the original banks also performed another function – they would lend out some of the money held in their vaults. Most modern legal definitions describe banks as institutions that receive money from individual depositors and lend that money to other borrowers. In the US,

> the term 'bank," means a bank or trust company … a substantial part of the business of which consists of receiving deposits and making loans and discounts.[39]

Similarly, in the UK and EU, the statutory definitions of banks reflect these deposit-taking and lending functions. The UK's Banking Act 2009 defines a bank as a:

> UK institution which has permission … to carry on the regulated activity of accepting deposits.[40]

While EU law refers to 'credit institutions', rather than 'banks', it defines them as:

> an undertaking the business of which is to take deposits or other repayable funds from the public and to grant credits for its own account.[41]

Strictly speaking, only commercial banks fully embody the definitions stated above. The commercial banker accepts 'from his customers loans of money of deposit, that is to say, loans for an indefinite period upon running an account, repayable as to the whole or any part thereof upon demand by the customer …'.[42]

Having thus received the deposits, the banks become the owners of the funds and can use those funds to issue loans in their own name and at their own risk. It is difficult to create a secondary market for these loans because of the privity of contract between the lender and borrower.[43] The loans created by banks are

[39] 26 US Code § 581.

[40] Banking Act 2009, s 2.

[41] Regulation (EU) No 575/2013 of the European Parliament and of the Council of 26 June 2013 on prudential requirements for credit institutions and investment firms and amending Regulation (EU) No 648/2012 OJ. L 176/1, Art 4(1).

[42] Diplock LJ in *United Dominions v Kirkwood* [1966] 1 All ER 968.

[43] Apart from the legal constraints which prevent the creation of a secondary market, there are also information constraints. Loan creation or generation is based on information about the potential borrower, such as their payment record or internal workings if the borrower is a corporation. Banks ecuritiza in collecting and processing this private information and so can determine the creditworthiness of a particular borrower and the relative value of a loan to that customer. The need for this ecuritizat information makes it difficult to create a secondary market for loans, because potential purchasers cannot collect and process this information. The level of information regarding a borrower is asymmetrical as between the bank and potential purchasers of the loans. Douglas Diamond, 'Financial Intermediation and Delegated Monitoring' (1984) 51(3) *Review of Economic Studies* 393.

generally illiquid because they cannot be sold quickly and easily. Furthermore, they are usually of a long-term nature, for example mortgages, in contrast to their source of funding, or liabilities, which are largely short-term deposits. By performing this maturity transformation function, banks can offer depositors part of the benefits of higher returns associated with long-term investments.[44] Thus, they perform a *liquidity and maturity transformation* function, by changing liquid deposits that can be demanded at any time, into illiquid assets with a longer maturity date.

Bank deposits are a form of demandable debt in that the bank contracts to pay a fixed sum of money to the depositor on demand.[45] The bank is then free to use the funds deposited for its own investment activities. Most savers want to be able to liquidate their investments at short notice in case they suffer financial shock. However, many of the bank's investments are illiquid, meaning the bank will have to incur some losses if savers attempt to get their money back at a moment's notice. To avoid this situation, banks maintain some liquid assets to meet short-term demand, the most liquid being cash.

This contrasts with the bank's profit-maximising objectives, which can only be achieved by lending as many of the funds held by the bank as possible, thus converting the cash into less liquid assets. Still, commercial banks give savers the assurance that they will be able to withdraw their deposit on demand. They ride on the assumption that the savers' liquidity needs are not correlated, thus the bank need only maintain in reserve a fraction of the funds deposited, leaving it free to lend out the rest, and still be able to meet demands for payment as and when they arise.[46] This is the essence of fractional reserve banking. Banks use the law of large numbers to predict the likely level of withdrawals at any one time with a reasonably high degree of confidence, and only maintain this amount as cash or equally liquid assets.[47]

(b) How Does Insolvency Occur?

(i) Liquidity Risk

Fractional reserve banking only works as long as depositors are confident the bank will be able to fulfil its promise to pay on demand. It is, essentially, a confidence trick, and once doubts arise about the bank's ability to meet its liabilities, then depositors will be justifiably concerned about their deposits and may seek to withdraw them.[48] But it is difficult to tell what can trigger this loss of confidence, as

[44] Armour et al (n 7), 277.

[45] H Mandanis Schooner and MW Taylor, *Global Bank Regulation: Principles and Policies* (Elsevier, 2010), 5.

[46] Armour et al (n 7), 28.

[47] X Freixas and JC Rochet, *Microeconomics of Banking* 2nd edn (MIT Press, 2008).

[48] Freixas and Rochet, ibid. See also Armour et al (n 7) 275.

Diamond and Dybvig point out, this loss of confidence and a subsequent run on the bank can be the result of anything really, from an earnings report, a run at another bank or a government forecast.[49]

A perception that the bank is insolvent, and any delay in demanding your deposit might result in not being paid back, since withdrawals are honoured on a first-come-first-served basis, prompts a mad rush to withdraw funds by all the depositors all at once.[50] However, because the bank only holds a fraction of its assets in reserve as cash or equally liquid assets, it may not be able to meet the demand. This is the *funding liquidity risk* that banks face, the risk that they may not be able to settle obligations with immediacy because of illiquidity.[51] Meanwhile, the bank may, in fact, have a healthy balance sheet with performing loans, and is only facing temporary liquidity constraints, as all firms do.

Faced with a sudden high demand for liquidity, and after exhausting its liquid assets, a bank will be forced to cut back its loans or sell its illiquid assets. However, the information asymmetry that exists between the bank and potential buyers of bank assets makes the assets unattractive. The bank will be forced to sell the assets at a lower price to offset the risk faced by the potential buyer.[52] The greater the liquidity demand, the more assets the bank is forced to sell at fire-sale prices, effectively writing off those assets, even though they were performing well. In an ordinary firm, the firm's equity should provide a cushion against such adverse shocks. Any reduction on the asset side of the bank's balance sheet should be covered by a reduction on capital, which represents the firm's liabilities towards shareholders. However, banks' capital usually represents a small portion of their liabilities as they are mainly funded through debt, in the form of deposits, which makes them highly leveraged.[53]

This thin cushion leaves banks vulnerable to the risk that they will not be able to meet any of their debts in the long run. If a significant portion of the assets is written off, this will wipe out capital, leaving the bank insolvent. For a bank to remain solvent, the value of its assets must quite simply exceed the value of its liabilities. We see here that what starts off as a temporary liquidity problem, or cash flow insolvency, may quickly degenerate to balance sheet insolvency.[54] Dalhuisen

[49] Diamond and Dybvig, 'Bank Runs' (n 8).

[50] Ibid. The coordination problem amongst bank depositors was captured in the D-D model.

[51] M Drehmann and K Nikolaou, 'Funding Liquidity Risk: Definition and Measurement' (12 July 2010) BIS Working Papers No 316. Available at: www.bis.org/publ/work316.htm.

[52] See Akerlof's market for lemons model.

[53] When leverage is combined with limited liability for shareholders it creates an incentive for managers to take on excessive risk because shareholders can reap all the benefits of high-risk high return projects, while shifting the risk of failure onto the bank's creditors, ie its depositors. See Schooner and Taylor, *Global Bank Regulation* (n 45) 22.

[54] JH Dalhuisen, *Dalhuisen on Transnational Comparative, Commercial, Financial and Trade Law: Financial Products, Financial Services and Financial Regulation* Vol 3, 7th edn (Hart Publishing 2019) 471.

contends that it is not lack of capital, but illiquidity that is the true or immediate killer of banks.[55]

To cope with liquidity risk, banks can access alternative funding on the interbank market, where banks holding an excess of central bank reserves lend them to those that are in short supply, and the capital markets, for example by issuing commercial paper. On the interbank market banks can either source funds via repo agreements, where the loans are fully collateralised and the solvency of the counterpart is a minor issue, or the unsecured market where lending is short term, often only overnight. As a result, prior to the crisis, liquidity risk was a secondary concern because it was believed the interbank market would help a solvent bank to stave off a bank run by providing liquidity at the market interest rate.

In addition, the market for securities constitutes a further mechanism for banks to raise funds.[56] Changes to the banking model, which began in the 1980s,[57] allowed banks to move from a relatively simple model, in which banks took deposits and made loans, and where they rarely engaged in cross-border transactions because currencies were not freely tradable,[58] to a model which allowed cross-sectorial investments and cross-distribution of products.[59] The removal of

[55] Ibid.

[56] Freixas, Laeven and Peydró, *Systemic Risk and Crises* (n 35) 117.

[57] In the US this culminated in the enactment of the Financial Services Modernization Act of 1999, also known as the Gramm-Leach-Bliley Act, which allowed a financial holding company to engage in activities that are 'financial in nature or incidental to such financial activity; or is complementary to a financial activity and does not pose a substantial risk to the safety or soundness of depository institutions or the financial system generally'. The process had begun much earlier in the UK, with the 'Big Bang' on 27 October 1986, a massive deregulation drive which, among other measures, allowed participation on the stock exchange by entities that were part of a wider financial group. Interestingly, in Europe, the combination of banking and other activities already had a long history, either in the form of *Allfinanz* or *Bancassurance*, which combined banking and insurance, or the *Universal Bank Model*, in which commercial banks would trade in the capital markets on behalf of clients and on their own account.

[58] Furthermore, banking was strictly segregated from other forms of financial activity, like insurance and securities underwriting and trading. The most prominent example of ring-fencing from this era was the US 1933 Banking Act 12 USC § 227, popularly known as the Glass-Stegall Act, which separated commercial banking from investment banking, and prohibited banks from trading in securities for their own account. Glass-Stegall was enacted in the wake of the banking crisis of 1929–1933. Even where legislation separating the two activities did not exist, as in as the UK, banking was kept separate from securities business by a network of custom, practice and club rules. For instance, Rules 27 and 38 of the London Stock Exchange required that members should be independent, neither they nor their wife should be engaged in other businesses and they could not partner with anyone outside the Exchange. Rules 27 & 38. See Rudolph E. Melsheimer and Walter Laurence, *The Law and Customs of the London Stock Exchange: With an Appendix Containing the Rules and Regulations Authorised by the Committee for The Conduct of Business* (Henry Sweet 1879) 129, 132.

[59] The convergence through cross-sectoral investments and cross distribution also brought with it a new type of financial firm, the financial conglomerates. These groups tend to engage in both regulated and un-regulated activities, at wholesale and retail level. The flagship business differs, so in some conglomerates, like the AXA Group, it may be insurance; or it may be banking, as in the case of Nordea; or the group can dominate all sectors, such as Citi Group, ING Group, Credit Suisse Group and Deutsche Bank. Financial conglomerates became popular because of the economies of scope which could be achieved via the business model. The model allows firms to streamline the

barriers allowed commercial banks to broaden their funding base, and diversify their source of income, in capital markets by issuing debt, like other corporates, in the form of certificates of deposit and short-term commercial paper. Furthermore, commercial banks increasingly engaged in proprietary trading in the capital markets, acting as underwriters and market makers.

Freixas et al show, however, that liquidity can also dry up in these alternative markets in a manner akin to bank runs. As described earlier, funding liquidity constraints may force banks to engage in fire sales. If a number of banks in the system have been forced to sell their assets in this manner at the same time this pushes down the price of the assets and the market's appetite for those assets.[60] This decreased appetite for those assets creates *market liquidity risk*, the risk that the holder of the assets cannot easily sell them off because there is not enough demand on the market or the market is experiencing a disruption, and therefore cannot meet its obligations to creditors.[61]

The decreasing market liquidity will lead to higher price volatility for the asset, and prompt prudent lenders in the repo market to either increase the haircut on collateral, ask the debtor bank to post more collateral, or reduce or cut off lending altogether. Any of these actions reduces the debtor bank's access to funding liquidity.[62] This is called a margin run and is akin to a bank run.[63] The bank, faced with reduced liquidity, becomes reluctant to take any further positions in high haircut assets, aggravating market illiquidity and volatility, which forces an increase in the haircut, so the negative cycle of deleveraging and more sales continues.[64]

Finally, the unsecured market can become illiquid if other banks either suddenly begin hoarding liquidity to prevent a liquidity shock or they refuse to lend because they suspect that counterparties on the interbank market are holding toxic assets and are insolvent.

Once depositors start a run on one bank, there is a risk of it becoming a generalised run on all banks, either through a *pure panic contagion* or as an *information-based* run. Under the former type of generalised run, the collapse of one bank may generate panic about the health of other banks because depositors cannot differentiate between solvent and insolvent banks, leading to a run on all

provision of multiple products and services, by leveraging the bank's branch network, IT systems and customer base. It allows greater diversification of the firm's portfolio and revenue streams, thus spreading its risk. Tripartite Group of Bank, Securities and Insurance Regulators, 'Supervision of Financial Conglomerates' (Report, July 1995). Available at: www.bis.org/publ/bcbs20.pdf, accessed 10 June 2018.

[60] Schooner and Taylor, *Global Bank Regulation* (n 45) 44.

[61] Basel Committee on Banking Supervision, *Principles for Sound Liquidity Risk Management and Supervision* (BIS, 2008).

[62] Schooner and Taylor (n 45) 44.

[63] Repurchase agreements, securities loans, commercial paper, money market funds, and uninsured bank deposits were the objects of runs and fire sales during the crisis. See Office of Financial Research, 'Financial Stability Assessment' [2016] *Financial Stability Report* 7, 16.

[64] Markus K Brunnermeier and Lasse H Pedersen, 'Market Liquidity and Funding Liquidity' (2009) 22(3) *The Review of Financial Studies* 2201.

banks regardless of their differences or similarities. An information-based run, on the other hand, arises because of perceived similarities between a failed bank and other banks.[65]

(ii) Credit Risk

Even if the failure of one bank does not develop into a generalised run, it can lead to failure of other banks due to credit risk, which is the potential of a borrower or counterparty to a loan failing to meet their repayment obligations.[66] As already highlighted above, banks regularly trade with each other on the interbank market, repo and capital markets and are linked in a web of assets and liabilities they owe to each other. The failure by one bank to meet its obligations to another, because it is insolvent, can affect that bank's balance sheet and so on. And when a borrower fails to repay, regardless of whether that borrower is another bank or not, the bank must write off that loan. This reduces the value of the creditor bank's assets on its balance sheet and in turn requires a reduction in the creditor bank's capital. If a substantial number of borrowers fail to repay, the non-performing loans could wipe out the bank's entire capital.[67] Loan losses can drive a bank into insolvency.

The payment function of banks adds another dimension to the risk of insolvency faced by banks. The lag between commitment to transfer and actual transfer exposes banks to credit risk. After calculations, a bank with a negative net position might not be able to settle its debts, but the other bank, with a positive net position and expecting payment, would only discover this the following business day, at least by midday, after it has spent half the day making more payments on behalf of the defaulting bank.

While the time lag is an important determinant of the risk faced by banks in payments systems, the existence of risk is also affected by whether the banks can secure collateral from the other participants in the payment system, whether a payment lacks finality because it can be revoked or is made conditional, for instance upon the receipt of funds; or how the legal system will enforce netting agreements, particularly in bankruptcy of one of the participants. The bottom line is the failure by a participating bank to settle its commitments can affect the solvency of its counterparties on the payment system if their exposure is sufficiently large. Payment systems are connective tissue through which shocks can be propagated.

[65] See C Calomiris and J Mason, 'Contagion and Bank Failures During the Great Depression: The June 1932 Chicago Bank Panic' (1997) 87(5) *American Economic Review* 863. Their work shows that, despite the theory of depositor irrationality, runs occurred on banks that were already insolvent, therefore the runs were justified.

[66] Basel Committee on Banking Supervision, 'Principles for the Management of Credit Risk' (Guidelines, 27 September 2002), 1. Available at: www.bis.org/publ/bcbs75.htm.

[67] Schooner and Taylor (n 45).

(iii) Market Risk

A bank's assets do not consist solely of loans, it also invests in securities. Thus, it may fail not because of exposure to other banks as counterparties, but because of common exposure in the capital markets. The movement in prices of securities due to fire sales as described above, also affects the balance sheet of the bank holding similar assets because accounting rules require that such assets be valued according to current market prices, they are marked to market. This is in contrast to traditional bank assets, in the form of loans, which are valued based on their historical cost. A bank's capital will therefore have to be reduced to absorb the losses generated from a reduction in asset values which, as stated before, could lead to the bank's capital being completely wiped out.

(iv) Operational Risk

Sometimes, however, the pressures on the bank's balance sheet which lead to insolvency may not be from the sudden withdrawal of liquidity, failure of a counterparty, or market risk but because of operational failures caused by people, faulty processes and systems, or external events.[68] This is the *operational risk* that banks live with, but excludes strategic and reputational risk.[69] Operational risk had always been regarded as a residual risk, not covered by credit or market risk, but, by the end of the 1990s, it had acquired widespread currency in the wake of the destruction of Barings Bank by the 'rogue trader' Nicholas Leeson, and the losses in excess of $1 billion suffered by Daiwa Bank due to the actions of Toshihide Iguchi. Moreover, as banks became larger and more complex, the challenges of managing and controlling the operations of large, complex, geographically far-flung organisations also grew, increasing operational risk.[70]

Contagion thus has two channels.[71] On the one hand there are bank runs, precipitated by a fear that a bank will not be able to meet its obligations to all depositors and resulting withdrawal of deposit funds or liquidity in capital markets, either of which leads to insolvency. On the other hand, there is connectedness, which can ignite a small failure at one bank into a huge flame engulfing the whole system.[72] Interconnections amongst banks can be direct, via banks assets, because they lend to other banks, or via their liabilities, because they borrow from other banks. Failure of a counterparty on the asset side can lead to depletion of capital, while failure on the liability side reduces the bank's funding liquidity and, as we saw, reduced funding liquidity eventually affects market liquidity. The

[68] Legal risk includes, but is not limited to, exposure to fines, penalties, or punitive damages resulting from supervisory actions, as well as private settlements. See Basel Committee on Banking Supervision, *Basel II: International Convergence on Capital Measurement and Capital Standards: A Revised Framework – Comprehensive Version* (BIS June 2006) 144. Available at: www.bis.org/publ/bcbs128.pdf.

[69] Ibid.

[70] Schooner and Taylor, (n 45) 175.

[71] D Schoenmaker, *Contagion Risk in Banking* (LSE Financial Markets Group, 1996).

[72] HS Scott, *Connectedness and Contagion: Protecting the Financial System from Panics* (MIT Press, 2016), 3.

issue of market liquidity also reveals an indirect form of interconnection amongst banks – common exposure. The failures via interconnections are exacerbated by the size of banks in the network. The bigger a bank, the greater the impact and reach of its failure.

3.2.3.2. Financial Imbalances

Financial crises tend to occur following periods of rapid credit growth and asset price bubbles, particularly in real estate.[73]

(a) Credit Booms

The literature shows that there is a strong correlation between *ex ante* credit booms and financial crises.[74] The type of credit boom may vary from crisis to crisis, being concentrated in the household sector, in the corporate sector, or in the public sector.

Any number of factors can trigger a credit boom, such as increased levels of productivity following periods of sustained economic growth; increased capital flows from international financial markets; and economic policies, such as accommodative monetary policy, which lowers interest rates and encourages more spending.[75] Alternatively, structural factors such as financial liberalisation and innovation can also lead to credit booms, as they encourage greater risk taking.[76] The abundance of liquidity makes debt cheaper and therefore an even more than normal attractive source of funding for banks, which in turn encourages them to engage in not only more leveraged lending, but also excessive maturity mismatches. Eventually, however, everything goes bust when liquidity withdraws from the market.[77]

Alternatively, as Freixas et al assert, the increased leveraging and maturity mismatches are the result of correlated risk choices by individual financial intermediaries, households and investors. By this account, excessive risk-taking in

[73] Freixas, Laeven and Peydró (n 35) 73.

[74] C Reinhart and KS Rogoff, *This Time Is Different: Eight Centuries of Financial Folly* (Princeton University Press, 2009); O Jorda, M Schularick, and AM Taylor, 'Financial Crises, Credit Booms and External Imbalances: 140 Years of Lessons' (2011) 59(2) *IMF Economic Review* 340; M Schularick and AM Taylor, 'Credit Booms Gone Bust: Monetary Policy, Leverage Cycles, and Financial Crises' (2012) 102(2) *American Economic Review* 102; O Jorda, M Schularick, and AM Taylor, 'When Credit Bites Back: Leverage, Business Cycles, And Crises' (2013) 45(2) *Journal of Money, Credit and Banking* 3; O Jorda, M Schularick and AM Taylor, 'Leveraged Bubbles' (August 2015) Federal Reserve Bank of San Francisco Working Paper Series Working Paper 2015-10.

[75] S Claessens and MA Kose, 'Financial Crises: Explanations, Types, and Implications' (2013) IMF Working Paper WP/13/28, 10. Available at: https://www.imf.org/external/pubs/ft/wp/2013/wp1328.pdf.

[76] Ibid.

[77] Freixas, Laeven and Peydró (n 35) 24.

banking has been interpreted as stemming from either of two root causes. The first explanation is based on time-varying risk appetites, bankers and consumers of financial products are buoyant in good times, to the point of neglecting tail risks, but cautious in bad times and therefore less willing to take on risk.[78] The second explanation is the moral hazard created by the limited liability that banks enjoy, coupled with the ability to engage in high leveraging, and the presence of explicit and implicit government guarantees and deposit insurance should it all come crashing down. These perverse incentives fuel excessive lending by bankers, safe in the knowledge that they can reap the high benefits if their risk-taking pays off; if not, they have a safety net. They can privatise gains but socialise a large part of losses.[79] Therefore, one way to prevent future systemic financial crises may be to design policies that dampen the appetite for risk. Regulatory responses will therefore depend on which is the favoured view on causes of credit booms and busts.[80] These endogenous factors do not, however, exists in a vacuum. There must be an initial run-up in wealth that increases the funding available with which to take risks. Therefore, endogenous and exogenous factors are reinforcing, and combine to make debt and leverage more attractive.

The market failure of credit booms in good times comes from excessive credit supply, while a credit bust in the bad times is a result of the contraction of the pool of aggregate liquidity (a reduction in funding and market liquidity), followed by widespread deleveraging, as described above in 3.2.3.1. (b)(i). Liquidity, our old nemesis, reappears. Therefore, what is needed is a policy instrument that limits both the *likelihood* of systemic crises, by (i) limiting availability of liquidity, the attractiveness of debt and the extent of maturity mismatch, as well as (ii) limiting the *cost* of systemic crises, by ensuring there is still sufficient liquidity for the system to function after the bubble bursts. An objective of macroprudential policy would therefore be to address the cyclicality of the financial system and its resilience throughout the cycle.

(b) Asset-price Bubbles

Pre-crisis periods tend to experience not only credit booms but also asset price bubbles. Asset-price bubbles follow from an increase in the availability of credit for investment.

Collapse of real estate prices has been identified as the most important source of systemic risk.[81] This has been true both historically and in the most recent crisis.[82]

[78] Freixas et al term this the preference channel. See, ibid, 73.

[79] Freixas et al term this the agency channel. See ibid, 74.

[80] Ibid 75.

[81] Reinhart and Rogoff, *This Time Is Different* (n 74); C Kindleberger and R Aliber, *Manias, Panics and Crashes: A History of Financial Crises* 6th edn (Palgrave McMillan, 2011).

[82] Allen and Carletti, 'Systemic Risk from Real Estate' (n 33). Booms largely involving equity market activities appear to have lower risks of adverse consequences. The burst of the internet bubble of the late

Banks' exposures in real estate markets have mounted over the past 40 years due to the politicisation of real estate funding, particularly residential real estate.[83] This was particularly true in the US where mortgage risk was highly subsidised by government sponsored entities, the Federal National Mortgage Association, (Fannie Mae), and Federal Home Loan Mortgage Corporation, (Freddie Mac). Banks themselves also increased their funding investment in real estate, relying primarily on their short-term debt. Real estate bubbles are particularly dangerous, in comparison, say, to equity bubbles, because exposure to real estate is highly correlated with exposure to other assets. Since real estate is often used as security for other loans, any changes in real estate prices will be reflected in the value of the mortgages backing these assets.[84] Furthermore, because of the illiquid nature of real estate, the mortgage holders cannot sell them off quickly at their full value to cover their liabilities, they inevitably suffer losses, adding pressure to an already strained balance sheet.[85]

Like credit booms, not all asset price bubbles trigger financial crises; some may actually have a positive impact on economic growth. A systemic crisis arises when there is a sudden reversal in asset values, for instance, when assets are liquidated at fire sale prices. As described in section 3.2.3.1 above, a drop in the value of banks' assets is absorbed by capital. The drop in value also affects the ability of borrowers to use the assets as collateral to secure funding which, as we saw, has a feedback effect on market liquidity. The bottom line is in the face of reduced availability of liquidity, banks respond by reducing lending, leading to a decrease in household and firm investment, which slows down economic growth, feeding back into bank activity. It is a vicious cycle that cannot be stopped, unless someone steps in to break the loop, for instance by providing liquidity, recapitalising the banks, or directly funding economic activity.

3.2.3.3. Lessons from Contagion and Financial Imbalances

From the preceding discussion we have learnt that, on the one hand, systemic crises arise from the build-up of imbalances in the financial sector. The prudent approach would be to prevent the excessive risk taking which leads to the build-up of bubbles. However, as risk cannot be eliminated from finance completely, the policies targeting financial imbalances should also support the liquidity and capital positions of financial institutions, and consequently the flow of credit to

1990s, which largely involved only equity markets, was not very costly for the real economy. The main reason is that booms in the real estate sector involve leverage and banks, therefore when the bubble bursts, the flow of credit to the rest of the economy is interrupted. See Claessens and Kose, 'Financial Crises' (n 75).

[83] C Calomaris, 'Restoring the Rule of Law in Financial Regulation' (24 September 2018) *Cato Journal*. Available at: www.cato.org/cato-journal/fall-2018/restoring-rule-law-financial-regulation.

[84] ibid.

[85] ibid.

the real economy during the bust phases. Moreover, asset price bubbles, particularly in real estate, normally accompany the worst credit booms, so another way to prevent future systemic financial crises may be to design policies that reduce banks' exposure to one type of asset during the boom phase. On the other hand, financial crises may be the result of contagion, either informational-based contagion, which results in runs on banks, or credit-based contagion, which is a result of the connectedness of banks' balance sheets. To avoid crises precipitated by contagion would require two approaches, making the individual intermediaries more resilient to the illiquidity that can trigger insolvency and/or reducing the connections amongst banks through which failure is transmitted.

Regulation to contain financial instability should thus have two dimensions – (i) the time dimension, which reflects the financial system's tendency to provide more credit during a boom, usually towards a particular type of asset, and to suddenly withdraw that credit in a bust phase, and (ii) the cross-sectional dimension, which reflects the extent of connections in the financial system through which risk can spread. See Table 3.1 below which summarises the regulatory implications of contagion and financial imbalances. It is important to note that both dimensions of systemic risks are related and reinforce each other.

Table 3.1 Regulatory Implications of Contagion and Financial Imbalances

Source of Shock	**Features**	**Regulatory Targets/Tools**
Contagion	• Liquidity + Balance Sheet Solvency • Size • Concentration • Interlinkages	• Increase individual bank resilience – capital and liquidity strengthening, reduce leverage. • Reduce interconnections. • Stem crisis – lender of last resort; liability guarantees, capital injections, orderly resolution.
Financial Imbalance	• Credit boom • Asset price boom	• Controlling credit growth, maturity transformation and leverage at the top of the cycle – countercyclical measures (capital, liquidity, leverage). • Improve system resilience by building buffers to draw down in bad times – countercyclical measures.

Bank management could put in place mechanisms to manage the various types of risks.[86] However their incentive to manage risk more effectively is low, because

[86] For instance, to avoid insolvency and limit contagion effects, they may manage credit risk by spreading it, through securitization, diversity in loan portfolios and limiting counterparty concentration, or by obtaining guarantees including the use of credit default swaps. Market risk is commonly hedged using derivatives such as options, futures and swaps. To protect against liquidity

leveraged lending allows banks to take greater risks and maximise shareholder profits while externalising the costs of any failure. Unfortunately, episodes of financial instability have macro-economic costs, and are very damaging for households and companies, which cannot be reasonably expected to anticipate or solve such episodes. There is a case, therefore, for government intervention in the risk management of banks – in the interest of public policy – to prevent financial instability, or, at the very least, limit the fallout if financial instability becomes unavoidable.

3.3. Correcting Market Failures – Microprudential Regulation

Banks' fragility combined with the important function they perform engenders a belief that they need to be supervised and regulated. Although the terms regulation and supervision are often used interchangeably, they are different. Lastra distinguishes regulation as the process of rulemaking, either by public or private bodies, while supervision, *stricto sensu*, refers to the monitoring of the behaviour of financial firms, in particular risk monitoring and risk control.[87] Because banking supervision monitors the degree to which the banks abide by the rules, there is a connection between the two concepts. The very process of supervision is subject to regulation. Throughout this book, the term 'regulation' shall be used to refer to both processes.

3.3.1. What is Microprudential Regulation?

Regulation is usually organised along the lines of three concerns: (i) safety and soundness of the individual intermediaries; (ii) conduct of business; and (iii) market integrity. The first objective can be achieved by targeting the service provider. Regulation which is focused on the individual intermediaries aims to ensure that banks exercise more caution in their business activities, in other words,

risk, banks can seek more long-term loans in the capital markets, or issue commercial paper, which offers fixed deposits, thus reducing the type of funding which creditors can demand at any time. On the asset side, they can invest in more liquid assets, like treasury bills, which can be quickly converted to meet withdrawal demands from depositors. Risk in the payment system can be addressed firstly through stringent entry requirements for participating banks and, as a safety net, by requiring the banks participating in the payment system to assume the risk of non-paying participants. More recently banks have sought to limit their exposure from underwriting the payment system by moving to a Real Time Gross Settlement (RTGS) system, in which transactions are completed in real time, the Clearing House interbank Payment System (CHIPS) in the US and the Trans-European Automated Real-time Gross Settlements Express Transfer (TARGET) in Europe are examples of such systems.

[87] RM Lastra, *International Financial Law* (Oxford University Press, 2015), 113–15.

that they be more 'prudent', thus safeguarding the public who are consumers of financial products and services. This is micro-prudential regulation.

Microprudential regulation begins before the bank even enters the market, by imposing licensing requirements, and throughout its life the bank is required to maintain those requirements on capital, liquidity, and general risk management to retain its licence. In the event the bank fails, microprudential regulation also mitigates losses and stops the spread of failure to other banks. Microprudential regulation was used as the tool for maintaining financial stability, because the failure of individual institutions can have spill-over effects – the contagion risk discussed above. However, its true objective remains the resilience of individual banks.

Microprudential regulation is to be distinguished from client protection and market abuse regulation. Policies in the area of client protection are mostly embedded in private law, namely contract and banking laws, agency and property law, disclosure rules and dispute resolution mechanisms. Clients have private law remedies available to them when they are wronged by financial intermediaries, however this is only after the fact and it may be costly for each individual client to enforce their rights, leading to inefficient markets.[88] Additional protection is provided through business conduct rules that mandate the fair treatment of customers and regulate the sale of risky products.

Typical business conduct rules may be proscriptive, such as those imposing advertising restrictions, duties in managing conflicts of interest and communicating to clients the conflict-of-interest policy, accepting limited inducements; or they may be prescriptive, such as requiring production and labelling of investment research, segregating and handling client money and assets so that these may be identifiable and ring-fenced in the event of firm insolvency, giving suitable or appropriate personal recommendation to clients in investment advice or other services, aiming for best execution when transacting orders for a client, and the duty to make fair and informative communications.[89]

The other type of regulation, market abuse regulation, arises because for financial markets to allocate resources efficiently, they require efficient pricing of the products and services. This is achieved through rules obliging sellers of securities to release certain information, while prohibiting insiders from acting and benefiting from information which is not publicly available (insider trading), or engaging in generally anti-competitive behaviour.[90] Much like client protection,

[88] See IH-Y Chiu, 'The Nature of a Financial Investment Intermediary's Duty to his Client' (2008) 28 *Legal Studies* 254, discussing the interface between private enforcement and public regulation in client protection.

[89] See, for instance, European Parliament and Council Directive 2004/39/EC of 21 April 2004 on markets in financial instruments amending Council Directives 85/611/EEC and 93/6/EEC and Directive 2000/12/EC of the European Parliament and of the Council and repealing Council Directive 93/22/EEC [2004] OJ L145/1 (MiFID). FCA Handbook in the UK.

[90] Group of Thirty, *The Structure of Financial Regulation: Approaches and Challenges in a Global Market Place* (G30, 2008).

many of these issues are resolved not through regulation *stricto sensu*, but through criminal and corporate law sanctions such as rules against market manipulation, insider dealing, money laundering, annual reporting and accounting principles. Financial regulatory schemes further the goal of market integrity by mandating transparency of all material information to investors through disclosure of key information.[91]

3.3.2. Scope of Microprudential Regulation

Modern financial regulation distinguishes between banks and capital markets because of the dichotomy between market failures in banking and capital markets. As a result, regulators in either marketplace different emphasis on the three regulatory objectives and methodologies applied to the securities and banking sectors. Regulation of commercial banks has had quite a different focus, concentrating on the safety and soundness of banks, and ensuring they hold sufficient capital and reserves to weather risks. As such, bank regulation generally focuses on *prudence*, which seeks to prevent the failure of financial institutions to meet their promises, which may be caused by a number of risks such as market, credit and liquidity risk.

While bank regulation developed out of informal central bank oversight during the conduct of monetary policy, capital market regulation only became a distinct field after the separation of commercial and investment banking in the wake of the Great Depression, a process which began in the US with the Glass-Stegall Act, and was emulated years later in the EU as the European states embarked on the single market project.[92] Capital market regulation as a separate field arose out of the need to protect individual investors and the integrity of the markets, after the great depression revealed that these were lacking. According to the International Organisation of Securities Commissions, (IOSCO), the three objectives of securities regulation are: '(1) the protection of investors, (2) ensuring that markets are fair, efficient and transparent, and (3) the reduction of systemic risk.'[93]

[91] Coffee argues that voluntary disclosure is not likely to be sufficient for investors, hence there is market failure in the supply of optimal product information in the investment market warranting the imposition of mandatory disclosure. See JC Coffee Jnr, 'Market Failure and the Economic Case for a Mandatory Disclosure System' (1984) 70 *Virginia Law Review* 717. See also JN Gordon and LA Kornhauser, 'Efficient Markets, Costly Information and Securities Research' (1985) 60 *New York University Law Review* 761; M Kahan, 'Securities Law and the Social Costs of "Inaccurate" Stock Prices' (1992) 41 *Duke Law Journal* 977; Merritt B Fox, 'Rethinking Disclosure Liability in the Modern Era' (1997) 75 *Washington University Law Quarterly* 903, on views in support of mandatory continuous disclosure.

[92] Armour et al (n 7) 3.

[93] IOSCO Objectives and Principles of Securities Regulation and the IOSCO Assessment Methodology. Available at: www.iosco.org/library/pubdocs/pdf/IOSCOPD154.pdf.

Although regulators in different sectors emphasise different concerns, this does not mean that they completely ignore other issues. It is unavoidable in these times when the line between banking and capital market business has been blurred – banks are now sellers of securities, while capital market entities are engaging in what is essentially deposit taking and lending. As such, business conduct restrictions and market integrity rules are being applied to commercial banks more broadly, particularly in their dealings with retail customers.[94] Similarly, capital market regulators have begun to impose prudential standards, such as requiring collateral or margins to be posted for some activities, which mimic the capital buffer imposed on banks.[95] After the GFC, interest in the prudential regulation of capital market intermediaries increased, particularly because of the growth of the shadow banking system.

Figure 3.1 The Organisation of Regulation

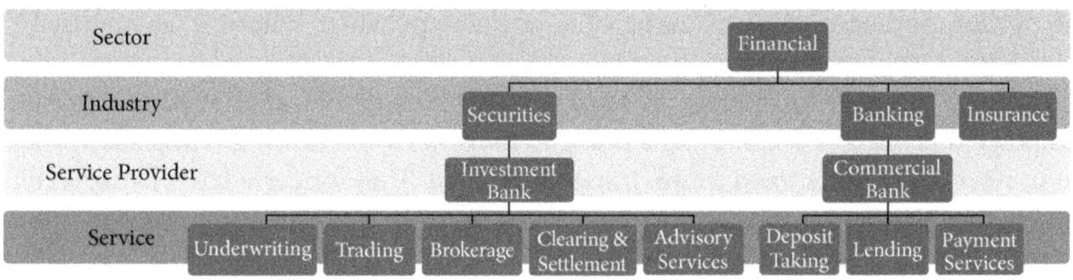

3.3.3. The Conduct of Microprudential Regulation

Regulation that safeguards the safety and soundness of individual financial intermediaries is, at its core, about quantifying and restricting the level of risk which financial intermediaries are permitted to take.[96] The object is to make banks more resilient. This is the risk-based approach to regulation, which acknowledges that risks cannot be completely removed from the financial system and regulatory responses should be targeted, proportionate and based on sound risk assessments.[97]

A risk-based approach implies two steps in setting regulatory objectives – formal risk assessment of probability and effect and prioritisation of risks to

[94] Group of Thirty, *The Structure of Financial Regulation* (n 30).

[95] See, for instance, the Securities Exchange Commission's Net Capital Requirement which imposes a minimum liquidity or net capital requirement. Similarly, Sec 731 of the Dodd-Frank Act imposes capital requirements for major swap participants.

[96] Gleeson contends that it is for this reason that financial regulation was a neglected area of law, because those who understood law were uncomfortable with the quantitative aspects of risk calculation, and those who understood risk quantification were generally not lawyers. See the preface of S Gleeson, *Gleeson on the International Regulation of Banking* 2nd edn (Oxford University Press, 2012).

[97] OECD, *Risk and Regulatory Policy: Improving the Governance of Risk* (OECD, 2010).

be targeted.[98] The types of risks prioritised under microprudential regulation can be identified in the first stage of prudential regulation – initial authorisation of the intermediary, which is granted based on meeting certain criteria. In the second stage, regulators then engage in continuous monitoring of the intermediary to ensure it maintains the criteria for licensing.

3.3.3.1. Licensing and Authorisation

The criteria for authorisation are reflective of the risks associated with operating financial intermediaries, as opposed to the risks connected to their services or products. A basic licensing regime includes an assessment of the firm's owners and its governance structure, the fitness and propriety of board members and senior management, the entity's strategic and operating plan, internal controls, risk management and projected financial condition, financial soundness in respect of capital, and any prior consent of a home supervisor where it is required[99] Licensing serves as a barrier to entry such that only firms that meet certain criteria will be allowed to operate as banks. Entry restrictions that seek to prevent, among other things, weak or dishonest managers from running banks also work to protect consumers from fraud or incompetence. This concern exists irrespective of whether the failure of that particular bank leads to a loss of confidence in other banks, thereby causing a systemic crisis.[100]

Initial licensing is supported by continuous supervision of financial institutions. The continuous supervision is more-or-less consistent with the initial criteria used for licensing. Supervisors monitor the bank's adherence to the minimum standards prescribed by the regulations relating to the bank's risks.[101]

These prudential standards are maintained via three main tools – capital adequacy, liquidity and leverage requirements. The Basel Committee on Banking Supervision's Basel Capital Accords, an internationally recognised benchmark framework in risk assessment for bank capital, form the bedrock of modern prudential requirements.[102] The three Basel Accords are soft law and do not have binding force in international public law, although they have been transposed into

[98] AL Beaussier, et al, 'Accounting for Failure: Risk-Based Regulation and The Problems of Ensuring Healthcare Quality in the NHS' (2016) 18(3–4) *Health, Risk and Society* 205.

[99] Basel Committee on Banking Supervision, *Core Principles for Effective Banking Supervision* (BIS September 2012), Principle 5. Available at: www.bis.org/publ/bcbs230.pdf.

[100] Schooner and Taylor, (n 45) 89.

[101] BCBS, *Core Principles for Effective Supervision*. The requirements cover a bank's corporate governance, risk management process, capital adequacy, credit risk, problem assets, provisions and reserves, concentration risk and large exposure limits, transactions with related parties, country and transfer risks, market risk, interest rate risk in the banking book, liquidity risk and operational risk. See Principles 14–29.

[102] These are Basel I: International Convergence of Capital Measurement and Capital Standards; Basel II: International Convergence on Capital Measurement and Capital Standards: A Revised Framework and Basel III: A Global Regulatory Framework for More Resilient Banks and Banking Systems.

hard law by most countries. They are the result of agreements between the central banks and regulatory agencies of the world's top 10 economies, represented on the Basel Committee on Banking Supervision, (BCBS). However, the Accords have been adopted widely around the world, owing mostly to the operation of peer pressure and their use by financial market participants, including equity analysts and ratings agencies.

3.3.3.2. Capital Adequacy

The original import of regulatory capital requirements was to diminish credit risk exposure. As stated before, if the value of a bank's assets declines below the level of its liabilities, the bank's capital should absorb the losses and still meet its liabilities. If, however, the capital is insufficient, the bank will end up insolvent. As such, bank supervision focused on building an adequate capital cushion to absorb both expected and unexpected losses from creditor defaults on assets. The aim was to protect the bank, either while it is a going concern, for the purpose of maintaining confidence in the financial system and avoiding disruption, or in a gone concern scenario, protecting depositors, bond holders and other senior creditors, while shareholders bear the losses in a wind up. Furthermore, the idea was that by preventing the failure of an individual institution, the buffer simultaneously reduces contagion risk.

The model adopted in the Basel Accords to manage capital is generally referred to as *risk-weighted capital requirements* (RWCR), which means that capital is calculated against the relative amount of risk the bank bears in its assets. As such, less risky assets have a lower or no risk weighting at all, thereby requiring less offsetting capital, while riskier assets have a higher or 100% weighting, therefore requiring more offsetting capital.

The first Basel Accord of 1988 was fairly straightforward and assigned the on-balance-sheet assets of a bank one of four broad risk-weighting categories.[103] Depending on the nature of the counterparty, an asset could either be zero-weighted if the counterparty was the central government of an OECD member country, or have a 20 per cent weighting if the counterparty was a bank incorporated in an OECD country; or a 50 per cent weighting on mortgages secured on residential property are weighted, or a 100 per cent weighting on many other assets, including commercial lending. The same risk-weighting categories were applied to off-balance sheet exposures, such as contingent liabilities (eg standby letters of credit, acceptances, or revolving underwriting facilities) and derivatives (eg swaps), with the exception that these had to be first converted into their credit equivalent amount before a risk weighting was assigned, by multiplying the nominal value of the contract by a conversion factor that varied from 0 to 100 per cent,

[103] Basel Committee on Banking Supervision, *International Convergence of Capital Measurement and Capital Standards (Basel I)* (BIS, July 1988). Available at: www.bis.org/publ/bcbs04a.pdf.

depending on the original maturity of the facility and whether it could be unconditionally cancelled.

The bank was then required to set aside capital which was 8 per cent of the risk-adjusted assets, which was famously set at that level because '7% sounded too low and 9% too high' – it was as good as guess work.[104] Regardless, the capital to be set aside was divided into core capital (Tier 1), which comprised, primarily, paid-up share capital and reserves; and supplementary capital (Tier 2), which included various forms of subordinated debt, both perpetual and term, plus general provisions. Total Tier 2 capital could not exceed total Tier 1 capital. Additionally, term-subordinated debt could not exceed 50 per cent of Tier 1 capital and was required to have a minimum original maturity of five years and one day and be fully amortised in its final five years prior to maturity. There is much debate surrounding the definition of what qualifies as capital in the banking context. Traditionally, capital meant share capital, however, with financial innovation, the definition has expanded to include instruments that perform the function of capital without having its legal form.[105]

Basel I proved, however, to be too blunt an instrument. The broad categories of risk did not adequately differentiate between assets with different risk characteristics, and lumped assets together. For instance, the risk of a loan to a start-up and a well-established corporation were both pegged at 100 per cent simply because they both fell into the bracket of 'commercial loan'. In reality, though, the risk of default on the two assets differs significantly, and the bank can charge higher interest for the riskier one. This encouraged banks to engage in regulatory arbitrage, by substituting assets in the same risk category whose risk weights were, in fact, too high for assets whose risk weights were, in reality, too low and therefore riskier.[106] Furthermore, Basel I only concentrated on credit risk, even though we have identified a myriad of risks to which banks are exposed.

The Accord evolved over time to try and counter some of these shortcomings. It was amended in November 1991 to more precisely define the general provisions or general loan loss reserves that could be included in the capital adequacy calculation.[107] The Committee amended the Accord in April 1995 and then again in April 1996, to recognise the effects of bilateral netting and multilateral netting of banks' credit exposures in derivative products respectively, and to expand the matrix of add-on factors.[108] A framework to address risks other than credit risk was added in January 1996, through the Market Risk Amendment, (MRA), which incorporated, in the capital calculation, market risks arising from banks' exposures to foreign exchange, traded debt securities, equities, commodities and options.[109]

[104] Gleeson, *Gleeson on the International Regulation* (n 98) 23.
[105] BCBS, *Basel I*.
[106] Robert Bichsel and Jürg Blum, 'Capital Regulation of Banks: Where Do We Stand and Where Are We Going?' (2005) 4 *Swiss National Bank Quarterly Bulletin* 42.
[107] See 'History of the Basel Committee'. Available at: www.bis.org/bcbs/history.htm.
[108] ibid.
[109] ibid.

As highlighted in previous sections, while a lender and a securities holder are technically both creditors, the lender is exposed to the risk of non-payment for the whole life of the loan, credit risk, whereas a securities holder can sell the security and therefore discard the risk of non-payment. The bigger risk for the securities holder is that a change will occur in the prices for the asset before he can sell it, therefore he is exposed to market risk. As banks extended their involvement with the capital markets beyond traditional bank lending activities, market risk could no longer be ignored. Firstly, the MRA divided the bank's assets into the banking book, containing traditional bank assets like mortgages, which were originated to hold, and the trading book, containing assets that are tradable such as bonds and derivatives.[110] The second step was to set capital against the trading book's market risk. To do this, the MRA adopted the *Building Block Approach* which divides market risk into two components: (i) specific risk, which is the risk of a negative price change due to the specific characteristics of the issuer of securities, and (ii) general market risk, which is the risk of a negative price movement in an instrument due to factors affecting all banks. The two types of risks are calculated on an instrument-by-instrument basis, with different rules for the treatment of bonds, equities, commodities-based instruments and foreign exchange securities. The capital charges for each category are then added up – hence the building block approach.

The most important innovation of the MRA, though, was that it allowed certain banks to devise their own models for calculating market risk, known as Value at Risk models, (VaR). This was provided the bank had sound risk management systems, which are integrated into management decisions; it conducted regular stress tests; and had an independent risk management unit alongside external audits. The VaR models function on the premise that, firstly, capital markets are both positively and negatively correlated, meaning it is rare that different assets can all decline in value at the same time; instead, as demand for one declines, demand for another usually rises.[111] Secondly, future markets will resemble past markets, meaning price relationships will persist. Based on these assumptions, the VaR model calculates the maximum projected losses for an asset portfolio, based on past market price trends, with a 99 per cent probability of loss, called the confidence interval. The bank must then set aside capital which is higher than either the previous day's VaR or the average VaR over the last 60 business days, in either case multiplied by a scaling factor, which is a minimum of three times the VaR. Scaling is intended to provide additional protection against unexpected losses which historical data cannot predict.[112] The VaR approach requires banks to correctly

[110] Of course, the line between banking book and trading book assets may be blurred, for instance through securitization or because traded assets used to hedge against risk in banking book assets are held in the banking book.

[111] Schooner and Taylor (n 45).

[112] Nassim Nicholas Taleb argues in his book, *The Black Swan: The Impact of the Highly Improbable*, that even with scaling, VaR models cannot adequately predict the losses resulting from rare but extreme market events – black swans.

identify the pertinent risk factors, possess an adequate time series of data on these risk factors, and set the right parameters for mapping these risk factors onto the extent to which a given portfolio will suffer losses.

Amendments to the Capital Accord continued in 2004 with the publication of a new capital adequacy framework, Basel II, which comprised three pillars: (i) minimum capital requirements, (ii) supervisory review and (iii) market discipline.[113] The Pillars introduced the following requirements:

Basel II maintained the basic approach to capital measurement under Pillar 1 but made two changes. Firstly, more risk-sensitive methods were introduced for measuring credit risk, which were finely calibrated to banks' actual risks. Banks had three options to calculate credit risk, they could either use the standardised approach where risk weightings were derived from credit rating agencies, or they could choose between the Foundation internal ratings-based approach and the Advanced internal ratings-based. The internal ratings-based approaches, (IRB), use the bank's own internally developed risk assessment system. The IRB was in response to complaints by banks that argued that the methodology for calculating the capital charge was not sensitive to banks' different risk profiles, or even the risk profiles of different assets within a single bank.[114] The use of IRB was, however, limited to larger banks that had the capacity to develop complex rating systems.[115]

To Pillar I there was also added a charge for operational risk. Operational risk is, however, notoriously difficult to calculate. It is a multivariate category of risk and operational failures are generally too infrequent for there to be much reliable data from which to calculate probabilities. Regardless, Basel II created a methodology to try and reign in operational risk. As with credit and market risk, banks have three options for calculating operational risk – *The Basic Indicator Approach, Standardised Approach* and the *Advanced Measurement Approach*. The Advanced Measurement Approach allows the larger and more sophisticated banks to devise their own internal systems for assessing their operational risk and arrive at the required quantum of capital.

The second Pillar of Basel II was designed to push banks to move their capital beyond the minimum required under Pillar I, by taking into account additional risks which are dependent on the nature of its business, the strength and quality of its management, and a variety of other firm-specific factors. These included risks that were not considered or fully captured under the first pillar, such as interest rate risk in the banking book and credit concentration risk respectively; or risks that were external to the bank, such as economic conditions.

[113] Basel Committee on Banking Supervision, *Basel II: International Convergence on Capital Measurement and Capital Standards: A Revised Framework – Comprehensive Version* (BIS, June 2006). Available at: www.bis.org/publ/bcbs128.pdf.

[114] M Power, 'The Invention of Operational Risk' (June 2003) ESRC Centre for Analysis of Risk and Regulation Discussion Paper No 16.

[115] BCBS, *Basel II*.

Pillar III formalised the role of market discipline in regulation, which is meant to bolster the minimum capital requirements and the supervisory review process. It forced banks to disclose more about the ways in which they assess risk. This would allow market participants to understand the adequacy of each bank's capital position. If a financial institution did not provide enough information about how it was measuring risk, it would have to set aside 20 per cent of its revenue to cover losses or possible trading risks.

While Basel II was clearly more risk sensitive, it was not without its shortcomings, some of which were discussed in Chapter 1 of this book. It seems Basel II was doomed from the start, due to its reliance on credit rating agencies; inconsistent outputs due to the IRB methods; failure to capture endogenous risk; fostering of regulatory arbitrage; missing tail risk; ignoring liquidity and leverage but, most importantly, its procyclicality. All these flaws were brought under the spotlight by the GFC, which provided a spur for reforms. The result was Basel III, which made three major changes to microprudential regulation – it made changes to the calculation and quality of capital, introduced a leverage ratio and, most importantly, a new liquidity requirement.[116]

Firstly, credit risk calculation was made more sensitive and robust. The IRB approach was constrained through an output floor, meaning that the capital set against credit risk using internal models should not fall below 72.5 per cent of the amount that would be reached using the standardised model. Input floors were also introduced, meaning the value of factors used to calculate credit risk, such as probability of default and loss-given default, must not fall below certain minimum levels, so called 'input floors'. Apart from the method of calculating capital, Basel III also made changes to the quality and level of capital. While the total required capital against credit risk remains at 8 per cent of risk-weighted assets, the level of required equity was increased to 4.5 per cent of risk-weighted assets after deductions.[117] The rest of Tier 1 capital amounts to 1.5 per cent of risk-weighted assets, to achieve a minimum Total Tier 1 of 6 per cent of risk-weighted assets. This leaves Total Tier 2 capital at 2 per cent of risk-weighted assets. Additional equity is also required for a capital conservation buffer of 2.5 per cent of risk-weighted assets, bringing the total common equity available to absorb losses to a minimum of 7 per cent. If a bank's capital falls within the buffer range, management is restricted from distributing dividends. Basel III also tightened the definition of capital, by (i) making Tier 1 capital fully loss absorbent on a going-concern basis, in the form of common equity and some equity-like debt instruments which are

[116] I mention here specifically those changes which affected microprudential regulation because, as we shall see, some of the changes introduced under Basel III fall into the realm of macroprudential policy.

[117] Basel Committee on Banking Supervision, *Basel III: A Global Regulatory Framework for More Resilient Banks and Banking Systems* (BIS 2011). Available at: www.bis.org/publ/bcbs189.htm.

subordinated and where dividend payments are discretionary;[118] (ii) removing distinctions within Tier 2 capital; and (iii) abolishing Tier 3 capital.

The standardised approach to calculating operational risk was also enhanced, while the option to use an internal approach was completely removed. Lastly, the Basel Committee also revised the market risk framework, through the fundamental review of the trading book (FRTB) and introduced an incremental risk capital charge (IRC) for unsecuritised credit products, significantly higher capital for trading and derivatives activities and complex securitisations held in the trading book, as well as a stressed value-at-risk framework to help mitigate procyclicality.

Despite the widespread usage of capital requirements to regulate banks, their effectiveness is doubtful; the banks at the centre of the GFC all fell despite meeting regulatory capital requirements.[119] High capital was not a reliable indicator of their resilience. As Gleeson contends, effective risk management, rather than high capital, is more useful to building a bank's resilience.[120] Which of these risks presents the biggest threat? The literature of the financial crisis generally describes the beginning as the moment when investors will not purchase securities or savers withdraw their deposits, forcing the bank to engage in fire-sales, the effects of which are felt through the economy.[121] The bank failures at the heart of the GFC were triggered by runs, either a margin run as in the case of Lehman Brothers or a good old-fashioned bank run as in the case of Northern Rock. Capital requirements did not mitigate the risk of bank or margin runs – which are essentially a problem of liquidity. It may well be, as Dalhuisen contends, that liquidity is the true killer of banks.[122]

3.3.3.3. *Liquidity Requirements*

Holding adequate capital may help steady the nerves of depositors and investors by providing assurance against balance sheet insolvency, however it does not insure against liquidity risk. In the past, many central banks addressed liquidity risk through *reserve requirements*, which obliged banks to keep a portion of deposits in the form of cash, in their vaults or as a deposit at the central bank.[123] Modern liquidity requirements prescribe that banks should maintain a minimum

[118] This does not include goodwill, deferred tax assets, bank investments in its own shares or in other banks, financial institutions and insurance companies, provisioning shortfalls and other deductions, such as projected cash flow hedging.

[119] See generally E Scott, *Capital Adequacy Beyond Basel* (Oxford University Press, 2005); Barth Caprio and Ross Levine, *Rethinking Banking Regulation* (Cambridge University Press, 2006) Daniel Tarullo, *Banking on Basel* (Patersen Institute, 2008).

[120] Gleeson (n 96) 20.

[121] Reinhart and Rogoff (n 74).

[122] Dalhuisen, *Transnational Law* (n 57).

[123] Reserve requirements also served a monetary purpose, by constraining banks' ability to create new credit, and consequently money supply growth.

stock of liquid assets (not just cash), which are a ratio of the deposits. Among the assets considered *liquid* are government bills, some government bonds, certificates of deposit issued by highly rated banks, and other forms of highly rated commercial paper. In some cases, a liquidity conversion factor will be applied to the assets to reflect the fact that the bank may not be able to realise their full value when the assets are sold.[124] The type of assets required will differ in each jurisdiction depending on approaches to monetary control or the structure of money markets.

Basel III provides a uniform method for calculating liquidity risk. Banks must maintain a liquidity coverage ratio, (LCR), at a specified level. The LCR ensures that banks hold sufficient liquid assets to withstand 30 days of stressed funding. Supervisors regularly determine what constitutes 'stressed funding'. In addition, Basel III also proposes a net stable funding ratio (NSFR) which will limit banks' ability to fund long-term assets using short-term liabilities. Both requirements act as a deterrent to bank runs, either by increasing a bank's long-term funding sources, like the NSFR does, or by forcing the bank to hold enough liquid assets to meet its short-term obligations, without resorting to fire sales, as the LCR does.[125]

3.3.3.4. Leverage Requirements

The crisis also highlighted how liquidity risk experienced by banks is exacerbated by over leveraging. Compared to other types of firms, banks are typically at least 25 times geared.[126] The Miller-Modigliani theorem helps to understand why banks are highly geared.[127] In a perfect market, debt and equity are equally priced because there are no asymmetries of information, no transaction costs and no taxes – credit is available to all at the market rate. In reality, of course, markets are imperfect, and three factors contribute to making debt more attractive.

Firstly, debt has tax advantages compared to equity, because interest is tax deductible and allows firms to enjoy greater after-tax profits. While the tax advantage of debt over equity is true for all firms, two other factors specific to banks make it more attractive. The second advantage is that a large share of banks' debt consists of demand deposits and other very short-term liabilities, which are extremely liquid and therefore attract a lower interest, rendering them cheaper. Thirdly, banks' creditors are protected by an extensive safety net in the form of deposit insurance and the lender of last resort, which act as a subsidy to bank debt.[128]

[124] Schooner and Taylor (n 46) 195.

[125] M Hoerova et al, 'Benefits and Costs of Liquidity Regulation' ECB Working Paper Series No 2169 (July 2018).

[126] Gleeson (n 96) 27.

[127] F Modigliani and MH Miller, 'The Cost of Capital, Corporation Finance and the Theory of Investment' (1958) 48(3) *American Economic Review* 261.

[128] Schooner and Taylor (n 45) 134.

A leverage ratio, which imposes an upper limit to a bank's debt can restrict excessive leveraging in boom periods and ensure a bank has sufficient capital to absorb shocks. Hence it can target both the cyclical and structural aspects of systemic risk. The leverage ratio can either be expressed as a ratio of the bank's debt to equity or assets to equity, which considers the extent to which a bank may be funding its activities with equity. Unlike Basel III's credit, market and operational risk requirements, the leverage ratio is non-risk based. It is calculated by dividing, a bank's Tier 1 capital by the bank's total exposures, which include (a) on-balance sheet exposures; (b) derivative exposures; (c) securities financing transaction exposures; and (d) off-balance sheet exposures.[129] The minimum leverage ratio is set at 3 per cent, meaning a bank must hold a minimum buffer of Tier 1 capital which amounts to 3 per cent of the bank's exposure. The higher the ratio, the safer the bank.

3.3.3.5. Remedial Measures

In some cases, managing the risk faced by banks may not be enough to prevent financial instability, in which case it will be necessary to eliminate the fallout from individual bank failure. *Crisis management* enables the financial system to continue playing its credit allocation role, even during periods of crisis. Potential tools in the armoury here include direct liquidity support and deposit guarantee schemes, which provide a safety net and, more importantly, special resolution regimes which enable orderly intervention at institutions in distress. Crisis management curbs disruptions to the financial system and ultimately to the real economy.[130] Four tools are used to achieve this: the Lender of Last Resort, Deposit Guarantee Schemes, Fiscal Support and Resolution. The first three form a safety net of sorts, while the last one aims to eliminate the source of systemic risk altogether.

(a) Lender of Last Resort

While liquidity buffers are meant to protect banks from the effects of a bank run, they may not completely eliminate the problem. Once the bank exhausts its own liquidity, its first line of defence is to seek funding from the lender of last resort,

[129] Basel Committee on Banking Supervision, *Basel III Leverage Ratio Framework and Disclosure Requirements* (BIS 2014). Available at: www.bis.org/publ/bcbs270.pdf.

[130] De Nederlandsche Bank, 'Towards a More Stable Financial System: Macroprudential Supervision at DNB' (7 May 2010). Available at: www.dnb.nl/en/binaries/Towards%20a%20more%20stable%20financial%20system_tcm47-236522.pdf. Goodhart and Perotti argue, however, that ex-post crisis interventions, such as central bank liquidity injections or government recapitalisations fail to address the root causes of the systemic crisis and can even cause higher *ex ante* risk taking, by disregarding moral hazard, thereby increasing the likelihood of a systemic financial crisis. See CAE Goodhart and E Perotti, 'Preventive Macroprudential Policy' (2013) 1(1) *Journal of Financial Management, Markets and Institutions* 115.

a concept which was developed by Henry Thornton and Walter Bagehot.[131] The lender of last resort stands as an institution that is willing to provide liquidity to cover sudden and unexpected withdrawals of deposits, when no other lender is willing or able to lend.[132] In circumstances where the private sector fails to provide as much of a good or service as would be socially optimal, we look to the public sector to step in and provide it instead. Central banks provide this last resort lending.

Central banks are best placed to provide this support because they can create legal tender without limit (in theory at least, of course considerations of price stability prevent them from printing money indiscriminately.) When the central bank makes a loan to a commercial bank the loan is reflected on the bank's balance sheet as an increase in liabilities (and a corresponding increase in the central bank's assets). In this way the bank's reserves held at the central bank are increased and it can use these to make more loans to its customers. The bank borrows against its more illiquid assets. Thus, the central bank only lends to an institution that is solvent, but going through a temporary problem, and protects itself against the risk of loss. Central banks are usually restrictive about the type of collateral they are willing to accept, these include government bonds and bills, highly rated bonds, and other low-credit risk-liquid instruments.

Recent experience suggests, however, that Bagehot's classical approach needs to be supplemented to take into account the fact that more and more non-bank financial institutions are taking over the credit provision function. A credit crunch or liquidity squeeze can now manifest itself in a completely different way from when the lender of last resort function was established. The strategy that central banks have adopted to curb the spread of fear and panic emanating from financial markets is an outright purchase of assets of marketable securities from the market. This means dealing with counterparties such as money market mutual funds and investment banks. This was the approach adopted by central banks in the wake of the GFC through the so-called quantitative easing (QE) programmes

(b) Deposit Protection Schemes

Even with the lender of last resort in place, there is still the risk that the bank will fail, because, as highlighted in previous sections, a liquidity crisis can quickly devolve into a solvency crisis. The next layer of the financial safety net is depositor insurance. Depositor insurance compensates depositors for losses suffered in the event of bank failure, up to a prescribed maximum. This removes uncertainty that depositors may not be repaid in the event of the bank failing and relieves some of the pressure that leads to bank runs. The deposit insurer aims to make payments

[131] H Thornton, An *Enquiry into the Nature and Effects of the Paper Credit of Great Britain* 1802 and Walter Bagehot, *Lombard Street: A Description of the Money Market* (Wiley, 1999).

[132] AH Meltzer, 'Financial Failures and Financial Policies' in GC Kaufman and RC Kormendi (eds), *Deregulation of Financial Services: Public Policy in Flux* (Ballinger, 1986).

within a short time of the trigger event and will then assume the depositor's position in insolvency proceedings.

A deposit protection scheme, however, can only provide a safety net for a few at any given time. It is not designed to deal with simultaneous failure of the whole system. It cannot resolve a systemic banking crisis by itself.[133] Unlike the central bank it cannot create money and instead relies on contributions paid in by participating institutions. In the face of imminent systemic collapse, governments must step in and provide a guarantee because they are the only entities with the resources to meet the large funding requirements.

(c) Fiscal Support

Fiscal support provides the third layer of the financial safety net. When the government steps in to bail out a bank, it provides it with equity capital. If the central bank were to provide equity capital it would run the risk of compromising its own balance sheet; moreover, it would create a serious conflict of interest in cases where the central bank is also the financial regulator of all banks.[134]

Unfortunately, like other forms of insurance, the financial safety net suffers from the problem of moral hazard. In essence, the safety net removes the need for depositors to charge a risk premium on the deposits they provide to banks and to reduce their already low level of monitoring, safe in the knowledge that their deposits are insured, while the banks themselves are likely to engage in riskier lending secure in the knowledge that they will be bailed out. The problem of moral hazard is particularly acute in banks that are deemed too big to fail (TBTF).[135] It is believed that the failure of certain large banks would have a significant negative impact on the rest of the financial system through contagion. In fact, TBTF is not a problem unique to commercial banks. For instance, during the GFC, the US government had to step in and bailout the insurance company AIG because of its strong presence on the credit default swaps market. It was considered too interconnected to fail.

Two mutually reinforcing strategies can be adopted to counter moral hazard. One strategy is to adopt constructive ambiguity, where the central bank and government keep banks guessing as to whether they are likely to provide liquidity support or bailout and, if so, the circumstances in which it will be provided. Alternatively, the deposit insurance scheme can be designed in a way that reduces

[133] Financial Stability Forum, 'Guidance for Developing Effective Deposit Insurance Systems' (September 2001) *Policy Document*. Available at: www.fsb.org/wp-content/uploads/r_0109b.pdf.

[134] Schooner and Taylor (n 45) 59.

[135] The term was coined by the United States' Comptroller of the Currency describing the 11 largest banks in the wake of the Continental Illinois failure in 1984. See House of Representatives Committee on Banking, Finance and Urban Affairs, 'Inquiry into The Continental Illinois Corp. and Continental Illinois National Bank' (Hearings Before the Subcommittee on Financial Institutions Supervisors, Regulation and Insurance, Serial 98-111, US Government Printing Office 1984).

moral hazard. This includes limiting the scope of deposit insurance coverage, subjecting depositors to a deductible, also known as co-insurance; or requiring risk-adjusted deposit insurance premiums.

These various mechanisms for limiting moral hazard are, at best, likely to be partially successful and, in fact, can encourage risk taking. The moral hazard problem leads some economic theorists to argue that the financial safety net should be completely dismantled or significantly pared back and that markets should be left alone to decide how to address the inherent risks. The assumption behind such thinking, which derives from the Efficient Markets School, is that government interference actually creates distortions in the markets. This reaction, however, would be rather extreme. Instead, the idea that took hold was to create a bank resolution and recovery mechanism that would allocate losses fairly between the bank's owners and its depositors, and minimise the costs to taxpayers, while preserving the incentive for infusion of new capital.

(d) Resolution

The failure of high-profile banks, which occurred during the GFC, highlighted how the safety net perpetuates moral hazard. The only other alternative would have been to allow the banks to fail. However, most countries' traditional insolvency regimes could not contain the fallout from the failure of multiple banks. In other industries the winding up of a failed firm can take years and the firm can easily be replaced, without the market suffering any disruptions. In the case of bank failure, however, speedy resolution, maintaining the system's critical functions and stability are of the essence.[136] The problem of resolving a bank quickly and with minimal disruption is compounded when that bank operates in numerous jurisdictions, because generally insolvency regimes differ. In response to these unique requirements for speed, continuity, stability and cross-border co-operation, the European Parliament enacted the Bank Recovery and Resolution Directive, while their counterparts in the US introduced similar resolution provisions in the Dodd-Frank Act, as did the UK with the Banking Act 2009.

The Bank Resolution and Recovery Directive ('BRRD') is a common framework guiding the recovery *and* resolution of credit institutions, investment firms, insurance undertakings and financial holding companies in the EU.[137] The Directive encourages regulators to attempt to save a failing institution first, that is when it

[136] Preamble (4) of Directive 2014/59/EU of the European Parliament and of the Council of 15 May 2014 establishing a framework for the recovery and resolution of credit institutions and investment firms and amending Council Directive 82/891/EEC, and Directives 2001/24/EC, 2002/47/EC, 2004/25/EC, 2005/56/EC, 2007/36/EC, 2011/35/EU, 2012/30/EU and 2013/36/EU, and Regulations (EU) No 1093/2010 and (EU) No 648/2012, of the European Parliament and of the Council OJ 2014 L173/190 (BRRD).

[137] See TC Maguze, 'EU Bank Recapitalisation and the Bail-in Option: An Analysis of the Effects of Mandatory Bail-in on Creditors' Property Rights' (2016) 5(2) UCL *Journal of Law and Jurisprudence* 1.

is close to, or already has, breached its licensing requirements, is facing cash-flow insolvency, and/or it requires a bail-out from the government.[138] If their interventions are unsuccessful, then orderly resolution of the firm follows. The resolution framework aims to ensure continuity of critical functions; avoid the destabilisation caused by contagion and protect public funds, client funds and assets and depositors.[139] The framework grants independent financial regulators the power to either (i) sell viable portions of the business; (ii) transfer viable portions to a bridge institution and wind-down the failed bank; and (iii) separate the bank's assets or bail-in the bank.[140]

The US created a similar framework, under the Title II of the Dodd-Frank Wall Street Reform and Consumer Protection Act of 2010, (Dodd-Frank Act), called the Orderly Liquidation Authority (OLA). The Act, the Federal Deposit Insurance Corporation (FDIC), is empowered to resolve a failing bank, with authority of federal regulatory agencies and the Treasury Secretary. When the FDIC was created it could only take failed banks into receivership, which was determined in conjunction with the bank's primary regulator. Now, it repays depositors in the failed bank up to the insured amount of US$250,000, then manages the rest of the assets. These activities are paid for out of a pre-funded pool of funds to which banks contribute called the Deposit Insurance Fund. The Dodd-Frank Act extended the FDIC's power to resolve bank holding companies and all systemically important financial institutions (SIFIs).

Where a subsidiary within a bank holding company is being resolved, the regulators adopt a 'Single Point of Entry' approach, (SPOE), which means that only the holding company is resolved. The subsidiaries are allowed to continue running by writing down the debt issued by the subsidiary to the parent company, while simultaneously writing down debt issued to the public by the holding company, essentially passing on the loss to investors. The FDIC then establishes a bridge company to which some of the failed company's assets and liabilities are transferred. The new company would be capitalised by bailing in a pre-arranged class of debt, converting it into equity. The resolution process is funded through contributions made by SIFIs to the OLA, after failure has occurred.

In the UK, the Bank of England was appointed the resolution authority for British banks, building societies, certain investment firms and their holding companies. In terms of the Banking Act 2009, resolution will be initiated if the firm is failing or is likely to fail, an assessment which is made by the Prudential Regulation Authority, and resolution action would save the firm, an assessment which is determined by the Bank of England in consultation with the Treasury and the Financial Conduct Authority. Resolution occurs, however, only if it is judged that it would be in the public interest to save the failed firm. The Treasury

[138] BRRD, art 32(4).
[139] BRRD, art 31.
[140] ibid, art 39.

is consulted primarily because resolution may involve the use of public funds, and it may veto a decision to resolve a firm.[141] The statutory regime permits the use of three resolution strategies – (i) bail-in, which is most appropriate for large complex firms, allowing them to remain solvent and continue to provide critical functions; (ii) partial transfer of assets, which is most suited to small and medium-sized firms whose failure could disrupt the system, but whose assets can be sold off quickly and easily; and (iii) insolvency, mostly used on small firms which likely do not qualify for resolution. Depositors of a small bank would be paid out of a Financial Services Compensation Scheme, up to the insured amount, or have the same transferred to another institution.[142] The UK also adopts a single point of entry approach when resolving failing subsidiaries in a holding company. As in the US where there are living wills, the Bank of England, with the bank's management, develops resolution plans and strategies for firms that are subject to the resolution regime.[143]

It is doubtful if the regulator and government can muster the political will required to allow systemically important institutions to fail and, even if they could, they may not be able to use these tools more than once considering the controversy they generate. A case in point is the bail-in tool, which has proved the most controversial of the resolution tools. Bail-in is a statutory power to restructure the balance sheet of a distressed bank by converting and/or writing down its liabilities to equity.[144] The aim of the bail-in tool is to counter the problem of moral hazard, by removing the safety net provided by taxpayers, and forcing investors to absorb the losses.

Bail-in compels investors to closely monitor the risk-taking activities of banks, thus introducing market discipline; investors will also price risk more accurately which, in turn, promotes a more efficient allocation of funds.[145] Bail-in is carried out on a going-concern basis, which means that the bank continues to operate and provide essential services to its customers while it is being recapitalised.[146] This will help to limit disruption and maintain public confidence in the banking system. However, in countries where this tool has been used, it has been followed by a flurry of lawsuits from disgruntled investors who suddenly woke

[141] See HM Treasury, *Memorandum of Understanding on Resolution Planning and Financial Crisis Management* (October 2017).

[142] At the time of writing, this is £85,000.

[143] Bank of England, 'The Bank of England's Approach to Resolution' October 2017. Available at: www.bankofengland.co.uk/-/media/boe/files/news/2017/october/the-bank-of-england-approach-to-resolution.

[144] J Zhou et al, 'From Bail-out to Bail-in: Mandatory Debt Restructuring of Systemic Financial Institutions' (April 2012) IMF Staff Discussion Note 12/03 6.

[145] B Cœuré, 'The Implications of Bail-In Rules for Bank Activity and Stability' (Opening Speech at ECB Conference on 'Financing the recovery after the crisis – the roles of bank profitability, stability and regulation', Milan, 30 September 2013). Available at: www.ecb.europa.eu/press/key/date/2013/html/sp130930.en.html.

[146] Zhou et al 'From Bail-out to Bail-in' (n 144) 6.

up to find themselves holding equity which was, in reality, worth less than their original investment.[147] See, for instance, the lawsuits in Portugal, Slovenia and Austria.[148]

3.4. Why Microprudential Regulation Cannot Prevent Financial Instability

Microprudential regulation should ideally remove the risk of insolvency, and thus limit the threat of contagion, by improving banks' resilience. The global financial crisis is evidence, however, that microprudential regulation can neither end nor slow down the risks associated with banking. In the decade after the crisis many jurisdictions in the western world remained exposed to systemic risk and the threat of financial instability. Some of the harsher critics even argue that modern regulation appears largely irrelevant to redress systemic risk.[149] An assessment of Basel III, sheds light on why the microprudential approach may be unsuitable to regulating financial stability. As Martin Wolfe observed, post-crisis regulatory efforts were incremental, but this would not be enough to create a safe system – the *mouse will never roar loudly enough.*[150]

The next section looks at why microprudential regulation will not roar. There are gaps that allow both contagion and financial imbalances to slip through.

3.4.1. Why Contagion Remains a Problem

3.4.1.1. Flawed Regulatory Tools

(a) Flawed Capital Calculation Tools

It has already been argued that it is doubtful that capital ever saved a bank and liquidity is the true problem. Basel III, the benchmark for regulation, does little to save the reputation of capital-based regulation. It is haunted by ghosts of Christmas

[147] Maguze, 'EU Bank Recapitalisation and the Bail-in Option' (n 137).

[148] See, for instance, *Goldman Sachs International and Others v Novo Banco SA* [2015] EWHC 2371 (Comm); Case C-526/14 *Kotnik and Others* [2016] ECR I-000, Opinion of AG Wahl; Jonathan Gould, Andreas Kroener and Maria Sheahan, 'Germany's NRW Bank Sues Over Austrian Bad Bank Bonds' *Reuters* (Frankfurt, 14 April 2015). Available at: www.reuters.com/article/nrw-bank-heta-asset-lawsuit-idUSL5N0XB47O20150414.

[149] See, for instance, Dalhuisen (n 54) 790. See also MM Prates, 'Why Prudential Regulation Will Fail to Prevent Financial Crises. A Legal Approach' (November 2013) Banco Central do Brasil WP 335.

[150] MN Wolf, 'Basel III: The Mouse that Did Not Roar' *The Financial Times*, 14 September 2010. Available at: www.ft.com/cms/s/0/966b5e88-c034-11df-b77d-00144feab49a.html#ixzz2pbNNFtQ2.

past, as it has inherited flaws from previous iterations of the capital adequacy rules, which failed to prevent the most recent episode of financial instability:

(i) Static Risk Weights which Mask Endogenous Risk of Underlying Assets

The use of risk weights remains debatable given the inherent opaqueness of banking activities, due to our old friend, asymmetric information. Despite bank regulators' access to comparatively greater information than other third parties, bank regulators also suffer difficulty in assessing the degree of risk in banks' assets. Not only must they ensure that banks correctly assign the appropriate risk weight to their assets, but they must also set risk weights that accurately measure the risks to which a bank is exposed. It appears risk weights are just the watered-down result of political compromise; as a result, low-risk weightings are often applied to assets that are favoured by politically powerful groups.[151]

Bankers have an incentive to relax their lending standards for assets favoured by the regulators, as was the case with asset-backed mortgages in the period leading up to the GFC. Conversely, however, risk weights do not shift to match the deteriorating asset quality.

(ii) Focus on Idiosyncratic Risk which Encourages Arbitrage

A corollary to the problem created by attaching risk weights to counter idiosyncratic risks is that it may simply lead to repackaging and shifting of the same aggregate risk to other assets within the same firm. For instance, by securitising subprime mortgages, and essentially purchasing them back as AAA-rated mortgage-backed securities which are perceived as less risky and therefore require less capital. Worse still, banks can simply shift these risks to the shadow banking system, which is beyond the purview of bank regulators. A further outcome is that risk in the system as a whole may become more correlated as all the banks shift to these 'less risky', and lower-risk-weighted assets. Thus, while an assessment of individual banks would give the impression that they are safe, a cross-sectional analysis would reveal systemic linkage through homogenous portfolios.[152]

(iii) Minimum Capital which is Too Low

The minimum capital level remains far too low at 8 per cent. The effect is that a minor reduction of total assets, not just risk-weighted assets, can result in all the equity being wiped out.[153] Capital would be better controlled if the minimum

[151] G Benston, *Regulating Financial Markets: A Critique and Some Proposals* (Institute of Economic Affairs, 1998), 113.

[152] Chen Zhou, 'Why the Micro-Prudential Regulation Fails? The Impact on Systemic Risk by Imposing a Capital Requirement' (July 2010) DNB Working Paper No 256. While these studies focused on the impact of capital regulation on systemic risk, Zhou stresses that the results apply to all microprudential tools which are applied in a unified manner to all financial institutions in a system.

[153] Anat Admati and Martin Hellwig, *The Banker's New Clothes: What's Wrong with Banking and What to Do About It* (Princeton University Press, 2013) 183.

equity amount were raised to a more significant level, such as the 30 per cent suggested by Admati and Hellwig, and if it were measured against total assets as opposed to risk-weighted assets alone. Admati and Hellwig blame the low level of capital on the lobbying efforts of bankers, based on the flawed argument that higher capital requirements would reduce bank profitability – their banker's new clothes.[154] However, as Gleeson points out, as long as banks have a statutory monopoly over deposit taking (since it requires a licence), they can remain profitable or even become super profitable.

(iv) Reliance on Credit Rating Agencies

The standardised method for calculating credit risk still relies on credit rating agencies, therefore banks using the IRB are still exposed to the possibility of procyclical and unreliable ratings.[155]

(v) Opaque Risk Calculation Models

Furthermore, because banks can still develop their own internal ratings models, which regulators and the market cannot monitor due to their complexity, the possibility of manipulation and regulatory arbitrage still exists.[156] Banks can concentrate on assets which regulators regard as low risk in order to reduce the level of capital held or simply manipulate the level of risk attached to an asset.[157]

(b) Liquidity Measures Encourage Arbitrage

All the adjustment factors and weights used to calculate the liquidity coverage ratio and net stable funding ratio have their counterparts in the risk weightings of capital ratios. Therefore, like capital ratios, the liquidity ratios will simply push banks to arbitrage towards seemingly more liquid assets. There is a danger that supposedly liquid assets may turn out to be illiquid. By way of example, banks are likely to purchase more government bonds, which traditionally have been favoured as highly liquid. However, as the sovereign debt crisis that followed the GFC proved, sovereign bonds can be highly risky and even subject to default. Alternatively, by encouraging the holding of more liquid assets, banks' returns may be lowered simultaneously encouraging excessive risk taking in other areas to cover the shortfall.

Furthermore, the liquidity requirements, which are primarily microprudential in nature, depend on an institution's idiosyncratic run risk and may underestimate the required holdings of liquid assets in a systemic liquidity spiral.

[154] Ibid.
[155] Avgouleas, *Governance of Global Financial Markets* (n 9).
[156] ibid.
[157] For instance, by investing in 'hybrid securities' which treat some debts as equity simply because there is a proviso that the borrower may withhold interest payments to creditors in a year when it does not make any profits, much like the case of dividends with shareholders.

(c) Perverse Incentives Created by Leverage Ratio

The leverage ratio treats all bank exposures in the same way. It is non-risk-based, therefore it treats high risk and low risk assets the same. This creates a basic incentive problem because they are not penalised for engaging in more risky activities. There is, of course, much debate over the extent of impact of these perverse incentives, with some arguing that the movement to high-risk activities is negligible.[158]

3.4.1.2. Interconnections are Ignored

As highlighted previously, the contagion equation has two channels of transmission. It can either be informational contagion, resulting from bank runs or run-like behaviour in capital markets; or contagion can be the result of extensive connections amongst banks, exacerbated by the size of banks within the network. The microprudential regulations focus on just the first source of contagion, by seeking to make individual institutions more resilient to runs, and completely ignoring the second aspect, the connections that propagate the disruption.

3.4.1.3. Remedial Measures which Encourage Moral Hazard

The remedial measures fare no better, the safety net provided by the lender of last resort, deposit protection and fiscal support only lead to moral hazard which perpetuates risk taking, while recovery and resolution mechanisms could possibly lead to reduced availability of financial services.

3.4.2. Why Financial Imbalances Remain a Problem

3.4.2.1. Procyclicality

The microprudential model appears at odds with a financial stability goal that seeks to lean against credit and asset-price booms and busts and build enough resilience to be able to withstand the busts. The capital requirements are cyclical, rising with the perceived risk in bad times and falling in good times. Thus, there may not be a sufficient buffer built up in good times to absorb losses during a downturn, nor do they discourage risk taking in the good times. Similarly, the liquidity requirements

[158] See R Haynes et al, 'Assessing the Impact of the Basel III Leverage Ratio on the Competitive Landscape of US Derivatives Markets: Evidence from Options' (June 2018) *CFTC Policy Brief*. Available at: www.cftc.gov/sites/default/files/About/Economic%20Analysis/oce_leverage_and_options.pdf; and J Acosta Smith, M Grill and J Hannes Lang, 'The Leverage Ratio, Risk-Taking and Bank Stability' (June 2017) *ECB* Working Paper Series No 2079/June 2017. Available at: www.ecb.europa.eu/pub/pdf/scpwps/ecb.wp2079.en.pdf?97048db54786167f5a45a6426ffd80d7.

are fixed, therefore they move with the cycle.[159] In other words, microprudential regulation is procyclical. There are mechanisms built into the risk calculation methodology or IRB, which attempt to dampen this procyclicality.[160] But they are not enough.

3.4.3. Summary

While the flawed microprudential tools and unsustainable remedial measures are a cause for concern, the fundamental issues, which the microprudential approach to financial stability fails to address, are interconnectedness and procyclicality. These gaps render microprudential regulation incapable of maintaining financial stability.

This narrow focus on individual institutions results in regulations which (i) do not account for cases of systemic risk arising primarily through common exposures to macroeconomic risk factors across institutions; (ii) ignore the possibility that the rational actions of an individual bank could have an adverse aggregate effect, in essence that risk to the financial system is also endogenous (for instance a bank selling off its assets to manage its liquidity could precipitate a downward spiral of prices in the market for those assets); and (iii) follow the financial cycle, meaning regulatory requirements are loosened at the top of the cycle when everyone is exuberant and any risk to the individual is perceived as low, encouraging even more risk taking, and tightened in a downturn, discouraging lending when it is most needed. This is the model followed by microprudential regulation.

Dalhuisen suggests that a continued focus on micromanaging the banks would require more radical action, perhaps even leading to some form of narrow banking.[161] This would entail creating a system with similar institutions. Microprudential regulation would be able to curb risk because the whole system is uniform. This, however, is likely to have serious consequences in terms of growth and employment, and by extension any social justice goals we may hope to achieve. As Dalhuisen cautions, narrow banking is not in line with current societal needs for credit. In any case, our current reality consists of heterogeneous financial institutions, products, services and customers. We are therefore faced with Hobson's choice – we either learn to live with a financial system in which we cannot eliminate risk or abandon it altogether.

[159] See JP Landau, 'A Liquidity-Based Approach to Macroprudential Policy' (September 2016) BIS Papers No 86. Available at: www.bis.org/publ/bppdf/bispap86s.pdf. See DC Hardy and P Hochreiter, 'A Simple Macroprudential Liquidity Buffer' IMF Working Paper WP/14/235. Available at: www.imf.org/external/pubs/ft/wp/2014/wp14235.pdf.

[160] For instance, calculating probability of default using inputs from longer run date and forward-looking provisioning based on an expected losses model when setting aside capital.

[161] Dalhuisen (n 54) 664–65.

An alternative may be to move away from the traditional model of the financial system that relies heavily on banking. Financial technology, (Fintech), may facilitate this move. FinTech has experienced a rapid growth and provides financial services solutions at both retail and wholesale level, providing an opening to households and business which would otherwise have not been able to access (i) payments, clearing and settlement; (ii) deposits, lending and capital raising; (iii) insurance; (iv) investment management; and (v) market support.[162]

At this point in time, however, it does not appear to be fundamentally changing the essence of intermediation in the financial system. For instance, the various mobile payment systems still require a deposit of fiat currency with a bank at some point along the payment chain. P2P lending and crowdfunding are unable to keep up with the rising credit appetite of retail customers, let alone the wholesale market. Likewise, cryptocurrencies at the moment have limited connection with the real economy, low-scale usage and a narrow user base.[163] Furthermore, while Fintech brings with it many opportunities, it also has its risks, including risk to financial stability from the usual sources of contagion and procyclicality.[164] These threats may not be imminent, according to the FSB, but they could arise in future.[165] Which brings us back to square one.

3.5. Conclusion

This chapter has attempted to demonstrate that the nature and magnitude of financial market failures necessitates government intervention in financial markets. However, before intervening, it is critical to identify and calibrate appropriate regulatory solutions because badly designed regulations are likely to cause just as much harm as financial market participants.

The way the financial system generates risk, the speed at which this risk migrates across the system (between banks and non-banks alike), and the inadequacy of pursuing financial stability via the safety and soundness of individual institutions suggest that regulations for financial stability should have a different objective, specifically the maintenance of the safety and soundness of the whole system, and ultimately avoid costs to the broader economy.

A regulator with a bird's-eye view of the financial system would require tools that can be calibrated at macro level. Moreover, the tools should be able to tackle the

[162] Financial Stability Board, 'Financial Stability Implications from FinTech: Supervisory and Regulatory Issues that Merit Authorities' Attention' (27 June 2017), 8. Available at: www.fsb.org/wp-content/uploads/R270617.pdf.

[163] European Central Bank, *Virtual Currency Schemes* (October 2012). Available at: www.ecb.europa.eu/pub/pdf/other/virtualcurrencyschemes201210en.pdf?941883c8460133b7758f498192a3ed9e.

[164] FSB, 'Financial Stability Implications from FinTech' (n 162) 20–21.

[165] The FSB highlights 10 issues for regulators to look out for in future, which mostly relate to Fintech regulatory governance than the provision of FinTech itself. See FSB, ibid, 31–32.

cross-sectional and time dimensions of financial instability. In other words, they should work to reduce interconnections and common exposures to macro risk, while at the same time operating in a countercyclical manner to dampen exuberance during an upswing, but still provide a cushion that allows banks to continue operating should a downswing occur. This is not to say that policy makers should reinvent the wheel and devise completely new tools, current tools in the prudential armoury may suffice if appropriately calibrated and deployed.

After the GFC, the world turned to macroprudential policy to fill the gap left by microprudential regulation. Macroprudential policy, as already stated in Chapter 1, uses primarily prudential tools to limit system-wide financial risk, and so prevent disruption to key financial services and the economy. A lot of energy has been dedicated to designing the agencies that decide macroprudential policy and the appropriate tool kit, to meet the objective of limiting system-wide distress and output costs to the broader economy.

The result has been the creation of new macroprudential agencies through either the transfer of responsibilities between existing organisations, the amalgamation of standalone agencies into other organisations, or the establishment of new bodies, which are better able to manage financial stability through macroprudential oversight. These agencies are armed with an arsenal of what are traditionally microprudential tools, which are, however, calibrated to operate in a countercyclical manner, reduce common exposure and factor in the size of institutions that propagate systemic risk. Some of these tools have been included in Basel III, such as the counter-cyclical capital buffer and surcharge on systemically important financial institutions, while others are designed at national level. The next chapter provides an overview of macroprudential policy and how the policy addresses the dual sources of shocks to the financial system. The ultimate goal is to demonstrate how this approach to regulating the financial system and maintaining stability justifies its delegation to an independent policy maker.

4

What is Macroprudential Oversight?

The concept of macroprudential financial oversight gained popularity in the aftermath of the Global Financial Crisis (GFC), however it was by no means a novel concept. Central bankers were using macroprudential policies well before the crisis without referring to them as such.[1] The term made its first appearance as far back as the 1970s at a meeting of the Cooke Committee.[2] More focused academic and policy work in developing a macroprudential framework began with Andrew Crocket's call for a macroprudential approach to financial stability.[3] Crockett distinguished between the macroprudential approach, which limits disruptions to the financial system and the broader economy, from the microprudential approach, which limits disruptions in individual financial institutions and the lives of depositors.

According to the Financial Stability Board (FSB), the International Monetary Fund (IMF) and the Bank for International Settlements (BIS), the key features of macroprudential policy are its (i) purpose (limiting the risk of disruption to the financial system); (ii) reach (the whole financial system and areas where the system intersects with the real economy); and (iii) tools and their governance (prudential tools calibrated to address systemic risk and assigned to macroprudential authorities).[4] Macroprudential policy heavily interacts with microprudential regulation and other macroeconomic policy areas, namely monetary and fiscal policy.

[1] J Caruana, 'Macroprudential Policy: What We Have Learned and Where We Are Going' (Keynote Speech at the Second Financial Stability Conference of the International Journal of Central Banking, Madrid, 17 June 2010). Available at: www.bis.org/speeches/sp100618a.pdf.

[2] A Lamfalussy, 'The Use of Prudential Measures in the International Banking Markets' (24 October 1979) BISA 7.18(15) – Papers Lamfalussy, LAM25/F67.

[3] A Crockett, 'Marrying the Micro- and Macroprudential Dimensions of Financial Stability' (Remarks before the Eleventh International Conference of Banking Supervisors, held in Basel, 20–21 September 2000). Available at: www.bis.org/speeches/sp000921.htm.

[4] FSB-IMF-BIS, 'Macroprudential Policy Tools and Frameworks: Progress Report to G20' (27 October 2011). Available at: www.fsb.org/wp-content/uploads/r_111027b.pdf.

Since the GFC, experience with macroprudential policy has grown, and macroprudential institutions have become commonplace. This includes the three jurisdictions that were the epicentre of the GFC and play a significant role as international financial centres, namely, the UK, the US and the EU. In the UK, responsibility for macroprudential oversight has been given to the Financial Policy Committee, (FPC), which functions as a committee under the auspices of the Bank of England; in the US it is the Financial Stability Oversight Council, (FSOC), a multiagency body constituted by representatives of all the financial regulators and the Treasury; while in the EU the responsibility has been granted to the European Systemic Risk Board, (ESRB), also a multi-agency body, but at transnational level.

The remainder of this chapter provides an overview of macroprudential policy and how the policy addresses the dual sources of shocks to the financial system – contagion and financial imbalances. The goal is to demonstrate how this approach to regulating the financial system justifies the delegation of its governance to an independent policy maker, but one with an explicit mandate to also consider non-economic effects of macroprudential policy, because of the unavoidable distributional effects of the policy.

4.1. Macroprudential Policy or Macroprudential Regulation?

The legal frameworks for macroprudential oversight in the UK, US and EU point to two separate stages to 'limiting system-wide risk and preventing disruption to key financial services and the economy',[5] namely (i) *calibration* of instruments in response to movements in the financial cycle and to manage inter-linkages amongst financial institutions; and (ii) *implementation through regulations*, which give direction to individual intermediaries. The first stage of macroprudential oversight is conducted as pure policy because the main actions required at this stage are, firstly, monitoring the system and, secondly, deciding when and by how much to activate the counter-cyclical measures, like capital buffers, liquidity ratios and leverage ratios, and reducing interconnectedness across the whole financial system. This is the act of 'calling the moment', as Dalhuisen calls it.[6] See Figure 4.1.

[5] De Nederlandsche Bank considers crisis management as a third stage to macroprudential supervision. However, crisis management is calibrated and applied at individual firm level, therefore is more appropriately a microprudential approach.

[6] JH Dalhuisen, *Dalhuisen on Transnational Comparative, Commercial, Financial and Trade Law: Financial Products, Financial Services and Financial Regulation* Vol 3, 7th edn (Hart Publishing, 2019) 555–56.

Figure 4.1 Steps in Macroprudential Oversight

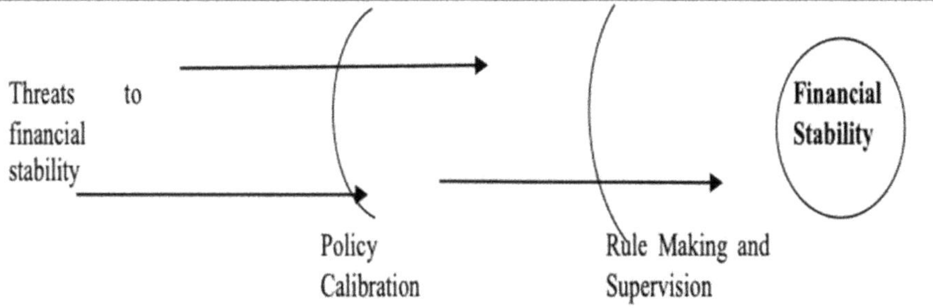

For example, the ESRB does not directly intervene in the financial markets nor does it issue instructions to individual firms. It was designed to be a 'reputational' body, with some form of moral authority to sway policy makers and supervisors.[7] The ESRB determines, collects and analyses relevant information; identifies and prioritises systemic risks; and issues non-binding warnings and recommendations for remedial actions where systemic risks are deemed to be significant. The recommendations are directed at either the EU, the European Supervisory Authorities, (ESA), national governments, national supervisory authorities or the European Commission, and their compliance is monitored through reports submitted to the ESRB. However, the ESRB cannot enforce compliance from an addressee of a recommendation. If it feels the action taken is inadequate it can only inform the Council of the European Union, or the ESA concerned. The UK's Financial Policy Committee performs similar functions monitoring levels of systemic risk, gathering and analysing data and issuing non-firm-specific directives or recommendations for remedial action to the prudential authorities – the Prudential Regulation Authority and Financial Conduct Authority. The FSOC in the US collects and evaluates data on SIFIs and recommends microprudential regulatory action. Its power to designate an institution as systemically important is, however, an exception to the largely policy-making role it occupies.

This does not mean that there are no rules guiding macroprudential authorities, rather the role of the rules is limited to establishing the authority and setting out its goals, functions and governance in generic terms. There is little detailed law governing operational aspects – much like monetary and fiscal policy – as policy decisions are largely discretionary, and therefore require the macroprudential authority to exercise their supervisory judgment.[8] In contrast, the second stage

[7] Commission, 'Proposal for a Regulation of the European Parliament and of the Council on Community macro prudential oversight of the financial system and establishing a European Systemic Risk Board' COM (2009) 499 final.

[8] In fact, the ESRB encourages authorities to use qualitative judgements to adjust instruments, even if the quantitative indicators have not yet been breached or are 'not showing unambiguous signals

of macroprudential oversight is essentially regulatory as it involves the setting, adjustment and control of capital, liquidity and leverage levels of individual intermediaries, albeit in reaction to the policy decisions, according to a set of rules, such as the EU's CRR/CRD IV, the UK's PRA Rule Book and the US Basel III Final Rule on Capital Standards.[9]

The distinction between 'policy making' and 'regulating' is a fine one; however, it exists in that policy makers define the fundamentals, parameters and direction of regulatory action.[10] Furthermore, as we will see later, the choice between a policy and a regulatory approach has implications for the governance models, which are at the centre of this book.

A policy-driven approach to managing financial stability allows supervisors to focus on 'big picture' issues, rather than the daily goings-on of individual firms. Moreover, rather than focusing on past failures and trying to prevent those, supervisors are more forward looking and react to issues as they arise. The use of discretion in policy making allows a flexible and prompt reaction to ever-shifting risks in the financial sector.

4.2. Objective of Macroprudential Policy

The overall objective of macroprudential policy is financial stability, however, frameworks vary across jurisdictions in respect of how the financial stability objective is interpreted. As noted in Chapter 3, systemic risk has two dimensions: (i) excessive time varying credit cycles – credit booms in good times which come from excessive credit supply, followed by a credit bust in the bad times as a result of deleveraging, deposits runs and/or credit crunches, and (ii) contagion – direct and indirect linkages and exposures amongst firms which spread failure like a wildfire across the system, depending on the importance of the firm(s) that has failed and whether its activities can be substituted or the extent of connections. Therefore, what is needed is a policy instrument that limits both the *likelihood* of systemic crises, by limiting the attractiveness of debt, and the *cost* of systemic crises, by limiting its spread. The instrument would address the cyclicality of the financial system and its resilience, as well as improve the solvency and liquidity of banks,

for such action'. See ESRB Instruments Working Group, *The ESRB Handbook on Operationalizing Macroprudential Instruments* (ESRB, 2018).

[9] The directives and recommendations issued by the macroprudential authorities are executed by microprudential regulators. In the US, this is the Federal Reserve Board, ('the Fed'), Securities Exchange Commission, Commodity Futures Trading Commission and the Housing Finance Agency. In the EU, like in the US, authority to intervene and issue directions to individual institutions has been vested in the European Central Bank and national supervisors in terms of Art 5 of the Single Supervisory Mechanism Regulation. The UK's Prudential Regulation Authority and Financial Conduct Authority are responsible for prudential regulation, and therefore executing regulatory measures to mitigate systemic risk.

[10] AC Brown, 'Regulators, Policy Makers, and the Making of Policy: Who Does What and When Do They Do It?' (2003) 3(1) *International Journal of Regulation and Governance* 1.

or reduce their size, concentration of activities and connections. In effect these actions also strengthen the resilience of the system.

In some jurisdictions, emphasis is placed on building the resilience of financial institutions, markets and infrastructures, which refers to the ability of the financial system to exclude or absorb shocks; while in others the aim is to more actively reduce the amplitude of the financial cycle by leaning against financial imbalances, in other words the build-up of credit and asset booms.[11] This is in contrast to microprudential regulation, which only has as its objective improving the resilience of individual financial intermediaries, using capital-based instruments.

The choice of objective is important because one does not seek to do more than to constrain the pace of credit and asset growth, while the other *accepts* that busts may occur and builds defences during the boom to be drawn down during the bust or reduces the channels for transmission of disruptions. Building resilience appears to be the more prudent of objectives, given that not all credit and asset price booms are bad, as some may be due to strong fundamentals, and distress may also arise because of severe problems that are not related to procyclicality, but may still be amplified via contagion.

Table 4.1 Macroprudential Policy Objectives in the UK, the US and the EU

	Financial Stability Objective	**Emphasis On**
UK	To protect and enhance the stability of the financial system of the United Kingdom. The responsibility of the Committee in relation to the achievement by the Bank of the Financial Stability Objective relates primarily to the identification of, monitoring of, and taking of action to remove or reduce, systemic risks with a view to protecting and enhancing the resilience of the UK financial system.[1]	Building resilience
US	Reducing the risk of financial disruptions that are sufficiently severe to inflict significant damage on the broader economy.[2]	Building resilience/ leaning against the cycle[3]
EU	To strengthen the resilience of the financial system and limit the build-up of vulnerabilities, to mitigate systemic risk and ensure the ongoing effective provision of financial services to the real economy.[4]	Building resilience/ leaning against the cycle

*Adapted from the Committee on the Global Financial System, 'Objective-setting and communication of macroprudential policies' (November 2016) BIS CGFS Papers No 57.

[1] Bank of England Act 1998, ss 2A(1) and 9C(2); [2] Janet Yellen, 'Pursuing Financial Stability at the Federal Reserve' (Speech, at Fourteenth Annual International Banking Conference, Chicago, 11 November 2011); [3] Janet Yellen, 'Monetary Policy and Financial Stability' (Speech at the Michel Camdessus Central Banking Lecture, Washington, DC, 2 July 2014); [4] ESRB Instruments Working Group, *The ESRB Handbook on Operationalizing Macroprudential Instruments* (ESRB, 2018), 7.

[11] Bank for International Settlements, 'Objective-setting and Communication of Macroprudential Policies' (November 2016) CGFS Papers No 57. Available at: www.bis.org/publ/cgfs57.pdf.

Building resilience and leaning against the cycle can be made more tangible through intermediate targets that focus on specific links in the transmission chain of systemic risk. For instance, in the UK, the FPC is required:

> to identify, monitor and take action to remove or reduce systemic risks attributable to structural features of financial markets, such as connections between financial institutions, systemic risks attributable to the distribution of risk within the financial sector, and unsustainable levels of leverage, debt or credit growth.[12]

In the US, intermediate objectives include strengthening the resilience of banking organisations; reducing fluctuations in the supply of credit; lowering the probability of default for a financial firm whose failure could undermine financial stability and cause outsize negative externalities, creating incentives for Global Systemically Important Banks, (G-SIBs), to shrink their systemic footprint and to offset any funding advantage that a financial firm has on account of it being perceived as too big to fail. Finally, in the EU the ESRB's objectives include:

> mitigating and preventing excessive credit growth and leverage, mitigating and preventing excessive maturity mismatch and market illiquidity, limiting direct and indirect exposure concentrations; and limiting the systemic impact of misaligned incentives with a view to reducing moral hazard.[13]

While narrowing down the objectives provides a powerful way of tracking macroprudential oversight, unlike monetary policy, these narrow objectives are directional and have not been further reduced to a numerical target that is more accessible to legislators and the public, to whom policy makers must answer.[14] This leaves us with questions about how much 'lowering' 'mitigating', 'limiting' or 'ensuring' is enough. It is to be expected that financial stability is difficult to reduce to a single indicator, unlike price stability, and, in any case, it may not be desirable given the constant (and often quick) shifts that occur in the financial system; the target for 'stability' also needs to be just as flexible.

Creating a framework for monitoring systemic risk to determine when to take action, in other words for measuring financial stability, is a critical component of macroprudential policy. The establishment of an effective monitoring system to detect tail-risks, improbable and severe events, is the first step at this stage.[15] The irony, though, is that such events cannot be reliably predicted.

[12] ESRB Instruments Working Group, *ESRB Handbook* (n 12) 7.

[13] Bank of England Act 1998, s 9C (2), (3).

[14] Bank for International Settlements, *Central Bank Governance and Financial Stability* (Ingves Report) (BIS, 2011).

[15] D Kohn, 'Macroprudential Policy: Implementation and Effectiveness' (Speech, Frankfurt, 27 April 2016). Available at: www.brookings.edu/wp-content/uploads/2016/07/speech902.pdf.

4.3. The Importance of Data

The literature on risk analysis for financial stability emphasises the role of timely and accurate data as a key component in devising policy actions and monitoring their effectiveness.[16] Data enables us to see and hear what is happening in the financial world. The sort of data required to identify systemic risks, comes in both aggregated and individual form. Aggregated data provides information on overall trends and common risk exposures in the markets, while data on individual firms provides insight on the interlinkages, risk concentrations and feedback mechanisms within the market.[17] Formal data collection mechanisms have been set up, which rely on firm-specific information provided by microprudential regulators.

4.3.1. Data Collection

The ESRB, for instance, relies on national microprudential regulators, central banks and statistical offices for information which it uses to assess the level of threat to EU financial stability. The type of data that these agencies must provide is summarised in the ESRB Decision on Data.[18] Given that the ESRB is a policy-making body making broad decisions for the system, the information it receives never identifies individual firms. Making decisions targeting individual firms would place it squarely in the realm of regulation, which has different legal implications. The ESRB can make reasonable requests for information concerning individual firms or request ad hoc surveys, but an ad hoc survey can only be carried out if the desired information is not available from other sources.

In the case of requests for dis-aggregated data, the ESRB must ensure that the request is justified and proportionate, which means seeking approval of the Board of Supervisors of the relevant ESA through two consultations.[19] In practice, the legal framework for the provision of information to the ESRB has proven to be weak, leading to delays, and irregular and partial provision of

[16] SG Cecchetti, I Fender and P McGuire, 'Toward a Global Risk Map' (May 2010) BIS Working Paper No 309. Available at: www.bis.org/publ/work309.pdf.

[17] JM Israel et al 'Statistics and Indicators for Financial Stability Analysis and Policy' (April 2013) ECB Occasional Policy Paper No 145/ April 2013. Available at: www.ecb.europa.eu/pub/pdf/scpops/ecbocp145.pdf.

[18] Decision of the European Systemic Risk Board of 21 July 2015 on the provision and collection of information for the macroprudential oversight of the financial system within the Union and repealing Decision ESRB/2011/6 (ESRB/2015/2) OJ C 394/4.

[19] Article 15(6)–(7) of Regulation (EU) 1092/2010 of the European Parliament and of the Council of 24 November 2010 on European Union macro-prudential oversight of the financial system and establishing a European Systemic Risk Board [2010] OJ L 331 (ESRB Regulation).

data, particularly when the ESRB requests information for ad hoc surveys and individual institutions, which involve complex procedures and the release of confidential information.

The UK has the least-complicated method for data collection. The FPC uses a functional process for identifying systemic risk and mapping risks into policy action. Risk assessment is conducted through quarterly surveillance processes, relying on market intelligence as well as supervisory insights and analysis by Bank of England Staff, which includes the Prudential Regulation Authority, (PRA), and the Financial Conduct Authority, (FCA). Market intelligence is drawn from an extensive contact base, including a wide range of financial agents and institutions. It provides insights beyond publicly available data.

The US went a step further and established a specialist agency to collect and analyse data relating to the financial sector. The Office of Financial Research, (OFR), which was established in terms of the Dodd-Frank Act,[20] delivers 'high-quality financial data, standards, and analysis for the FSOC, the Council members and the public'.[21] The actual research on intermediaries and markets is conducted by the OFR's Research and Analysis Centre.

4.3.2. Processing/Organising the Data

The analysis of data to measure the level of risk has generally proceeded using a combination of four methods, namely distributional models and stress testing, which seek to identify common exposures and interlinkages; financial stability indicators, (FSIs), which focus on cyclicality; and vulnerabilities analysis that combines elements of the three other models.[22] Of the four, stress testing and FSIs are the most widely used methods.

Distributional models measure systemic risk by estimating the probability of default of individual firms, and the correlation of default events. As such they serve a dual purpose, they can alert regulators to firm-specific risk, and the distribution of system-wide risk.[23]

Stress testing models, in contrast, measure the resilience of the financial system to shocks. Stress testing occurs at two levels: (i) at firm level, where the regulators test whether individual firms would survive in a stressed scenario, and then (ii) at sectoral level where the same test is repeated. As such, it relies heavily on

[20] Dodd-Frank Wall Street Reform and Consumer Protection Act PubL 111–203, 124 Stat. 1376–222, sec 154 [sec 152].

[21] See www.financialresearch.gov.

[22] Cecchetti et al, 'Toward a Global Risk Map' (n 16).

[23] ibid.

detailed and accurate supervisory information. Bernanke lauded stress tests for their forward-looking approach (they essentially predict the likelihood of future survival), as opposed to relying on past data to try and prevent future events, how they promote supervisory consistency (by giving supervisors a horizontal views of banks) and how they promote transparency (by providing the public with information on bank and financial system resilience).[24]

The third method of organising data, via financial stability indicators, preoccupied policy makers even before the onset of the GFC.[25] FSIs enable policy makers to identify and measure misalignments in the financial sector, which point to the build-up of systemic risk, and provide warnings of financial sector distress. FSIs, such as movements in credit-to-GDP ratios and asset prices, act as early-warning signals of adverse developments in the financial sector.[26]

While FSIs have been lauded for their effectiveness in summarising current financial conditions, there is still some scepticism regarding their ability to forecast macroeconomic conditions. FSIs are constructed using historical data, and, as we know the financial and economic environment is constantly evolving, influenced by non-repeating events (like deregulation) and pricing is often based on estimates of future interest rates and term premiums. In short, it is an environment of substantial uncertainty. But for all their shortcomings, financial stability indicators still encourage policy makers to make their decisions in a more systematic way, which also makes it easier to exercise political oversight and enforce accountability over the independent macroprudential authorities.

It is important to remember, while these techniques are helpful in shaping the views of policy makers and public understanding, they are merely indicators of instability and not the end result that macroprudential authorities should pursue.

Finally, macroprudential authorities can use vulnerability analysis to measure systemic risk. The technique, which is a more intuitive approach to measuring risk, combines quantitative techniques mentioned above as well as qualitative techniques to gauge the type and level of systemic risk. Policy makers track developments for a wide variety of markets using movements in prices and quantity. For example, financial risk could be inferred from movements in option prices, which indicate volatility.[27]

[24] B Bernanke, 'Stress Testing Banks: What Have We Learned?' (Speech at 'Maintaining Financial Stability: Holding a Tiger by the Tail' Financial Markets Conference, Georgia, 8 April 2013). Available at: www.federalreserve.gov/newsevents/speech/bernanke20130408a.htm.

[25] Reinhart and Rogoff's 'This Time is Different' presents the most extensive of recent studies. See C Reinhart and KS Rogoff, *This Time is Different: Eight Centuries of Financial Folly* (Princeton University Press, 2009).

[26] See IMF Financial Soundness Indicators. Available at: data.imf.org/?sk=51B096FA-2CD2-40C2-8D09-0699CC1764DA.

[27] Cecchetti et al (n 16).

4.4. Macroprudential Policy Instruments

There are over 1,313 macroprudential instruments in use across the globe,[28] including soft tools like communication which is used to provide forward guidance to firms and transparency with the public.[29] The tools can be placed into two broad categories depending on the policy objectives outlined earlier, although in practice they may address both dimensions of systemic risk: (1) instruments tailored to mitigate the time-varying dimension of systemic risk, in other words controlling credit growth plus attendant asset price increases, and building resilience for the bad times; and (2) instruments tailored to mitigate the cross-sectional dimension of systemic risk, by improving the liquidity or solvency of systemic institutions, and/or limiting concentrations and interconnectedness, also to improve resilience.[30]

Figure 4.2 The Classification of Macroprudential Instruments

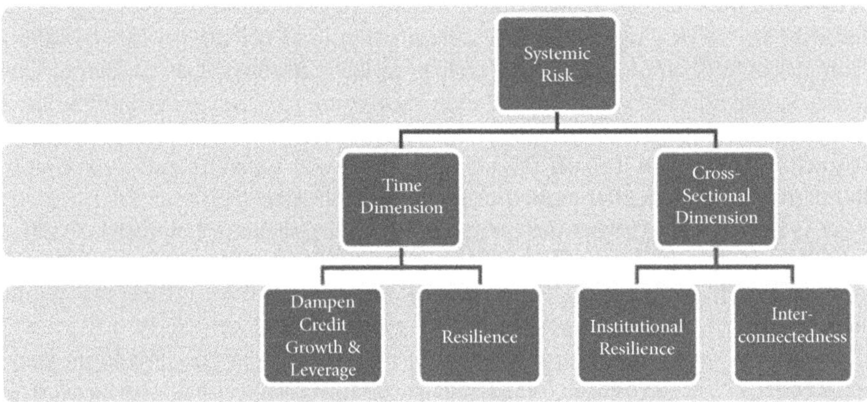

The core instruments of macroprudential policy are traditional microprudential instruments with a macroprudential add on, designed to reduce excessive

[28] For a summary see the IMF database, International Monetary Fund, 'Macroprudential Policy Survey' www.elibrary-areaer.imf.org/Macroprudential/Pages/Home.aspx. The tools fall into six categories covering liquidity and foreign exchange (FX) mismatches, the household sector, the corporate sector, structural risks, non-banks and broad-based tools applying to all exposures.

[29] Rochelle Edge and Nellie Liang, 'New Financial Stability Governance Structures and Central Banks' (August 2017) Hutchins Center Working Paper No 32. Available at: www.brookings.edu/wp-content/uploads/2017/08/es_20170808_liang_newfinancialstabilitygovernancestructures.pdf. However, the impact of communication tools, such as the financial stability report, (FSR), is doubtful, given their focus on historical data and a lack of clarity about their aims and objectives. See M Čihák, S Muñoz, S Teh Sharifuddin, and K Tintchev, 'Financial Stability Reports: What Are They Good For?' (January 2012) IMF Working Paper WP/12/1. Available at: www.imf.org/external/pubs/ft/wp/2012/wp1201.pdf.

[30] This is not the only method of classifying instruments; for instance, they can be classified according to the intermediate objective being pursued; the transmission channel of the

procyclicality or increase resilience in the financial system, by targeting systemically important institutions with higher impact, risk concentration and interconnectedness. Macroprudential authorities may also turn to other macroeconomic policy instruments, such as fiscal, monetary, foreign exchange and even administrative policy.[31]

In order to acquire a macroprudential label, policy tools must have a macroprudential add-on, meaning (i) they either operate counter-cyclically and/or specifically target systemically important institutions and activities, and (ii) they are operated by the designated macroprudential policy maker.[32] The tools work on either the liabilities side of the financial institution's balance sheet, by altering their cost or composition, or the tools can target the asset side, shifting the composition and risk profile of assets (including by managing the borrower's credit risk).[33]

The following discussion looks at a selection of instruments from the international framework, as well as from the UK, the US and the EU. This sample only details a fraction of the instruments that are used across the globe and is intended to demonstrate the transmission channels between the macroprudential instruments, and the objectives described above.

These instruments mainly target banking institutions. A more prudent approach would be for policy to target activities rather than institutions. Entity-specific regulation and supervision can create competitive distortions, and, worse still, it will just encourage dangerous activities to move to the shadow banking system. The US, as we shall see, has adopted an activities-based approach in Dodd-Frank, and in March 2019, the FSOC issued a proposed Interpretive Guidance that would prioritise 'Activities-Based' macroprudential policy. Focus would only shift to individual institutions if regulating activities fails.

instrument or whether they alter the credit, liquidity or capital of the firm. For other methods of classification see ESRB Instruments Working Group, *ESRB Handbook* (n 8); X Freixas, L Laeven, and JL Peydró, *Systemic Risk, Crises, and Macroprudential Regulation* (MIT Press, 2015) and C-H Lim et al, 'Macroprudential Policy: What Instruments and How to Use Them? Lessons from Country Experiences' (October 2011) IMF Working Paper No 11/238. Available at: www.imf.org/external/pubs/ft/wp/2011/wp11238.pdf.

[31] Lim et al, 'Macroprudential Policy: What Instruments and How to Use Them' (n 30).

[32] Microprudential instruments may have a macroprudential effect even if they are not calibrated as such – an example would be the leverage ratio which deters the build-up of leverage. If an additional leverage ratio is applied to an institution based on its size and interconnectedness, then the ratio would acquire macroprudential qualities. Similarly, if a liquidity coverage ratio or net stable funding ratio are applied in a time-varying manner, then they become macroprudential and work to dampen the build-up of credit over time and build resilience by creating a liquidity buffer that can be released in bad times.

[33] There are several strategies that macroprudential authorities can adopt in the deployment of tools. Tools are often used in combination, and they may be broad-based or targeted. This points to an underlying weakness in the macroprudential approach – the lack of a clearly defined, numerically or otherwise, policy target.

4.4.1. International Time-varying and Cross-Sectional Instruments

Basel III, together with national legislation like the CRR/CRD IV in the EU, the Financial Services Act in the UK and the Dodd–Frank Act in the United States, draws on the tools listed in the IMF survey to manage systemic risk and maintain financial stability. Basel III introduced three kinds of capital buffers with an explicit macroprudential orientation. Although, as we shall see, some of its other typically microprudential instruments may also be recalibrated by introducing a macroprudential add-on.

Basel III introduced two instruments targeted at dampening the upswing of the financial cycle and building resilience to withstand a downswing. The first is a capital conservation buffer, (CCB), equal to 2.5 per cent of risk-weighted assets. Combined with the ordinary 4.5 per cent capital required for credit risk, it brings the total common equity standard to 7 per cent.[34] The buffer is designed to expand during buoyant periods and can be drawn down during periods of stress. A bank will be prohibited from making discretionary profit distributions if its buffer falls below the 2.5 per cent. This will increase overall sector resilience and provide the mechanism for economic recovery. Thus, the financial system will not experience a disruption to credit supply during a downturn, or at least the effects of a downturn are reduced. In this way, the CCB counters the procyclicality of the system.

The second type of capital buffer is the countercyclical capital buffer, (CCyB), which allows regulators to impose a further capital requirement amounting to 2.5 per cent of risk-weighted assets if the regulator judges systemic risk to be building up.[35] The buffer is released when system-wide risk crystallises. While Basel III suggests a minimum CCyB, the regulators may use their discretion in setting the CCyB, provided it is accompanied by an explanation to the public.[36] In fact macroprudential authorities are required to disclose to the public every time they make changes to the CCyB, including a breakdown of all the jurisdictions in which the country's banks have extended private sector loans.

The Basel Committee's guidance to national authorities on operating the countercyclical buffer, uses the credit-to-GDP gap as a predictor for systemic risk, since financial crises have been linked to credit bubbles.[37] The Guidance sets out criteria to determine the maximum point in the credit-GDP gap at which firms

[34] Basel Committee on Banking Supervision, *Basel III: A Global Regulatory Framework for More Resilient Banks and Banking Systems* (BIS, 2011) paras 122–35. Available at: www.bis.org/publ/bcbs189.htm.

[35] ibid, paras 139–45.

[36] In the UK, for instance, CCyB has been hovering between 0.5% and 2% since 2016.

[37] Basel Committee on Banking Supervision, *Guidance for National Authorities Operating the Countercyclical Capital Buffer* (BIS, December 2010). (BCBS). Available at: www.bis.org/publ/bcbs187.pdf.

should build up the buffer, and the minimum level at which the buffer should be released to keep the financial system and economy going.[38]

An individual bank's buffer is the weighted average of the buffers in effect in all the jurisdictions where the bank has lent money/the final guarantors of the loans reside.[39] Like the CCB, the CCyB consists entirely of Common Equity Tier 1 capital and if the minimum buffer requirements are breached, profit distribution constraints will be imposed on the bank.[40] Basel member countries are expected to reciprocate the CCyB rate in order to avoid banks from one jurisdiction gaining an unfair advantage over others, because they are subject to lower capital requirements. Therefore, the home country of a bank is not allowed to set a CCyB lower than that being applied by the host country where the bank has credit exposures. The only exception is in instances where the host country's buffer is set at a level higher than the minimum 2.5 per cent. So, for instance, if the host regulator sets the buffer at 3 per cent, other regulators are only obliged to reciprocate the buffer level up to 2.5 per cent of risk-weighted assets (RWA).

Counter-cyclical capital requirements provide a measure to reduce the time dimension of systemic risk. The CCyB forces banks to hold more capital, either by raising more Tier 1 capital or reducing their risk-weighted assets. This can serve the objective of dampening the financial cycle, by reducing the amount available for lending. Alternatively, if banks are forced to fund their activities with more equity capital than debt, then the more expensive form of funding may make credit too expensive for banks' customers, thus reducing the appetite for credit, even if it is available.

The CCyB also helps banks build resilience to periods of distress. The extra capital built up during good times will be used to absorb losses and/or continue lending during a downturn. Loosening the capital buffer, thus releasing the supply of credit to households and businesses, activates the cushion. Of course, there needs to be strong coordination with microprudential regulators who may be acting in the opposite direction, by raising capital levels in reaction to perceived risks. The increased resilience of domestic systems can have positive spill-over effects on the global financial system, given the global interconnections.

In addition, Basel III introduced a capital surcharge for systemically important banks (SIBs). Every year, the Basel Committee works with the Financial Stability Board and national regulators to develop a list of global systemically important banks (G-SIBs), with a score for each bank that is a measure of systemic losses that would be suffered should the bank fail. G-SIBs are identified using the indicator-based measurement approach, which includes both quantitative indicators and

[38] ibid, Annex 1.

[39] As opposed to where its loans are booked. The weight attached to the jurisdiction is the sum of bank's credit risk charges arising from its exposures to the private sector in that jurisdiction.

[40] BCBS, *Basel III*, (n 34) para 147.

qualitative elements.[41] Five qualitative and quantitative indicators were chosen to reflect the common features amongst banks whose failure would lead to financial instability, namely (i) size, (ii) interconnectedness, (iii) substitutability in the market, (iv) global footprint and (v) complexity. Some of the indicators were further subdivided, in essence defining what each indicator means. Each indicator is given an overall weight of 20 per cent, and where there are two or three subdivisions each one is also weighted, 10 per cent where there are two indicators and 6.67 per cent where there are three.

Table 4.2 G-SIB Risk Weighting

Category	Indicator	Weight
Cross-jurisdictional activity	Cross-jurisdictional claims	10%
	Cross-jurisdictional liabilities	10%
Size	Total exposures as defined for use in the Basel III leverage ratio	20%
Interconnectedness	Intra-financial system assets	6.67%
	Intra-financial system liabilities	6.67%
	Securities outstanding	6.67%
Substitutability/financial institution infrastructure[1]	Assets under custody	6.67%
	Payments activity	6.67%
	Underwritten transactions in debt and equity markets	6.67%
Complexity	Notional amount of over-the-counter derivatives	6.67%
	Level 3 assets	6.67%
	Trading and available for sale securities	6.67%

*Basel Committee on Banking Supervision, '*Global Systemically Important Banks: Updated Assessment Methodology and the Higher Loss Absorbency Requirement*.' (BIS, July 2013).

[1] In 2019 the BCBS issued a revised framework which added trading volume as a fourth sub-indicator to the substitutability category. From 2021, underwritten transactions in debt and equity markets and trading volume will each carry a weight of 3.33%.

The value for each sub-indicator for a single bank is divided by the total calculated for all banks in a sample and multiplied by 10,000 to express it in terms of basis points. The value for the main indicator is a simple average of all the sub-indicators, just as the final score for each bank is an average of its five indicator scores.

There is, however, a subjective element to the calculation of systemic importance. Firstly, national regulators may add banks to the sample used as a

[41] Basel Committee on Banking Supervision, *Global Systemically Important Banks: Updated Assessment Methodology and the Higher Loss Absorbency Requirement* (BIS July 2013). Available at: www.bis.org/publ/bcbs255.pdf.

proxy for the banking sector based on supervisory judgement. Secondly, the results of the indicator-based approach can be adjusted also based on supervisory judgement, gleaned from qualitative analysis of banks. Thus, both quantitative and qualitative evidence of systemic importance is captured.

As at the end of 2019, banks with a score of 130 basis points and above were considered G-SIBs and made subject to a higher loss absorbency requirement, which can range from 1 per cent to 2.5 per cent of Common Equity Tier 1. The SIB surcharge acts as a deterrent to banks from increasing their global systemic importance (by increasing their size, interconnections etc.). Commentators have, however, criticised the surcharge for being too low. Passmore and Hafften, for instance, estimate that to be more effective, the systemic risk surcharge should increase from 3 to 8.25 per cent, or even higher for G-SIBs who finance their activities with short-term funding.[42]

The BCBS also issued a framework for determining domestic systemically important banks, (D–SIBs), intended to limit similar externalities at national level from banks that are locally, but not globally.[43] The framework is not as detailed as that for G-SIBs, and simply provides principles for country regulators to take into account when designing an assessment methodology and determining higher loss absorbency levels. This framework puts national discretion at the forefront, given the variances amongst countries' banking sectors.

All three of the standards issued by the BCBS are capital based. Capital-based instruments have the double advantage of (i) building resilience, because forcing banks to hold more capital improves their loss-absorption, and (ii) dampening the supply of credit and asset prices. The Basel III instruments for macroprudential oversight are fewer, however, when compared to the more standardised core instruments of microprudential regulation. For the most part, jurisdictions have developed additional macroprudential instruments that target country-specific systemic risks, usually by employing a macroprudential add-on to traditional microprudential instruments.

4.4.2. Examples from National Legal Frameworks

4.4.2.1. EU

Between September 2011 and December 2016, the ESRB made 13 public recommendations in relation to specific systemic risks, although three of them were amendments of previous recommendations. The most significant of these recommendations is Recommendation ESRB 2013/1 on intermediate objectives and

[42] W Passmore and AH von Hafften 'Are Basel's Capital Surcharges for Global Systemically Important Banks Too Small?' (2019) 15(1) *International Journal of Central Banking* 107.

[43] Basel Committee on Banking Supervision, *A Framework for Dealing with Domestic Systemically Important Banks* (BIS, October 2012).

instruments of macroprudential policy.[44] The Recommendation then establishes five intermediate objectives for macroprudential policy and classifies instruments according to the objective they address, namely:

(a) to mitigate and prevent excessive credit growth and leverage;
(b) to mitigate and prevent excessive maturity mismatch and market illiquidity;
(c) to limit direct and indirect exposure concentrations;
(d) to limit the systemic impact of misaligned incentives with a view to reducing moral hazard; and
(e) to strengthen the resilience of financial infrastructures.[45]

Instruments to address objectives (a) and (b) fall in the category time-varying instruments, meant to target the cyclicality of the financial system, while instruments targeting objectives (c) to (e) are more obviously in the cross-sectional category as they seek to improve the solvency of intermediaries whose failure would have a systemic impact, or limiting concentrations and interconnectedness.

The following instruments recommended by the ESRB target the time dimension:

(i) counter-cyclical capital buffer;
(ii) sectorial capital requirements (including intra-financial system);
(iii) macro-prudential leverage ratio;
(iv) loan-to-value requirements;
(v) loan-to-income/debt (service)-to-income requirements;
(vi) liquidity coverage ratio;
- net stable funding ratio
- loan-to-deposit ratio

(vii) margin and haircut requirements.[46]

On the cross-sectional side, the ESRB recommends the use of:

(i) large exposure restrictions;
(ii) CCP clearing requirement;
(iii) SIFI capital surcharges;
(iv) margin and haircut requirements on CCP clearing I;
(v) increased disclosure; and
(vi) structural systemic risk buffer.[47]

[44] European Systemic Risk Board Recommendations ESRB/2013/1 of 4 April 2013 on Intermediate Objectives and Instruments of Macroprudential Policy [2013] OJ C 170/1. (Recommendation on Intermediate Objectives).
[45] A2(a)–(e) Recommendation on Intermediate Objectives.
[46] See Table 4.1.
[47] ibid.

The method for calibrating instruments is contained in the Capital Requirements Directive (2013/36/EU) (CRD) and the Capital Requirements Regulation (575/2013) (CRR), (collectively CRR/CRD IV). The Directive requires national implementation measures, while the Regulation is directly applicable across the EU. For measures covered by the CRR/CRD IV room for national discretion is restricted since it pursues maximum harmonisation.

Macroprudential instruments contained in the CRD/CRR, are divided into Pillar 1 instruments, which apply to the banking sector, and Pillar 2 instruments. Pillar 1 instruments are similar to those outlined in the BCBS global framework, namely the CCyB, CCB, and an additional buffer for Globally Systemically Important Institutions, (G-SII), or Other Systemically Important Institutions, (O-SII), with a slight deviation on the method for calculating buffers for O-SIIs.

The EU built on the principles provided by the BCBS and issued guidelines on the criteria to determine the conditions of O-SIIs. The basic methodology is similar to that for identifying G-SII, there are four main indicators each with a weight of 25 per cent, which are further divided and weighted accordingly. Any institution that scores 350 basis points or higher is considered an O-SII. Macroprudential authorities may raise the cut-off point to 425 basis points or reduce it to 275 basis points, making it more sensitive to local conditions in the Member State's financial system. The relevant authorities may also add firms to the sample pool based on supervisory judgement, which includes both quantitative and qualitative considerations.

Macroprudential authorities may also apply, under Pillar 1, higher sectoral capital requirements for assets in the real-estate sector, which target exposure concentrations, such as a systemic risk buffer, (SRB) increasing risk weights on real estate assets or shifting the Loss Given Default, (LGD) parameters. Whereas the G-SII and OSII target systemic risks from an institutional perspective, the SRB attacks it from a product/service perspective by penalising large and common exposures in the real-estate sector. Different buffer levels may be applied to different banks or sets of banks. As an alternative to imposing an SRB, macroprudential authorities may require banks that use the Standardised Approach for calculating credit risk to increase the risk weights attached to loans backed by mortgages on residential or commercial property from 35 and 50 per cent respectively, to 150 per cent, or impose other stricter requirements.[48] The financial stability concerns warranting such intervention are specified in regulatory technical standards (RTS).[49]

[48] CRR, art 124(2).

[49] European Banking Authority, 'Draft Regulatory Technical Standards on the conditions that competent authorities shall take into account when determining higher risk-weights, in particular the term of "financial stability considerations" under CRR, art 124(4)(b) and the conditions that competent authorities shall take into account when determining higher minimum LGD values under CRR, art 164(6) CRR' (6 July 2015) Consultation Paper EBA/CP/2015/12.

Alternatively, for banks that used the IRB method for calculating credit risk, macroprudential authorities may request that they apply a loss given default value which is higher than 10 per cent for loans secured by residential mortgages and 15 per cent for commercial mortgages. Again, the EBA has drafted regulatory technical standards to provide guidance on determining such higher LGD floors. In principle, a targeted increase in capital can be applied to any category of loans that are the subject of a credit boom. In the decade since the crisis this has been in the real estate sector.

Where the Pillar 1 instruments do not adequately address an identified systemic risk, then Member States may introduce 'national flexibility measures' via national legislation. These national flexibility measures enable the use of several microprudential instruments calibrated for macroprudential purposes, such as those used to manage credit and liquidity risk, interconnections, or public disclosures. National authorities, however, will require the approval of the European Council, to implement the additional measures. The ESRB and EBA must also be notified and give their opinion on the envisaged national measures.

Table 4.3 EU National Flexibility Measures

National Flexibility Measure	Transmission Channel
LCR & NSFR	Measures address the fundamental elements to financial imbalances, liquidity and maturity transformation. As highlighted in Chapter 3, the BCBS introduced internationally harmonised minimum liquidity requirements in the form of the Liquidity Coverage Ratio, (LCR) and the Net Stable Funding Ratio, (NSFR).[50] These minimum requirements can serve a macroprudential purpose, even though they are not explicitly calibrated for that function, by forcing banks to hold more liquid assets and finance their activities with more long-term funding than demand deposits. As a consequence, reducing their need for frequent refinancing, especially via fire sales, may also result in market illiquidity and contagion. Time-varying adjustments to the LCR and NSFR may work to (i) reduce credit growth in an upswing if the longer-term funding sources are sufficiently more costly than deposits and (ii) increase resilience by allowing banks to draw down on the liquidity buffer in a downswing.
Capital Conservation Buffer	Improves banks' future loss absorption capacity and curbs excessive credit growth and leverage insofar as holding the buffer increases the cost of lending.

(continued)

[50] Application of LCR and NSFR – Article 412 CRR, as read with Commission Delegated Regulation (EU) 2015/61 of 10 October 2014 to supplement Regulation (EU) No 575/2013 of the European Parliament and the Council with regard to liquidity coverage requirement for Credit Institutions [2015] OJ L 11/1.

Table 4.3 *(Continued)*

National Flexibility Measure	Transmission Channel
Public Disclosure Requirements	Strengthen the resilience of the system by facilitating public scrutiny of financial institutions.
Large Exposure Requirements	Target risk from high counterparty concentration and interconnectedness. A counterparty exposure is considered 'large' if its value is equal to or exceeds 10 per cent of the bank's eligible capital. Counterparty exposures should not exceed 25 percent of eligible capital, or €150 million in the case of exposure to other banks, whichever is the higher. The macroprudential measure would reduce the value of what is considered large, remove exemptions to exposures and tighten models and mitigation techniques for calculating the exposures.[51] The instrument puts an upper limit on losses that a bank may suffer because of exposure to certain counterparties or encourages the diversification of risk.
Limits on Intra-financial Exposures	These work in a similar way as limits on large exposures, working on both dimensions of systemic risk. Their primary purpose, however, is to limit the extent of lending between banks and therefore interconnectedness. The measures simply involve the application of a broad range of macroprudential instruments to risk exposures, such as securitisations, to other financial intermediaries, not just banks.

The application of Pillar 2, like national flexibility measures, is left to the discretion of Member States, when they appear to offer the most effective and efficient solution. The only condition is that the macroprudential authority must demonstrate through stress tests – namely the bank's Internal Capital Adequacy Assessment Process (ICAAP) and Supervisory Review and Examination Process (SREP) – that a bank being targeted through a Pillar 2 measure poses a systemic risk.[52]

The main difference between Pillar II and national flexibility measures is that, whereas national flexibility measures are designed to apply to all the firms in a territory, Pillar 2 measures are firm specific and act as a targeted 'add-on' to the other macroprudential instruments, whether this is through a liquidity surcharge and limitations on borrowers via the LTV, LTI and DTI ratios.

The liquidity surcharge is a risk premium charged on the difference between a bank's liquidity position and the national or EU mandated liquidity and stable funding requirements. The macroprudential authority may charge it, taking into account the bank's business model and liquidity management strategy, stress-test results and overall state of liquidity in the Member State.

[51] *ESRB Handbook* (n 8).
[52] ibid, 134.

The other important Pillar II measures, the LTV, LTI and DTI ratios, also work on dampening the credit cycle. These instruments are not harmonised under the CRR/CRD IV and are therefore implemented at national discretion. They are different from the capital-based instruments in that instead of targeting the bank's balance sheet, they target borrowers by restricting the amount they can borrow relative to the value of any security provided against the loan or the borrower's income. By doing so they can curb credit growth and therefore debt driven demand and prices in the targeted sector, of which emphasis in the decade since the crisis has been on the real estate sector. This emphasis is justified by experience from previous financial crises, which showed the link between real estate price booms and financial instability, as highlighted in Chapter 3. In addition, both the bank and borrower resilience to downturns is improved by reducing the likelihood of the borrower defaulting and the bank suffering losses as a result.

4.4.2.2. UK

The UK's macroprudential instrument framework was designed pre-Brexit, but largely remains similar to that of the EU.[53] The FPC has in its arsenal instruments that target the liability side of firms' balance sheets, such as countercyclical capital buffers; capital conservation buffers and buffers for SIBs;[54] minimum, supplementary and countercyclical leverage ratios; and those that target the asset side of the balance sheet, like LTV and ICR limits for mortgages on buy-to-let properties; LTV and DTI limits for mortgages on owner-occupied properties; and sectoral capital requirements for exposures in housing and financial sectors. The FPC is empowered to issue directions to the PRA and FCA on the use of these instruments, and it issues a policy statement for each of its macroprudential powers, explaining what instrument has been assigned and how and when it will direct or recommend its use.[55]

The CRR was directly applicable to firms in the UK, while CRD was implemented through national law. Therefore, the policy strategy for calculation of the CCyB, capital conservation buffer, additional capital for G-SIIs and O-SIIs, and sectorial capital requirements follows the same methodology. On the other hand, the FPC has developed its own approach to sectorial LTV, LTI, ICR and DTI ratios, as well as the leverage ratio.

[53] A general policy was put in place to ensure a smooth transition in the post-Brexit era, after the UK left the EU. See Bank of England, 'The Bank of England's Amendments to Financial Services Legislation under the European Union (Withdrawal) Act 2018' (June 2019) Bank of England Policy Statement | PRA Policy Statement PS5/19. Available at: www.bankofengland.co.uk/paper/2019/the-boes-amendments-to-financial-services-legislation-under-the-eu-withdrawal-act-2018.

[54] The Capital Requirements (Capital Buffers and Macro-prudential Measures) Regulations 2014, SI 2014/894 and Prudential Regulation Authority, *PRA Rulebook* (27 January 2020).

[55] See the FPC's approach to setting the countercyclical capital buffer; the FPC's powers to supplement capital requirements; the FPC's powers over leverage ratio tools; and the FPC's powers over housing policy instruments, Available at: www.bankofengland.co.uk/financial-stability.

Table 4.4 FPC Macroprudential Instruments

Tool type	Date	Description
Borrower Resilience	June 2014	15% LTI flow limit for owner-occupier mortgages
Borrower Resilience	June 2014	Affordability tests for mortgages
Borrower Resilience	June 2017	Update affordability tests for mortgages
Bank Resilience	Annual since 2014	Stress test scenario design
Bank Resilience	Quarterly	Set CCyB
Bank Resilience	June 2015	Introduction of a UK leverage ratio framework
Market Resilience	June 2013	Contingency planning for LIBOR and other benchmark rates disappearing
Market Resilience	March 2015	Asked the Bank and FCA to address data gaps and build a common understanding of vulnerabilities in capital markets and asset management activities; report back by September
Market Resilience	June 2015	Asked the Bank, PRA and FCA to ensure firms at the core of the UK financial system, including financial market infrastructure, completed their cyber vulnerability tests and adopted resilience action plans.
Market Resilience	Semi-Annual	Financial stability report risk identification chapters
Brexit mitigants	Quarterly since 2017	Checklist laying out risks to banks, borrowers and markets

Prominent Examples from FPC Tools and Decisions. From Anil K Kashyap, 'My Reflections on the FPC's Strategy' Speech given at the 50th Anniversary of the Journal of Money, Credit and Banking, Frankfurt, 28 March 2019. Available at: www.ecb.europa.eu/pub/conferences/shared/pdf/20190328_financial_intermediation/Panel_Kashyap_slides.pdf.

The UK framework places more emphasis on the time dimension of systemic risk. Although the FPC insists that its target is to build resilience, its approach is balanced and involves leaning against the cycle. Half of the tools which have been granted to the FPC are trained towards imbalances that can arise within the system, tools such as the LTV and DTI, which have been applied to new mortgage transactions, excluding the refinancing of existing mortgages, to arrest further growth imbalances. The FPC's reluctance to explicitly state that it actively leans against the cycle may be because of how politically sensitive the issue of controlling credit supply is. It appears not to want to be seen to be making distributional choices beyond its purview, which can be the result of borrower-targeted macroprudential tools.

Regardless, the FPC has a very clear focus on the time dimension of systemic risk and the effects of the financial system on the real economy, likely because the proponents of macroprudential policy in the UK recognised the inevitability of procyclicality in the financial system. The reluctance to leave the market to self-correct may also be the result of factors like the financial sector's contribution to the economy and the extent of leverage amongst UK banks.[56]

4.4.2.3. US

The US macroprudential framework is detailed in the Dodd-Frank Act and, in contrast to the UK, this seems to focus solely on the cross-sectional aspect of systemic risk, particularly, on:

> preventing or mitigating risks to the financial stability of the United States that could arise from the material financial distress, failure, or on-going activities of large, interconnected financial institutions.[57]

The FSOC, which is the designated guardian of financial stability, can designate non-bank financial companies as Systemically Important Financial institutions, opening the way for application of other macroprudential tools through stricter regulation by the Board of Governors of the Federal Reserve System, (hereinafter 'the Fed'). The Dodd-Frank Act itself only provides directional guidance on the criteria for meeting the statutory standard for designation; however, the FSOC issued a final rule and interpretive guidance for the process of designation.[58]

The rule provides the procedure to be followed by FSOC when designating a non-bank financial firm as a SIFI, while the interpretive guidance provides the methodology for determining systemic importance, including key terms and concepts, the quantitative thresholds for qualification and statutory standards for evaluation. The method is broken down into two steps, firms are first measured against a set of uniform quantitative thresholds which indicate that further evaluation is required; they are then evaluated in terms of a six-category framework, which is the essence of the statutory standards for a determination.[59]

The Council further issued supplemental procedures to the Rule and Guidance related to non-bank financial company determinations[60] and a staff guidance

[56] For instance, the LSE's Financial Markets Group and influential individuals like Andrew Crockett, a former Bank of England official and General Manager of the Bank for International Settlements. See Andrew Baker, 'Political Economy and the Paradoxes of Macroprudential Policy' (September 2017) SPERI Paper No 40.

[57] Dodd-Frank Act, secs 112, 115 and 165.

[58] FSOC is required to 'consider' certain issues. Dodd-Frank Act, sec 113.

[59] Authority to Require Supervision and Regulation of Certain Nonbank Financial Companies, 12 US Code § 5323 (2010).

[60] Financial Stability Oversight Council, 'Supplemental Procedures Relating to Nonbank Financial Company Determinations' (4 February 2015). Available at: www.treasury.gov/initiatives/fsoc/designations/

relating to methodologies for Stage 1 assessment of the designation process.[61] The staff guidance provides numerical values that will trigger an escalation to Stage 2 of the assessment. While the interpretive guidance provides more clarity and certainty on the likely actions to be taken by the Council, the fact is the designation is largely discretionary, although it is required to give explanations and the designation decision may be appealed.

The *MetLife* case demonstrates the ambiguity of the standards that guide designation. In 2014, MetLife was one of the first intermediaries to challenge its designation by FSOC, raising constitutional and procedural concerns about the process employed by FSOC. Judge Collyer seemingly rejected the use of unlimited and inconsistent discretion in regulation, finding that:

> During the designation process, two of FSOC's definitions were ignored or, at least, abandoned. Although an agency can change its statutory interpretation when it explains why, FSOC insists that it changed nothing. But clearly it did so. FSOC reversed itself on whether MetLife's vulnerability to financial distress would be considered and on what it means to threaten the financial stability of the United States. FSOC also focused exclusively on the presumed benefits of its designation and ignored the attendant costs, which is itself unreasonable under the teachings of Michigan v. Environmental Protection Agency, 135 S. Ct. 2699 (2015). While MetLife advances many other arguments against its designation, FSOC's unacknowledged departure from its guidance and express refusal to consider cost require the Court to rescind the Final Determination.[62]

In addition to the power to designate non-banks entities as systemically important, the FSOC may also recommend tighter prudential regulation for both bank and non-bank SIFIs, using the usual arsenal of capital, leverage, liquidity, and resolution instruments.[63]

Again, the Dodd-Frank Act does not provide detailed rules on how the FSOC arrives at recommendations on prudential standards, but merely sets out a long list of issues that the Council should take into consideration.[64] Upon receiving recommendations from the FSOC, or of its own accord, the Fed is empowered to subject SIFIs to the more stringent risk-based requirements.[65] The only exception to SIFIs under the Feds purview, are Financial Market Utilities, (FMUs), that are

Documents/Supplemental%20Procedures%20Related%20to%20Nonbank%20Financial%20Company%20Determinations%20-%20February%202015.pdf.

[61] Financial Stability Oversight Council, 'Staff Guidance Methodologies Relating to Stage 1 Thresholds' (8 June 2015). Available at: www.treasury.gov/initiatives/fsoc/designations/Documents/FSOC%20Staff%20Guidance%20-%20Stage%201%20Thresholds.pdf.

[62] *Metlife v FSOC* 177 F Supp 3d 219 (DDC 2016) (Opinion of Rosemary M Collyer), 29.

[63] Dodd-Frank Act, sec 115. The threshold for a Bank Holding Company to qualify as a SIFI was initially set at $50 million when the Dodd-Frank Act was enacted. This was raised to $100 billion, which was raised further to $250 billion after 18 months.

[64] The criteria are similar to those for designating non-bank financial companies as SIFIs.

[65] Dodd-Frank Act, sec 165.

registered derivative clearing organisations and clearing agents.[66] These are subject to prudential regulation from the Commodities Futures Trading Commission and the Securities Commission respectively. In addition, the Fed is empowered to prescribe regulations for the recovery of distressed non-bank financial companies before they fail.[67] However, the recovery measures do not include financial assistance.

The FSOC may also recommend limits or prohibitions of financial *activities* if it deems them to be systemically risky.[68] There is little further guidance beyond these principles, apart from regulators also being required to consider the long-term effects on economic growth from any limitations they impose. Specifically, Federal banking agencies are free to develop the heightened standards to be imposed.[69] It is debatable, though, whether the increased prudential requirements are the best way to guard against risk emanating from interconnectedness, even though they increase the resilience of the intermediaries.[70]

As part of measures to minimise the effects of contagion, by strengthening the resilience of firms, large and internationally active banking organisations are subject to the Basel III Liquidity Coverage Ratio (LCR).[71] In September 2014 the Fed, Office of the Comptroller of the Currency (OCC), and the Federal Deposit Insurance Corporation (FDIC) adopted a final rule implementing the LCR. Like the Basel Committee's LCR, the US requirement is also designed to improve banks' liquidity risk profile, and therefore their resilience to shocks from financial and economic stress.[72] Under the rule, large and internationally active banks are required to maintain high-quality liquid assets that are equal to or greater than their total net cash outflows over a 30-day period. Smaller bank holding companies and savings and loan companies are subject to a modified version of the LCR which is less stringent in terms of the percentage liquid assets required and the frequency at which it is calculated for reporting purposes.

[66] Financial market utilities (FMUs) provide a system for 'transferring, clearing, and settling payments, securities, and other financial transactions among financial institutions or between financial institutions and the system'. See www.federalreserve.gov/paymentsystems/designated_fmu_about.htm.

[67] Dodd-Frank Act, secs 166 and 168.

[68] Dodd-Frank Act, sec 120. From its inception to the end of 2018 the FSOC has only *proposed* one recommendation, that the Securities and Exchange Commission proceed with structural reforms of MMFs, which was rejected.

[69] Sec 171(b)(7)(A)–(B). The rules usually target activity in the markets for derivatives, securitised products, financial guarantees, securities and repurchase/reverse repurchase agreements. The rules also address concentrations in assets whose value is derived from models, as opposed to historical cost or current market prices; and concentrations in activities whose interruption would disrupt the financial system.

[70] E Avgouleas, *Governance of Global Financial Markets: The Law the Economics the Politics* (Cambridge University Press, 2012), 278.

[71] These are bank holding companies, certain savings and loan holding companies, and depository institutions with US$250 billion or more in total assets or US$10 billion or more in on-balance-sheet foreign exposure and to their consolidated subsidiaries that are depository institutions with US$10 billion or more in total consolidated assets.

[72] Liquidity Risk Measurement Standards 12 CFR Part 50 § 50.10 (2019).

Other aspects of the US macroprudential arsenal outside of the Dodd-Frank Act, also target the time-varying dimension of systemic risk. As part of its Basel III implementation, the Fed also applies the CCyB.[73] In terms of the rule implementing the CCyB, the capital requirements for internationally active banking organisations will be raised whenever there is a perceived elevated risk of excessive losses from the banks' activities or markets to which they are exposed.

The US also applies a leverage ratio with a macroprudential add on. All banking organisations in the United States that are subject to consolidated capital requirements are subject to a minimum 4 per cent leverage ratio requirement, which is the ratio of Tier 1 capital to average total consolidated assets. This requirement has been in place for decades in the United States. In 2014 the Fed announced a 3 per cent supplementary leverage ratio that is consistent with the Basel III leverage ratio and applies to all banks that use the Advanced Internal Ratings Based method to calculate credit risk. The supplementary leverage ratio is calculated by dividing the bank's Tier 1 capital by its total leveraged exposures, both on and off-balance sheet. G-SIBs have a higher leverage ratio threshold of 5 per cent, which is a combination of the minimum 3 percent and an additional 2 per cent buffer. If the additional buffer is breached, the bank will be prohibited from making capital distributions and certain discretionary bonus payments. The banking subsidiaries of GSIBs that enjoy deposit guarantees are subject to an even higher leverage requirement of 6 per cent. These supplementary ratios act as macroprudential add-ons to the leverage ratio, making it more targeted towards dampening leverage during the upswing of the financial cycle.

Although statements issued by policy makers in the US purport that they pursue dual objectives of leaning against the cycle and resilience emphasis seems to be placed on building resilience of institutions to shocks and disturbances. In particular, the US approach is to treat systemic risk as an issue of size. However, as some commentators have pointed out, exposure in small banks is also a big source of risk and instability has been a feature of developing world economies before the advent of financial conglomerates.[74] For instance, banking crises experienced in the US during the 1980s were the result of losses on real-estate assets experienced by small banks.

The approach is in stark contrast to the UK's resilience focus. The US approach indicates a preoccupation with the effect of macroeconomic shocks on individual financial institutions, while the effect on the rest of the economy is a subsidiary issue. Many macroprudential advocates in the US, unlike their counterparts in Europe, are not sold on the notion of procyclical financial markets, and place

[73] The Federal Reserve Board's Framework for Implementing the Countercyclical Capital Buffer 12 CFR Appendix A to Part 217.

[74] CW Calomiris and Stephen H. Haber, *Fragile by Design: The Political Origins of Banking Crises and Scarce Credit* (Princeton University Press, 2014) chaps 6–7.

greater faith in financial markets' capacity to self-correct, as long as its institutions are stable.[75] The market is not always right, however, and is susceptible to mispricing risk.

4.4.3. Macroprudential Policy in Action: Reactions to COVID-19

Between 2020 and 2021, barely a decade after being set up, macroprudential policy instruments were put to the test when the global coronavirus pandemic hit. In contrast to 2008, policy makers had been pushing countercyclical measures to build resilience in the financial system and buffers to draw down in bad times. The bad times came in the form of COVID-19. The coronavirus pandemic was a public health crisis, but it affected financial sector stability because lockdowns slowed down economic activity and led to job losses in some areas, resulting in an increase in credit default risk.

In response, policymakers activated a combination of tools that focused on the liabilities side of lenders' balance sheets, to make capital more available. In the past, banks would have responded to the prospect of default by reducing lending even further and regulators by tightening capital requirements to make institutions stronger. This time, however, policy makers in the US, the UK and the EU asked banks to release the countercyclical capital buffers that had been built in the preceding 10 years.[76] The FPC in the UK directed banks to use the capital to cover expected losses and to continue supporting lending in the economy. Dividend restrictions were also imposed in all three jurisdictions.

Apart from releasing the CCyB, to free up capital, policymakers in the US also allowed the largest bank holding companies to temporarily exclude reserves and Treasury securities from their calculation of total assets for determining the supplementary leverage ratio and to draw down on their liquidity buffer if it was for lending, in a safe and sound manner. Meanwhile, banks in both the EU and UK were allowed to temporarily operate below the liquidity coverage ratio.[77]

Regulators also tried to ease tension on the asset side by providing creditor forbearance or repayment moratoria, especially for mortgages, whose massive

[75] A Persaud, 'The Locus of Financial Regulation: Home Versus Host' (2010) 86(3) *International Affairs* 637.

[76] S Benediktsdóttir, G Feldberg and N Liang, 'What Macroprudential Policies Are Countries Using to Help Their Economies Through the COVID-19 Crisis?' (Monday, 6 April 2020, Brookings Institute). Available at: www.brookings.edu/blog/up-front/2020/04/06/what-macroprudential-policies-are-countries-using-to-help-their-economies-through-the-covid-19-crisis/.

[77] Benediktsdóttir, Feldberg and Liang, 'What Macroprudential Policies Are Countries Using', ibid. See also the Prudential Regulation Authority, 'Q&A on the use of Liquidity and Capital Buffers' 20 April 2020 (updated 6 July 2020). Available at: www.bankofengland.co.uk/-/media/boe/files/prudential-regulation/publication/2020/qanda-on-the-use-of-liquidity-and-capital-buffers.pdf?la=en&hash=151DF13BD8CA7E3755D515BC5A44F9A299C1235D.

defaults triggered the previous financial crisis – although these measures are not true macroprudential tools.[78] Regardless, all these strong policy responses appear to have successfully reduced risk and prevented a sharp tightening of credit.[79] In addition to activating existing tools, a slew of new instruments were also added to the macroprudential armoury of national policy makers between 2020 and 2021.[80]

4.5. The Future of Microprudential Regulation in a Macroprudential World

One may well ask if there is any role left for microprudential regulation seeing as macroprudential policy has taken over all the tools in the microprudential armoury. Tensions and confusion are likely to arise from the current set up where micro and macroprudential policy are conducted separately.[81] Disagreement can arise over who is the final arbiter over an instrument or the direction in which the instrument should be adjusted.

Even if there are instances where both micro and macroprudential authorities use the same tools, they are not used with the same degree of granularity, and hence will complement each other. For instance, macroprudential measures, like the countercyclical buffer, which are applied evenly across the board, could help mask unhealthy banks and keep them alive if it appears that, overall, the system is safer. Micro-prudential supervision still serves the purpose of identifying and managing idiosyncratic risk. It is safe to say, at least in the case of capital requirements, that microprudential rules will continue to address the core/basic requirements. The macroprudential authority can only control the counter-cyclical add-on or the systemic risk buffer for G-SIBs, both of which have separate, well-articulated frameworks in Basel III, that have been adopted in numerous jurisdictions. There are some instruments that only microprudential regulators control and vice versa.

[78] Prudential Regulation Authority, 'Covid-19: IFRS 9, Capital Requirements and Loan Covenants'. Available at: www.bankofengland.co.uk/-/media/boe/files/prudential-regulation/letter/2020/covid-19-ifrs-9-capital-requirements-and-loan-covenants.pdf?la=en&hash=77F4E1D06F713D2104067EC6642FE95EF2935EBD; or the European Banking Authority, 'Our Response to Coronavirus (Covid-19)'. Available at: www.eba.europa.eu/coronavirus.

[79] See T Adrian, 'Macroprudential Responses to the COVID-19 Pandemic and Outlook' (Speech at IMF Fifth European Systemic Risk Board Annual Conference, 'Strengthening the Financial System Post-COVID-19', 8 December 2021) and D Igan, A Mirzaei and T Moore, 'Does Macroprudential Policy Alleviate the Adverse Impact Of COVID-19 on the Resilience of Banks?' (2023) 147 *Journal of Banking and Finance* 2.

[80] See International Monetary Fund, 'Macroprudential Policy Survey Database'. Available at: www.elibrary-areaer.imf.org/Macroprudential/Pages/Home.aspx.

[81] J Osiński, K Seal, and L Hoogduin, 'Macroprudential and Microprudential Policies: Toward Cohabitation' (June 2013) IMF Staff Discussion Note SDN 13/05.

Osiński et al suggest that to benefit from the complementarities between micro and macroprudential policy, there needs to be maximum clarity on the mandates, functions and allocation of toolkits for either policy area.[82] This should be coupled with mechanisms that promote information exchange, open discussion, and cross-participation of policy makers in both domains. Greater understanding between the two policy makers not only helps to align policies along the financial cycle, but also promotes the will to act in an uncertain environment, rather than taking a wait and see approach as instability builds up.[83] Coordination and cooperation can be encouraged via either the (i) governance structure (for instance creating an interagency committee where regulators meet and discuss the policies or a legal obligation to comply or explain non-compliance with recommendations from the macroprudential authority); (ii) creating a policy hierarchy (giving one authority powers of direction or override over the other); or (iii) an obligation to publish a general policy guidance. As we shall see in Chapter 5, all these methods have been adopted to varying degrees in the jurisdictions under review.

4.6. Evaluation of Macroprudential Instruments: Unintended Consequences of Macroprudential Instruments

In Chapter 3, doubts were raised about whether capital has ever saved a bank, which does not augur well for the mostly capital-based macroprudential instruments. However, this time may well be different because capital buffers are being built in good times to be drawn down in bad times, not the other way around, which was a fundamental problem identified with the microprudential approach. Furthermore, in building the buffers, the process has the added effect of damping credit growth and rising asset prices, a key driver of systemic risk and financial crises. This provides much-needed support to the leverage ratio, which performs a similar function under the microprudential regime. The macroprudential armoury also expands to the asset side of a bank's balance sheet to build resilience and dampen the credit cycle, through LTV and LTI ratios.

Initial evidence from cross-country studies on experiences with macroprudential policies, though limited, is positive and suggests that many macroprudential tools can achieve their intended objectives.[84] Literature shows that lending restriction measures, such as the LTV and LTD ratios, have largely

[82] ibid.

[83] ibid.

[84] See Lim et al (n 30) 15; and E Cerutti, S Claessens, and L Laeven, 'The Use and Effectiveness of Macroprudential Policies: New Evidence' (2015) IMF Working Paper WP/15/61.

succeeded in dampening the appetite for credit and asset prices,[85] a time-varying LCR provides protection from negative externalities during a downturn by forcing the holding of liquidity during the upswing and releasing the liquidity when it is most needed;[86] countercyclical capital requirements can significantly affect the supply of credit.[87]

However, these studies mostly measure the effects of single instruments on intermediate objectives, not the aggregate effect of combined instruments, which is how they are being deployed. More importantly, while the benefits of macroprudential policy are slowly becoming more apparent with time, so are the costs.

4.6.1. Reduced Economic Growth, Welfare and Equality

It was demonstrated that capital-based instruments, whether of a time-varying or cross-sectional nature, dampen the credit cycle, however there is the danger that the credit supply may be reduced more than warranted. To meet the additional capital requirements, banks could either raise new capital or cut back on lending to retain capital. If they choose the latter, the result is a tightening of credit, which adversely affects economic growth, welfare standards and equality, when the withdrawal of credit is too tight. Tightening the capital buffers may actually precipitate a bust. Phasing in the capital buffer during periods when raising new capital is relatively cheap, so banks turn to this option instead mitigates the effect.

The time-varying capital tools present an additional problem in that even if they are calibrated to just the appropriate level, that does not have an adverse effect on the credit supply, the danger of inappropriate timing remains. Release the capital buffer too early, and there will not be a sufficient buffer to absorb losses. Conversely, tightening too early stifles recovery as banks withhold capital to rebuild buffers. In any case, inappropriate timing of the buffer results in a tightening of credit conditions and a reduction in economic growth and welfare. Appropriate timing and phasing-in of implementation is therefore crucial to the success of capital-based instruments.

[85] E Wong et al, 'Loan-To-Value Ratio as a Macroprudential Tool: Hong Kong's Experience and Cross-Country Evidence' (2011) *Hong Kong Monetary Authority Working Paper 01/2011*; T Poghosyan, 'How Effective is Macroprudential Policy? Evidence from Lending Restriction Measures in EU Countries' (March 2019) IMF Working Paper WP/19/45. Available at: www.imf.org/en/Publications/WP/Issues/2019/03/01/How-Effective-is-Macroprudential-Policy-Evidence-from-Lending-Restriction-Measures-in-EU-46640. Poghoysan found that the impact was not immediate and was only felt after almost three years. The policy met its targets more during the tightening phase than in the loosening phase.

[86] J Willem Van den End and M Kruidhof, 'Modelling the Liquidity Ratio as Macroprudential Instrument' (2012) DNB Working Paper 342.

[87] S Aiyar, CWCalomiris, and T Wieladek, 'Does Macro-pru Leak? Evidence From a UK Policy Experiment' (2014) 46 *Journal of Money, Credit and Banking* 181.

4.6.2. Leakages and Arbitrage

Leakages can occur within one jurisdiction or across borders. Banks simply avoid holding extra capital by:

(i) transferring their exposures to non-regulated entities, ie moving them off-balance sheet;
(ii) increasing exposures to what are perceived as low-risk weight assets, thus concentrating risk in one type of asset;
(iii) liquidity-based instruments can also prompt a shift towards more liquid assets, which can have the counterproductive effect of reducing their market liquidity and that of other asset classes in the process;
(iv) drawing down their voluntary buffers to cover the compulsory buffers, thus negating their effect; and
(v) banks using the IRB model to calculate credit risk can reduce their capital charge by adjusting the parameters of the model, since they design the models themselves (the irony is that only banks that are large enough can use internal models; those banks are likely to be the most systemically risky and therefore most in need of structural buffers).

In addition, the increased cost of borrowing from banks encourages the movement of financial transactions toward the shadow banking system, which is outside the purview of bank regulators.[88] Regulatory arbitrage shifts and masks systemic risk. This raises questions about the boundaries of financial regulation and whether it should extend to all levered institutions. The US framework seems to have overcome this problem by enabling the FSOC to designate even non-bank firms as systemically important, bringing them under the purview of the Fed. However, the designations have been challenged at every turn, as a lot of it depends on discretion, not just a firm meeting of the minimum monetary value, which shrouds the process in ambiguity.

The global presence of banks also opens a channel to arbitrage by moving jurisdictions. This has a two-fold effect: it reduces the supply of credit in the first country; and leads to a boom in the new host due to the influx of capital. The EU reciprocity rules reduce the incentive to arbitrage in this way. However, there is an alternative problem, banks may simply choose to reduce their lending to all jurisdictions to meet a higher overall capital requirement. Again, this adversely affects the supply of credit in several jurisdictions.

[88] T Ahnert et al, 'Macroprudential FX Regulations: Shifting the Snowbanks of FX Vulnerability?' (November 2018) Bank of Canada Staff Working Paper 2018-55. Available at: www.bankofcanada.ca/wp-content/uploads/2018/11/swp2018-55.pdf; C Dassatti, JL Peydro and F Rodriguez-Tous 'Macroprudential and Monetary Policy: Loan-Level Evidence from Reserve Requirements' (March 2019) *Universitat of Pompeu Fabra Barcelona Working Paper No 1650*. Available at: econ-papers.upf.edu/papers/1650.pdf.

Results are mixed on the effects of leakages. Aiyar et al, in a study of countercyclical capital requirements on UK banks, found substantial leakage. Resident foreign branches, which were not subject to the same requirements as local banks, stepped in to fill the gap and increased their lending, while local banks reduced lending as intended by the policy.[89] In contrast, Bianchi and Bengui found that, on average, leakages and arbitrage had a negligible effect on both the severity and frequency of financial crises and aggregate welfare.[90]

4.6.3. Distributional Effects

Apart from the problems of excessive deleveraging, leakages and arbitrage associated with macroprudential instruments, there is a more fundamental issue raised by lending ratios. As noted earlier, the LTV, LTI and DTI instruments target borrowers by restricting the amount they can borrow depending on their income or the value of any security they can provide. Thus, they have a direct distributional effect, as they can influence the ability of borrowers with low income to purchase a house, use that house as collateral against other investments, or increase wealth from rising house prices. It ceases to be a clean mathematical calculation and introduces a social variable to the decision on whether to activate the instrument.

This pushes macroprudential authorities towards inaction for fear of exceeding their remit. Popular pressure also acts on the macroprudential authorities' willingness to implement policy. In the good times, when memories of the previous crisis have receded, there will be pressure to relax policy standards. After all, why should an authority adopt a policy where the costs are immediate while the benefits may not appear for years (or are not apparent since the success of the policy means the absence of crisis). The opposite is true at the height of a crisis. Rajan contends that the loosening of capital buffers in busts may, in fact, be of no consequence because a risk-averse market may want banks to hold more capital in the downturn, and 'its will naturally prevails.'[91]

Calibrating macroprudential instruments is therefore not so straightforward. We are left here with three risks from macroprudential policy – (i) the potential slowing down of economic growth, (ii) shifting and masking of systemic risk that will eventually materialise and (iii) distributional effects. This raises serious questions about how far and when macroprudential authorities should intervene. The success of the policy hinges on the policy maker's ability to make appropriately timed and calibrated policy.

[89] Aiyar, Calomiris, and Wieladek, 'Does Macro-pru Leak?' (n 87).

[90] J Bianchi and J Bengui, 'Macroprudential Policy with Leakages' (September 2018) Federal Reserve Bank of Minneapolis Working Paper 754. Available at: www.minneapolisfed.org/research/wp/wp754.pdf.

[91] RG Rajan, 'The Credit Crisis and Cycle-Proof Regulation' (2009) 91(September) *Federal Reserve Bank of St Louis Review* 397.

4.7. The Governance Structure Required for Macroprudential Policy

4.7.1. The Importance of Unfettered Discretion

Čihák highlights a time inconsistency problem for macroprudential policy, in the style of Kydland and Prescott; and Barro and Gordon, which may be solved by appointing an independent macroprudential institution.[92] A macroprudential authority can assert *ex ante* that it will take a tough stance in the event of a financial crisis. If, however, its statements are not credible, economic agents will not believe that the authority will take a tough stance and that it will, instead, be *ex post* more efficient for the authority to be lenient – to engage in regulatory forbearance, pump liquidity into insolvent institutions, or be silent about weaknesses in the financial system.[93] Rationally behaving economic agents will factor in this leniency and it fuels moral hazard as financial firms are tempted to take on riskier projects in the hope that they will be rescued by the authority, in other words they take a 'gamble for resurrection'. As such, in a situation of growing financial instability, any perceived leniency of the macroprudential authority may lead to financial crisis.[94]

The bias toward inaction or failure to act in a timely manner can be motivated by three factors that are closely connected. Firstly, asymmetry of the policy means the benefits of a policy action may be uncertain *ex ante* and will only be felt in the medium term, while the costs are often more obvious and immediate.[95] For instance, additional capital requirements may increase the cost of financial intermediation, forcing banks to compensate for the loss in profits by taking on higher risk; measures may shift systemic risk from one segment of the market, to less tightly regulated segments of the market, masking risk; countercyclical actions limiting credit booms and higher liquidity requirements may have negative effects for credit supply and, in turn, aggregate output, employment and welfare; and measures that are designed to improve the quality of borrowers have implications on equality and welfare.

Political cycles restrict politicians' vision to the short term, therefore a policymaker may wish to avoid the plethora of immediate adverse effects highlighted above which may ruin chances of re-election. Adair Turner testified to this likely influence of macroprudential policy whilst speaking before the Parliamentary Treasury Select Committee, suggesting that if the FSA had aggressively challenged

[92] M Čihák, 'Price Stability, Financial Stability, and Central Bank Independence' [2010] *Oesterreichische Nationalbank 38th Economic Conference* 45.

[93] ibid 49.

[94] ibid.

[95] MD Knight, 'Marrying the Micro- and Macroprudential Dimensions of Financial Stability: Six Years On' (Address at the 14th International Conference of Banking Supervisors, Mérida, 4–5 October 2006). Available at: www.bis.org/speeches/sp061005.htm.

banks to reduce their mortgage lending in 2004, the FSA would have faced pushback, with many preferring them not to hold back extending credit to ordinary people or to prevent the democratisation of home ownership.[96]

Turner's sentiments were echoed by the then Governor of the Bank of England, Mervyn King, who believed regulators would have been alone in calling for a stricter approach and government and parliament would have faced strong lobbying.[97] Similarly in the US, the Fed's hands were tied, as far as its microprudential duties went, by the government policy to increase home ownership, and it could not react to the ever-growing number of subprime mortgages.[98]

This is not to say that financial crises are not politically dicey waters, because they also have electoral consequences, and the resultant accumulation of debt constrains governments' wider policy implementation. However, crises are few and far between, and memories are short.

Apart from pressure from the electorate, the policy maker also faces intense lobbying pressure from the financial industry whose profitability will be affected by policy actions. Politicians can also be captured by powerful stakeholders beyond the electorate, most likely in the direction of lax policies. Industry players have different forms of capital which can be used to influence policy makers to which voters do not have access, including financial capital to fund political campaigns, academic research and the hiring of lobbyists.[99] The financial industry also possesses relationship capital, through its constant interaction and consultations with policy makers, some of whom are former financiers themselves, creating what Bengston refers to as 'cognitive alignment'.[100] The result of this is an institutionalisation of discourses, concepts and terminologies of both the regulators and the regulated. The financial industry also possesses human capital and organisational advantages that enable them to share information and coordinate lobbying.[101] In contrast, voters face information, coordination, and collective action problems.

In short, macroprudential policy actions will be unpopular with both the electorate and private sector, unlike monetary policy actions, because there are many who dislike inflation but few who dislike the feeling of getting richer when credit is plentiful.[102] The macroprudential authority's ability to establish a credible track record of being tough is made more difficult by the fact that financial crises are

[96] Joint Committee on the Draft Financial Services Bill, Draft Financial Services Bill (2010–12, HL 236, HC 1447) Q2168.

[97] Joint Committee on the Draft Financial Services Bill, Q2354.

[98] See S Mallaby, *The Man Who Knew: The Life and Times of Alan Greenspan* (Bloomsbury Publishing, 2015).

[99] J Armour et al, *Principles of Financial Regulation* (Oxford University Press, 2016) 557–58.

[100] E Bengtsson, 'Macroprudential Policy in the EU: A Political Economy Perspective' (2019) *Global Financial Journal* 567–80.

[101] Armour et al, *Principles of Financial Regulation* (n 99) 557–58.

[102] C Borio, 'Implementing a Macroprudential Framework: Blending Boldness and Realism' (2011) 6(1) Article 1 *Capitalism and Society* 1.

less frequent, so authorities may never get a chance to demonstrate their strategy during their term.[103]

These factors combine to create an inaction bias, which in turn puts a premium on governance arrangements that foster a willingness to act on the part of the macroprudential authority.[104] Since the government is quite obviously susceptible to the time-inconsistency problem, it is not the first choice for a macroprudential policy maker. Of course, the government's willingness to act can be signalled through some form of credible commitment to a rule.

To avoid the costs of inaction, or adverse action, policy makers could simply follow simple feedback rules, like the Taylor rule which is used to direct monetary policy in some jurisdictions, or microprudential regulation, which is cast in detailed, prescriptive rules which set out the minimum prudential requirements that banks must meet and maintain to be licenced to operate.[105] In theory, once a certain threshold is breached, then a predetermined policy kicks in. This rules-based approach relies on detailed, prescriptive rules, which set the standards for both regulated firms and the regulators in enforcing the rules. As such, a rules-based approach promotes equal treatment and reduces arbitrariness and bias in decision makers, which in turn allows for predictability and precision, depending on the degree of specificity in the rule.[106]

While rules may be touted for their ability to foster certainty and equal treatment, they lack flexibility and may encourage loophole behaviour or gaming.[107] Even if regulators are able to identify these issues, they have little room to react since rules can only evolve either through a lengthy statutory amendment, or at best 'creative' enforcement, which essentially disguises the exercise of discretion in a non-transparent, unaccountable manner. A rule-based approach cannot keep up with the complexity and constant innovation that characterise the modern financial system.

Furthermore, a successful rule-based approach requires the setting of thresholds which would trigger action. However, unlike inflation, which has been reduced to a numerical target and can be manipulated using short-term interest rates, it is more difficult to quantify the threshold for systemic risk that warrants intervention and the specific actions that will be taken in each situation. A number of factors combine to make it difficult to detect and measure systemic risk: systemic risk has multiple drivers, there are complex interactions within the financial system

[103] Čihák (n 92) 50.

[104] EW Nier, 'On the Governance of Macroprudential Policies' in S Classens (ed) *Macroprudential Regulatory Policies: The New Road to Financial Stability?* (World Scientific Publishing, 2012) 183, 197.

[105] The Taylor rule is a mathematical formula devised by John B Taylor and is intended to serve as a guideline for the US Federal Reserve and other central banks for adjusting short-term interest rates, in response to changes in economic conditions like inflation and gross domestic product. See JB Taylor, 'Discretion Versus Policy Rules in Practice' (1991) 39 *Carnegie Rochester Conference Series on Public Policy* 195.

[106] CR Sunstein, 'Problems with Rules' (1995) 83 *California Law Review* 953, 961.

[107] C Ford, 'Principles-Based Securities Regulation in Wake of the Global Financial Crisis' (2010) 55(2) *McGill Law Journal* 257, 263.

and between the financial system and the rest of the economy, and the rarity and non-linearity of financial crises makes it difficult to use past experiences to devise future measures.[108] The situation is further complicated by the existence of a wide array of tools that may be used to counter risk. Setting explicit objectives may result in useful policy options being inadvertently ruled out.

A rules-based approach will not work for macroprudential policy, which requires flexibility. The alternative is a principles-based approach, which was a reaction to the constraints posed by strict adherence to rules in the face of new threats to the financial system. By adopting a principles-based approach, regulators move away from micromanaging banks via prescriptive rules.[109] This does not mean that rules are completely thrown out the window, rather, the legislation contains directives that are cast in more general language and regulators look to principles as a guide in enforcing the legislation.[110]

The main difference between the principles-based and rules-based approaches is the level of discretion granted to regulators; the former is more outcome-orientated than process-orientated when it comes to intermediaries fulfilling statutory requirements; and there is increased involvement of firms' senior management in regulation.[111] This last point suggests a level of self-regulation. Ford cautions against conflating self-regulation and principles-based regulation since the latter requires a robust and capable regulator to interpret and enforce rules. It should not mean that industry is allowed to dictate to the regulator.[112]

The UK's Financial Services Authority was one of the most notable regulators to move to the principles-based approach,[113] citing its effectiveness, compared to detailed rules which have not prevented misconduct in a range of areas; its durability, because focusing on final outcomes rather than processes allows regulators to adjust to changes in the environment; its accessibility, especially to smaller firms, since principles are plainly spelt out and not hidden in a mass of detailed statutes; and its fostering of substantive compliance rather than box ticking, which is likely to be the result of requiring compliance with a multitude of rules.[114] The popularity of the principles-based regulation waned, however, after the GFC

[108] ibid.

[109] Financial Services Authority, *Principles-based Regulation Focusing on the Outcomes That Matter* (FSA April 2007) 4.

[110] Ford (n 107) 266.

[111] FSA, *Principles-based Regulation* (n 109).

[112] Ford (n 107), 285.

[113] The FSA was not the only financial regulator to explore principles-based regulation in its regulatory regime. At the time the EU Commission was also extolling the virtues of the approach, while the US Treasury had proposed a Blueprint for a Modernised Financial Regulatory Structure, which formalised a principles-based approach to the regulation of capital markets.

[114] FSA (n 109). These arguments for a principles-based approach are generally echoed in the academic literature. See, for instance, P Schlag, 'Rules and Standards' (1985) 33 *UCLA Law Review* 379; A Scalia, 'The Rule of Law as a Law of Rules' (1989) 56 *University of Chicago Law Review* 1175; KM Sullivan, 'The Justices of Rules and Standards: Foreword, The Supreme Court, 1991 Term' (1992) 106 *Harvard Law Review* 22; L Kaplow, 'Rules versus Standards: An Economic Analysis' (1992) 42 *Duke Law Journal* 557; CR Sunstein, 'Problems with Rules' (1995) 83 *California Law Review* 953; F Schauer, 'The Tyranny of Choice and the Rulification of Standards' (2005) 14 *Journal of Contemporary Legal Issues* 803.

revealed the inadequate risk-management practices of banks and other financial intermediaries. Causes of this failure are wide ranging, from misplaced regulatory faith in industry, in a 'shocking abdication of responsibility',[115] to lack of certainty created by principles, arbitrary regulatory conduct, overreaching, and retrospective interpretation of norms.[116] Julia Black identifies seven paradoxes of the principles-based regulation, which may explain its failure to keep financial instability at bay.[117] A simpler explanation for why a principles-based approach cannot manage financial stability is that it is designed to manage the conduct of business, not the safety and soundness of individual firms.

Consequently, the principles-based approach was replaced by the 'judgement-based' approach, again pioneered by the UK regulator. Under the judgement-based approach, 'the nature and intensity of supervision will depend on the risks posed by each firm. Supervisory effort and resources will focus particularly on "big picture" issues with potential systemic impact'.[118] This approach is not bound to rules that were designed based on past experiences, allowing regulators to be more forward looking and consider a wider range of possibilities. Judgement-based regulation is related to principles-based regulation in so far as it looks at the spirit of the regulation, rather than the rules, and allows the use of discretion albeit based on transparent rules. However, unlike the principles-based approach, it is more concerned with stability, which is achieved through more flexible, and prompt reaction to ever-shifting risks in the financial sector. Although allowing complete discretion in supervision has been criticised for amounting to direct involvement of regulators in the running of financial institutions, which they are ill-equipped to do.[119]

Invariably, regulatory decision making in most jurisdictions falls along a continuum and cannot be neatly placed in one category or the other. Cunningham illustrates the difficulty of classifying systems as solely rules based, principles based, or judgement based.[120] All systems are a blend of rules, principles and judgement in varying proportions. The FSA, for instance, called its approach '*more* principles-based'.[121] In fact, it is necessary to combine approaches since different problems in the financial system require different solutions. In any case, the methods are not isolated from one another, but are mutually reinforcing. For macroprudential policy, the result has been a 'guided discretion' approach.

This approach has been adopted in the macroprudential frameworks of the UK, the US and the EU. They use a combination of statutes, like the Bank of

[115] G Soros, 'The Worst Market Crisis In 60 Years' *Financial Times* (22 January 2008).

[116] SL Schwarcz, 'The "Principles" Paradox' (2009) 10 *European Business Organization Law Review* 175.

[117] These are the interpretive paradox, the communicative paradox, the compliance paradox, the supervision and enforcement paradox, the internal management paradox, the ethical paradox and the trust paradox. See J Black, 'Forms and Paradoxes of Principles-based Regulation' (2008) LSE Law, Society and Economy Working Papers No 13/2008.

[118] HM Treasury, *A New Approach to Financial Regulation: The Blueprint for Reform* (Cm 8083, 2011).

[119] Dalhuisen, *Transnational Law* 560.

[120] L Cunningham, 'A Prescription to Retire the Rhetoric of Principles-Based Systems in Corporate Law, Securities Regulation and Accounting' (2007) 60 *Vanderbilt Law Review* 1411.

[121] FSA (n 109).

England Act 1998, Dodd-Frank, and CRR/CRD IV; and formal extra-statutory devices, such as memoranda of understanding, exchanges of letters, and general statements of policy to indicate *benchmark reference rates and principles* to guide the judgement of supervisors. In practice, a substantial amount of judgement still needs to be exercised, reference rates and principles cannot possibly capture all the risks to the financial system given how dynamic systemic risk is.

If the policy powers were to remain with the government, however, neither guided discretion, nor principles and judgement-based decision making for that matter, provide sufficient insulation against time inconsistency that a rules-based approach would provide. Only a policy maker insulated from the political cycle can be trusted to make a credible commitment to its pronouncements on future macroprudential policy, even if they exercise a significant amount of discretion. Therefore, macroprudential policy must be vested with an independent policy maker.

4.7.2. Accounting for Distributional Effects in Policy

As we saw in Section 4.6 above, macroprudential policy may also have unintended distributional effects. It is difficult to draw a clean line between macroprudential policy and its social consequences. The decision to activate macroprudential policy should not be solely based on highly rationalised and strongly quantitative reasons, because this risks real social concerns becoming de-personalised. Macroprudential authorities cannot afford to take policy actions that would run contrary to *any* of the values and ideals of society if they are to maintain legitimacy.

This raises questions about the non-economic values that ought to guide macroprudential policy. One may easily conclude that society desires macroprudential policy to pursue democratic values However, as demonstrated in Chapter 2, there are three sets of values founding the legitimacy of financial policy makers – allocative efficiency, democracy and social justice.

Figure 4.3 Intersection of Societal Values

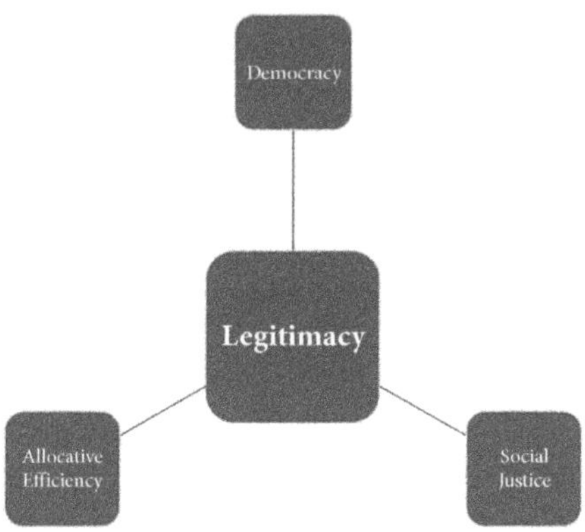

If it is to be considered legitimate, the governance of macroprudential policy should ensure that these three values are met. At the same time, macroprudential policymakers must remain independent to be effective at their primary mandate – maintaining financial stability. So how do we ensure that macroprudential policy resonates with other societal values besides allocative efficiency?

The impossibility of avoiding distributional consequences means that the (i) independent policy makers will need to be given (ii) an explicit mandate to consider social justice in policy making and (iii) held accountable according to that mandate. Accountability and transparency arrangements are the proper counterfoil to independence – to ensure independent policy makers are not straying too far from society's values.

4.8. Conclusion

Macroprudential policy undoubtedly helps improve the resilience of financial systems and dampens the financial cycle because the framework is more dynamic and adaptive to risks in the financial system which evolve over time. This is its main advantage over the more static, myopic microprudential approach. There is the risk, however, that in exercising this discretion macroprudential authorities may impose social costs on the system and population. Regulators may well be tempted to simply not act, to avoid responsibility when 'things fall apart'.

Since macroprudential policy is susceptible to problems of time-inconsistency and credible commitment, it appears that an independent institution which is insulated from the political cycle and other powerful vested interests is the optimal policy maker.

Independence usually means the policy makers cannot make distributional decisions; however, as we saw, macroprudential policy has the potential to directly affect changes in society. The policy maker therefore needs to be held accountable for the distributional effects of any policies it makes. These two elements, independence and accountability, are embodied in the governance structure of the macroprudential policy maker.

A lot of energy has gone into designing and testing different policy tools, while little attention has been paid to the suitability of governance arrangements. This is surprising, given the evidence of a positive correlation between regulatory governance and effective financial regulation. The proposition that governance matters was the impetus of this book and sets the frame of reference for the discussion in the following chapter, which studies the governance of macroprudential authorities – more specifically the legitimacy of those governance arrangements. Chapter 5 discusses and evaluates the mandate, independence, accountability and transparency of policy makers in the UK, the US and the EU, as a benchmark for good governance and legitimacy in macroprudential policy.

5

Independence, Accountability and Transparency in Macroprudential Policy

The question of the entities that formulate, monitor and enforce policy is equally important as the nature of macroprudential policy itself. As the operating environment changes, the governance of the policy makers ceases to be an ancillary concern and deserves equal attention as the rules themselves. Indeed, financial crises have been linked to political interference in the regulatory process, forbearance and weak regulations, which Das and Quintyn identify as symptoms of weak regulatory governance. While the opposite is also true – there is statistical evidence confirming a positive correlation between strong regulatory governance and a sound financial system. Good governance is the first tenet of effective financial supervision. It reinforces the credibility and moral authority of policy makers, while the opposite is true, where the policy makers lack credibility and authority, it fosters unsound practices in financial intermediaries. In other words, governance arrangements can make or break the legitimacy of a policy maker.

This chapter begins by laying out the tenets of good governance for an independent policy maker, or regulatory agency, namely operational independence, accountability and transparency. Before assessing whether macroprudential policy makers meet this standard of good governance, the institutional framework for macroprudential policy will be laid out using examples from the UK, the US and the EU. The next section will be dedicated to discussing how the principles of independence, accountability and transparency are applied within the macroprudential policy legal framework, in the three case studies and evaluating whether they actually meet the standard of good governance when compared to similar independent policy makers – central banks conducting monetary policy.

The second part of this chapter evaluates the effect current governance structures have on the legitimacy of macroprudential policy makers and concludes that firstly there is a political obsession with controlling financial policy which will ultimately compromise the technocratic effectiveness of the macroprudential authorities, which is the actual basis of their legitimacy. Secondly, the accountability and transparency mechanisms do not account for the fact macroprudential policy may have distributional effects – in other words there is no way of ensuring that policy makers are considering the social effects of policy outputs and holding them to account for it. The two problems are related, it appears in a bid to ensure that social justice concerns are considered in macroprudential policy (and not democracy as some might think), political interference has increased, but this raises the question about how these genuine concerns can be reconciled with concerns for credible commitment. How can the social justice and economic norms which bolster legitimacy co-exist, if we are going to find ways to avoid a 'legitimacy gap' in macroprudential authorities, which would eventually result in their claims being rejected by those they seek to govern.

5.1. Independence as a Standard of Good Governance

The link between the governance of financial regulation and financial markets received little economic analysis until the mid-1990s, which is surprising considering the unique nature of financial sector regulators, when compared to regulators in other sectors.[1] Das and Quintyn attribute this to the subdued post-Second World War markets, where the condition of regulatory governance made little difference.[2] It is now recognised that the strength of financial systems is not only the result of sound intermediaries and efficient market infrastructure, but also the governing practices of regulators and supervisors.[3]

Regulatory governance is a subset of the much broader public sector governance. There is no generally agreed definition of governance in the public sector: the definitions are varied and generally tailored towards the mandate of the specific organisation which is expounding the definition and may vary over time.[4] However, the definitions have in common two elements: they talk about the traditions and institutions that direct how authority is exercised.

This definition of governance considers (i) the functional/organisational structure (ie how decision makers are appointed and how they function), (ii) how the

[1] M Quintyn and MW Taylor, 'Regulatory and Supervisory Independence and Financial Stability' (March 2002) IMF Working Paper WP02/46. Available at: www.imf.org/external/pubs/ft/wp/2002/wp0246.pdf.

[2] US Das and M Quintyn, 'Crisis Prevention and Crisis Management: The Role of Regulatory Governance' in RE Litan, M Pomerleano, and V Sundararajan (eds), *Financial Sector Governance: The Role of the Public and Private Sectors* (Brookings Institution, 2002) 163.

[3] ibid.

[4] For a literature review of the definitions adopted by international organisations see the International Monetary Fund, 'The Role of The Fund in Governance Issues – Review of The Guidance Note – Preliminary Considerations – Background Notes' (August 2017) IMF Policy Papers. This contrasts with the concept of corporate governance which has a more precise and agreed definition as the system by which business corporations are directed and controlled. Like public sector governance, corporate governance determines the organisational and functional structure of the business, and relationships amongst the different stakeholders (management, board, shareholders and other stakeholders). See Organisation for Economic Co-operation and Development, *OECD Principles of Corporate Governance* (OECD, 1999).

appointed decision makers manage resources under their stewardship and formulate policies and regulations, and, lastly, (iii) how various interests are accorded a place in decision making (ie respect of citizens and state).[5] However, this definition is value neutral, it simply describes the process of governance. There is a further need to define the qualities that influence its effectiveness, in other words what makes for 'good governance'.

Recognising the importance of regulatory governance, numerous international standards for financial sector regulatory governance have been promulgated, much like the Basel prudential standards. These include the IMF's Code of Good Practices on Transparency in Monetary and Financial Policies; the Basel Committee on Banking Supervision, (BCBS), Core Principles for Effective Bank Supervision, the Committee on Payment and Settlement Systems, (CPSS), Core Principles for Systemically Important Payment Systems; the International Organization of Securities Commissions, (IOSCO), Objectives and Principles of Securities Regulation; and the International Association of Insurance Supervisors, (IAIAS) Core Principles. The standards are used as a benchmark for designing supervisory systems and practices. The standards also form a component of the Financial Sector Assessment Program, (FSAP), which is an evaluation of financial system resilience and development in IMF and World Bank member countries.

In the first systematic study of the link between financial system regulators and financial stability, the 'governance nexus', Das and Quintyn identified independence as one of the four ingredients for good regulatory governance which is derived from the standards, alongside accountability, transparency, and integrity.[6] The components are complementary. Independence is the counterfoil to accountability, while transparency upholds independence by shining light on regulatory activities and reducing the chances of interference. In the same way transparency also establishes integrity for agency staff. Independence and integrity are also mutually reinforcing; independence allows regulators to make decisions which may be unpopular but in the best interests of the system, without fear of punishment. Finally, accountability and integrity are mutually reinforcing, because while regulators are independent, they remain accountable for their actions, which encourages them to maintain their integrity. The four principles interact and reinforce each other. The key to good governance lies in the combined application of these principles in designing the legal framework of macroprudential policy.

The regulatory standards outlined above focus on agency independence as the starting point for good regulatory governance in finance, with the exception of the IMF's MFPs which focus on transparency. Independent regulatory authorities are

[5] See Das and Quintyn, 'Crisis Prevention and Crisis Management' (n 2). See also Daniel Kaufmann, Aart Kraay, and Pabl Zoido-Lobaton, 'Governance Matters' (October 1999) World Bank, Policy Research Working Paper, No 2196.

[6] Das and Quintyn (n 2).

generally viewed as the most suitable method for regulating complex markets that require a high level of technical expertise, such as money, securities, energy, transport, telecommunications and the environment.[7] One of the features associated with the rise of the regulatory state has been the re-distribution of governmental control and power from majoritarian to non-majoritarian institutions. Lastra describes independent regulators as 'miniature governments' who govern, make rules and settle disputes arising from said rules.[8] This, of course, raises questions about whether such institutions and the rules they promulgate should be considered legitimate. Macroprudential policy makers are no exception as they have also been structured as independent agencies.

The US has a long history with independent financial regulators, while other developed and developing countries largely adopted this framework in different iterations throughout the 1980s and 1990s.[9] The move towards independent regulators was largely spurred by research on the effect of independence on price stability, which began with the seminal work of Bade and Parkin.[10] Although this initial research was preoccupied with monetary policy, researchers began to extend their studies to financial regulation, in the search for the ideal model for regulatory governance, which has to do with the allocation of power on the one hand and with the exercise of power on the other.[11]

By the 2000s, independence in financial regulation was the gospel of the day, promoted right from the top, at international level, by institutions like the Basel Committee on Banking Supervision and the International Monetary Fund, which includes agency independence amongst the measures of financial development during its Financial Sector Assessment Programmes.[12] Supervisory independence is now the second core principle of effective banking supervision. Principle 2 requires that supervisors have operational independence, transparent processes, budgetary autonomy, accountability and legal protection embedded in the legal framework. When it came to framing the independence of macroprudential authorities, it followed more closely the central bank model, than that for financial regulators, because there is a significant difference between policy making and

[7] F Amtenbrink and RM Lastra, 'Securing Democratic Accountability of Financial Regulatory Agencies – A Theoretical Framework' in RV de Mulder (ed), *Mitigating Risk in the Context of Safety and Security. How Relevant is a Rational Approach?* (Erasmus School of Law and Research School for Safety and Security (OMV), 2008) 115, 117.

[8] RM Lastra, *International Financial and Monetary Law* (Oxford University Press, 2015), 83.

[9] S Gadinis, 'From Independence to Politics in Financial Regulation' (2013) 101 *California Law Review* 327.

[10] R Bade and M Parkin, 'Central Bank Laws and Monetary Policy' (1987) *University of Ontario*, Department of Economics Discussion Paper.

[11] RM Lastra, 'The Governance Structure for Financial Regulation and Supervision in Europe' (2003) 10 *Columbia Journal of European Law* 50.

[12] MW Taylor, MG Quintyn, S Ramirez, 'The Fear of Freedom: Politicians and the Independence and Accountability of Financial Sector Supervisors' (February 2007) IMF Working Paper WP07/0. Available at: www.imf.org/en/Publications/WP/Issues/2016/12/31/The-Fear-of-Freedom-Politicians-and-the-Independence-and-Accountability-of-Financial-Sector-20155.

regulation. Differences exist in the articulation of independence for regulation and policy and macroprudential authorities are more analogous to the other macroeconomic policy maker – central banks.

There is a dearth of empirical studies, in the style of Bade and Parkin, which disaggregate independence and measure the effect of varying levels of each component on financial stability objectives and on different types of macroprudential authorities using solely macroprudential tools. A survey of the literature shows that attention has been concentrated on the impact of central bank independence on financial stability, often carried out using monetary policy tools, and scholars seem to take for granted the desirability of independence in macroprudential policy conducted by a committee under the central bank or interagency committee.[13] Regardless, the results from the research are telling. For instance, Klomp and de Haan, found a negative relation between central bank independence and financial instability, which is mostly due to political independence as opposed to economic independence.[14] Ueda and Valencia, found in their empirical analysis that neither a dual mandate central bank (in charge of both price and financial stability) nor a separate macroprudential authority delivers socially optimal policy when they lack political independence.[15] Balls et al, make a case for operational independence, arguing that given the plurality of macroprudential policy instruments, it is more susceptible to political pressures.[16] The consensus is that, as with monetary policy, the political economy considerations favour a strong operational independence and limited political independence.

5.2. The Institutional Framework for Macroprudential Policy

5.2.1. Traditional Institutional Arrangements for Financial Regulation

The set of institutions that today provide the architecture for the regulatory and supervisory system all emerged over time in response to events, most often to past crises. Financial regulation is characterised by a wide variety of institutional

[13] See, for instance, J Klomp and J de Haan, 'Central Bank Independence and Financial Instability' (2005) 5 *Journal of Financial Stability* 321.

[14] ibid.

[15] K Ueda and F Valencia, 'Central Bank Independence and Macro-Prudential Regulation' (April 2012) IMF Working Paper WP/12/101. Available at: www.imf.org/external/pubs/cat/longres.aspx?sk=25872.0.

[16] E Balls, J Howat, A Stansbury, 'Central Bank Independence Revisited: After the Financial Crisis, What Should a Model Central Bank Look Like?' (April 2018) M-RCBG Associate Working Paper Series No 87. Available at: www.hks.harvard.edu/sites/default/files/centers/mrcbg/working.papers/x87_final.pdf.

models, reflecting differences in countries' traditions; political and social history; and size and structure of the financial system.[17] There are broadly four models for regulation:

(i) the institutional model, where different types of financial firms (banks, securities firms, insurers etc.), may be regulated differently and by different agencies;
(ii) the functional model, which separates regulation by activity although one organisation may be performing several activities;
(iii) the objective-based model, where regulatory functions are divided according to the public goals of financial regulation, thus one regulator is responsible for all prudential supervision while another oversees conduct of business. This model is alternatively known as the 'twin peaks' model; and
(iv) the unified model, where one regulator oversees the whole financial system.

The institutional model is the most popular, usually organised along the lines of banking, capital markets and insurance because, traditionally, these firms only focused on one of these activities and rarely ventured into other areas. Thus, the type of firm was synonymous with the activities it carried out. The regulator for the institution would be responsible for prudential requirements, conduct of business and market integrity. More interestingly, for our purposes, this meant that each regulator would also be responsible for financial stability (via prudential regulation) within an individual industry since intermediary is synonymous with industry.

The institutional approach to regulation became untenable, however, as the lines between sectoral activities carried out by different firms blurred, in the face of innovative products and organisational structures, such as conglomerates. In its place, the popularity of the functional model grew. The functional model, however, is not without its faults, as it may lead to inconsistent supervisory treatment of functionally equivalent products and services. Overall, both the institutional and functional models are weakened by the potential for jurisdictional conflicts between regulatory authorities, and fragmented supervision by the various agencies, which can prevent a more holistic view of risks in the financial sector and their effects.

As the institutional and functional models faced criticism, the integrated model rose in popularity in the 1990s and 2000s because it could potentially produce economies of scale and scope. The unified regulator oversees safety and soundness, conduct-of-business and market integrity regulation for all the industries in the financial sector. Thus, one regulator is responsible for financial stability. Like the other models, it too has its pitfalls, namely that it concentrates power in the hands of a single agency, which could lead to the marginalisation of other important agencies, like the central bank. Conversely it stretches the resources

[17] CAE Goodhart et al, *Financial Regulation: Why, How and Where Now?* (Routledge, 1998).

of a single regulator, which could lead to the neglect of important risks; lastly, prudential regulation and conduct of business regulation are too significantly different to mix. The failures of the UK's FSA, which was viewed as the epitome of the unified model, exemplify these shortcomings. Prior to the global financial crisis, it had prioritised consumer protection ahead of the safety and soundness of individual institutions.[18] The unified model may, however, be more suitable in small economies where a complex structure would be unnecessary and costly.

Llewellyn argues that, ultimately, the structure of a regulatory agency must be guided by the principles of effectiveness, meaning how far it helps meet the objectives of regulation, and efficiency, meaning the objectives are met in a way that does not impose unnecessary costs on the public and regulated firms.[19] Therefore, an objectives-based model would be most appropriate, because the agency's objectives are clearly defined, and it can be held accountable. The regulatory objective of safety and soundness, and consequently financial stability, of all financial intermediaries would be under the direction of one regulator, while another takes care of the conduct of business. Once again, financial stability becomes the responsibility of one regulator overseeing all intermediaries.

In real life, of course, the regulatory models are rarely stratified this neatly. As highlighted at the beginning of this section, the development of models is path dependent. As a result, some systems combine elements of more than one model and cannot be placed in one category. The US regulatory structure, for instance, is notoriously difficult to classify.

A key issue in the discussion of institutional structures is the role of the central bank in prudential regulation. There are opposing views on the wisdom of assigning central banks prudential authority. The main argument raised against this structure is that giving the central bank a dual mandate may result in conflicts of interest. For instance, downward adjustment of interest rates by the central bank may fuel financial excesses that eventually lead to a financial crisis; conversely, in order to unwind those financial excesses and rescue the financial system, the central bank may be forced to engage in quantitative easing which increases inflation. Furthermore, the high level of discretion afforded to central banks makes it difficult to hold them accountable for regulatory activities, even though regulation has replaced managerial discretion in financial firms up to a point.

Be that as it may, there is no doubt that the central bank has a role to play in financial stability in countries where it manages the payment system and, of course, as lender of last resort. Furthermore, it has a vested interest in the overall

[18] E Ferran, 'The Break-up of the Financial Services Authority' (2011) 31 *Oxford Journal of Legal Studies* 455 discussing Financial Services Authority, *The Turner Review: A Regulatory Response to the Global Banking Crisis* (FSA, 2009).

[19] DT Lleywellyn, 'Institutional Structure of Financial Regulation and Supervision: The Basic Issues' (Aligning Supervisory Structures with Country Needs Seminar Washington DC, June 2006). Available at: www. siteresources.worldbank.org/INTTOPCONF6/Resources/2057292-1162909660809/F2FlemmingLlewellyn.pdf.

safety of the financial system because of its relationship to monetary policy. As a result, while international experience varies, in many jurisdictions, the central bank has historically been responsible for the microprudential regulation and supervision of banks, in addition to monetary policy, given the complementary nature of the two functions.

5.2.2. Suitability of Traditional Institutional Arrangements

The Global Financial Crisis (GFC) exposed weaknesses in these institutional arrangements, such as the high fragmentation in the US, which allowed high-risk activities to slip through the regulatory cracks, or, at the opposite end of the spectrum, high levels of integration in the UK, which led to the prioritisation of consumer protection over prudential regulation or, somewhere in the middle, a loosely structured arrangement in the EU, which could not respond to a rapidly evolving and complex crisis.[20] Given that microprudential regulation focuses on individual intermediaries, the resultant governance models give regulators a limited field of vision, particularly where they have adopted an institutional or functional model. Apart from jurisdictions where a unified model has been adopted, it would be safe to assume that in all other models, regulators lack authority over many parts of the financial system, and therefore cannot effectively detect and/or counter the build-up of vulnerabilities and financial instability.

The institutional implications of adopting a broader financial stability objective are that a unified regulator would be best suited to monitor the whole system. This overarching agency would, however, not be a regulatory agency but a policy-making agency, given that its decisions are to be calibrated at macro level as opposed to institutional level. It is with this history in mind that institutions for macroprudential policy were designed.

5.2.3. Institutional Framework for Macroprudential Policy

Since the GFC, experience with macroprudential policy has grown, and along with it, institutions for implementing the policy. The development of institutional arrangements for macroprudential policy is path dependent, there is no 'one size fits all' approach.[21] There are, however, three broad considerations when designing effective institutional arrangements, namely (i) access to information and

[20] D Awrey, 'Law, Financial Instability and Institutional Structure of Financial Regulation' in Anita Anand (ed) *Systemic Risk, Institutional Design, and the Regulation of Financial Markets* (Oxford University Press, 2016) 61, 79.

[21] IMF-FSB-BIS, 'Elements of Effective Macroprudential Policies Lessons from International Experience' (31 August 2016), 1. Available at: www.bis.org/publ/othp26.pdf.

experts skilled enough to interpret the data; (ii) motivation for timely and effective intervention; and (iii) opportunities for regulators to cooperate, but without compromising autonomy in their primary policy areas.[22] Several models for the governance of macroprudential policy and supervision have emerged, which build on existing institutional frameworks by assigning the macroprudential mandate to either (i) a central bank; (ii) a committee within the central bank; (iii) an inter-agency body, in which the central bank participates and several regulators share the mandate; and (iv) the microprudential authority, which also carries out macro-prudential policy.[23] This book focuses on the first three models.

5.2.3.1. Central Bank-based Model

In the IMF-FSB-BIS's taxonomy of macroprudential institutional frameworks, the first model assigns the function to the central bank, while the bank's governor or board makes decisions regarding macroprudential policy. This model is preferred where financial regulatory and supervisory powers are already concentrated in the bank; and where regulatory and supervisory powers reside outside the central bank then a coordinating mechanism compliments the assignment of the mandate to the central bank. Such coordinating mechanisms may include a committee chaired by the central bank, agreements to share information or the authority to recommend actions to other bodies. In 2010, the International Monetary Fund, (IMF), conducted a survey of macroprudential policy frameworks and found that, in the majority of countries, the independent central bank was granted the sole mandate for macroprudential policy.[24] Subsequent studies have also found a bias towards placing the macroprudential policy function with the central bank.[25]

Macroprudential policy is thought to be best placed with independent central banks because they already play such a big role in the financial system – managing monetary policy, payment systems, microprudential regulation (where this is

[22] EW Nier, J Osiński, LI Jácome, and P Madrid, 'Institutional Models for Macroprudential Policy' (11 November 2011) IMF Staff Discussion Note SDN/11/18. Available at: www.imf.org/external/pubs/ft/sdn/2011/sdn1118.pdf.

[23] IMF-FSB-BIS, 'Elements of Effective Macroprudential Policies' (n 21).

[24] International Monetary Fund, 'Macroprudential Policy: An Organising Framework' (March 2011) IMF Policy Papers. Available at: www.imf.org/external/np/pp/eng/2011/031411.pdf.

[25] See, for instance, E Egawa, A Otani and T Sakiyama, 'What Drives Institutional Arrangements for Macroprudential Policy' (June 2015) Institute of Monetary and Economic Studies, Discussion Paper No 2015-E-3. Available at: www.imes.boj.or.jp/research/papers/english/15-E-03.pdf. This study builds on the 2010 study by the IMF by expanding the sample group to 66 countries and updating the information. They found that, of those countries in which macroprudential policy is specifically pursued, the mandate for the policy was given to a single agency in 76% of countries. Amongst the advanced economies, 63% gave the macroprudential mandate to the central bank, while 42% gave the mandate to a committee. In emerging market economies 78% chose to assign the mandate to the central bank, while 44% deposited the mandate with a committee. In countries where the broader financial stability is pursued, the mandate is shared amongst different agencies in 67% of the countries surveyed.

housed under the central bank) and as lender of last resort.[26] It allows the harnessing of institutional expertise available at the central bank. Central banks have ready access to information and the expertise in information analysis to identify systemic risks that can inform macroprudential policies, as well as a platform for communicating those risks to the markets and the public, and co-ordinating responses with other policy and regulatory functions.[27]

In any case, the central bank's price stability mandate and financial stability are complementary. For instance, downward shifts in interest rates can result in asset booms, which eventually end in financial crises when the bubble bursts.[28] On the other hand, in order to unwind financial excesses caused by poor macro-prudential oversight, a central bank may be forced to engage in quantitative easing, such as recent asset purchase programmes, which can result in inflation as the central bank effectively creates new money to purchase the assets.[29] Thus, there is need to co-ordinate and balance monetary policy and macroprudential policy and the central bank has a clear incentive to carry out both. If, however, macroprudential policy is delegated to a government agency, such coordination can be challenging, or, worse still, the central bank's independence over monetary policy will be eroded as it works with the government to maintain financial stability.

The Reserve Bank of New Zealand, (RBNZ), is an example of the central bank model for macroprudential policy. The RBNZ is responsible for 'promoting the maintenance of a sound and efficient financial system'[30] and this has been interpreted as a mandate for macroprudential policy. The RBNZ's macroprudential objective is to manage movements in the credit cycle or liquidity conditions.[31]

Some authors strongly disagree with this commingling of competencies, especially the mixing of microprudential powers with other discretionary powers.[32] As Dalhuisen rightly observes, while central banks may be information hubs and are certainly manned by experts in monetary policy, this may mean little for other policy areas because the analysis required for each type of policy differs. Furthermore, it is conceivable that, at times, monetary and macroprudential policy

[26] See Nier et al, 'Institutional Models' (n 22); IMF, 'An Organizing Framework' (n 24); IMF-FSB-BIS, 'Elements of Effective Macroprudential Policy' (n 21); Bank for International Settlements, Central Bank Governance and Financial Stability (Ingves Report) (BIS, 2011).

[27] Masciandaro and Volpicella found that microprudential supervisory powers are a proxy of the information advantages available to the central bank, as the greater the micropowers, the more likely the central bank is granted macroprudential powers. See D Masciandaro and A Volpicella, 'Macro Prudential Governance and Central Banks: Facts and Drivers' (2016) 61 *Journal of International Money and Finance* 101–19.

[28] AS Duff, 'Central Bank Independence and Macroprudential Policy: A Critical Look at the US Financial Stability Framework' (2014) 11 *Berkeley Business Law Journal* 183.

[29] ibid.

[30] Reserve Bank of New Zealand Act 1989, s 1A(1)(b). (RBNZ Act).

[31] Memorandum of Understanding between the Minister of Finance and the Governor of the Reserve Bank of New Zealand, 13 May 2013. Available at: www.rbnz.govt.nz/-/media/c6ed4cf89bed-4f1198ea687f7ba713ec.ashx.

[32] See JH Dalhuisen, *Dalhuisen on Transnational Comparative, Commercial, Financial and Economic Law* Vol 3, 6th edn (Hart Publishing, 2016), 823–25.

will diverge, and this may not necessarily be a bad thing. In fact, trying too hard to balance the trade-offs from the two policies may leave them blunt. Most worrying is that accumulating competencies under the central bank ultimately reduces the level of transparency because policy makers could hide conflicts of interest or conceal mistakes made in one policy through another.

The second institutional model described below provides a compromise between leveraging on the expertise and information reservoirs of central banks; and maintaining autonomy and transparency in the execution of different mandates. The following discussion explains how maintaining separate committees for each policy function under the auspices of the central bank may overcome the problems cited above.

5.2.3.2. Central Bank Committee Model

The second model is a variation of the first and assigns the macroprudential mandate to a committee within the central bank, therefore it inherits some of the key strengths of the first model, namely access to vast data and expertise in risk analysis. Furthermore, the structures for monetary policy and macroprudential policy are separated, so there is less likelihood of duplication of efforts, but there is still some coordination since responsibility for both policies is under one roof. The committee structure also allows participation in decision making by regulatory and supervisory authorities that are separate from the central bank, as well as industry experts and stakeholders. The committee thus benefits from a wide range of perspectives and knowledge and the central bank is disciplined in the exercise of its powers.[33]

An example of this model is the UK's Financial Policy Committee, (FPC), which functions under the auspices of the Bank of England. In the UK, the Bank of England is vested with a Financial Stability Objective, which is defined as 'protecting and enhancing the stability of the financial system' of the country.[34] The Bank achieves the objective in a number of ways, namely:

(i) acting as lender and market maker of last resort at times of financial stress;
(ii) reinforcing trust and confidence in money itself;
(iii) promoting the safety and soundness of individual financial institutions (via the Prudential Regulation Authority);
(iv) removing or reducing risks to the financial system as a whole;
(v) supervising financial market infrastructure; and
(vi) safely resolving failing financial institutions in collaboration with other UK financial authorities to support UK financial sector business continuity and operational resilience.

[33] IMF (n 24).
[34] Bank of England Act 1998, s 2A.

While some of these activities belong in the realm of monetary policy and microprudential regulation, there are some clearly macroprudential functions, in particular, removing or reducing risks to the financial system as a whole. The FPC directly addresses systemic risk issues and functions as a sub-committee at the Bank of England, chaired by the Governor of the Bank, in terms of the Bank of England Act 1998. The FPC's aims are to further the Bank's financial stability objective and the government's economic policy, and it does this by identifying, monitoring, and removing or reducing systemic risks to the UK's financial system.[35]

The Bank of England Act defines systemic risk as a risk to the stability of the whole or part of the UK financial. It also acknowledges that systemic risk has two dimensions, there are:

> systemic risks attributable to structural features of financial markets, such as connections between financial institutions, systemic risks attributable to the distribution of risk within the financial sector, and unsustainable levels of leverage, debt or credit growth.[36]

As far as its duty to support economic policy is concerned, the FPC receives written notice each year from the Chancellor of the Exchequer on the government's economic policy and how the FPC is expected to contribute towards achieving these goals. The government also makes recommendations about matters that the FPC should consider when pursuing its financial stability objective and its responsibilities in relation to that objective, as well as any other issues that affect the FPC's functions in general.[37]

The FPC is vested with two powers to achieve its mandate: the power to either (i) give *directions* to implement instruments that have been prescribed by the Treasury and approved by Parliament; or (ii) issue *recommendations* for measures to mitigate risks to the Prudential Regulation Authority, (PRA) and the Financial Conduct Authority, (FCA).[38] The PRA and FCA are part of the UK's twin peaks approach to microprudential regulation. Viewed as the poster child for the objectives-based model, the UK overhauled its supervisory structure by creating twin peaks in the regulatory structure after the financial crisis and in the face of strong public criticism of the FSA. On the one hand, there is the PRA, which is an operationally independent subsidiary of the Bank of England and is responsible for the prudential regulation of banks and designated investment firms. On the other hand, there is the FCA, which took over from the FSA and regulates conduct for both banks and investment firms generally, as well as prudential regulation of all other investment firms which are not designated.

Neither one of the FPC's powers may be directed at specific financial institutions, this is the realm of regulation which has been left to the PRA and FCA, nor

[35] Bank of England Act 1998, s 9C.
[36] ibid.
[37] Bank of England Act 1998, s 9E.
[38] Bank of England Act 1998, ss 9L & 9N.

can the FPC specify the exact actions and timing for implementing Directions.[39] The FPC may only make recommendations on these last two issues. Directions remain in force for a specified period or until revoked, while the regulators are free to consider the recommendations as and when they deem appropriate. While they are not obliged to comply with the recommendations, they must, however, explain why they have chosen an alternative course of action.

The FPC can also make Recommendations to other agencies. Within the Bank of England, it can advise on the Bank's provision of financial assistance to distressed institutions and the way in which the Bank oversees the payment and settlement systems. While outside the Bank, the FPC may make recommendations to Treasury in several areas, including macroprudential powers that Treasury ought to extend to the FPC, and to other entities whose policy work could affect financial stability. Again, such recommendations do not target a particular institution, however they are not made on a 'comply or explain' basis.

5.2.3.3. *Inter-Agency Committee Model*

The third model assigns the macroprudential mandate to an interagency committee outside the central bank, although it still participates in the committee. The interagency committee coordinates policy action and facilitates information sharing. In particular, this model can accommodate stronger participation in macroprudential policy by the Treasury, which not only bolsters the committee's political legitimacy, but also allows for coordination with fiscal policy.[40]

The US has adopted an inter-agency model for macroprudential policy under Title I of the Wall Street Reform and Consumer Protection Act, (the Dodd-Frank Act). The Dodd-Frank Act seeks to address the issue of financial stability in two ways, through the establishment of the Financial Stability Oversight Council (FSOC) and the creation of a two-tier supervision system, under which the financial institutions most likely to cause system-wide problems in the event of failure are subjected to a more intensive supervisory regime than other institutions. FSOC is a committee of microprudential regulators and independent industry experts, sitting under the Chairmanship of the Secretary of the Treasury. In terms of the Dodd-Frank Act, FSOC's mandate is to:

- (i) identify risks to the financial stability of the US that could arise from the material financial distress or failure, or on-going activities of large complex financial institutions;
- (ii) promote market discipline by eliminating expectations of federal financial support for failing institutions; and
- (iii) to respond to emerging threats to the stability of the US financial system.[41]

[39] Bank of England Act 1998, s 9H(4) & 9Q.
[40] IMF-FSB-BIS, 'Elements of Effective Policy' (n 21), 20.
[41] Section 112(a) (1).

The FSOC's primary responsibilities include regulatory coordination amongst heads of the financial system regulators, data collection and evaluation; designation of either non-bank financial companies or financial market utilities, (FMUs), as systemically important; and reporting to the US Congress annually on its activities, significant market developments and threats to US financial stability. To execute these responsibilities, it was assigned broad powers to collect information, including reports from systemic Bank Holding Companies (BHCs) and systemic nonbanks concerning their financial condition and the extent to which their activities could undermine financial stability in the US. In this regard, it is supported by the newly created, and independent, Office of Financial Research (OFR) which was set up specifically to collect extensive data and provide objective analysis.

The FSOC's second, and arguably most important power, is the power to designate an institution as systemically important for heightened supervision. The Dodd-Frank Act already provides that Bank Holding Companies will be considered systemically important if they hold more than $50 million in assets. The criteria to be applied by FSOC in designating a non-bank institution as systemically important is outlined in the 'Authority to Require Supervision and Regulation of Certain Non-Bank Financial Companies' of 3 April 2012.[42] This second power feeds into FSOC's third power, the power to make recommendations to microprudential regulators regarding enhanced supervision standards, particularly where the case concerns a specific systemically important financial institution, (SIFI). While the former power, designation of SIFIs, is clearly laid out in law there is little guidance for making recommendations since the law does not provide metrics for financial stability. Like the FPC, the FSOC largely relies on discretion. Consequently, regulatory actions by microprudential regulators in fulfilment of such recommendations will also be judgement based.

Responsibility for implementation of macroprudential policy still rests with the microprudential regulators, who include the Fed, Securities Exchange Commission, Commodity Futures Trading Commission, and the Housing Finance Agency. The FSOC itself has limited tools to manage systemic risk. Changes were introduced to the mandates of existing agencies to consider the new objective of financial stability, and the Fed exercises, by far, the greatest macroprudential regulatory powers. Upon receiving recommendations from the FSOC, the Fed is empowered to subject firms to stricter risk management techniques, public disclosure requirements and capital requirements for leverage, liquidity, and credit risk. It may also require short-term debt limits; contingent capital instruments or enhanced public disclosure. In addition, designated firms will be required to submit resolution plans. In essence, the Fed can pick and choose from the whole armoury of microprudential tools to effect macroprudential changes. The only exception

[42] 12 US Code § 5323.

to SIFIs under the Feds purview, is FMUs that are registered derivative clearing organisations and clearing agents. They are subject to prudential regulation from the Commodities Futures Trading Commission and the Securities Commission respectively.

It should be noted that not all banks in the US are directly regulated by the Fed. Prudential regulation of banks is conducted by three Federal banking agencies, namely the Fed, the Office of the Comptroller of Currency, (OCC) and the Federal Deposit Insurance Corporation, (FDIC). The Fed regulates and supervises:

(a) bank holding companies, and the subsidiary bank if it is a member of the federal reserve system;
(b) financial holding companies;
(c) US branches, agencies, and representatives of foreign banking organisations, except where the branch or agency holds a federal charter in which case it is regulated by the OCC; and, more recently after the introduction of the Dodd-Frank Act; and
(d) savings and loan holding companies and non-bank systemically important financial institutions.

The FDIC and chartering state supervise all other state banks that have not joined the Federal Reserve System, while the OCC supervises national banks that hold federal charters. Similarly, a Savings and Loan Association can be regulated by either the OCC, if it is federally chartered, or the FDIC if it is state chartered. The subsidiaries of financial holding companies remain subject to the authority of their primary regulators.

5.2.3.4. Transnational Interagency Model

In the EU, an interagency model has also been adopted, the difference being that it is on a transnational scale. Financial regulation is conducted under the auspices of the European System of Financial Supervision, (ESFR), which brings together national and EU-level financial supervisors. Within that system, the ESRB is responsible for macroprudential monitoring systemic risk in the EU.[43] The governance structure of the ESRB consists of a General Board, a Steering Committee, a Secretariat, an Advisory Scientific Committee, (ASC) and an Advisory Technical Committee, (ATC).[44] Decisions are made by the General Board, which is chaired by the president of the European Central Bank, (ECB), and made up of members

[43] Regulation (EU) No 1092/2010 of the European Parliament and of the Council of 24 November 2010 on European Union macro-prudential oversight of the financial system and establishing a European Systemic Risk Board, [2010] OJ L 331/1 (ESRB Regulation).
[44] ibid, art 3(c)–(d) & 18(3).

of the European System of Central Banks, (ESCB).[45] The rest of the bodies offer support services:

1. The Steering Committee supports the decision-making process of the General Board by doing the preparatory work for meetings.[46]
2. The ECB provides the Secretariat services, which means it is responsible for the day-to-day administrative and logistical functions of the ESRB – drawing on support of the ESAs, national central banks and supervisory authorities.[47]
3. The ASC is a 15-member expert body offering advice and assistance to the ESRB on relevant issues. The members are appointed based on their skills, experience, and general competence.[48]
4. The ATC provides additional technical support, beyond that provided by the Secretariat. Its membership includes representatives from the ESAs, national central banks and supervisory authorities, the ECB, and the European Parliament.

The ESRB leverages on the plurality of its membership for resources and analytical capabilities, to make a functional macroprudential body.[49] Furthermore, the inclusive arrangement lends legitimacy to the General Board's decisions. Apart from the collective knowledge of the home organisations, individuals appointed to key posts in the ESRB structure boast of impressive general competence, skills and experience. The ESRB's input legitimacy seems to have been built around individuals or personalities. Although they are highly skilled and experienced, the problem is that their financial stability/systemic risk preferences are relatively unknown when compared to, for instance, monetary policy where inflationary preferences of independent central bankers have been studied over time and are more or less known. The implications of this will become clearer when legitimacy is analysed and how macroprudential authorities are encouraged to rely on their discretion.

There are also several concerns with the structure of the ESRB, starting at the top with the chair of the General Board. Because of their other role as President of the ECB, the time of the ESRB's Chair is constrained, which may inhibit their effectiveness, level of engagement and, ultimately, the ESRB's operational efficiency.

[45] ibid, art 5(1). In the Euro Zone, monetary policy is conducted under the auspices of the Eurosystem, which is made up of the European Central Bank, (ECB) and the national central banks, (NCBs), of the 19 countries that use the euro. When the Eurosystem and the NCBs of those Member States that do not use the euro work together, they do so as the European System of Central Banks (ESCB).

[46] ESRB Regulation, art 4(3).

[47] Council Regulation (EU) 1096/2010 of 17 November 2010, arts 2 and 3 conferring specific tasks upon the European Central Bank concerning the functioning of the European Systemic Risk Board [2010] OJ L 331/162.

[48] ESRB Regulation, art 12(1).

[49] S Ingves, '"It takes all sorts …" – Macroprudential Oversight in the EU' (Keynote Address First ESRB Annual Conference 22–23 September 2016). Available at: www.bis.org/review/r161024c.pdf.

For instance, during the ESRB's first year of existence, which also happened to be the height of the euro area crisis, it was reported the Chair had left General Board meetings at times to tend to his central bank duties. The European Parliament has suggested in the past that an independent Chair whose time is dedicated to conducting ESRB work would better serve the ESRB. Furthermore, such an individual would have greater incentive to deliver the ESRB's targets because their professional standing and reputation would be tied to its failure or success. Despite recommendations the president of the ECB continues to hold the dual mandate, albeit the mandate was limited to the first five years of the ESRB in Article 5(1).

Apart from problems with the leadership, the General Board's size also presents an impediment to the effective functioning of the ESRB. Currently the Board consists of 67 members, including National Central Bank Governors and Heads of National Supervisory Authorities; representatives from EU institutions, including the Council and the European Commission and the ESAs; as well as chairs of the ESRB's committees. This restricts the scope for in-depth discussion of systemic risks and possible policy interventions. The ATC's expansive membership also creates challenges for it, although of a slightly different nature. One of the problems noted is that ATC members tend to represent national positions regarding risk prioritisation, therefore some systemic risks are in danger of being neglected. The European Parliament's review of the work of the ESRB recommended the appointment of an independent and dedicated Chair, with experience in monetary policy, financial stability and financial supervision, who would prioritise financial stability and its management. The first Chair of the ATC was Riksbank governor Stefan Ingves – once described as a 'sadomonetarist' by fellow economist Paul Krugman.

In contrast, the steering committee only consists of 14 members; this has led to feelings of discontent amongst some members of the General Board who feel that the agenda for Board meetings represents the narrow interest of the 14 members since the steering committee supports the organisation of the Board's meetings. The ASC also suffers from a narrow representation, despite a provision in the ESRB regulation which mandates that the ASC shall be composed of representatives from academia, small to medium-sized enterprises, trade unions, the financial sector and the public. The current committee, however, is composed mostly of academics.[50]

The ESRB does not intervene directly in financial markets; instead, it makes recommendations to other EU and national authorities, who in turn craft and implement macroprudential policy. As already stated the ESRB was conceived as '[…] a "reputational" body with a high-level composition that should influence the actions of policymakers and supervisors by means of its

[50] See www.esrb.europa.eu/about/orga/asc/html/index.en.html.

moral authority'.[51] The ESRB relies on two main policy instruments to exert its 'moral authority' – public or private, non-binding warnings and recommendations, directed at either the EU as a whole, the ESAs, national governments, national supervisory authorities or the Commission. In some instances, the ESRB has used other tools, including occasional papers, annual reports, speeches, press releases and macro-prudential commentaries. While compliance with warnings and recommendations is not mandatory, it is encouraged via a 'comply-or-explain' mechanism similar to that used in the UK. The ESRB monitors compliance based on reports from its addressees, and where it feels the action taken is inadequate it informs the Council or ESA concerned – however, it does not have enforcement tools or powers.

Hence the second pillar of macroprudential supervision in the EU consists of national macroprudential and microprudential supervisors. The European Central Bank and national designated authorities or national competent authorities have been vested with the macroprudential mandate in terms of Article 5 of the Single Supervisory Mechanism Regulation.[52] The ESR's Recommendation on the macroprudential mandate of national authorities provides guidance for national institutional frameworks.[53] Since 2013, institutional frameworks have developed exponentially, from just nine in 2013 to 25 in 2016.

The European Banking Authority (EBA) drafts the prudential rules that are enforced by the ECB and national competent authorities, which is one of the three European Supervisory Authorities.[54] The EBA's core task is the creation of a single set of rules, the Single Rule Book, to be used by supervisors across the EU. The Single Rule Book is the foundation of the EU's banking union.

The European Commission created the legal framework for the single rulebook, while the EBA fleshes it out through technical standards for implementation and regulation, as well as guidelines and recommendations to EU banks and supervisors. Even then, the EBA's technical standards are not automatically binding on national supervisors, but must be examined and endorsed by the Commission, the Council and the EU parliament. The strong political influence in the regulatory process can be explained by the Meroni doctrine.[55] According to the doctrine,

[51] European Commission, 'Proposal for a Regulation of the European Parliament and of the Council on Community Macro Prudential Oversight of the Financial System and establishing a European Systemic Risk Board' COM (2009) 499 final, 5.

[52] Council Regulation (EU) No 1024/2013 of 15 October 2013 conferring specific tasks upon the European Central Bank concerning policies relating to the prudential supervision of credit institutions, [2013] OJ L 287/63. (SSM Regulation).

[53] Recommendation ESRB/2011/3 of the European Systemic Risk Board of 22 December 2011 on the macro-prudential mandate of national authorities [2013] OJ C 41/1.

[54] The EBA is part of the European System of Financial Supervision (ESFS), which also includes the European Securities and Markets Authority (ESMA), the European Insurance and Occupational Pensions Authority (EIOPA); the ESRB; the Joint Committee of the ESAs; the ECB; and the Member States' competent supervisory authorities.

[55] M Andenas and IH-Y Chiu, *The Foundations and Future of Financial Regulation: Governance for Responsibility* (Routledge, 2013).

EU agencies can only hold a limited amount of delegated power and discretionary powers may not be delegated to them. They do not enjoy the same level of autonomy as EU institutions and must remain under the supervision of the Commission. The EBA's independence and rule-making powers are, therefore, severely checked by political organs. Which brings into question whether the resultant rules are the most ideal.

Responsibility for implementation of the Single Rule Book has been split between the ECB and National Competent Authorities, who function as a Single Supervisory Mechanism (SSM). The ECB supervises 'significant credit institutions' from Eurozone Member States and those who have opted to closely cooperate, while national competent authorities supervise 'less significant credit institutions.' The ECB's Supervisory Board plans and executes the ECB's duties under the SSM, although decision-making remains the remit of the ECB's General Board. Joint Supervisory Teams, (JSTs), manned by staff from the ECB and NCAs, carry out the actual day-to-day supervisory activities. The ECB may develop its own methodologies and common standards for supervision, although it must take care to maintain consistency with the Single Rule Book.

5.3. Legal Articulation of Independence in the Macroprudential Institutions

Independence of macroprudential authorities, like that of central banks, manifests in the legal framework. Lastra's taxonomy for legal articulation of central banks divides legal safeguards into organic and functional safeguards.[56] Organic legal safeguards direct the organisation of the macroprudential authority (eg, procedures for appointment of the board, terms of office, dismissal, suitability and salary, prohibitions while in office and restrictions after leaving office) and define its interactions with government. This is, in essence, political independence. Functional legal safeguards, on the other hand allocate the functions of the macroprudential authority (conduct of macroprudential policy and/or monetary policy, exchange rate policy and banking supervision) and scope of powers of the authority (regulatory powers, financial autonomy, decisional autonomy and limitations on lending).

It should be noted the legal framework might not capture all the dynamics of independence. Gaps may exist between de facto and de jure independence. A focus on de jure measures of independence provides a convenient smoke screen to cover significant government interference with the work of the independent agency.[57] Independent agencies, like central banks, are inherently political

[56] See RM Lastra, *Central Banking and Bank Regulation* (LSE Financial Markets Group 1996) 25–58.

[57] TF Cargill, 'The Myth of Central Bank Independence' (October 2016) Mercatus Working Paper. Available at: www.mercatus.org/system/files/mercatus-cargill-central-bank-v1.pdf.

institutions established by governments. Therefore, a more complete assessment of independence would also include an assessment of practical measures, such as turnover in leadership. However, de facto independence, though relevant, is difficult to measure, at least quantitatively, therefore it has been less emphasised in economic studies. The various legal safeguards outlined above come together in the framework to create five broad categories of independence in macroprudential policy as follows.

5.3.1. Goal Independence

Goal independence is the macroprudential authority's freedom to unilaterally decide its policy objectives. In all three jurisdictions reviewed, there is limited goal independence because the objective, financial stability, is specified by the legislature in the macroprudential policy statutes. In the EU, the legal framework goes further and sets out the intermediate targets of macroprudential policy to be pursued by the ESRB. Setting the goal is rightly a political responsibility. Minimising goal independence provides democratic legitimacy to the independent macroprudential policy makers. This negates the argument that control over macroeconomic policy with distributional effects is in the hands of unelected officials who cannot be held accountable. By designating the parameters for policy actions in legislation, Parliament retains control over the policy, and the public, via the ballot, can hold politicians accountable.

Despite giving the impression that goal independence is limited, in all three jurisdictions, the goal is framed very broadly, leaving it to the macroprudential authority to interpret not just the meaning of targets like 'protecting and enhancing' financial stability or 'reducing expectations' of assistance, but the term 'financial stability' itself, which is nebulous. This is not a fatal flaw however, after all it is difficult to hardwire into the legislation a specific target given the differences in not just the forms of threat, but in the forms of finance itself. The broadly framed goal reflects a need to maintain flexibility in the face of an ever-changing financial system.

The FPC also presents a slight departure from the other two jurisdictions. Apart from the financial stability goal, the FPC is also required to consider the government's broader economic policy when deciding macroprudential policy. It is logical that macroprudential authorities should have regard to greater issues of growth, after all, a stable financial system should not respond to shocks by causing further material economic harm. Financial stability should be balanced against the freedom to take the sort of risks that drive investment and growth. Treasury provides annual guidance on its economic policies, however, there is no guidance in the legislation as to how or to what extent economic policy considerations should influence macroprudential policy decisions. This could make it difficult to hold authorities accountable (see Annexure 2).

5.3.2. Institutional Independence

Institutional independence in macroprudential policy refers to the structural and functional autonomy of the macroprudential authority. Firstly, although the government controls the selection and nomination of members in all three macroprudential authorities, independence can be achieved through a pluralistic appointment process. This means that the agencies are composed of economic agents from various sectors. On paper, all three agencies appear to be pluralistic, as voting members represent different sectors of the financial system and/or members come from outside the regulatory system and there is merit-based appointment of members. In the EU, however, there is a disconcerting concentration of central bankers amongst the voting members of the ESRB. Out of the 38 voting members, only eight are non-central banks. Ironically, national competent authorities, defined as the designated authorities responsible for macroprudential policy in member states, sit as non-voting members. Essentially central banks have been granted more influence over financial policy by default.

In all three jurisdictions, there is also a significant addition to the composition of the governance structure – a member of the executive. In the UK a member of the treasury sits as a non-voting member of the FPC, while the ESRB includes a member from the European Commission. The US actually goes so far as to make the Secretary of Treasury the chairperson of the FSOC, forcing the Fed to work with and under the direction of a government representative.

Decision making in macroprudential policy also appears to be more influenced by politicians than it is in monetary policy, at least in the UK and US. The EU has maintained the general rule that the policy makers shall avoid taking instructions from government agents. In the UK, the treasury can make recommendations about the FPC's responsibilities that the committee must comply with or explain. Or, it can give directions when the bank exercises its stabilisation powers, such as provision of assistance to a distressed bank, if it feels the UK's financial stability is under threat. Similarly, the Fed requires Treasury approval to establish programs that provide credit to distressed financial institutions (see Annexure 2).

Variations also exist in the level of cooperation required by law between the macroprudential authority and treasury. There appears, however, to be consensus across the board on the need for closer cooperation in the conduct of macroprudential policy. In all three jurisdictions, it is explicitly stated that the macroprudential authority will generally aim to work with the treasury. There are detailed rules concerning attendance of policy meetings, regular updates on activities and exchange of opinions. In the US and EU, the rules go further by allowing a member of the executive branch of government to vote on macroprudential policy (see Annexure 2).

5.3.3. Instrument Independence

Instrument independence is the macroprudential authority's freedom to choose which policy instruments to use and how to use them. In all three jurisdictions the macroprudential authority has the discretion to decide on the combination of instruments to be employed from a list designated by parliament in the legislation. The lists of available instruments are, however, exhaustive and the use of additional policy tools requires prior approval of either the treasury or parliament. The EU even imposes a hierarchy for application of the policy tools that have been harmonised.

Furthermore, there is a separation between formulation and implementation of policy. It appears, since policy instruments are applied directly to individual firms, either the macroprudential authority must also be a microprudential regulator to implement the policy or another regulator must implement it. In the EU implementation at national level is carried out by the ECB and National Authorities responsible for macroprudential regulation, with more binding powers than the ESRB. These National Authorities happen to be national central banks in only 13 Member States. In the UK, the Prudential Regulation Authority plays the role; while in the US, it is the Fed that regulates banking activity (see Annexure 2). In fact, in the sample of countries used in this study, only one macroprudential authority, the UK's Financial Policy Committee (FPC), has any sort of hard powers.[58] It can issue directions to the PRA and FCA regarding instruments under the FPC's purview.[59]

The government has limited the FPC powers of direction over very specific regulatory aspects, which can only be trained towards the whole system and not individual firms. The rest of the FPC's powers are either semi-hard, being recommendations issued on a comply or explain basis, or simply soft powers. To date, the FPC has operated mostly via its recommendation powers, apart from setting and enforcing the CCyB. The FSOC in the US also has a hard power in that it may designate systemically important financial institutions. The rest of its powers are largely soft. The ESRB has a range of semi-hard to soft powers; it cannot directly intervene in the financial markets or issue instructions to individual firms but can issue non-binding warnings and recommendations to EU and national regulators,

[58] The IMF/FSB/BIS report classifies the types of powers that macroprudential authorities may possess in three categories: 'hard', 'semi-hard' or 'soft' powers. When policymakers have hard powers, they can manipulate tools directly or compel other regulatory authorities to use the tools in a particular way. In contrast, with semi-hard powers, limit policy action to non-binding recommendations to the actual implementing regulators, on a 'comply or explain' basis, while with 'soft' powers policymakers can offer their opinion, a warning, or a recommendation, but without any power to compel compliance or an explanation for inaction. Comply or explain powers are viewed as the most suitable when further judgment at micro level is necessary, where a policy action may have distributional effects, and broad accountability and transparency are needed.

[59] See 4.4.2.2 on UK Macroprudential Instruments.

on a 'comply or explain' basis. As stated earlier, this is because it was conceived as a reputational body empowered only with moral authority. The ESRB monitors compliance based on reports from its addressees, and where it feels the action taken is inadequate it informs the Council or ESA concerned – however it does not have enforcement tools or powers.

Between September 2011 and December 2016, the ESRB made 13 public recommendations in relation to specific systemic risks, although three of them were amendments of previous recommendations. The most significant of these recommendations was Recommendation ESRB 2013/1 on intermediate objectives and instruments of macro-prudential policy. In some instances, the ESRB has used other tools, including occasional papers, annual reports, speeches, press releases and macro-prudential commentaries.

In effect, the new macroprudential institutions are devoid of any real power, and appear more to be fora for sharing information and coordination regulatory activities.[60] While current institutions are better placed to watch for financial instability, they may not be able to prevent financial instability.[61] That said, Bodestein *et al* found that the improved information sharing and coordination facilitated by macroprudential authorities could still lead to improved policy outcomes.[62]

5.3.4. Financial Independence

Financial independence is autonomy in the management of the macroprudential authority's finances. In the UK, the macroprudential authority functions under the auspices of the central bank, therefore, it is subject to the same financial arrangements. The government holds stock in the Bank of England. However, the stock does not carry voting rights. The Bank of England is responsible for raising further funding for activities through a combination of open market operations, levies and reserve requirements imposed on financial institutions; and it is free to decide how its income is used to meet operating expenses.

There is a similar set up in the EU, the ECB provides human and financial resources as the ESRB's Secretariat. In turn, contributions from national central banks consisting of foreign reserves, euro contributions, IMF reserve positions and special drawing rights fund the ECB. NCBs can make further contributions to capital. The ECB is guaranteed autonomy in the management of its finances under

[60] R Edge and N Liang, 'New Financial Stability Governance Structures and Central Banks' (August 2017) Hutchins Center Working Paper No 32. Available at: www.brookings.edu/wp-content/uploads/2017/08/es_20170808_liang_newfinancialstabilitygovernancestructures.pdf.

[61] ibid.

[62] M Bodenstein, L Guerrieri, and J LaBriola, 'Macroeconomic Policy Games' (2014) Finance and Economics Discussion Paper No 2014-87.

the TFEU. In the US, the Office of Financial Research covers any expenses of the FSOC. In turn, the OFR is funded by a specially set up Financial Research Fund. Initially, the Fed financed the Fund; two years after it was set up it began receiving 'assessments', in essence levies, from SIFIs. Funds in the Financial Research Fund are not considered to be government funds or to have been allocated by Congress, and Congress does not decide how the funds are to be used. In other words, the funds are not subject to appropriation and apportionment. The OFR is free to invest any excess funds as it sees fit.

An adjunct to financial independence is that lending to the government is also limited, through provisions that prohibit or limit the financing of public sector deficits and monetising of public debt. There are no such direct provisions in relation to macroprudential authorities, most likely because they do not themselves control any funds. Where, however, the macroprudential authority receives its funding from the central bank, insulation is provided via limitations on lending which are applicable to the central bank. The ECB is prohibited from lending to regional, local and central governments, or their public undertakings. The Bank of England was prohibited from monetary financing as part of the European System of Central Banks (see Annexure 2).

5.3.5. Personal Independence

Personal independence safeguards the agency members' impartiality. This requires, firstly, that appointees to the agency be suitably qualified. Once suitable officials have been appointed, their positions are secured through sufficiently long terms of office, which do not coincide with the political cycle and limit politicisation and short-term perspectives. Limitations on terms of office are coupled with well-defined grounds for dismissal – the existence of which is determined by courts of justice and not the government. These include criminal offences, serious misconduct, permanent incapacity or a serious lack of fulfilment of obligation. Finally, to ensure full-time dedication and avoid any conflict of interest, members of the agency are subject to incompatible/disqualifying activities such as offering financial advisory services to members of parliament. Restrictions are carried over even after leaving the agency by limiting, for a reasonable period following a term of office, the ability to pursue private employment in credit and financial institutions or become government officials. These two measures preclude susceptibility to capture.

The UK legislation explicitly requires the appointment of individuals whose professional skills correspond to their functions and who have demonstrable professional independence. Members of the FPC are appointed for a term of three years and not more than twice. However, they may be dismissed before completion of their tenure if they are absent from meetings for more than three months without consent, or become bankrupt and unable to discharge their functions as a member. Finally, Executive members of the FPC are required to give their exclusive services to the Bank, while non-executive directors may have other roles outside. There are, however, no restrictions after leaving office.

The EU presents slight deviations, in that, firstly, the tenure of leadership for the macroprudential policy body matches that of the political cycle. At the inception of the ESRB, the ECB president's tenure as chairperson was set at five years, as was that of the vice-chairperson of the ESRB. However, in 2017, a proposal to amend the ESRB suggested that the President of the ECB should become the permanent chairperson of the ESRB, which would align the terms of office for both monetary policy and macroprudential policy. Secondly, the new legislation creates additional restrictions while in office by forbidding members of the General Board (whether voting or non-voting) from working in the financial industry and using non-public information for private gain, although they can take up teaching and scholarly activities.

Suitability and salary, as well as dismissal from the ESRB are, however, not covered by the regulation establishing the ESRB. This is not necessarily a problem given that other members may be guaranteed personal independence in terms of legislation constituting the agency which they represent, for instance, the ECB, which arguably has the most extensive duties and powers in relation to macroprudential policy. Members of the ECB Executive Board are appointed based on their standing and experience in monetary or banking fields. The ECB's Governing Council sets salaries, pensions and other social security benefits, based on recommendations from a committee comprising members appointed by the Governing Council and the European Council. Members of the ECB Executive Board can be dismissed if they no longer qualify for appointment or are found guilty of serious misconduct. However, only the Court of Justice, on application by the Governing Council or the Executive Board, may confirm this. The executive or legislature of a Member State may dismiss other members of the Governing Council on the same grounds, although this may be appealed to the CJEU.

The US presents a similar problem to the EU in that the macroprudential authority is composed of heads from different agencies. The legislation establishing the FSOC only provides guidance in relation to the independent member of the Council. The independent member is required to have insurance expertise, and has a limited term of six months, and, although the US legislation does not explicitly define grounds for dismissal, case law has established that the President may not dismiss an executive branch official, outside the core executive departments, for purely political reasons.[63] As stated above, the fact that there are no uniform rules covering personal independence is not necessarily a problem given that this may be guaranteed by other legislation for all the other voting members of the FSOC. All, that is, except for the Secretary of Treasury, who also Chairs the Council. This becomes a cause for concern.

[63] See, for instance, in *Wiener v United States* 357 US 349 (1958).

5.4. Legal Articulation of Accountability and Transparency of Macroprudential Authorities

Accountability is to be distinguished from control, which is a broader concept. Control can involve both (i) a requirement that an agent report on its activities *and* (ii) compelling certain behaviour through punishment or reward. The latter does not necessarily require the addressee to explain and justify their conduct, they must simply follow instructions to the letter.[64] In contrast, accountability is limited to just the first type of activity – a requirement that an agent report on its activities. Therefore, although mechanisms of accountability can be included amongst mechanisms of control, doing the reverse – imposing mechanisms of control as part of accountability all in the name of ensuring legitimacy, would undo the whole point of creating independent regulatory agencies, which is a prerequisite for them to effectively function.[65]

Regardless, we cannot continue to ignore the criticism levelled against independent macroprudential authorities, that they lack democratic legitimacy. Politics cannot be completely avoided in financial regulation because regulators require some popular support to effectively administer rules in the present and future.

Accountability mechanisms can be used to draw them back into the light. Narratives of legitimacy based on democracy emphasise political forms of accountability that make public officials responsible for their actions through mechanisms such as parliamentary and executive oversight, judicial review, or through electoral punishment. Since independent regulators cannot be held accountable via the ballot, that leaves parliamentary, executive and judicial oversight. These mechanisms are based on the principle of separation of powers and rule of law, which are central features of democracies. While it is accepted that experts know best, their discretion needs to be checked, so that (a) no one person holds more power than any other in society, in other words, independent regulators are placed within the system of checks and balances, and (b) their discretionary powers are not exercised in an arbitrary and unreasonable manner.[66]

Amtenbrink and Lastra identify four core elements of accountability, namely:[67]

(i) a party to whom power is delegated, the accountable;
(ii) the authority to whom the power holder is answerable;

[64] M Bovens, 'Analyzing and Assessing Public Accountability. A Conceptual Framework' (16 January 2006) European Governance Papers No C-06-01, 14.

[65] C Zilioli, 'Accountability and Independence: Irreconcilable Values or Complementary Instruments for Democracy? The Specific Case of the European Central Bank' in G Vandersandern (ed) *Melanges en homage a Jean-Victor Louis* (Vol 2, ULB 2003) 400.

[66] Economists, on the other hand, tend to favour performance-based accountability, which focuses on quantifiable output measures, and transparency. However, critics of the mechanism argue, that its focus on the technical, reduces public involvement and the equality and fairnesss which that embodies.

[67] Amtenbrink and Lastra, 'Securing Democratic Accountability' (n 7).

(iii) the content of the obligation. It is worth highlighting here that there are three obligations that the independent regulator owes. They are required (i) to give an account of their decisions, (ii) to explain and justify the decision and course of action taken, and (iii) where harm or error is proved, to take responsibility and provide amends or redress. This could actually be translated as *how* accountability is to be given. While the third obligation can only necessarily be fulfilled ex post facto, the other two can be fulfilled before or during the process of taking a decision or action. As such, accountability can take the form of ex ante/input accountability or ex post/output accountability; and

(iv) criteria for assessment.

Contemporary discussions of accountability are often accompanied by discussions of transparency. In a transparent institution the objectives and activities towards meeting those objectives are relayed to the public in a manner that is accessible and easy to understand. Typically, this type of information is made available through mandatory disclosures, reporting requirements, investigative powers or a general right to information. The growing emphasis on transparency can be attributed to the shift from the welfare state to market-based economies.

While it is a 'good' in itself, transparency also serves the purpose of enhancing the effectiveness of accountability. It facilitates education and understanding of policy activities, not just by the legislature and executive, but, more importantly, by the public. With better understanding, the public can engage the independent regulator in a way that resonates with deliberative democracy. Public evaluation of independent regulators creates an extra layer of political accountability.

Calls for greater public participation in social policy are ubiquitous. There is extensive scholarship on the subject of public participation in policy formation and monitoring. Generally, scholars agree that public participation, facilitated by transparency, improves the public's perception of the legitimacy of regulatory processes in two ways – by either improving perceptions of procedural fairness and equity, or substantive fairness and equity. If policy reforms are to succeed, the public, who bear the costs of these changes, needs to understand the rationale for the reforms.[68] Therefore, if macroprudential policy reforms are to be meaningful, and legitimate, contemporary expert led governance should be balanced with public input.

Public participation embodies deliberative democracy, a different incarnation of democracy, and enables different stakeholder groups to deliberate policy issues in a meaningful, fair and reasoned manner – all of which are indicative of the 'value of mutual respect', a prerequisite for democratic legitimacy.[69] Public participation gives people a greater sense of ownership over policy, because it opens the door

[68] HP Minsky *Stabilizing an Unstable Economy* (Yale University Press, 1986) 321.

[69] A Gutmann and D Thompson, *Why Deliberative Democracy?* (Princeton University Press, 2004).

to a wider constituency to participate in decision making, including minority perspectives, which may prompt acceptance of policy outcome.[70]

Apart from strengthening perceptions of procedural fairness, opening up policy to public scrutiny can also change attitudes towards the same. Deliberation can reveal common interests or help the public overcome cognitive biases towards policy, in other words convince them that it is substantively desirable.[71]

The next section of this chapter details how accountability and transparency is framed in the three jurisdictions under review and whether this should satisfy those clamouring for more democratic legitimacy. The accountability mechanisms do well to outline *who* owes accountability, to *whom* accountability is owed, and *how* it is to be enforced. However, things become a little hazy when it gets to *what* they are accountable for – the criteria for assessment. While it is important to establish those first three factors, it is meaningless if the independent regulator is not aware of *all* that society expects them to achieve. The result is they may be perceived as lacking legitimacy if they are not meeting these goals.

5.4.1. Core Element #1 – Who is Accountable for Macroprudential Policy

The answer to the question of who is accountable in the three jurisdictions under review appears obvious. We have seen how macroprudential policy has been assigned to new bodies created specifically to maintain financial stability, namely the Financial Policy Committee in the UK, the Financial Stability Oversight Council in the US and the European Systemic Risk Board for the EU. That would be the end of that, except, as you will recall, actual implementation of policy has been separated from the policy maker, and instead placed in the hands of micro-prudential authorities. This was unavoidable given that macroprudential policy is essentially a manipulation of microprudential tools for system-wide benefit.

The problem posed by this structure becomes apparent if one attempts to use the judicial review method of accountability. Who is the proper respondent where a micro-prudential authority is merely articulating and enforcing the policy issued by a macroprudential authority?[72] This may not be a problem in the context of the EU where the ESRB has virtually no powers and is limited to issuing Recommendations and Warnings, or in the US for that matter where the FSOC is

[70] J Nash and DE Walters, 'Public Engagement and Transparency in Regulation: A Field Guide to Regulatory Excellence' (June 2015) Research Paper Prepared for the Penn Program on Regulation's Best-in-Class Regulator Initiative.

[71] J Rossi, 'Participation Run Amok: The Costs of Mass Participation for Deliberative Agency Decisionmaking' (1997) 92 *Northwestern University Law Review* 173.

[72] JH Dalhuisen, 'Management of Systemic Risk from a Legal Perspective' in M Andenas and G Deipenbrock (eds), *Regulating and Supervising European Financial Markets* (Springer International Publishing, 2016) 365.

also limited to giving recommendations to the Fed and other sectoral regulators. The FSOC is only directly responsible for designation decisions and has already been held accountable at least once for decisions made under those powers, as we saw in the MetLife case. The situation is a little more complicated in the UK where the FPC not only has non-binding powers to issue guidance to the PRA and FCA, but it also has binding powers to issue Directions. The question then becomes who is accountable should the orders contained in the Direction prove wrong, the issuer of the Direction or the implementer? Thus, accountability mechanisms, meant to bolster democratic legitimacy, falter at the first hurdle.

5.4.2. Core Elements # 2 & 3 – To Whom is Accountability Owed and What is the Content of the Obligation?

A legal framework that spells out clearly the accountability arrangements with respect to the three branches of government and all other stakeholders can bolster the functional legitimacy of macroprudential authorities.[73] Macroprudential authorities would become part of the state's system of checks and balances – which means answering to the judiciary, executive and legislature – and making them answerable to the public as well. These elaborate forms of oversight were heavily influenced by the US model and experience, which served as a blueprint for regulatory governance scholarship generally in the industrialised world. Political accountability is a key element of macroprudential policy infrastructure.[74] The scrutiny is essential when a single body holds all the rule-making power and the power is discretionary.

Executive and legislative accountability can be exercised in a number of ways including recommendations from treasury, meetings with treasury, annual reports and regular appearances before the legislature. As for judicial review, it follows naturally that as administrative agencies acting on authority set out in statute, macroprudential authorities are subject to ex-post judicial review.[75] They are accountable before the courts for their actions. To the extent that macroprudential authorities have exceeded their legal authority, they should be held liable and affected parties should be able to obtain redress. This form of accountability proves problematic, however, because intermediaries and third parties seeking recourse via judicial review would be hard pressed to prove any wrongdoing on the part of

[73] Lastra, *Central Banking* (n 56).

[74] This is in contrast to the economic approach, which emphasises performance control and disclosure. Performance control is concerned with the efficiency of the agency, based upon the objectives and targets imposed on it. It is a more technical approach to accountability. Lastra, *International Financial and Monetary Law* (n 8) 90.

[75] International Monetary Fund, 'Implementing Macroprudential Policy – Selected Legal Issues' (17 June 2013) IMF Board Paper. Available at: www.imf.org/external/np/pp/eng/2013/061713.pdf.

a policy maker endowed with discretionary powers.[76] In theory it might be easier to make a claim against a macroprudential *regulator* for decisions taken against individual firms.

In fact, accountability for policy and accountability for regulation are different. The realm of regulation presents distinct challenges from that of policy making because it has different nature, goals, instruments, and personnel.[77] Thus, the two capacities require different models of accountability. Output-based accountability is preferred for policy makers, since they operate with clear performance objectives, which can easily be measured, while input-based accountability is preferred for regulators, which focuses on processes adopted, since they often have broad powers, but their performance or outputs are often hard to measure.[78] The last decade has seen a steadily growing body of academic literature on the issue of financial regulatory independence and accountability. The literature advocates for stronger, more complex accountability mechanisms for financial regulators.[79]

As explained above, transparency has also been granted a prominent position in the legal framework. In the financial stability realm, transparency is important not just for accountability reasons, but it helps to foster credibility and build public confidence in a relatively new policy area.[80] Nowhere was this more apparent than during the first round of stress tests in the US during the GFC. Bernanke believed that disclosure of stress test results enabled the public to judge the condition of banks for themselves and helped to re-establish the public's faith in the US banking system.[81] The disclosures included information on projected losses and revenues, any objections to a firm's capital plan that the Fed had raised and banks own estimates of losses and revenues in a stressed scenario.[82] The estimates provided by banks not only gave an alternative perspective on the test results but were very telling about the amount of risk banks were willing to take on and how well they managed this risk.[83]

In turn, post-crisis policies benefit from public solicitation of feedback, which macroprudential authorities can incorporate to produce more effective policy.

[76] The European Court of Justice has previously pronounced that the rights of individuals within monetary policy are extremely limited in relation to the state. See *Schülter v Hauptzollamt Lörrach* [1973] ECR 1135 at 1161. Therefore, it is conceivable that individual rights of recourse in relation to macroprudential policy may be limited also.

[77] Quintyn and Taylor (n 1).

[78] Lastra (n 7).

[79] Amtenbrink and Lastra (n 7).

[80] For an example of the role of accountability and transparency in financial stability see Jerome Powell, 'Financial Stability and Central Bank Transparency' (Speech at Sveriges Riksbank Anniversary Conference, Stockholm, 25 May 2018).

[81] Ben Bernanke, 'Stress Testing Banks: What Have We Learned?' (Speech at 'Maintaining Financial Stability: Holding a Tiger by the Tail,' Financial Markets Conference Georgia, 8 April 2013). Available at: www.federalreserve.gov/newsevents/speech/powell20180525a.htm.

[82] ibid.

[83] ibid.

However, transparency needs to be balanced against confidentiality constraints on the commercial data it uses to reach its decisions, and the market's tendency to react to any hint of bad news, thus becoming a self-fulfilling prophecy. Also, enhanced disclosure of certain policy decisions may draw the macroprudential supervisor into discussion of broader economic policies and hence impinge on its valued independence. It may also have a destabilising effect on the free flow of discussion, particularly where its governing body is composed of national representatives with differing and, at times, conflicting interests.

5.4.2.1. The FPC and Political Accountability

(a) Executive Accountability

In the United Kingdom, executive and parliamentary review are key elements of the new financial stability infrastructure. Firstly, the FPC receives annual recommendations from the Treasury on additional issues it should consider when deciding policy and the responsibility this entails, especially how it can support the Government's economic policy. These instructions fall into the category of *ex ante* accountability. The FPC is not bound by Treasury recommendations, but is required to comply or explain, to the extent that the FPC rejects Treasury's recommendations. The recommendations and responses are published and laid before Parliament.[84] The duty to explain or comply falls in the category of *ex post* accountability.

Ex post accountability to the Executive is also achieved via audits. Historically, there was a strong resistance against external scrutiny of the Bank of England's activities, which of course now include macroprudential policy and supervision. The Bank of England was outside the purview of the National Audit Office, (NAO), however in July 2015 the Chancellor of the Exchequer launched the Bank of England Bill, which sought to increase the BoE's transparency and accountability by bringing the Bank under the purview of the NOA. The Bill was criticised as giving a false sense of accountability because it gave the Court of the BoE veto powers over what the NAO may scrutinise, supposedly to maintain the independence of the Bank.[85]

(b) Parliamentary Review

In addition to executive accountability, members of the FPC are required to regularly appear before the Parliament's Treasury Select Committee, (TSC), to explain

[84] Bank of England Act 1998, s 9E.

[85] F Giuglian, 'Proposal to Open Bank of England Books to Auditors Causes Unease' *Financial Times* (9 September 2015). Available at: www.ft.com/intl/cms/s/0/522be5a2-5702-11e5-9846-de406c-cb37f2.html#axzz3wUfEPQtl; Ferdinando Giuglian, 'Auditor calls Bank of England regulation bill "unacceptable"' *Financial Times* (15 October 2015). Available at: www.ft.com/intl/cms/s/0/a28001cc-7328-11e5-a129-3fcc4f641d98.html#axzz3wUfEPQtl.

their assessment of risk and policies. The TSC evaluates the FPC's performance through scrutiny of the FPC's financial stability reports, much in the same way it scrutinises the reports of the Monetary Policy Committee.

(c) Judicial Review

Provisions for judicial review of macroprudential supervisors are not explicit in the UK. It is to be presumed that aggrieved financial firms can seek review of regulatory decisions and make appeals to the Tax and Chancery Chamber of the Upper Tribunal.[86] The Upper Tribunal, which is part of the administrative justice system of the UK, is a superior court of record, equivalent to the High Court, with powers of judicial review.

Third parties, like depositors and investors, face an additional hurdle because 'they have no immediate standing except in conduct of business issues when they may be given special private protection through redress in ordinary civil courts or in special ombudsman facilities … (at most) they may still try to sue regulators for negligence as a matter of their civil liability if all goes wrong'.[87] In the past, cases have been brought against the Bank of England, in its capacity as regulator, on the basis of misfeasance in public office.[88] The limitation of liability is based on the principle of 'proximity', which states that liability towards an aggrieved party for the breach of a legal rule only arises if the said rule was designed to protect the interests of the aggrieved party. If the rationale of the prudential rule in question is financial stability, then it is inconceivable that third parties can claim the breach of a rule.

(d) Transparency

The FPC's main tool for facilitating transparency is the financial stability report, (FSR). The FPC prepares and publishes an FSR twice a year. The FSR details the development of risks to the UK Financial system, as well as actions being taken by the FPC in response. The Governor of the Bank and the Chancellor of the Exchequer meet after the publication of a report, to discuss the FPC's findings and proposals to tackle any systemic risks identified. The report is also presented to parliament, which uses it as the basis for evaluating the FPC.

As part of its communication requirements, the FPC also publishes the minutes of its meetings, including those meetings between the Governor and the Chancellor following the publication of an FSR. The records contain details of all decisions and deliberations. Any Directions and/or Recommendations that have

[86] Tribunals, Courts and Enforcement Act 2007.
[87] Dalhuisen, 'Management of Systemic Risk' (n 72).
[88] *Three Rivers District Council & Ors v The Governor & Company of The Bank of England* [2004] EWCA Civ 218.

been issued must also be communicated not only to those on whom the duty of execution falls, but also to the public.

5.4.2.2. *FSOC and Accountability*

(a) Congressional Accountability

Congressional accountability is tied to transparency mechanisms. The FSOC is required to publish an annual financial report to Congress. The report details the FSOC's activities and provides an assessment of potential threats to US financial stability and recommendations to enhance the system's safety, promote market discipline and maintain investor confidence.[89] The FSOC's voting members individually sign off the report, indicating their agreement that the Council is doing all it can to ensure the stability of the US financial system and if they disagree they must provide reasons and specify what further actions they believe should be taken.

(b) Judicial Review

Unlike the UK and EU where it is difficult to see how the macroprudential authority may be held accountable before the courts, in the US it is possible, at least in as far as FSOC exercises its designation powers that are directed at individual firms. In the US, a non-bank financial company can institute an action for the rescission of designation as a SIFI;[90] in 2014 MetLife was one of the first intermediaries to challenge its designation by the FSOC, raising constitutional and procedural concerns about FSOC's process.[91] The Dodd-Frank Act, however, does not provide for judicial review of macroprudential supervisory decisions that are carried out by microprudential regulators.

(c) Transparency

The Council maintains a transparency policy and, in terms of that policy, it has committed to open its meetings to the public, at least twice a year, via a live web stream. However, depending on what is being deliberated, the Chairperson or a majority of Council members may decide to close off the meeting, or parts of it, from public scrutiny. Council members may challenge this when it comes from the Chairperson only.

The public is entitled to at least seven days' notice of a meeting. Such notices are published on the Council's website and they include the agenda, and details on

[89] Dodd-Frank Wall Street Reform and Consumer Protection Act Pub. L. 111–203, 124 Stat. 1376–222, s 112 (Dodd-Frank Act).

[90] Dodd-Frank Act, s 113(h).

[91] *Metlife v FSOC* 177 F Supp 3d 219 (DDC 2016).

the time and place of any open meeting, or when the meeting is closed, notification that the meeting is closed and the reasons thereof. Where the Council is scheduled to vote on a proposed or final rule, then details of that proposal or final rule shall also be published along with the notice. Details of each meeting are made available on the Council's website as soon as possible after the meeting. The Council also releases minutes of meetings immediately following its next regularly scheduled meeting. The minutes record all votes of Council members, but the Chairperson can order those parts of the minutes be redacted.

In September 2015, Scott Garrett, the Chairman of the Financial Services Subcommittee on Capital Markets and Government-Sponsored Enterprises in the US Congress, sought to increase transparency via the Financial Stability Oversight Council (FSOC) Transparency and Accountability Bill.[92] The Bill proposed creating a more formal obligation for transparency by subjecting the FSOC to the Government Sunshine Act. The Sunshine Act requires that meetings of federal agencies with multiple members must be open to public scrutiny.[93] The Bill also proposed allowing members of Congress from the Committee on Financial Services and the Committee on Banking, Housing, and Urban Affairs to attend and participate in *all* meetings of the Council.

5.4.2.3. The ESRB and Accountability and Reporting Requirements

(a) Executive Accountability

The ESRB has limited accountability obligations to the European Council. As will be recalled, the ESRB has the power to issue Recommendations and Warnings. Article 18 of the ESRB Regulation requires that if the General Board intends to make public a Recommendation or Warning, then it must inform the Council sufficiently in advance so that it is able to react.

(b) Parliamentary Review

Parliamentary review is the primary accountability mechanism. The Chair of the ESRB appears before the European Parliament annually to present the ESRB's report, or more frequently when the EU is going through a financial crisis. The ECB faces similar reporting requirements in the execution of its duties as prudential supervisor and therefore must account for macroprudential supervisory decisions.[94]

The ESRB's accountability mechanism involves a lot of meetings between the head of the ESRB and the government. The Chair of the ESRB holds confidential

[92] H.R.3557–114th Congress (2015–2016).

[93] The Act goes as far back as 1976 and is codified in 5 USC § 552.

[94] Article 20 Council Regulation (EU) No 1024/2013 of 15 October 2013 conferring specific tasks upon the European Central Bank concerning policies relating to the prudential supervision of credit institutions, [2013] OJ L 287/63. (SSM Regulation).

meetings with the Chair and Vice-Chairs of the Economic and Monetary Affairs Committee of the European Parliament at least twice a year and they may also be asked to sit in on meetings of Committees of the European Parliament.

Presumably, an additional executive control measure, although not explicitly stated, are the operational audits conducted by the European Court of Auditors. The Court of Auditors, which is established by Article 285 of the Treaty on the Functioning of the European Union (TFEU) and the Financial Regulation for the general budget of the EU, is responsible for monitoring the finances of the EU.

(c) Judicial Review

The ESRB's macroprudential policy is unlikely to come under judicial review since it does not actually exercise any rule making powers. Its powers are confined to recommendations, which the addressees may choose to follow or not. Presumably the ECB and national authorities remain accountable for any macroprudential regulation decisions they take.

This is clear in the case of the ECB, which is granted macroprudential powers under Article 5 of the SSM Regulation. In terms of the same regulation, the ECB's regulatory actions are subject to review by the ECJ, but this is without prejudice to the 'margin of the decisions with the regulation discretion left to the ECB to decide on the opportunity to take these decisions'.[95] Still, where ECB decisions adversely affect third parties, it is required to make good any damage caused by it under 'the general principles common to laws of Member States'.[96] There is also provision for review at institutional level in terms of Article 22 of the SSM Regulation, which requires the observance of due process, such as hearings for aggrieved persons, and an administrative board is set up in terms of Article 24 precisely to accord aggrieved parties a chance to be heard. The Board, however, only conducts administrative reviews of the ECB's procedural and substantive decisions.

(d) Transparency

In terms of Article 19 of the ESRB Regulation, the ESRB is required to publish a report to the European Parliament at least once a year, and the report is also made available to the public. In addition to general information on the ESRB's assessment of financial stability in the EU, the report can also contain any warning or recommendations that it has made public. According to Keller, the ESRB has actually been proactive in disseminating information, going beyond the statutory

[95] SSM Regulation, Preamble 60.
[96] ibid, Preamble 61.

requirements by regularly conducting press conferences and publishing on its website quarterly risk dashboards reports of the ESRB committees and working papers.[97]

5.4.3. Common Problems with Core Element #3

On paper, the existing accountability mechanisms allow the executive, legislature, judiciary and public to observe and evaluate policy actions, and for the macroprudential authorities to explain and justify their actions. This provides for democratic legitimacy and thus negates the need for increased political involvement in macroprudential policy and regulation.

Upon closer inspection, however, several gaps can be observed which render formal accountability mechanisms insufficient to bolster the democratic legitimacy of macroprudential authorities. The legal provisions on macroprudential accountability reads more like a litany of 'best practices for central bank accountability,' but several factors combine which make a case against using similar accountability mechanisms for both monetary and macroprudential policy. See Table 5.1.

Table 5.1 Differences Between Monetary Policy and Macroprudential Policy

	Monetary policy	**Macroprudential policy**
Target	Single	Multiple
Measurability	Numerical target	Directional target
Criteria to measure priorities may change	No	Yes
Confidentiality	Forward guidance is a key tool	May be critical to prevent panic
Regulatory function	None	May make decisions on individual firms

Using a central bank template for accountability models results in gaps. The following are the most conspicuous issues.

5.4.3.1. Lack of Sanctions or Override Mechanism

Statutory accountability arrangements in the ESRB are limited to the exchange of information and reporting requirements and lack any substantive

[97] A Keller, 'Independence, Accountability and Transparency: Are the Conventional Accountability Mechanisms Suitable for the European Systemic Risk Board?' (2017) 5 *International Company and Commercial Law* Review 176.

accountability.[98] Substantive accountability would impose consequences for the way the ESRB exercises its powers. The same can be said of the FPC and the FSOC. Arguing for stricter accountability for the ESRB, Keller makes a case that such mechanisms exist in several legal systems, which punish or reward monetary policy makers in response to their performance, therefore the same can be applied to macroprudential authorities. However, it is difficult to see how this would work in practice for macroprudential authorities given the indeterminacy of the macroprudential goal. As highlighted before, it has not been reduced to a quantitative measure, which makes it difficult to measure performance.

5.4.3.2. The Oxymoron of Opaque Transparency Mechanisms

In theory, explaining the policy decisions to the general public results in a basic understanding of those decisions and their rationales which, in turn, fosters greater acceptance of said policy decisions. In reality, however, the FSRs are too technical and long-winded for the public to understand. FSRs issued straight after the crisis were particularly lengthy, averaging 100 pages. The penchant for complex and lengthy reports may simply be an attempt to preserve the mystique of the 'technically adept policy maker' which was a source of their legitimacy. However, it may actually have the opposite effect and foster distrust of policy makers. In defence of macroprudential authorities though, some of these macroprudential tools, such as stress testing, are simply too complicated to communicate in an effective manner to the public. As a result, transparency and accountability may suffer.

Furthermore, while macroprudential authorities in all three jurisdictions are required to publish minutes of their meetings, they may redact sections of the minutes with information considered sensitive or which, if released, could trigger financial instability. The macroprudential authority has the final decision on the type and amount of information to be released to the public. This has raised the ire of members of Congress in the US, who have repeatedly condemned the secrecy of FSOC and its uncooperative behaviour. At a 2015 hearing of the FSOC before the Financial Services Committee, Committee Chairman Jeb Hensarling opened the hearing with a scathing attack on FSOC, stating:[99]

> FSOC has earned bipartisan condemnation for its lack of transparency. Two-thirds of its proceedings are conducted in private. Minutes of those meetings are devoid of any useful substantive information on what was discussed. Even Dennis Kelleher, the CEO of the left-leaning Better Markets, has said 'FSOC's proceedings make the Politburo look open by comparison. At the few open meetings they have, they snap their fingers and it's over, and they are all scripted. They treat their information as if it were state secrets.

[98] ibid.

[99] House of Representatives Committee on Financial Services, 'Oversight of The Financial Stability Oversight Council' (Serial 114-65, 8 December 2015).

His sentiments were echoed by Congressman Scott Garrett who stated:[100]

> You all have gotten to know each other pretty well because you meet regularly in closed door sessions, where the public is not allowed, to basically discuss to fundamentally change the U.S. economy. So I thought I'd just take this minute to introduce ourselves to you. We're the U.S. Congress. We were created by Article One of the U.S. Constitution. We're the ones who are actually elected representatives of the American public. And we're the ones who send you all those pesky letters that you all routinely ignore.
>
> And I know you're probably confused by this setting: That the public is here; that there's TV cameras here. So this is probably unusual for you. But this is what we do. We're open to the American public … So if there is one thing you take away today and that's the way you run your hearings, and that's the way you conduct yourselves. You need to become more like us …

The reality does not match the aspirations in the legal framework. The work of policy makers remains shrouded in secrecy and mystery and, while this may be necessary at times to avoid the self-fulfilling effect of announcing the prospect of financial instability, it creates a barrier between the accountable and the principal. More importantly, under such conditions, the transparency measures cannot be credibly expected to bolster public participation.

5.4.3.3. Poor Public Participation

Assuming the transparency issue highlighted above were to be redressed, it still may not be enough to increase public participation because the public is too dispersed to offer a coherent contribution. There is a need to create a more organised and explicit role for the public and there are four possible types of public-interest representatives that could participate in the regulatory process, namely:[101]

- public interest groups;
- members of the public appointed to regulatory agencies or separate officially appointed public-interest-monitoring agencies;
- scientific or technical expert councils; and
- special advisory commissions.

In the US and EU there is already legal provision for special advisory commissions and scientific expert councils respectively. The Dodd-Frank Act makes provision for the appointment of special advisory, technical, or professional committees to assist the FSOC. The committees may consist of State regulators, members of the Council, or individuals coming from outside.[102] Likewise, the ESRB's General

[100] ibid.
[101] S Omarova, 'Bankers, Bureaucrats, and Guardians: Toward Tripartism in Financial Services Regulation' (2012) Cornell Law Faculty Publications. Paper 1010. Available at: scholarship.law.cornell.edu/facpub/1010.
[102] Dodd-Frank Act, sec 111(d).

Board is assisted by the Advisory Scientific Committee (ASC), which conducts research to inform macroprudential decisions. The ASC consists of 15 experts who bring a variety of skills, experience, and expertise to the Committee. These advisory bodies are not, however, truly representative of the public as they are dominated by individuals from more or less the same background. For instance, all the ASC's members are economists.[103]

Of the four options, public-interest groups appear to be the strongest form of public-interest representative. Their key strength lies in that they emerge organically, from the efforts of affected citizens, thus they hold a stronger claim to democratic legitimacy as compared to the other institutions that owe their existence to the government. Furthermore, regulatory capture could be effectively combated by empowering public interest groups, while allowing the system to retain the benefits of consultations between the regulators and industry.[104] The use of public interest groups rests, of course, on the assumption that there exists interest groups with the necessary knowledge and pursuing interests that are aligned to the regulatory objectives (Chiu and Andenas suggest the 'Occupy Movement' as a possible public interest representative in finance.[105]) Public interest groups would be empowered by giving them:

(i) access to the same information the regulator uses to make decisions;
(ii) the right to participate in any negotiations between the regulator and financial firms, where compromises on regulatory standards are made; and
(iii) the same *locus standi* as the regulator.[106]

In the wake of the GFC, one of the boldest suggestions came from economist Ross Levine, who has strongly argued that one of the main causes was governance failure in the form of regulatory capture, which, in turn, produced policies that encouraged excessive risk taking and misallocation of society's resources towards unproductive ends.[107] He criticised the reform process at the time for its near exclusion of the public from the regulatory process and instead proposed the creation of a 'Sentinel' – an independent financial regulatory commission representing the public interest, manned by experts in economics, law, accounting and finance. The Sentinel's job would be to assess the substance of financial regulation and deliver a report of its findings to the legislature and executive. Its overall objective would be to promote transparency and open debate. The Sentinel would be funded from the Federal Reserve's budget.

[103] This is as its inception to June 2023.
[104] I Ayres and J Braithwaite, *Responsive Regulation: Transcending the Deregulation Debate* (Oxford University Press, 1992), 34–100.
[105] M Andenas and IH-Y Chiu, *The Foundations and Future of Financial Regulation: Governance for Responsibility* (Routledge, 2013).
[106] ibid 57–58.
[107] R Levine, 'The Governance of Financial Regulation: Reform Lessons from the Recent Crisis' (2012) 12(1) *International Review of Finance* 39.

There is only one problem with the Sentinel – it excludes any actual public interest groups; despite being premised on the idea that regulatory governance failed because the public interest was neglected. Also, the fact that the Sentinel would rely on funding from one of the agencies it is supposed to be monitoring appears counter intuitive.

In contrast, Omarova proposed an independent 'Public-interest Council', located outside of the legislative and executive branches of government much like independent central banks.[108] The Council's mandate would be to safeguard the public interest in financial stability and limit the damaging effects of systemic risk. Financial regulation experts, mainly academics, prominent non-political figures, members of consumer councils and representatives of other public-interest groups would man the Council. They would participate in *ex ante* accountability procedures, like taking part in rule making, and requesting regulatory action to address public concerns, and it would also be of the *ex-post* accountability via reviews of information on relevant developments in financial markets, and a right to receive activity reports from regulatory agencies.

The Public Interest Council was certainly more representative than Levine's Sentinel, and it also had a lot more bite than bark, a little too much in this writer's opinion. In particular, extending the right to participate in regulatory rule making overstepped the bounds of an accountability mechanism and placed the Council squarely in the realm of a control mechanism. What is required is a more moderate entity that is representative, but has its role limited to enforcing accountability.

While increased public participation aligns independent agencies to democratic values, by allowing more citizen influence, we must remain mindful of its negative effects. In practice, it may slow down and complicate the regulatory process. Furthermore, improving public participation, or any of the other accountability gaps identified for that matter, may be of little use if macroprudential authorities are not aware of what it is they are being held accountable for. The criteria for assessment are evaluated in the next section.

5.4.4. Core Element #4 – Criteria for Assessment

There are two criteria for assessment. The first is to evaluate whether policy activities achieve the desired policy output, ie financial stability, and the second is to evaluate whether the policy activities align with or promote societal values.

5.4.4.1. Issues with Measuring Output

First and foremost, legislative, and executive accountability pre-supposes some measure against which parliamentarians can easily judge the actions of

[108] Omarova, 'Bankers, Bureaucrats, and Guardians' (n 101).

macroprudential policy makers. However, as highlighted in previous chapters, no one single indicator is sufficient to measure the presence or extent of systemic risk in the system, against which the effectiveness of the macroprudential authority could be reasonably assessed. In contrast, when it comes to monetary policy there is a clear remit from Parliament, usually a target of 2 per cent consumer price inflation, which can be used to measure central bank performance month in month out with published inflation numbers. There is no danger of the Central Bank imposing any other standard. For macroprudential policy, authorities generally determine threats to stability using presumptive indicators of financial imbalances like excessive leverage and credit expansion.

Alternatively, output can be measured by stress testing the resilience of the financial system, in other words the ability of the financial system to withstand a severe downturn. The UK, for example, has a resilience target for each area of the system at each point in time and for each threat, with flexibility hardwired into it to allow adaptability as the financial system evolves. In banking for instance, the FPC balances its financial stability objective, which is maintaining resilience, and ensuring that it does not negatively affect growth over the medium to long-term by conducting a cost and benefit analysis. On the benefit side of the ledger, the FPC considers the fact that the system will not magnify severe downturns. On the cost side of the ledger, the FPC considers the drag on growth that comes the rest of the time from forcing banks to fund more of their lending with capital rather than deposits.

The resultant resilience target is expressed in the severity of the economic scenario the FPC expects banks to be resilient to. In 2022 this was defined as a situation in which the UK Bank Rate rises rapidly to 6 per cent in early 2023 before later being reduced gradually to under 3.5 per cent; unemployment rises to over 8.5 per cent; the output of the economy falls by nearly 5 per cent, the global economy falls by 2.5 per cent and house prices fall by 31 per cent.[109] The FPC is conscious that the resilience target should be flexible – if the economy becomes more fragile, the stress scenarios will be tightened and the capital levels needed to pass them will increase, or the opposite, in a downturn the capital buffers that have been built up will be run down to absorb losses without cutting lending.

The real test of this measure of resilience, however, only comes when the system receives a shock. But such systemic events are few and far between, which would mean the FPC's performance could only be measured in periods of crisis, negating the whole accountability mechanism.

5.4.4.2. Output not Wholly Aligned with Societal Values

With monetary policy the values that policy makers must align themselves with are clearly established – allocative efficiency. With macroprudential policy on

[109] Bank of England, 'Stress Testing the UK Banking System: Guidance on the 2022 Stress Test for participants' Available at: www.bankofengland.co.uk/stress-testing/2022/stress-testing-guidance-2022-for-participants.

the other hand, it is less clear. One can make some estimation of how the broad outputs of macroprudential policy, reducing financial instability, will align with society's economic values, in other words expectations for allocative efficiency. But it is less clear when it comes to unintended outputs, the distributional effects of macroprudential policy, and how much these align with society's noneconomic values, social justice. For instance, when one considers sectoral based policies like the LTV and DTI limits on mortgages, that will not only affect allocative efficiency, but also affect the ability of individuals to achieve dreams of homeownership. As we saw, most macroprudential policy is likely to have this redistributive effect, on top of its effects on allocative efficiency, even if such outcome was not intended. This has been glossed over in the formal accountability mechanism's criteria for assessment and is a fundamental problem.

There are no guidelines for how policy makers can ensure they are aligned with all of society's values, or if they should be striving to be aligned at all, therefore there is no way for stakeholders to keep track of how policy makers are making distributional decisions or compel them the make such decisions if they should.

5.5. Differences in the Articulation of Independence between Monetary Policy and Macroprudential Policy

It was established in this book that the powers of macroprudential authorities cannot be justified by reference to the typical democratic processes. An alternative source of legitimacy must be found, and the automatic response has been to treat macroprudential authorities like independent central banks. Arguments favouring independent macroprudential authorities are based on the technocratic nature of macroprudential policy, and the need for an arm's-length oversight body in conducting financial policy. Some of the tools used by macroprudential authorities target particular sectors or loan types, and while it may be beneficial to target specific areas of risk for policy intervention, such an approach may be susceptible to popular pressures from vested interests.[110] This lends credence to the idea that it is best handled by a body that is removed from the political cycle and third party influences, and that can offer a credible commitment to policy. This suggests that macroprudential authorities are only legitimate to the extent that they are independent.

The legal framework for macroprudential policy, when compared to that of monetary policy, as far as they articulate independence, has largely maintained the same levels of goal and financial independence. The level of *goal independence* is similar as a matter of principle. For both policy fields, the objectives of price

[110] AG Haldane, 'Macroprudential Policies: When and How to Use Them?' (Re-Thinking Macro Policy II: First Steps and Early Lessons conference Washington DC, April 2013).

stability are explicitly set in legislation in the UK, US and EU. The only difference, however, between goal setting for macroprudential policy and monetary policy is that in addition to the broad policy goal there is a fixed inflation target, typically set at 2 per cent, which is determined by either the government or is agreed bilaterally, although it is communicated outside the statute. Despite the explicit target, the central banks are given leeway to set the horizon for monetary policy and deviate from the target due to unexpected events. In contrast, the objectives of macroprudential policy are often expressed as directional, rather than absolute targets, this leaves a lot of room for macroprudential authorities to exercise discretion in interpreting the goal.

Financial independence, on the other hand, remains unchanged as a matter of practicality because both monetary and macroprudential policy rely on the same financial administration systems and human resources. Governments do not contribute to the finances of the macroprudential policy institutions, and none of the available macroprudential tools can be used to directly finance public debt or monetise deficits.[111]

There are, however, significant differences between the institutional, instrumental and personal independence of monetary policy and that for macroprudential policy. Firstly, *institutional independence* has been attacked for not creating a truly pluralistic policy maker, especially in the US. Compared to the homogeneous FSOC membership, the appointments to the Fed must yield a 'fair representation of the financial, agricultural, industrial, and commercial interests and geographical divisions of the country'.[112]

Secondly, institutional independence has been reduced in all three jurisdictions by the inclusion of treasury in the structure, greater allowance being given to politicians to make recommendations, give directions and approve policy action, and government representatives being allowed to vote on policy. In contrast, members of Treasury do not participate in the monetary policy making body. The exception to this arrangement is the UK, where a representative of the Treasury has always sat on the Monetary Policy Committee as a non-voting member. Furthermore, central banks are generally prohibited from taking instructions from government officials and can pursue objectives that potentially conflict with those of government, although the circumstances and conditions under which such conflict is permitted are limited. Therefore, the central banks are subject only to non-binding consultations with the government in making policy-related decisions. This does not, however, bar all liaisons between the central banks and the government. In all three jurisdictions, some interchange is required between staff of the central bank and treasury, usually by granting

[111] Although macroprudential regulatory treatment of sovereign exposures could encourage private sector funding of government debt, at the expense of other borrowers. Every time the government is in distress, so is financial stability. See, for instance, Bank for International Settlements, 86th Annual Report 2015/16 (26 June 2016), 92–93.

[112] Federal Reserve Act, sec 10.

a right to attend meetings and important discussions of either party, but not to participate in voting and decision making. In the UK and EU, this interaction has been formalised by including it in statute, while in the US it is less formal, although traditions have been built up over years which encourage interaction and exchange of ideas, such as the weekly luncheons hosted for the Fed and Treasury senior staff. These arrangements ensure consistency in economic policy. See Annexure 3.

Similarly, *instrument independence* has undergone some changes, the most significant being that there is no recourse to policy instruments outside those prescribed by the legislature. In all three jurisdictions the central bank has discretion to conduct monetary policy through an array of market instruments, chiefly open market operations, without administrative regulation or political interference. Although the central bank statutes list the policy tools that the central banks may employ, the list is not exhaustive and leaves room to use 'other operational methods of monetary control'. The authority is complemented by rule-making powers. Thus, the central banks have sole responsibility for formulating and implementing monetary policy (see Annexure 3). Macroprudential authorities, on the other hand, do not have responsibility for implementation of policy, as this has been handed over to microprudential supervisors.

Consequently, the importance of ensuring supervisory independence has also increased. This is the agency's freedom to exercise discretion in supervisory activities like licensing, monitoring, enforcement of rules and penalising deviations. In all three jurisdictions, the microprudential supervisors have been granted the final word on who can enter the system, and this has not been affected by the introduction of a macroprudential mandate. At the monitoring stage, microprudential supervision is generally conducted autonomously, but guided by predetermined prudential regulations that are applied uniformly. Likewise, the supervisory agencies also enjoy autonomy to sanction wayward firms and enforce those sanctions, again based on predetermined rules.

There is an attempt to balance rules and discretion in the conduct of supervision because it affects the rights of financial firms directly, therefore supervised firms should be able to ascertain what standards are being applied to them, and also an idea of what will happen when those standards are breached. The introduction of macroprudential duties has increased the level of discretion, given that the exact rules to be applied are not predetermined in legislation, but enhanced rules may be issued on a cyclical basis, and directed at particular firms, as and when deemed necessary by the supervisory agency. Which is at odds with the largely rules-based approach of microprudential supervision in the application of rules, the system of sanctions and interventions. Given the 'intimacy' of the supervisory process, again there is the possibility of capture by the entities being supervised.

Only one aspect of *personal independence* is similar for both monetary and macroprudential policy as a matter of practicality – suitable qualifications and remuneration. The other two aspects, sufficiently long tenure and security from dismissal are compromised by the inclusion of Treasury representatives in the policy-making body. In contrast, the tenure for *all* central bank members of the monetary policy authority is longer than the political cycle and *none* of the members live in fear of the 'Damocles' Sword' of dismissal (see Annexure 3).

On the face of it, macroprudential authorities face the same political constraints but enjoy the same operational freedoms as monetary authorities. However, on closer inspection, the differences in the articulation of institutional and instrument independence in particular, points instead to reduced operational independence. This raises two important questions, what has prompted the need for greater political intervention in financial regulation and, what does it mean for its legitimacy. More importantly, how do these almost inconspicuous changes affect the functional legitimacy of macroprudential authorities, which is predicated on policy output, ie its effectiveness. As has been alluded to in the Introduction, legitimacy is important because it is a critical element in motivating behavioural responses for effective policy changes.

5.5.1. Why are We Gravitating Back Towards More Political Control?

5.5.1.1. Ordinary vs Extraordinary Times

During financial crises there have always been both procedural and substantive reasons justifying a role, if not a demand, for the political leadership to step in and develop and implement strategies to contain the crisis. In a crisis, strict adherence to normal decision-making processes, to which independent policy makers are bound, may be untenable given the time-sensitive nature of the emergency. Flexibility and expediency could thus be temporarily prioritised over predictability. However, there must exist a relationship of trust between the polity and the policy maker to permit a departure from normal procedural constraints. It must be expedience and flexibility in the 'right' direction, whatever that may be. Unfortunately, faith in independent regulatory agencies was shaken when the crisis set in, and the polity could not trust, or have strong enough reasons to put aside its doubts, that independent policy makers would act in their best interests. Which brings us to the second, substantive, reason why in extraordinary times functional legitimacy may be less important.

While the actions taken to resolve financial crises are highly technical in nature, they also have politically sensitive content. The actions often require massive budgetary resources, to finance the restructuring of failing intermediaries for instance, and the breaking of vested interests, both of which require strong political support and legislative approval.[113] More importantly, the resolution of

[113] Das and Quintyn (n 2).

crises involves burden sharing and the redistribution of wealth, which require value judgements to be made about society's preferences.[114] Technical ability, for all its advantages, has its limits, especially when decisions made by policy makers could shape the very identity of a nation, and the focus instead shifts to other values.[115] For instance, how the British and US governments' reaction to the crisis was actually designed to serve the interests and security of the broader population, especially the middle classes.[116] In crisis situations, therefore, macroprudential authorities, like central banks, may be ill-equipped to make fundamental decisions about the welfare of the nation and, in extraordinary times, national interest may well supersede functional legitimacy.

The resolution of financial crises therefore is not just a technical exercise but requires the balancing of sensitive political trade-offs. For this reason, it makes sense to suspend the usual belief in the infallibility of independent regulators and allow political influence in the regulation of the financial system. In extreme cases, a crisis may lead to an independent agency being stripped of its influence altogether. In 1929, straight after the stock market crash, the unravelling of the gold standard and the Great Depression, central banks were stripped of their responsibility, status and power.[117] The period during and after the GFC was such an extraordinary time. Macroprudential authorities are a product of crisis, born at a time when decisions had to be made that went to the heart of the very identity of the countries in crisis. This may explain why independence has – surreptitiously – been wrested from macroprudential authorities. A decade on, however, the insidious hand of politics is still present in their governance structure, which begs the question why politicians have been reluctant to relinquish control in this macroeconomic policy area.

5.5.1.2. Unknown Preferences

Another key factor encouraging political involvement is that the preferences of the macroprudential authorities are actually unknown. In Chapter 4, I highlighted a time-inconsistency problem with macroprudential policy, which may be solved by appointing an independent policy maker. The assertion rests however on an

[114] ibid.

[115] Amtenbrink and Lastra (n 7).

[116] M Watson, 'Headlong in the Polanyian Dilemma: The Impact of Middle-Class Moral Panic on the British Government's Response to the Sub-prime Crisis" (2009) 11(3) *The British Journal of Politics and International Relations* 422 and P Langley, 'Toxic Assets, Turbulence and Biopolitical Security: Governing the Crisis of Global Financial Circulation' (2013) 44 (2) *Security Dialogue* 111. Although Thirkell-White points out policy makers' initial handling of the global financial crisis, through bailouts, also offended the popular values of justice as it appeared those who caused the crisis went unpunished and taxpayers had to carry the burden of their mistakes. See B Thirkell-White, 'Dealing with the Banks: Populism and the Public Interest in the Global Financial Crisis' (2009) 85(4) *International Affairs* 689.

[117] P Tucker, *Unelected Power: The Quest for Legitimacy in Central Banking and the Regulatory State* (Princeton University Press, 2018), 4.

assumption about the extent to which said independent policy makers are averse to financial instability. In the realm of monetary policy, it has been demonstrated that the differences in inflation preferences amongst central bankers have different effects on inflation and unemployment, thus partisan governments have preferences over the types of agents they appoint.[118]

In the absence of a method for measuring 'instability aversion' and given that there are still wide variations on the acceptable level of instability with which society is willing to live, it cannot be taken for granted that independent authorities will be conservative and seek to avoid financial instability. The difficulty of pinning down the policy maker's instability aversion is made even more difficult by the fact that financial stability exists along a continuum, as highlighted earlier. There is the danger that an unrestrained macroprudential policymaker's preferences will diverge from public interest.[119] For instance, where the macroprudential authority is the central bank, it might end up an inflation nutter,[120] at the expense of financial stability, or, worse still; the policy maker may begin wading into political debates that are outside its remit.[121]

5.5.1.3. Vagueness Surrounding the Goal

A key element of independence is that the government should set the goal of the regulatory agency, to ensure some minimum political control. On paper, this is clear – financial stability. The reality, however, is that macroprudential policy is a complicated, indeterminate and nascent policy domain, characterised by disagreements over the actual problem to be resolved, never mind the solution. Although 'financial stability' is repeatedly stated as the core objective of macroprudential policy, the term itself has numerous iterations.[122] The three jurisdictions used as case studies have broken down financial stability into intermediate targets; however, these targets are expressed in directional rather than in absolute terms: it is difficult to numerically approximate, for example, 'to lower', 'to mitigate', 'to limit' or 'to ensure'.

An unambiguous goal helps anchor the independence of the authority. Policy actions to constrain the upswing of the financial cycle will be unpopular because, essentially, they constrain credit when it appears plentiful. Therefore, there needs to be a compelling defence for seemingly unnecessary or costly actions when financial instability has not yet materialised. Even if it does, should the policy

[118] C Adolph, *Bankers, Bureaucrats and the Politics of Central Banks* (Cambridge University Press, 2013).

[119] Balls et al 'Central Bank Independence Revisited' (n 16).

[120] M King, 'Changes in UK Monetary Policy: Rules and Discretion in Practice' (1997) 39 *Journal of Monetary Economics* 81.

[121] W Buiter, 'Central Banks: Powerful, Political and Unaccountable?' (2014) Centre for Economic Policy Research Discussion Paper No 10223.

[122] HJ Allen, 'What is "Financial Stability"? The Need for Some Common Language in International Financial Regulation' (2013–2014) 45 *Georgetown Journal of International Law* 929.

actions fail then it may be difficult to hold policy makers to account for actions not taken if the goal against which actions are to be measured is vague.

The obvious reason for the lack of consensus is that macroprudential policy did not develop from a strong theoretical and empirical foundation but was a response to the crisis. Compared to monetary policy, there is hardly any public understanding of macroprudential policy. It follows that the politicians who represent the electorate also struggle to set a goal that they can be sure accords with the values of those they represent. If they cannot be sure of the parameters of the goal they are setting, then complete delegation becomes undesirable.

5.5.1.4. Policy Failure Contagion

In all three jurisdictions, macroprudential authorities are mainly composed of central bankers and microprudential regulators. The move to constrain its independence may arise from fears created by their failures in other policy functions, namely monetary policy and microprudential regulation. In the public's eyes it may not be prudent to completely handover a new set of powers to the same entities that failed to safeguard the financial system the last time round: 'it makes no sense to turn over control of the task of macro-prudential supervision to a set of institutions that have manifestly failed to do the job properly at the latest time of asking. They have no track record of competence in macro-prudential supervision.'[123] Although this may be true, Goldby and Keller feel that this is an unfair assessment, however, as numerous economists did raise the alarm.[124] Unfortunately these warnings went unheeded, either because central bankers did not have the right instruments to address the threat, or they lacked the will. The latter is more likely.

Still, in the aftermath of the GFC many were furious with financial regulators. On Capitol Hill for instance Members of Congress both on the left and right of the aisle were disappointed with the Fed, either for guaranteeing counterparties to the insurance giant AIG or for failing to protect borrowers from abusive lending practices.[125] The Fed was punished for it, as evidenced by the 112 legislative bills, criticising the Fed, which were introduced in Congress following the crisis.[126]

In the UK, this mistrust and displeasure were expressed by disbanding the Financial Services Authority, the once unitary microprudential regulator, accompanied by declarations that a crisis would not be allowed again. The Joint

[123] W Buiter, 'The Proposed European Systemic Risk Board is Overweight with Central Bankers' (Willem Buiter's Maverecon, 28 October 2009). Available at: blogs.ft.com/maverecon/2009/10/.

[124] M Goldby and A Keller, 'The Commission's Proposal for a New Systemic Risk Board: An Evaluation' (2010) 4(1) *Law and Financial Markets Review* 48.

[125] LM Goodhart 'Brave New World? Macro-prudential Policy and the New Political Economy of the Federal Reserve' (2015) 22(2) *Review of International Political Economy* 280.

[126] ibid.

Committee on the draft of the Financial Service Bill vowed, at the time proposals were being presented for a new Financial Policy Committee, that it would ensure stronger governmental control of the new Committee.[127]

Past failures and the resultant loss of trust in traditional independent regulators may explain the resultant structure of macroprudential authorities. Indeed, in the decade after the crisis, the story of the crisis and its causes has been retold many times, from the perspective of academics, central bankers, economists, lawmakers, financiers and lobbyists. The literature tends to vilify not only financiers, but also financial regulators. The exception being accounts written by former financial regulators, which tend to glorify them as hapless victims of a perfect storm, who, regardless, rose above it to save the financial system. The words of Henry Waxman, Chairman of the US House of Representatives Committee on Oversight and Government Reform, during a Congress Hearing soon after the crisis captured the sentiment of many, that, 'the list of regulatory mistakes and misjudgments is long, and the cost to taxpayers and our economy is staggering'.[128]

5.5.1.5. Fear of Regulatory Capture

An oft-repeated cause of these misjudgments and mistakes is that regulators fell prey to regulatory capture and could no longer be trusted to provide impartial services. The original theory on capture defined it as when private interest groups used their economic resources to purchase legal and regulatory outcomes from politicians. However, over time, it has become more ingenious, targeting policy makers' ethos and traditions, but still just as dangerous.[129] This form of regulatory capture is particularly pervasive in the financial sector because of the presence of large, well-organised firms, with immense economic and political power.

The belief is that in the decades preceding the latest crisis, the industry exerted so much influence, to the extent that regulators began to embrace more self-regulation and allowed innovation and complexity in the financial markets to thrive. Essentially, they willingly ceded control to the firms they were meant to regulate, which prevented them from spotting systemic risk. This narrative, however, ignores an alternative explanation, that the regulatory regime appeared 'captured' because the legislature that created this regime was itself captured by private interest and so had produced a regime predestined to capture.

Of course, this is not to say that regulators are unfairly demonised in the post-crisis literature. There is evidence of regulatory forbearance and misplaced focus.

[127] Joint Committee on the Draft Financial Services Bill, Draft Financial Services Bill (2010–12, HL 236, HC 1447).

[128] House of Representatives Committee on Oversight and Government Reform, 'The Financial Crisis and The Role of Federal Regulators' (Opening Address of Hon Henry A Waxman, US Representative for the State of California, Serial No 110–209, 23 October 2008).

[129] LG Baxter, 'Capture in Financial Regulation: Can We Channel It toward the Common Good?' (2011) 21 *Cornell Journal of Law and Public Policy* 176.

Particularly where the regulator was also the central bank, emphasis was placed on the central bank's role as lender of last resort, and therefore on managing crises, but not on avoiding crises to begin with, by ensuring safety and soundness through prudential regulation. Although this may have been the result of granting dual objectives without clarifying the hierarchy of objectives, or a hierarchy in which financial stability came second to maintaining price stability.[130]

However, if there was a perceived capture problem in financial regulation, then the appropriate reforms should have focused on taming the predator, industry influence, instead of the prey, the regulators. A more effective approach to combat capture, whether emanating from industry or the political establishment, and to win popular trust, is to improve accountability mechanisms and, despite the assertions of lawmakers, increasing political involvement in financial regulation does not make for improved accountability, they appear to be conflating accountability and control.

In any case, the accounts that emphasise regulatory capture have had a profound impact on the re-designing of the institutional framework for financial regulation, particularly the extent of independence in regulation. The response to the perceived governance problem has been a subtle move from less technocratic independent regulation, towards more democratic politically controlled regulation.[131]

5.5.1.6. The Rise of Populist Politics

The rising tide of anti-establishment, populist sentiment sweeping the world has only fuelled the suspicion with which regulatory independence is now viewed.[132] The media is awash with statements made by politicians criticising independent central bankers in particular. For instance, during the 2016 US presidential campaign, Donald Trump reproached the then Fed chair, Janet Yellen, for politicising monetary policy.[133] In France, Marine Le Pen pledged to minimise the influence of global financial institutions and return power to French citizens.[134] The then UK Labour Shadow Chancellor of the Exchequer, John McDonnell, wanted to subject interest rates to more democratic oversight.[135]

[130] B Bernanke's account of his time at the Fed is very telling in this regard. In *The Federal Reserve and The Financial Crisis* (Princeton University Press 2012), Bernanke only dedicates eight pages, out of 129, to the subject of bank regulation, despite the fact that this is one of the Fed's major mandates.

[131] In the case of the EU, one may argue that the design of macroprudential authorities was influenced by EU principles such as proportionality and subsidiarity, or the Meroni doctrine.

[132] CAE Goodhart and RM Lastra, 'Populism and Central Bank Independence' (2018) 29(1) *Open Economies Review* 49.

[133] S Liesman, 'Trump says Janet Yellen should be "ashamed of herself" so will she resign?' Available at: www.nbcnews.com/storyline/2016-election-day/trump-said-janet-yellen-should-be-ashamed-herself-so-will-n68158.1.

[134] 'Marine Le Pen Launches Presidential Campaign' *Financial Times* (4 February 2017). Available at: www.ft.com/content/a5519f64-eaeb-11e6-930f-061b01e23655.

[135] 'John McDonnell Labour Shadow Chancellor, In Quotes' *Financial Times* (14 September 2015). Available at: www.ft.com/content/6ec89ff6-5acd-11e5-9846-de406ccb37f2.

The loss of confidence is not just with financial regulators, but with the market-based economy as a whole. In his introduction to the 2015 Bank of England Open Forum, Mark Carney acknowledged how a crisis of solvency and legitimacy had eroded public trust in market mechanisms and the financial system.[136] The loss of faith in a system manifests either as pressure for government to exercise more control or to do away with the system altogether.

Calls for total abolition of the market-based system are few. However, there is strong evidence of public demand for more state intervention, especially right after the crisis hit.[137] Polls conducted by the Edelman Trust Barometer, FT/Harris and GlobeScan indicated amongst respondents a growing fear of globalisation and support for increased regulation by their governments of businesses activities.[138] Ironically, the general decline of trust in market-based economies and globalisation was not accompanied by a decline in citizens' confidence in government. This is not surprising, however, as there is empirical evidence suggesting a negative correlation between crises and citizens' confidence in their institutions of governance.

It appears that the anti-independence/anti-establishment sentiment surreptitiously crept into financial regulation reform as more caution was exercised in designing macroprudential authorities.

5.5.1.7. Distributional Effects of Policy Tools

Even if we were to assume that the public will accept the objective of 'financial stability' in its vagueness and that the independent macroprudential authority's stability preferences align with those of the public, there remains the concern that the tools used to achieve said financial stability may lead the macroprudential authority into areas of policy that are outside its purview. As demonstrated in Chapter 4, many of the tools in the macroprudential arsenal have redistributive consequences. Policy decisions will quite obviously benefit some and disadvantage others. In the name of pursuing the long-term goal of financial stability, macroprudential authorities may, in the short term, offend an electorate's sense of justice and reasonableness, for instance by denying them access to credit.

Although they were created to pursue society's economic objectives, macroprudential authorities undeniably affect its non-economic objectives. A condition of granting independence is that the apolitical and technocratic regulatory agency must leave distributional decisions to elected politicians. Inadvertently, however, the macroprudential authority wades into political and fiscal territory. Therefore, it was to be expected that macroprudential policy provoked a political response.

[136] M Carney, 'Introduction to the Open Forum' (London, 11 November 2015). Available at: www.bis.org/review/r151116c.htm.

[137] F Roth, 'The Effects of the Financial Crisis on Systemic Trust' (July 2009) CEPS Working Document No. 316/July 2009.

[138] ibid.

The distrust of apolitical technocratic authorities is compounded by the growing use of unconventional monetary policy tools by central banks, which also draw them beyond their mandate into the realm of fiscal policy. While quantitative easing may increase commercial banks' liquidity, it does not compel them to lend. Thus, its effects may be limited to increasing the value of assets, but not prices and wages. This can substantially influence levels of inequality, since the poor and middle classes tend not to own assets, and instead live on wages, salaries or pensions. Conversely, the savings of the poor and middle classes are eroded by the decrease in interest rates. In this way, quantitative easing appears to be a hidden tax, used to finance government activities, especially where the central bank mainly purchases government bonds under a quantitative easing programme. It becomes just 'fiscal policy dressed up'.[139] Unconventional monetary policy has significant distributive consequences, leading many to question whether it should not fall under the purview of government control, much like fiscal policy. Adding further discretionary macroprudential powers runs the risk of creating, as Tucker calls them, 'overmighty citizens'.

5.6. Between Scylla and Charybdis: An Evaluation of the Legitimacy of Macroprudential Authorities

All the factors described above have combined to create a general atmosphere of mistrust in independent policy makers: they cannot be trusted in extraordinary times; or that this time round their policies will be successful; or that they will not fall prey to industry capture; or that they are pursuing the right goals, in line with societal preferences for financial stability; and they certainly cannot be trusted with the boundless distributional powers that come with macroprudential policy. All these shortcomings could be palatable if citizens participated in the policy-making process, either by voting directly on policy, or if their chosen representatives chose the policy. In other words, if policy were arrived it in a way that respects the freedom and equality of all those affected. The increased government involvement creates a sense of increased citizen participation in the policy process.

But we must always keep in mind that the successful implementation of macroprudential policy demands, among other things, that macroprudential authorities have legitimacy. It has been argued in this book that macroprudential policy has similar legitimacy foundations to monetary policy. The legitimacy of the macroprudential authority is based on the extent to which they can demonstrate credibility and commitment to a policy direction, which is sustained by their

[139] See C Borio, '"Helicopter Money" – Reality Bites' (Commentary in Nikkei Asian Review, 4 September 2016). Available at: www.bis.org/speeches/sp160906.htm.

independence. If history has taught us anything, it is that any limitation on their independence, however minor it may appear, will have a negative effect.[140]

The FSOC's relationship with government sponsored entities is a case in point. FSOC has been accused of inaction in the face of mounting risk in real estate, preferring to focus on interconnectedness, because it was pandering to the continued political push to subsidise housing finance. The FSOC said nothing when the head of the Federal Housing Finance Agency, Mel Watt, loosened the down payment limit from 5 to 3 per cent on mortgages eligible for the government guarantees offered by government-sponsored entities.[141]

It appears that choosing one form of legitimacy over another is untenable in the case of macroprudential policy. Unlike other macroeconomic policy areas where the source of legitimacy falls more or less in either the economic or political basket, neither one nor the other can solely justify the legitimacy of macroprudential policy. There are trade-offs between functional and democratic legitimacy.

On the one hand, attempts to improve democratic legitimacy by increasing political interference leaves us with weakened policy makers who cannot effectively carry out their function. The independence of macroprudential authorities is premised on the notion that not only are they technically adept but are sufficiently insulated from political pressures to ensure credible commitment to difficult policy decisions. This commitment is particularly crucial in the face of financial instability, or importantly before it manifests, when they appear to be 'taking away the punch bowl when the party gets going'.[142] In fact, there is no guarantee that the increased political involvement will lead to outcomes which accord with democratic values either. We are reminded that electoral strategising, and industry lobbying still influences politicians' choices. Thus, their decisions may not be motivated by values of democracy at all. Macroprudential policy may be condemned to being simply reactive.

On the other hand, focusing on functional legitimacy, over democratic legitimacy, risks very valid concerns with the social effects of policy being ignored. It is the argument of this book that the governance structure of macroprudential

[140] J Dahger, 'Regulatory Cycles: Revisiting the Political Economy of Financial Crises' (15 January 2018) IMF Working Paper No 18/8.

[141] CW Calomiris, 'Restoring the Rule of Law in Financial Regulation' (24 September 2018) *Cato Journal*. Available at: www.cato.org/cato-journal/fall-2018/restoring-rule-law-financial-regulation. Calomiris blames this on the fact that the FSOC is composed of the heads of the various financial regulatory agencies, who can at any point in time be appointed by the same political party. The Secretary of Treasury at the time, Jacob Lew, could not be expected to criticise a head of agency appointed in the same administration. Such political diversity in the US is usually achieved through the system of staggered appointments to regulatory agencies such as the Fed, SEC, and the FDIC. However, the fact that the agencies which the FSOC members represent use a staggered approach to appointment provides a guard against the concentration of which Calomaris complains.

[142] A phrase coined by former Federal Reserve Chairman William McChesney Martin concerning the role of central banks.

policy can be understood with reference to this dilemma – in other words, it is the dilemma of representing popular concerns while at the same time promoting effective solutions. It appears we are sailing between Scylla and Charybdis.[143]

In trying to pacify political sensibilities, by directly participating in governance, governments have increased the democratic legitimacy of macroprudential authorities, but compromised their functional legitimacy. By fixing one problem we have created another. Ultimately, macroprudential authorities may lose democratic legitimacy if they cannot produce outcomes which accord with values of democracy, something that is almost guaranteed if macroprudential policy cannot be trusted to maintain financial stability. The two are intricately linked.

Even though consistently poor economic results from democratically elected policy makers undermine the acceptance of their authority, those affected by and bearing the cost of policies may accept poor results over time, as they have a sense of ownership over the decisions. However, as we saw, the costs of poor outputs such as financial crises can be devastating and are to be avoided. The almost unquestioned faith in the functional legitimacy of central banks is evidence that citizens are willing to forego any right to directly participate in policy making, as long as the output reflects society's preferences for allocative efficiency, which represent a different set of the community's accepted norms. However, it is clear that there is no constituency that is in favour of being stripped of democratic input if the resultant framework is not going to produce allocation efficiencies. The question then becomes, how do we move to a place in which democratic sensibilities are balanced with allocative efficiency, reflecting norms that are perceived as legitimate, and how this can be reflected in the legal framework for macroprudential policy?

The literature on legitimacy presents a ready bridge between the two types of legitimacy – democratic accountability and transparency. Democratic accountability mechanisms can lead macroprudential authorities to conduct a more thorough assessment of, and be more sensitive to, outputs, because they are being watched and will be required to explain their actions. Accountability moves policy decisions closer to the 'popular will'. Macroprudential authorities can therefore be left to conduct policy with minimal political intervention, while at the same time citizens participate in the policy process. The legal framework for accountability and transparency becomes a decisive factor in the legitimacy of macroprudential policymakers. But, as we saw in the preceding discussion on

[143] Scylla and Charybdis are monsters from Greek mythology who sit on either side of a stretch of narrow waters waiting to snatch whoever passes through. Odysseus must cross these waters during his journey, which is described in Homer's Odyssey, Book XII. Scylla is female creature with six heads, and from her cave devours whatever comes within reach. Charybdis is a creature who creates a whirlpool which sucks whole ships down into the sea three times a day. Odysseus can either ride his ship on the side of Scylla, which means he will lose six men, one for each head on Scylla, or he can choose to ride on the side of Charybdis and hope the entire ship is not sucked down into the chasm. Odysseus thinks he can kill Scylla, but Circe admonishes him for his pride and reminds him Scylla is immortal, the only course is flight. Odysseus chooses to sail close to Scylla and loses six men.

accountability and transparency, there are several gaps in the core elements in the UK, US and EU.

The gaps identified in the first three core elements are largely procedural; several solutions were proffered to address these. The real challenge to macroprudential legitimacy comes from the fourth core element – Criteria for Assessment, which is incomplete. Accountability mechanisms are meaningless if those being monitored have no idea what is expected of them – and society's other expectation of macroprudential policy, namely social justice, has not been taken into account.

One may argue, though, that once policy makers cross over to the socio-political realm, then we must quickly push them back to their rightful side and return such decisions to elected officials or at least agencies that report directly to them. Therefore, it is not the place of macroprudential policy makers to be pursuing social values and ideals. The independent policy maker's realm is defined typically by limiting their goal independence. However, as we saw in Chapter 4, unlike the case of monetary policy, it is virtually impossible to draw a clean line between macroprudential policy and distributional effects. Macroprudential policy straddles the line and cannot be exclusively measured in economic terms. It is unavoidable that macroprudential authorities should make policy with distributional effects. If we are to continue without clarifying the contours of non-economic values of which macroprudential authorities must be cognisant, separate from market values, then we risk creating confused policies.

Macroprudential authorities cannot afford to take policy actions that would run contrary to the values and ideals of society. It is not enough to have functional legitimacy, that functional legitimacy is underpinned by promoting social justice.

Figure 5.1 Legitimacy Preferences

	No Functional Legitimacy	**Functional Legitimacy**
No Democratic Legitimacy	✗	✓
Democratic Legitimacy	✓	✓ (shaded)

(shaded) Social Justice Considerations

Therefore, the macroprudential legal framework should explicitly articulate the non-economic values that policy makers must respect in the conduct of macroprudential policy. This begs the question, how are the values of social justice to be infused in the framework?

5.7. Conclusion

The analysis in Chapter 5 has highlighted that the functional independence of macroprudential authorities is greatly reduced when compared to similar policy making and regulatory agencies. While they may appear to hold all the power and the glory, they are, in fact, underpinned by extensive political control. In this chapter, several explanations were proffered for the shift in the nature of independence, which ranged from the lack of specific or numeric targets, unknown regulator preferences in the context of financial stability, regulatory failures before and during the crisis and the rise of populist sentiment. While it is true that macroprudential policy and regulation lack a strong theoretical and empirical foundation, or that macroprudential policy was developed during extraordinary times, this does not fully explain the increased political control because participation of the executive and legislature will not cure these problems. There is no evidence to show that politicians know any better than the independent policy makers. The more likely explanations, therefore, for the political obsession with controlling the policy-making process are the distributional consequences of macroprudential policy and rising populist sentiment.

This chapter has demonstrated how economic values no longer dominate the pursuit of macroeconomic policy, but the polity is reminding us that non-economic values, like social justice, which we had tried to sideline, are also important and will likely play an influential role in shaping macroprudential policy, especially when this touches on emotive subjects like home ownership. This is not to say economic values are not important; however, a broader view is necessary considering the concerns surrounding social justice.

The true concern is that macroprudential policy, beyond society's control, will have distributional effects that do not accord with societal values. A fundamental problem with macroprudential policy is that we cannot describe with certainty how *fairly* it will be used in achieving financial stability, and that is the source of the impending crisis of legitimacy.

Unfortunately, one cannot simply politely ask macroprudential authorities to avoid making redistributive choices, because one cannot draw a clean line between the economic and non-economic effects, unlike in monetary policy.[144] Increased political control reflects an attempt to ensure that likely distributional outcomes align with societal values.

[144] Although even this distinction in monetary policy has also been challenged in the past and more recently with the introduction of quantitative easing.

The increase of political participation in financial regulation should come as no surprise though. It precedes the crisis. For example, the actions of the US government in subsidising mortgage loans was an indication of raised expectations about access to credit over a life cycle as a social good, because it enhances one's welfare, that the state is responsible for enabling.[145] These expectations were built on past experiences with financial crises dating as far back as the Great Depression, which sparked significant institutional inventions for a particular social purpose, for instance the government-sponsored enterprises, like Fannie Mae, its smaller cousin Ginnie Mae, and Freddie Mac.[146] Once that social purpose became embedded in everyday life and institutions, subsequent financial innovations, like securitisation, simply built upon these platforms.[147]

Current reforms should be viewed in the same light, the most recent crises created expectations, which are being reflected in the institutional reforms, and we can expect future innovations in finance designed to meet those expectations. This leads one to the conclusion that macroprudential policy is a socio-political and economic concept. The decision to activate macroprudential policy should not be solely based on highly rationalised and strongly quantitative reasons, because this risks real social concerns becoming de-personalised. Baker argues that the very foundation of macroprudential policy, a rejection of the fallacy of composition, means that it is built on an acknowledgement of macro moralities and ethics, to which microprudential regulation was closed off by virtue of its focus on the individual entity's actions.[148]

Creating a social justice goal requires answering three questions: (1) What is being distributed? (2) To whom? and (3) Is the principle guiding distribution, for instance, based on need, just deserts, entitlement, pure equality, or proportionality? Only after dealing with these substantive issues can we devise a procedure for distribution.

Chapter 6 offers suggestions for reforming the macroprudential legal framework to include a social justice goal for macroprudential authorities, which offers both substantive and procedural guidance.

[145] L Seabrooke, 'What Do I Get? The Everyday Politics of Expectations and the Subprime Crisis' (2010) 15(1) *New Political Economy* 51.

[146] ibid.

[147] ibid.

[148] Andrew Baker, 'Macroprudential Regimes and the Politics of Social Purpose' (2018) 25(3) *Review of International Political Economy* 293.

6

Restoring the Legitimacy of Macroprudential Authorities

The previous chapter highlighted that the functional independence of macroprudential authorities is greatly reduced when compared to similar independent policy making and regulatory agencies. While they may appear to hold all the power and the glory, they are, in fact, underpinned by extensive political control. But it is not enough to restore the independence of macroprudential authorities, and thus their functional legitimacy, social justice must also be embedded within the pursuit of policy for that legitimacy to be complete.[1] While it appears counterintuitive to give these independent authorities distributive powers, if macroprudential authorities want to retain their independence and, therefore, their legitimacy, giving them a clear trackable social justice mandate reduces the need for political interference and demonstrates to the public how all their work, not just the financial stability aspect, is relevant to society. It is merely bringing accountability and transparency to outputs that are already being felt by the public, therefore bolstering the legitimacy of macroprudential policy makers.

Traditionally, theories of social justice have not figured in the design of financial regulation. However, the fact that social justice does not currently appear in the list of explicit objectives of macroprudential authorities should not blind us to the real possibility and necessity of requiring them to be actively concerned with it. The increasing demands for central bankers to tackle a wide range of social problems via monetary policy, including climate change, income and racial inequality, is a clear indication that the problem is not going away. For instance, in 2021, the US Congress introduced the Federal Reserve Racial Economic Equity Act, a Bill which, among other things, requires the Fed to carry out its duties in a way that supports the elimination of racial and ethnic disparities in employment, income, wealth and access to affordable credit. Fontan, Claveau and Dietsch's survey of the Bank of England, Federal Reserve Board and European Central Bank highlights a shift in central bankers' attitudes towards a belief in the intrinsic value of removing inequalities, beyond the instrumental role in promoting financial stability or

[1] You will recall in the discussion on how to found legitimacy in Chapter 2 that it does not matter if the decision maker is an elected official (pursuing equity and freedom) or an independent policy maker (pursuing allocative efficiency), both must be seen to also prioritise social justice (pursuing equal rights and liberties, equal access to opportunities and the greatest benefits to the least advantaged of society).

more broadly economic growth.[2] In other words, it is recognition that inequality not only hinders efficiency, but is also unjust in and of itself.

The attitudes of central bankers who were in charge in the wake of the global financial crisis (and essentially the architects of macroprudential policy) is also very telling. Mark Carney, governor of the Bank of England from 2013 to 2020, remarked that policy makers should take a broader view of the current and intergenerational effects of their decisions on equality of outcomes and opportunities.[3] Not just because these factors are good for growth and are important determinants of well-being, but also because they appeal to a fundamental sense of justice. In his view, any action taken in response would be to maximise the benefits of the least well off, in the tradition of Rawls. Over at the Fed, in the same year, Chair Janet Yellen stated at a conference at the Boston Fed that she was greatly concerned by the inequality in the United States which continued to increase and thought it was appropriate to question how compatible this was with widely held American values like equality of opportunity.[4]

For Yellen, the greatest dilemma facing American society was ensuring fair and just access to opportunities, because economic opportunities were the foundation for building wealth.[5] She offered no guidance however, on the principle to be followed in distributing opportunities. Yellen and Carney's counterpart at the ECB during the same period, Mario Draghi, was non-committal, only acknowledging that he could understand the dissatisfaction of the youth, poor and unemployed.[6] There was no discussion of any sort of redistribution of advantages or a principle that might guide as such, but policy makers could make sure they were convinced the choices they were making were the right ones.[7]

The rest of this chapter will discuss the practicality of pursuing social justice in economic policy, how social justice considerations can be introduced to macroprudential policy, and how the pursuit of social justice can be balanced with the macroprudential policy maker's primary mandate – financial stability – for instance via the cost–benefit analysis process or as a tiebreaker between policy instruments and/or levels of instrument calibration. I must hasten to add, this chapter does not provide an exhaustive list of potential methods, nor does it include a detailed empirical analysis of those proposed methods for incorporating social justice into macroprudential policy. However, the mere framing of the issue is a worthwhile

[2] C Fontan, F Claveau and P Dietsch, 'Central Banking and Inequalities: Taking off the Blinders' (2016) 15(4) *Politics, Philosophy and Economics* 319.

[3] M Carney, 'Inclusive Capitalism – Creating a Sense of the Systemic' (Speech at Conference on Inclusive Capitalism, London, 27 May 2014). Available at: www.bis.org/review/r140528b.pdf.

[4] JL Yellen, 'Perspectives on Inequality and Opportunity from the Survey of Consumer Finances' (Speech at the Conference on Economic Opportunity and Inequality, Boston, 17 October 2014). Available at: www.federalreserve.gov/newsevents/speech/yellen20141017a.htm.

[5] ibid.

[6] M Draghi, 'Introductory Statement' (Press Conference, Barcelona, 3 May 2012). Available at: www.ecb.europa.eu/press/pressconf/2012/html/is120503.en.html.

[7] ibid.

exercise as it highlights the *feasibility* of creating a legal mandate for social justice in macroprudential policy, having established the *desirability* of doing so in the previous chapters.

6.1. The Practicality of Pursuing Social Justice in Public Policy

An obligation to consider the public interest frequently appears in the legislative frameworks of different regulatory fields with an economic bias, for instance in the competition law and media context.[8] Competition authorities are often permitted to consider a range of non-economic, public interest factors relating to mergers, if controlling the merger not only affects allocative efficiency.

For instance, under Article 21(4) of the EU Merger Regulations, (EUMR), Member States can take action, in line with the general principles and provisions of EU law, to safeguard 'legitimate public interests' that the EUMR does not cover. The regulation lists public security, diversity in media service providers and prudential rules as the three public interest considerations that can be taken into account. Member States can consider other public interest concerns, provided they have been communicated to and assessed by the Commission. Similarly, the UK's Enterprise Act 2002 empowers the Secretary of State to intervene in mergers where the public interest in the same issues highlighted by the EUMR is under threat.[9] Of course, the presence of the phrase 'public interest' in the legal framework alone does not itself signify the establishment of a strong normative concept, it requires articulation.

The Enterprise Act goes further and defines public interest considerations in media mergers as,[10] in the case of a newspaper merger, (i) accurate reporting; (ii) safeguarding freedom of expression; and (iii) plurality in media. In the case of a merger between broadcaster or a broadcaster and newspaper, the public interest considerations are (i) plurality in media reflecting the diversity of audiences; (ii) availability of diverse high-quality broadcasting which appeals to a diverse audience; and (iii) the broadcaster's commitment to the country's broadcasting standards and objectives contained in the Communications Act 2003, s 319.[11] The repeated emphasis on free expression and maintaining a plurality of voices in the media industry resonates with the democratic values of liberty and equality.[12]

[8] M Feintuck, 'Regulatory Rationales Beyond the Economic: In Search of the Public Interest' in Mike Feintuck R Baldwin, M Cave, and M Lodge (eds) *The Oxford Handbook of Regulation* (Oxford University Press, 2010).

[9] Enterprise Act 2002, s 42(2) as read with s 58.

[10] Enterprise Act 2002, s 58.

[11] Ofcom's broadcasting standards govern various issues such as protection of minors, crime and disorder, impartiality, accuracy, offence, harm and manipulation.

[12] Surprisingly, the Enterprise Act 2002 says nothing about national security or financial stability. Feintuck gives a prime example of the inconsistencies that can arise when political values are not

The Enterprise Act points to another public policy area where public interest tests are frequently used, media law – a field that has historically engaged with political values. In the UK, like many other jurisdictions,[13] a public interest standard was embedded in the legal framework for media regulation. In terms of the Communications Act 2003, the UK's independent media regulator, the Office of Communications, (Ofcom), is required:

(a) to further the interests of citizens in relation to communications matters; and
(b) to further the interests of consumers in relevant markets, where appropriate by promoting competition.[14]

The reference to both interests of citizens and consumers points to a separation of political and economic values. In the execution of these functions, apart from competition considerations, Ofcom must have regard to the needs of the disabled, the elderly and low-income households; prevention of crime and disorder; consumers and general public needs; and the different concerns of different communities living in different geographic locations in the UK.[15] It is clear that these provisions are relevant in the present context because they recognise the media's broader importance to society, not just as another economic sector. The regulation of media in this case serves the values of democracy and social justice and can be used as a basis to hold regulators accountable if they are unwilling, or find themselves unable to defend, these values.

The entities driving macroprudential authorities are themselves no strangers to social policies. For instance, since 2019 when Christine Lagarde took over as President, the ECB has been driving action against climate change. Similarly, the Fed in the US has veered into environmental policy by requiring the banks it regulates to demonstrate that they are not overly susceptible to climate risk.

While it's encouraging that policy makers are already pursuing social justice in one form or another, relying on this sort of 'activism' or 'goodwill' from policy makers to get things done is not without its dangers. On the one hand, leaving policy makers to decide the content of social justice risks them departing from actual societal expectations, on the other hand, the policy maker might lack

clearly articulated, in the case of the UK government's handling of the takeover of the HBOS group by LloydsTSB. In 2008, the UK Government and Competition commission were prepared to instantly approve LloydsTSB's takeover of the HBOS group because it was in the 'public interest' to maintain the UK's financial stability. Seven years earlier, similar provisions in the predecessor to the Enterprise Act were used to deny Lloyds' takeover of a major rival, Abbey National.

[13] See, for instance, the United States' Communications Act 1934. It created the Federal Communications Commission, an independent regulator of electronic media, with a mandate to consider 'the public interest, convenience and necessity would be served' when granting broadcasting licences in terms of s 309 of the Act. Section 307 of the Act is even more explicit about the social justice mandate of the Communications Commission, as it requires that broadcasting licences shall be distributed equitably amongst the states to ensure equality of broadcasting services to which citizens are entitled.

[14] Sec 3(1).

[15] The list of issues is longer; however, these were the most salient for our purposes.

goodwill, not be an activist or simply be afraid to act because they lack a clear mandate.

6.2. Content of the Mandate

Simply declaring 'the macroprudential authority shall act in the interests of social justice when deciding policy', is likely to be met with criticisms for being excessively abstract, indeterminate, or analytically weak. To put this problem into context, consider the US Federal Communications Commission, which has faced similar problems with its public interest mandate. As the independent regulator of electronic media, it has a mandate to consider 'the public interest, convenience and necessity' under the Communications Act, s 309. Although this clearly has non-economic connotations, the Act itself does not give any further explanation of what is meant by public interest and the term has regularly been criticised for providing little guidance, even though it fulfils the constitutional requirement that the independent agency's mandate is set by the elected legislature.[16]

There is a need, therefore, to provide for enforceable guidelines in the application of social justice principles. Even though, as stated earlier, social justice has not traditionally featured as part of the financial policy-maker's mandate, this does not mean that existing mandates cannot be modified and/or extended accordingly to ensure that macroprudential authorities aim appropriately at the objectives that reflect society's values.

So, what should a social justice mandate in macroprudential policy look like? The actual goal/objective being pursued by macroprudential policy maker needs to be expressly articulated and emphasised to (i) give policymakers' direction and improve transparency; (ii) enable stakeholders to hold policy-makers accountable; and (iii) hopefully, reduce the need for increasing political involvement in macroprudential policy.

As with financial stability, identifying the general content of a social justice goal is no easy task. This is the fundamental problem with advocating for policy that pursues social justice. In the absence of a coherent vision of the underlying values and claims of social justice, it will be difficult to motivate its inclusion in the legal framework for policies like macroprudential policy. More disturbingly, though, we are likely to revert to the default narrower focus on monopolies, information asymmetries, agency problems and negative externalities, which do not capture the full range of society's justice concerns. Ultimately, the choice of which definition of social justice is to guide policy makers must reflect the public opinions about what is a fair or just society. The principle that a particular society will

[16] See SN Brotman, 'Revisiting the Broadcast Public Interest Standard in Communications Law and Regulation' (23 March 2017) Brookings Institute. Available at: www.brookings.edu/research/revisiting-the-broadcast-public-interest-standard-in-communications-law-and-regulation/.

settle upon will ultimately be the product of democratic participation and dialogue and will evolve through further legislation, judicial decision and other modes of norm creation.

In this book it has been argued that social justice considerations should be guided by the theory of justice as fairness – the Rawlsian perspective. To restate Rawls's view of social justice, if rational persons, acting behind the veil of ignorance, were to choose how to distribute primary goods, which are the fundamental resources needed to realise their life plans, they would reach two conclusions, namely, that (i) each person should have the equal right to engage in activities, as long as they do not infringe the rights of others; and (ii) social and economic inequalities should only be allowed if (a) they are going to maximise improvements for the least-advantaged members of society (the Difference Principle); and (b) there is equal access to opportunities (offices and positions) for all.[17]

From this perspective, macroprudential policy makers would seek to ensure that, firstly, policy decisions or outcomes promote (or at the very least do not hinder) each person's equal right to engage in activities, as long as they do not infringe the rights of others. Secondly, policy decisions should aim for equal distribution of primary goods; however, unequal distribution would be allowed when it advanced the least advantaged members of society in the long run and there was equal access to opportunities.

Primary goods in the financial context could be access to responsible and sustainable transaction accounts, whether with a conventional bank or mobile money, which allow individuals to save and make payments, access to credit and insurance services.[18] Access to credit in particular enables individuals to improve the quality of their lives by purchasing property, starting and expanding businesses, investing in education and health, managing risk, and weathering financial shocks.[19] Almost everything that happens in our lives is ordered around finance.[20]

Credit is, therefore, a resource in society, which ought to be subject to the demands of social justice in its allocation as it is so central to shaping social life. This is not to say that credit should be used as a palliative to address the deeper anxieties of the lower and middle classes.[21] As the recent and previous financial crises have proven, irresponsible excessive credit can be just as harmful, because those with lower income and wealth are hit harder when fortunes reverse, and the financial system becomes unstable. One of the most highlighted aspects of

[17] J Rawls, *A Theory of Justice* (Harvard University Press, 1971), 266.

[18] These are the foundational pieces of financial inclusion. Available at: www.worldbank.org/en/topic/financialinclusion/overview.

[19] ibid.

[20] WN Goetzmann, RJ Shiller, J Mendillo, DF Swensen, Z Chen, 'What Should Finance Do for Society?' (2 January 2014), Yale Insights. Available at: www.insights.som.yale.edu/insights/what-should-finance-do-society.

[21] As Rajan accuses pre-crisis governments of doing. See RG Rajan, *Fault Lines* (Princeton University Press, 2010) 9.

financial inclusion is access to cheap credit, in a manner that neither exploits nor harms borrowers.

This brings us to the second principle of justice as fairness – inequalities in financial policy may be allowed if they are arranged to the greatest benefit of the least advantaged members of society. How are policy makers to define 'least advantaged'? The legal frameworks for macroprudential policy provide a ready answer for this. For example, in the US, where macroprudential policy focuses on activities in the financial sector, there is also reference to the people most affected by the systemic risk those activities pose – namely low-income, minority, or underserved communities.

6.3. Operationalising Social Justice in Macroprudential Policy

While defining the content of the mandate is a powerful way of giving direction it is only one half of the equation – there is still the matter of how it is to be executed. You will recall that the third Core Principle of Accountability – Content of the obligation – requires policy makers to give an account of their decisions, to explain and justify the decision and course of action taken and, where harm or error is proved, to take responsibility and provide amends or redress. This translates to *how* accountability is to be given, which necessitates a decision-making mechanism that all stakeholders can follow and critically consider.

6.3.1. 'Justice Enhanced' Cost–Benefit Analysis

The UK is the most progressive when it comes to endorsing distributional concerns in macroprudential policy. The FPC has stated that it takes distributional concerns into account when weighing the benefits and costs of a proposed policy instrument. For instance, when the FPC exercises its powers over housing instruments, such as the LTI and DTI ratios, it considers amongst the consequences, the impact on economic activity, compliance costs to firms, leakages, competition implications, impact on financial products and *distributional impact*. An assessment of distributional impact includes whether a proposed Direction or Recommendation would disproportionately affect certain types of firms, such as mutual and private banks that lend less and therefore do not contribute to systemic risk to the same extent, or consumers like young borrowers and first-time buyers, who do not have enough income or assets to meet the ratio.[22]

[22] For instance, when the FPC was motivating for Treasury to grant it additional powers over the housing market, namely the LTI and DTI ratios. See Financial Policy Committee, 'Financial Policy Committee statement on housing market powers of Direction from its policy meeting, 26 September

Cost–Benefit Analysis (CBA) is a process often used by decision makers to evaluate alternative courses of action, by quantifying the costs and benefits of each one, and choosing the most appropriate alternative. Hopefully, by choosing rules that produce greater benefits than losses, the public interest is served. CBA is not, however, designed to be the sole basis for choosing a particular course of action; instead, it is a tool to support decision making. It does not supplant policy judgement; but provides important information to which the policy maker will have regard in reaching decisions likely to further its objectives.

On the one hand, CBA increases policy makers' understanding of the consequences of proposed decisions, compares actual outcomes to expected effects and determines causes from deviations that may need correction. On the other hand, it forces them to be more transparent and lay bare their assumptions about the effects of policy on the public, which also assists public understanding of the policy. Of course, not all the costs or benefits of a course of action can be monetised, but still, a legal mandate for policy makers to conduct CBA can still be useful for encouraging 'evidence-based' rather than intuitive decision making. While discretion is the bedrock of independent agencies, CBA allows more predictability in policy decisions, making compliance with changes less costly.

The quantified CBA of proposed rules is mandatory for all financial regulatory agencies in the UK. Unless they cannot reasonably estimate the costs and benefits or it would not be practical to do so, reasons for failure to conduct the CBA must be provided.[23] Such rulemakings and CBA are subject to judicial review, although judicial review has not generally been used to challenge rules for inadequate CBA.[24] The FPC's macroprudential policy decisions are no exception, and are also subject to cost–benefit analysis under the Bank of England Act, s 9F. The FPC must guarantee that:

> a burden or restriction which is imposed on a person, or on the carrying on of an activity, should be proportionate to the benefits.[25]

Any proposal for a new macroprudential instrument must include a CBA, unless the costs and benefits cannot be estimated, or it would be impractical to do so.[26]

2014' (Bank of England 2 October 2014). Available at: www.bankofengland.co.uk/-/media/boe/files/statement/2014/fpc-statement-from-its-policy-meeting-26-september-2014.

[23] Financial Services Act, 2012, amending, inter alia, the Financial Services and Markets Act 2000, ss 138I (Financial Conduct Authority) and 138J (Prudential Regulation Authority).

[24] Coates finds only one example of a court decision that even refers to CBA, namely *R (on the application of the British Bankers Association) v FSA et al* [2011] EWHC (Admin) 999 (Eng); wherein the court rejected the plaintiff's challenge to the assertion that the FSA principles created any obligations as between firms and customers in the context of 'payment protection insurance'. See JC Coates IV, 'Cost–Benefit Analysis of Financial Regulation: Case Studies and Implications' (2015) 4(124) *Yale Law Journal* 882.

[25] Bank of England Act 1998, s 9F.

[26] As far as I can tell, neither the ESRB nor FSOC is subject to a similar formal requirement to conduct CBAs. The FSOC may eventually become subject to a requirement though. Independent agencies in the US, in contrast to executive agencies, are not subject to an explicit legal CBA requirement. Despite the absence of a formal requirement, some independent agencies, on their own initiative, do conduct CBA

Macroprudential policy presents an ideal policy area for the conduct of CBA. Kohn highlights the numerous benefits and costs that macroprudential policy entails, such as avoiding damage to the economy and society and use of taxpayer funds on the benefits side, but at the same time increased costs of lending and lower credit availability on the costs side.[27] CBA provides a means for macroprudential authority to articulate the reasons behind policies with such polar effects.

Although CBA applies efficiency yardsticks, it is not entirely counterintuitive to use it as a guide for explicit redistributive purposes. In reality, the valuations that are the components of CBA are a product of the present distribution of wealth, which skews the value placed on products by different people.[28] CBA, which does not take into account distribution of costs and benefits, assumes that the present distribution is acceptable, and is likely to favour those who are economically better off. A justice enhanced CBA attempts to avoid the moral deficiencies of our current system, without abandoning its traditional strengths and benefits.

While FPC has stated that it takes distributional impact into account when conducting CBA, it does not specify how this is achieved. Presumably, the UK Treasury Green Book provides guidance. The Green Book recommends attaching distributional weights to costs and benefits in the analysis, unless the analyst can demonstrate it is undesirable to do so.[29] Distributional weighting adjusts costs

of proposed rules and, more importantly, include distributional concerns. The SEC, for instance, issued an internal guidance for economic analysis in rulemaking. The guidance directs that the agency should include, compliance costs, direct costs, and indirect costs. In general, types of indirect costs can include the distributional effects of the rule.

Calls have increased to subject independent agencies to the same formal requirements as executive agencies to conduct CBA, and several Bills have been introduced which would require agencies, like the FSOC, to conduct a CBA of decisions, starting with the Independent Agency Regulatory Analysis Bill of 2012. In terms of the Act, the President may impose on independent regulatory agency CBA requirements that are applicable to other agencies and choose rules based on the benefits relative to the costs. The president may also require economically significant rules to be subjected to CBA, to the extent that the costs and benefits can be quantified. It should also be noted that unlike in the UK, compliance or non-compliance with the cost–benefit analysis requirement shall not be subject to judicial review.

The Bill, however, makes no mention of the factors to be included in the CBA, including any distributive impacts. Distributional impacts will be considered when conducting a cost-effectiveness analysis. Cost-effectiveness analysis is distinct from cost–benefit analysis. Whereas the later seeks to identify the policy choice offering the greatest benefits, the former is a method for identifying an option with the lowest present value to meet the same level of objective.

Interestingly, the Bill proposes to exclude monetary policy from mandatory CBA. Coates posits that it is because there may be rules that are incapable of satisfying a cost–benefit test, such a rule may not be justifiable in quantitative terms but may still be valuable. In any case, as previously alluded to, hardwiring monetary policy decisions into legislation may not be a good idea. The exemption of monetary policy raises questions about the desirability of extending the same to another policy domain, specifically macroprudential policy.

[27] D Kohn, 'Institutions for Macroprudential Regulation: The UK and the US' (14 April 2014) *Brookings Institute*. Available at: www.brookings.edu/on-the-record/institutions-for-macroprudential-regulation-the-uk-and-the-u-s/.

[28] R Baldwin, M Cave and M Lodge, *Understanding Regulation: Theory, Strategy, and Practice* 2nd edn (Oxford University Press 2011).

[29] HM Treasury, *The Green Book: Central Government Guidance on Appraisal and Evaluation* (The Stationery Office, 2018).

and benefits by attaching weights to different CBA inputs. These inputs can reflect aspects of individuals' socio-economic status, like income, health, life expectancy, or environmental quality.[30] Those falling on the disadvantaged end of these inputs would receive larger weights.

There are, however, several reasons why distributional weights are difficult to justify (and in fact CBA in general) as a method for implementing social justice. The most often cited argument against weighted CBA is that the weights are arbitrary. Agencies may lack the information needed to calculate weights, because they are a measure of utility which is highly subjective. Alternatively, they may face resource and time constraints and, in the end, are forced to make rough justice decisions. In any case, the result of weighted CBA gives a picture of the aggregate distributional impact. In effect distributional concerns of individuals and groups are buried or overlooked in the aggregated results.

Given the limitations with CBA, the best strategy for ensuring a comprehensive analysis of policy, taking into account social justice, would be to analyse distributional consequences separately from CBA and in light of the government's wider distributional policies. The results may be referred to in the CBA summary. The FPC appears to have taken this approach of providing a separate qualitative analysis of distributional effects in the summary of the CBA. The June 2014 Financial Stability Report suggests that this is the actual method adopted by the FPC when considering distributional impacts.[31]

In 2014, the FPC provided a *qualitative* assessment to support its recommendation that firms' lending to borrowers with a loan to income ratio of more than 4.5 per cent should be limited to 15 per cent of the firm's total mortgage book. The FPC created two scenarios reflecting how the housing market and credit might evolve over three years and measured the costs and benefits of the recommendation in either scenario. Rather than conducting a weighted CBA, the FPC simply highlighted the potential distributional impact, on some borrowers particularly those buying more expensive houses and first-time buyers who rely heavily on borrowing to enter the property market.

How are policies to be evaluated if distributional outcomes point towards a different policy decision than efficiency outcomes would require? Goals will have to be prioritised. The prioritisation of social justice over economic efficiency may be a difficult sell however, given that the primary purpose of macroprudential policy is allocative efficiency. The argument thus far has been that allocative efficiency should not come at the expense of social justice, but that is not to say social justice should come at the expense of financial stability either.

[30] See M Adler and E Posner, *New Foundations of Cost–Benefit Analysis* (Harvard University Press, 2006) and M Adler, 'Cost–Benefit Analysis and Distributional Weight: An Overview' (2013) Duke Environmental and Energy Economics Working Paper Series EE 13-04.

[31] Bank of England, 'Assessing the Impact of the FPC's Recommendations on the Mortgage Market' (June 2014) Financial Stability Report 60.

6.3.2. Social Justice as a Tiebreaker

The tensions between financial stability and social justice could be avoided by using the social justice analysis as a tiebreaker between competing policy proposals. By using social justice values as a tiebreaker when considering different policy instruments, or calibration of instruments, policy makers can avoid the two values of allocative efficiency and social justice coming into direct conflict. Instead, the policy decision will follow a two-step process, the first step being an economic analysis, which can follow the conventional CBA and the second step being an evaluation of which option accords with government policy on social justice.[32] This effectively creates a hierarchy of values, where social justice is subordinate to allocative efficiency. This is not necessarily problematic because ultimately the raison d'être of macroprudential authorities is to maintain allocative efficiency of the financial system. Combining CBA with the tiebreaker approach will assist macroprudential authorities to choose policies that improve allocative efficiency *and* are fair as well.

The ECB, in its capacity as monetary authority, provides an example of the tiebreaker condition as part of its mandate. The Treaty on the Functioning of the European Union, Article 127(1) (the Lisbon Treaty) states that:

> [w]ithout prejudice to the objective of price stability, the ESCB [European System of Central Banks] shall support the general economic policies in the Union with a view to contributing to the achievement of the objectives of the Union as laid down in Article 3 of the Treaty on European Union.

Article 3 of the Treaty on European Union explicitly mentions social justice as one such objective. When selecting policy alternatives, price stability takes precedence, but also those alternatives that align with Union objectives laid out in Article 3.

6.4. Balancing Trade-offs with Competing Mandates

Introducing a social justice mandate will not come without its costs. Mr Draghi's reluctance to commit the ECB to a social justice goal in monetary policy, noted

[32] I have deliberately avoided framing the approach as a Multi-criteria Analysis, (MCA). MCA assists policy makers in selecting alternative projects, which have significant social and economic impact, taking into account several criteria. It is suited to decision making with more than one goal, advocated by different interest groups or stakeholders, and where trade-offs exist between the different goals. MCA enables policy makers to craft different options based on the extent to which different policies meet a set of criteria. The different criteria are scored and weighted according to their importance in achieving the overall policy objectives. The final score indicates the most effective, therefore preferable, option. The policy maker can choose to use one option or a mix of options. MCA is intuitively appealing because it highlights the political and economic effects separately, but provides a clean, mathematical method of combining the outcomes for easy measurement. However, it suffers from the same fundamental problem as CBA – the weighting system is prone to arbitrariness.

in the introduction to this chapter, may well be justified, when one considers the problems that could come with imposing multiple mandates on an independent central bank – particularly one on social justice – such as the impact of politics, the lack of sufficient financial literature, and the push and pull of financial stability and economic growth. The same concerns would extend to independent macroprudential authorities. Some of the more pressing include the following:

6.4.1. Macroprudential Policy is a Blunt Instrument

As with monetary policy, the argument could be made that macroprudential policy tools are too blunt. Being tools targeted towards *systemic risk*, macroprudential policy tools are, in effect, designed to aim at aggregate outcomes not to target subgroups of the population, in the same way as, for instance, micro-prudential regulation. In any case, the tax and transfer policy, administered by the central government, is better placed to reduce inequalities.

In response to the first objection, while macroprudential policy may be designed to address systemic risk, it is implemented via what are essentially microprudential tools; these can be fine-tuned to react to specific market segments. Prime examples are instruments that target borrower resilience, like the UK's LTV and ICR limits for mortgages on buy-to-let properties, or the LTV and DTI limits for mortgages on owner-occupied properties.

In response to the second objection, I borrow from Fontan et al's arguments in favour of monetary policy being used for distributional purposes. Firstly, the state's ability to impose taxes may be curtailed in the current environment characterised by capital mobility. Individuals may simply choose to operate in jurisdictions with favourable tax policies. There is no reason why macroprudential cannot step in and fill the gap. Secondly, and more importantly, direct tax and transfer policies can generate efficiency losses, by causing changes in the behaviour of market participants. For instance, higher taxes raise the prices of goods, leading buyers to consume less, while in the opposite case, a lowering of taxes may discourage sellers from producing. In either case the market is operating below the optimum equilibrium. Other policies can act as substitutes that avoid efficiency losses in the first place.

To be clear, my argument in this book does not deny the obvious point that there are less blunt instruments to address issues of social justice, such as fiscal policy. It is rather aimed at the assumption that macroprudential policy is completely divorced from such distributional discussions and is legitimated solely through its ability to maintain allocative efficiency. To continue to try and maintain a solid wall between economic and non-economic goals risks policy outcomes which diverge significantly from society's expectations. This is not to suggest that the wall should be completely torn down but, to use an analogy, windows may be built that let the light through and allow independent macroprudential policy makers to keep sight of other interests. Of course, this means that, on the other side of the wall, the interests must be clear for all to see.

6.4.2. Agency Drift

There is the danger that unelected macroprudential authorities, as agents, will drift from the principal, society's, standards of justice, which implies the need for greater control of the so-called independent agency. This runs contrary to the whole premise of independent agencies, that they can offer time-consistency and credible commitment because they remain autonomous. However, the danger of agency drift can easily be remedied via tightening accountability measures. As highlighted in Chapter 6, control and accountability are different concepts. Accountability allows the independent agency to retain its autonomy but provides an ex-ante or ex-post mechanism for the principal to ensure the agent is pursuing its mandate in a way that accords with the principal's values.

6.4.3. Effect on Other Policy Mandates

Macroprudential authorities will be faced with trade-offs between their financial stability and social justice goals. On the one hand, as we saw in Chapter 4, macroprudential policy can shape the distribution of credit, and therefore income and wealth.[33] The home mortgage is an example of where macroprudential policy and the demands of social justice intersect. Caps on loan-to-value ratios are being used to curb financial imbalances, by limiting credit growth in mortgage markets. However, lowering caps also affects individuals' access to housing, because they are required to post more collateral to get a mortgage, which may be impossible for individuals who already have low income and no assets, thus multiplying their disadvantage.

On the other hand, loosening mortgage lending standards in order to maintain a pathway to home ownership could promote the sort of pre-crisis profligacy of subprime mortgages that led to financial instability – the costs of which are felt more acutely by the poor. The legal framework in the US is cognisant of this, and the Dodd-Frank Act provides that when the FSOC designates a SIFI, per s 113, or recommends for more stringent regulation of a SIFI, per s 115, the Council should take into account whether the firm is

> a source of credit for households, businesses, and State and local governments … and … a source of credit for low-income, minority, or underserved communities, *and*

[33] For more empirical studies on the effects of macroprudential policy on income and wealth see J Frost and R van Stralen, 'Macroprudential Policy and Income Inequality' (May 2018) DNB Working Paper No 598/May 2018.

> *the impact that the failure of such company would have on the availability of credit in such communities* (emphasis mine).

There is also reference to low-income, minority, or underserved communities in s 120, which provides that the FSOC may recommend stricter regulation of a financial activity or practice if the Council determines that an activity could lead to 'problems spreading among ... low-income, minority, or underserved communities'. In short, prioritising short-term social justice at the expense of long-term stability can be just as detrimental as focusing solely on efficiency objectives. What is required is a fine balancing act.

Prioritising trade-offs is inherently a political task and the macroprudential policymakers should receive explicit guidance on which secondary objectives are the most relevant in a particular situation. Setting priorities between different objectives remains the preserve of elected officials. This is why a formal procedure involving elected officials should be used to specify and prioritise the policy areas where the macroprudential policy makers would be expected to deliver social justice.

In this manner, macroprudential policy makers would receive renewed legitimacy for an expanded set of goals. They could work efficiently, deploying their full toolkit towards a clear and politically defined set of policy objectives, guided by democratic institutions, but without the need for increased political involvement in policy making.

6.5. Conclusion

The previous chapters established the desirability of introducing an explicit social justice mandate to macroprudential policy, as a basis for strengthening the legitimacy of macroprudential authorities. Indeed, even amongst independent policy makers, there is recognition of the importance of tempering efficiency concerns with ideals of fairness and justice. There are, of course, arguments that can be raised against this. These arguments resemble the arguments of old, similar to those made against granting a financial stability mandate to an independent central bank that also holds monetary policy and microprudential regulation mandates. The issues raised by these arguments are certainly a cause for concern. Regardless, while these dangers are real, they should not deter us from leveraging macroprudential policy for social justice. Macroprudential authorities ought to make a substantive commitment to social justice. Of course, recognising the problem says nothing about how it is to be addressed, especially in light of the other objectives already pursued by macroprudential authorities.

This chapter suggested weighted cost–benefit analysis as a possible method for introducing social justice concerns. Alternatively, social justice considerations can be used as a tiebreaker when choosing from different, but equally attractive, macroprudential policy options. Naturally, the suggested methods are neither free from flaws, nor are they exhaustive. But even if the processes do not ultimately lead to justice, they can still contribute to knowledge building on policy trade-offs between the optimal level of financial stability and the likely distributional of benefits and burdens in society, or, alternatively, between the preferable distribution of benefits and burdens and possible efficiency losses. At the very least, information on distribution would provide grounds for better-informed debate with those who disagree on whether macroprudential policy ought to be used to support social justice goals in the first place, as well as to determine whether some sort of compensatory action is needed.

The most important outcome from the whole process, however, is that eventually we, as a society, will have to face, head-on, the question of what a just society means. For as long as this remains unspecified, it will be a fragile basis for intervention and likely to be ignored by those governing. The end result will be discontent amongst the governed, and a crisis of legitimacy, not only for macroprudential authorities, but also, possibly, for all forms of government.

7

Conclusion

Legitimacy is critical to the proper functioning of macroprudential policy because it justifies the exercise of authority which, in turn, motivates acceptance of the directives issued by the macroprudential authority. Evaluating the legitimacy of the independent macroprudential authorities involves two steps, firstly, determining how regulators acquire legitimacy in the first place, and secondly measuring the extent to which macroprudential authorities meet the requirements of legitimacy. To answer the first question, Chapter 2 examined the theoretical underpinnings of the concept of legitimacy.

It was concluded that the acceptance of authority is predicated on either descriptive or normative grounds. Between the two, normative sources of legitimacy which are derived from the value system of those who are subject to authority and whose compliance is sought, provide the most complete justification for the exercise of authority. Normative values can be further broken down into the political, such as democracy, economic, such as allocative efficiency, and the social. Institutions which govern society may be arranged in a way that allows us to best achieve those values. Therefore, their authority is based on those values. Thus, the authority of central government finds its basis in the values of democracy that are embodied by the electoral process.

However, in some areas of public policy, elected decision-makers may be susceptible to the time-inconsistency problem and struggle with credible commitment to policy, in order to pander to the electorate, leading to inefficient results. The solution is to shift responsibility for those policy areas to an alternative system of governance – independent policy makers. The move to the independent policy maker indicates that sometimes democracy does not exhaust society's values, and those other concerns may rank ahead of democratic values.

A prime example is in the field of monetary policy. Central bank independence is justified not by reference to principles of democracy, but values of allocative efficiency. Empirical evidence suggests that central bankers with operational independence produce more efficient results, than when political authorities implement monetary policy, because they are more consistent over time and can offer credible commitment to policy. Government still exercises political control as it sets the goal of the central bank, meaning central bankers have little political independence, however they can execute policy at their discretion. They are deemed better able to achieve the objectives of monetary policy than the political authorities, precisely because they are independent from and insulated against political pressures that may steer monetary policy in a less than optimal direction.

The authority of independent financial policy makers can also be justified by reference to the values of allocative efficiency. Chapter 3 explored the functions of the financial system, the need for regulation and the types of regulation that might be required. The main role of the financial system is to allocate financial resources; however, market failures may lead to its inefficient functioning. Financial regulators step in to right those failures, via regulations that address the safety and soundness of financial intermediaries, consumer protection, market integrity and financial stability. Macroprudential policy deals specifically with the market failures resulting in financial instability, namely excessive credit cycles and the network of interconnections amongst financial intermediaries that propagate failures.

As we saw in Chapter 4, macroprudential authorities employ a number of countercyclical and structural instruments, which seek to either dampen the credit cycle or build the financial system's resilience to shocks. The policy may prove to be unpopular, however, as it essentially withdraws the availability of credit during good times, when to the ordinary person it is seemingly unnecessary. However, as we witnessed in the Global Financial Crisis of 2007–2008, it is precisely during the good times that instability builds up. The fact that the policy is likely to be unpopular with the electorate makes it susceptible to time-inconsistency and credible commitment problems. Therefore, like monetary policy, macroprudential policy requires a policy maker who is free from the influence of the electoral cycle, one who operates independently. The legitimacy of macroprudential policy makers derives, therefore, from values of allocative efficiency as embodied in their independence.

Chapter 5 was dedicated to evaluating the independence, accountability and transparency of macroprudential policy makers. After broadly describing the different policy governance frameworks in use around the globe, I disaggregated and evaluated agency independence, accountability and transparency as articulated in the legislation of the UK, the US and the EU. Notable differences exist in the articulation of each. The differences suggest that, in fact, while macroprudential authorities might be more democratic than other independent agencies, they fall short in functional independence. Increasing political control of macroprudential authorities compromises their technocratic effectiveness and ultimately their legitimacy, which is largely a function of their consistency and credibility as independent experts, rather than their democratic credentials. Furthermore, in all three of the jurisdictions reviewed, common problems were identified in meeting all four criteria for an accountability mechanism. However, the biggest problem identified was vagueness surrounding the criteria for evaluation, which should consist not only of effective results, but also results which accord with societal values. The same values which legitimate authority.

Reasons behind the shift towards greater political involvement were explored in Chapter 5. Reasons ranged from the lack of specific or numeric targets, unknown regulator preferences in the context of financial stability, regulatory failures before and during the crisis and the rise of populist sentiment. The response has been to increase political control, however, there is no evidence to show that politicians know any better than the independent regulators. The more likely explanation for the political obsession with controlling the regulatory process are the distributional consequences of macroprudential policy and the lack of an accountability mechanism to ensure distributional effects of macroprudential policy align with social justice expectations.

To restore the legitimacy of macroprudential authorities, political influence must, therefore, be reduced. The next step is to realign policy makers' mandate with societal values.

It is taken for granted that as long as macroprudential policy achieves financial stability, ergo meeting the values of allocative efficiency, then it has achieved its objectives. That this is the sole criterion for evaluation. However, the increased political control we saw in Chapter 5 suggests that allocative efficiency is not the only value to which macroprudential policy must aspire. There is a range of values and ideals, which economic analysis cannot account for, and which are not satisfied by focusing on market efficiency alone. As we saw, boosting the democratic credentials of macroprudential authorities does not fully satisfy these non-economic values either.

Social justice was established early on as being a growing concern among citizens, who are dissatisfied with the pervasive inequalities propagated by the financial system. More and more, citizens are demanding that those who exercise authority over them must do so in a way that promotes social justice. And really, no convincing argument exists why this should not be so. It appears macroprudential policy is not immune to the pressure, especially since some policy instruments have a direct distributive impact. Thus, macroprudential policy needs to be aligned with the societal values of democracy, allocative efficiency *and* social justice. The legitimacy of macroprudential authorities relies on all three sets of values, and the excessive focus on allocative efficiency, which is a consequence of depoliticisation of the process, is likely to lead to the exclusion or marginalisation of other values, specifically social justice.

Viewed from this angle, post-crisis financial reform is not only about finding a superior technical fix to manage risk, but also how best to serve the broader population. Establishing a link between social justice and macroprudential policy, would not only reassert the interests of the collective alongside the dominant voice of the market, but boost the legitimacy of policy makers. If governments hope to enhance public backing for the macroprudential project, then they will have to grant macroprudential authorities the mandate to meet *all* society's expectations. Simply asserting the value of financial stability will not suffice. Furthermore, explicitly mentioning social justice in the goal framework also sets boundaries for how far distributional considerations should influence decisions, rather than pretend there are no distributional effects and leave ourselves subject to inconsistencies. This is not to say that expanding the mandate of macroprudential authorities is not without its costs. Cultivating social justice may very well erode macroprudential authorities' claims to technical, impartial and non-political oversight. A balance will have to be struck.

Articulating the additional mandate will require, firstly, a vision of what is socially just and secondly, connecting this vision to the empirical and quantitative processes of macroprudential policy. Chapter 6 demonstrated that it is easier said than done, to pin down the *general* substantive content of social justice and weave it into the policy-making process. Regardless, 'difficult' is not the same as 'impossible'. Social justice values have been invoked before in various shapes and forms, in numerous public policy arenas and, as the chapter also suggested, current methodologies in use, like the cost–benefit analysis, can be leveraged to introduce social justice concerns to macroprudential policy. Even if this thesis did not arrive at a final formula for articulating a social justice mandate, alongside one for financial stability, it is hoped that it at least provided the reader with some insights into the possibilities.

The argument advanced in this book was not a diatribe against the 'evil empire' but sought to highlight the need to rebalance the rationale for financial regulation. The bottom line is macroprudential policy demands taking into account a wider range of factors than are currently being considered. It may be the only way macroprudential authorities can achieve legitimacy and continue to enjoy the power and the glory.

ANNEXURE 1: SUMMARY OF THE LEGAL BASIS FOR IMPLEMENTATION OF MACROPRUDENTIAL POLICY TOOLS IN THE US, UK AND THE EU

	Time-varying Instruments	Cross-sectional Instruments
UK FPC may make recommendations and, in relation to macroprudential measures prescribed by secondary legislation, give directions to the Prudential Regulation Authority (PRA) and the Financial Conduct Authority (FCA) – BoE Act 1998, ss 9H & 9O. A 'macro-prudential measure' included in any direction to regulators shall be prescribed by the Treasury by order, approved by resolution of each House of Parliament – BoE Act 1998, s 9L Can only use tools from the range set out by the Minister of Finance and development of any additional macro-prudential instruments will be undertaken in consultation with the Treasury – BoE Act 1998, s 9H.	• CCyB – Capital requirements (Capital Buffers and Macro-prudential Measures) Regulations 2014 (2014/894) and Chapter 3, 'Countercyclical Capital Buffer' of the Capital Buffers Part of the PRA Rulebook • CCB – Capital Requirements (Capital Buffers and Macro-prudential Measures) Regulations 2014 (2014/894) • LTV and ICR limits for mortgages on buy-to-let properties – The Bank of England Act 1998 (Macro-prudential Measures) Order 2016 • LTV and DTI limits for mortgages on owner-occupied properties – the Bank of England Act 1998 (Macro-prudential Measures) Order 2015 • Countercyclical leverage ratio – The Bank of England Act 1998 (Macro-prudential Measures) (No 2) Order 2015	• Sectoral capital requirements for exposures in housing and financial sectors – The Bank of England Act 1998 (Macro-prudential Measures) Order 2013 • G-SII Buffer – (Capital Buffers and Macro-prudential Measures) Regulations 2014 (2014/894) • O-SII Buffer – (Capital Buffers and Macro-prudential Measures) Regulations 2014 (2014/894)

(continued)

(Continued)

	Time-varying Instruments	Cross-sectional Instruments
US	• CcyB • Supplementary leverage ratio	• FSOC may recommend tighter requirements for SIFIs in regard to risk-based capital requirements; leverage limits; liquidity requirements; resolution plan and credit exposure report requirements; concentration limits; a contingent capital requirement; enhanced public disclosures; short-term debt limits; and overall risk management requirements – Dodd-Frank Act, s 115 • FSOC may recommend more stringent regulation of a financial activity by the primary regulator, if the conduct, scope, nature, size, scale, concentration, or interconnectedness of such activity or practice could create or increase the risk of significant liquidity, credit, or other problems spreading among bank holding companies and nonbank financial companies, financial markets of the United States, or low-income, minority, or underserved communities – Dodd-Frank Act, s 120. • Fed can take action to mitigate threats to financial stability, including limiting mergers, acquisitions and certain financial products, terminating and imposing conditions on activities or force the sale and transfer of assets –Dodd-Frank Act, s 121.

(continued)

(Continued)

	Time-varying Instruments	Cross-sectional Instruments
		• In order to prevent or mitigate risks to the financial stability of the United States that could arise from the material financial distress or failure, or ongoing activities, of large, interconnected financial institutions, the Board of Governors shall, on its own or pursuant to recommendations FSOC, establish prudential standards for SIFIs that shall include risk-based capital requirements, liquidity requirements; overall risk management requirements; resolution plan and credit exposure report requirements; and concentration limits, contingent capital; risk committee, stress tests, leverage limitation, short-term debt limit, inclusion of off-balance sheet activities in capital computation – Dodd-Frank Act, s 165(a) • Fed can prescribe regulations establishing requirements to provide for the early remediation of financial distress of a nonbank financial company, excluding financial assistance – Dodd-Frank Act, s 166 • Minimum risk-based capital requirements on a consolidated basis for insured depository institutions, depository institution holding companies, and nonbank financial companies supervised by the Board of Governors – Dodd-Frank Act, s 171

(continued)

(Continued)

	Time-varying Instruments	Cross-sectional Instruments
		• Federal banking agencies shall develop capital requirements that address the risks that the activities of such institutions pose, not only to the institution engaging in the activity, but to other public and private stakeholders in the event of adverse performance, disruption, or failure of the institution or the activity – Dodd-Frank Act, s 171 • Liquidity Coverage Ratio
EU National competent/ designated authorities of Eurosystem Member States shall apply requirements for capital buffers and own funds to be held, including countercyclical buffer rates, and any other measures aimed at addressing systemic or macro-prudential risks set out of the CRR and CRD IV – SSM Regulation, art 5(1) ECB may apply higher requirements than those set by national competent/designated authorities of Eurosystem for capital buffers and own funds to be held, including countercyclical buffer rates, and any other measures aimed at addressing systemic or macro-prudential risks set out in the CRR and CRD IV – SSM Regulation, art 5(2)	• Countercyclical capital buffer – art 130; CRD, arts 135–140 • Sectoral RWs – CRR, arts 124(2), 103, 458(2)(d)(vi), • LDG floors – CRR, art 164 • Sectoral LTV, LTI and DTI – CRD, art 104, National Law • LTD, LTSF limits – CRD, art 104, National Law • Time-varying LCR and NSFR – CRR, art 458 • Leverage Ratio – National Law	• Capital buffers for G-SIIs and O-SIIs – CRD, Art 131, Guidelines on the criteria to determine the conditions of application of Directive 2013/36/EU, art 131(3) (CRD) in relation to the assessment of other systemically important institutions (O-SIIs) • Systemic risk buffer – CRD, arts 133–134 • Liquidity Surcharges – CRD, art 105 • Direct sectorial capital requirement – CRD, art 133; CRR, arts 458 and 92; CRD, art 103 • Large exposure requirements – CRR, art 458 • Measures for intra-financial sector exposures – CRR, art 458 • Increased capital conservation buffer – CRR, art 458 • Increased own funds requirements – CRD, art 106

ANNEXURE 2: LEGAL ARTICULATION OF INDEPENDENCE IN MACROPRUDENTIAL POLICY

	UK	US	EU
Objective	Bank shall protect and enhance the stability of the financial system of the United Kingdom – BoE Act 1998, s 2A Treasury may by notice in writing to the Financial Policy Committee specify what the economic policy of Her Majesty's Government is to be taken to be – BoE Act 1998, s 9D	FSOC goal is to identify risks to the financial system that may arise from large, complex financial institutions, promote market discipline by reducing expectations of federal financial support for failing institutions; and respond to emerging threats to the stability of the U.S. financial system – Dodd-Frank Act, s 112	ESRB seeks to mitigate systemic risks to financial stability – ESRB Regulation, art 3(1). Intermediate objectives are to mitigate and prevent excessive credit growth and leverage, and excessive maturity mismatch and market illiquidity; to limit direct and indirect exposure concentrations; to limit the systemic impact of misaligned incentives with a view to reducing moral hazard; and to strengthen the resilience of financial infrastructures – Recommendation A2(a) on Objectives and Instruments

(continued)

(Continued)

	UK	US	EU
Appointment	Governed by the same Court of Directors at the top. Pluralistic Financial Policy Committee, (FPC), consisting of the Governor and Deputy Governors of the Bank, excluding the COO; the Chief Executive of the Financial Conduct Authority; one member appointed by the Governor of the Bank after consultation with the Chancellor; five members appointed by the Chancellor; and a representative of the Treasury – BoE Act 1998, s 9B	Voting members include Secretary of Treasury, who sits as Chairperson and Chairpersons of the Fed, Commodity Futures Trading Commission, Federal Deposit Insurance Corporation, Federal Housing Finance Agency, National Credit Union Administration, Office of the Comptroller of the Currency, Securities and Exchange Commission, Consumer Financial Protection Bureau; and an independent member appointed by the President, by and with the advice and consent of the Senate, having insurance expertise – Dodd-Frank Act, s 111(b) 1&2 Non-voting members, who shall serve in an advisory capacity as a non-voting member of the Council, shall be the Director of the Office of Financial Research; the Director of the Federal Insurance Office; a State insurance commissioner, to be designated by a selection process determined by the State insurance commissioners; a State banking supervisor, to be designated by a selection process determined by the State banking supervisors; and a State securities commissioner (or an officer performing like functions), to be designated by a selection process determined by such State securities commissioners – Dodd-Frank Act, s 111(b) 1&2	Members include President and Vice-president of the ECB, governors of the NCBs of the Member States, one member of the European Commission, the Chairpersons of the three financial regulators (ie the EBA, EIOPA and ESMA), the chairperson and two vice-chairs of the Advisory Scientific Committee of the ESRB, and the Chair of the Advisory Technical Committee of the ESRB – ESRB Regulation, art 6 Non-voting members include one high-level representative per Member State of the competent national supervisory authorities, the President of the Economic and Financial Committee (EFC), the Governor of the national central bank of Iceland, the Governor of the national central bank of Norway, a high-level representative of the Ministry of Finance of Liechtenstein, a high-level representative of the competent national supervisory authority of the European Free Trade Association (EFTA) States, and a college member of the EFTA Surveillance Authority (whenever relevant).

(continued)

(Continued)

	UK	US	EU
Term	Non-Executive Members of the FPC appointed for three-year periods and not more than twice – BoE Act 1998, Sch 2A, para 1	Covered by constituting legislation of member agencies. Independent member of the FSOC, serves for six years, which may be extended for a further 18 months, while the non-voting members serves two years – Dodd-Frank Act, s 111(c)	President of the ECB chairs ESRB for a term of five years – ESRB Regulation, art 5(1) First vice-chairperson of the ESRB is limited to a term of five years, with the opportunity for re-election once – ESRB Regulation, art 5
Dismissal	Court of Directors can remove a member, subject to the consent of the Chancellor if they are absent from meetings for more than three months without consent, bankruptcy and unable to discharge their functions as a member – BoE Act 1998, Sch 3, para 9	Covered by constituting legislation of member agencies.	Covered by constituting legislation of member agencies.
Suitability & Salary	Appointment to FPC made based on the individual's knowledge or experience which are relevant to the Committee's functions – BoE Act 1998, s 9B(3) Remuneration Committee of the Court of Directors advises Court on the remuneration of the external members of the FPC.	Independent member must have insurance expertise – Dodd-Frank Act, s 111(b)(1)(J) Suitability of all others covered by constituting legislation. All members of the Council who are federal officers or employees serve without compensation in addition to that received for their services as officers or employees of the United States – Dodd-Frank Act, s 111(I)	Covered by constituting legislation of member agencies.

(continued)

(Continued)

	UK	US	EU
Restrictions In Office and After	Executive members are required to give their exclusive services to the Bank, while non-executive Directors may have other roles outside – BoE Act 1998, Sch 1, para 1(4) No restrictions after leaving office	Covered by constituting legislation of member agencies.	No member of the General Board (whether voting or non-voting) shall have a function in the financial industry – ESRB regulation, art 7(2) Members of the General Board may undertake teaching and scholarly activities as well as non-profit activities in their personal capacity – ESRB Code of Conduct, art 4 Members shall not use non-public information for furthering their own or another's private interests, particularly for private financial transactions. There are no restrictions placed on central bankers after leaving office.
Liaison with Government	In pursuing the Financial Stability Objective, the Bank shall aim to work with other relevant bodies (including the Treasury and the Financial Conduct Authority) – BoE Act 1998, s 2A(a) Treasury representative may attend meetings of the FPC, but may not vote; any view they express is disregarded in determining whether there is a lack of consensus and a matter should be taken to vote – BoE Act 1998, Sch 3, para 13	Secretary of Treasury and Fed President attend and vote at FSOC meetings together – s 111(b) 1	Member of the Commission sits on the General Board of the ESRB with a voting right – ESRB Regulation, art 6(1)(c) as read with Rules of Procedure, art 4(1) President of the Economic Policy Committee may attend meeting and sit at the main table at meetings but does not have a vote – Rules of Procedure, art 4(2)

(continued)

(Continued)

	UK	US	EU
	Governor and the Chancellor of the Exchequer meet to discuss the financial stability report, after its publication by the FPC, and any other matters relating to the stability of the UK financial system – BoE Act 1998, s 9X(1) Outside of meetings, the Bank generally aims to work with other relevant bodies, including the Treasury and the Financial Conduct Authority, in pursuing the Financial Stability Objective – BoE Act 1998, s 2A(a) Bank and Treasury must co-ordinate the discharge of their respective functions, and prepare a memorandum describing in general terms how they intend to achieve this co-ordination, so far as they relate to the stability of the UK financial system, and affect the public interest – Financial Services Act 2012, s 64(1)		Chairperson of the ESRB holds confidential oral discussions at least twice a year and more often if deemed appropriate, behind closed doors with the Chair and Vice-Chairs of the Economic and Monetary Affairs Committee of the European Parliament on the on-going activity of the ESRB – ESRB Regulation, art 19(5) Generally, the ESRB examines specific issues at the invitation of the European Parliament, the Council or the Commission – ESRB Regulation, art 19(3)
Limits on Lending	No provisions	No provisions	No provisions

(continued)

(Continued)

	UK	US	EU
Conduct of Policy	Court of Directors determines the Bank's strategy in relation to the Financial Stability Objective – BoE Act 1998, s 9A(1) FPC identifies, monitors and takes action to remove or reduce risks to the UK financial system – BoE Act 1998, s 9C(1) and 9G(1) FPC may make recommendations and, in relation to macroprudential measures prescribed by secondary legislation, give directions to the Prudential Regulation Authority (PRA) and the Financial Conduct Authority (FCA) – BoE Act 1998, ss 9H & 9O Can only use tools from the range set out by the Minister of Finance and development of any additional macro-prudential instruments will be undertaken in consultation with the Treasury – BoE Act 1998, s 9H	FSOC can designate non-bank financial companies whose size, complexity, or activities could pose systemic risk and ensure that those institutions are subject to consolidated supervision – Dodd-Frank Act, s 113 FSOC can recommend to the Fed standards to limit contingent capital, credit exposure, and a company's short-term debt, set broader public disclosure requirements or require a company to develop a resolution plan – Dodd-Frank Act, s 115 FSOC may recommend primary financial regulatory agencies to apply new or heightened standards and safeguards – Dodd-Frank Act, s 120 Fed carries out consolidated supervision under enhanced prudential standards which address liquidity requirements, risk management processes, resolution plan reports, credit exposure reports, and limits on risk concentration – Dodd-Frank Act, s 165 Fed can take action to mitigate threats to financial stability, including limiting mergers, acquisitions and certain financial products, terminating and imposing conditions on activities or force the sale and transfer of assets – Dodd-Frank Act, s 121	ESRB shall provide warnings and, where appropriate, issue recommendations for remedial action, including, where appropriate, for legislative initiatives – ESRB Regulation, art 16(1) The General Board shall decide whether a warning or a recommendation should be made public – ESRB Regulation, art 17 National competent/designated authorities of Eurosystem Member States shall apply requirements for capital buffers and own funds to be held, including countercyclical buffer rates, and any other measures aimed at addressing systemic or macro-prudential risks set out of the CRR and CRD IV -Art 5(1) SSM Regulation ECB may apply higher requirements than those set by National competent/designated authorities of Eurosystem for capital buffers and own funds to be held, including countercyclical buffer rates, and any other measures aimed at addressing systemic or macro-prudential risks set out in the CRR and CRD IV – SSM Regulation, art 5(2)

(continued)

(Continued)

	UK	US	EU
	Current tool kit has sectorial capital requirements and countercyclical capital buffers – Bank of England Act 1998 (Macro-prudential Measures) (No 2) Order 2015	Fed can impose new requirements for a company's leverage and risk-based capital investments ratios – Dodd-Frank Act, s 171	Member States are recommended to establish a legal framework that permits the macro- prudential authorities to hold the powers over the macro-prudential instruments from a long list which target each intermediate objective – Recommendation B on Objectives and Instruments Policy instruments in CRR and CRD IV follow a hierarchy: CRR, art 124/164, CCB, capital conservation buffer, G/O-SII, Pillar 2 and (2) SRB; CRR, art 124/164, Pillar 2, SRB and CCB and (2) CRR, art 458, and lastly Pillar 2 measures
Regulatory Powers	Bank is responsible for the application of capital requirements regulation so far as it relates to macro-prudential measures – BoE Act 1998, s 2AA FPC may make recommendations and, in relation to macroprudential measures prescribed by secondary legislation, give directions to the Prudential Regulation Authority (PRA) and the Financial Conduct Authority (FCA) – BoE Act 1998, ss 9H & 9O	The appropriate federal banking agencies shall establish minimum leverage and risk-based capital requirements on a consolidated basis for insured depository institutions, depository institution holding companies, and non-bank financial companies supervised by the Board of Governors – Dodd-Frank Act, s 171	ECB is exclusively competent to carry out prudential supervisory activities – SSM Regulation, art 4 The ECB has the power to grant and withdraw the authorisation of any credit institution and to assess the acquisition of holdings in credit institutions in the euro area. This is done jointly with NCAs – SSM, art 4(1)(a)

(continued)

(Continued)

	UK	US	EU
	A 'macro-prudential measure' included in any direction to regulators shall be prescribed by the Treasury by order, approved by resolution of each House of Parliament. Development of any additional macro-prudential instruments will be undertaken in consultation with the Treasury – BoE Act 1998, s 9H & S9L PRA may make rules applying to PRA-authorised persons with respect to the carrying on by them of regulated or unregulated activities – FSMA 2000, s 137G PRA may make rules supplementing any of the conditions, 'threshold conditions', which specify requirements which a person must satisfy in order to be regarded as satisfying a particular condition in relation to any regulated activities; and matters which are, or may be, or are not, relevant in determining whether a person satisfies a particular condition in relation to any regulated activities – FSMA 2000, s 137O	Not later than 180 days after determination by FSOC that a non-bank financial company is to be supervised by the Fed, such company shall register with the Fed, in prescribed forms, including such information as the Board of Governors, in consultation with the Council, may deem necessary or appropriate – Dodd-Frank Act, s 114 Fed has authority to issue regulations arising from the extra financial stability duties imposed on it as a result of the designation of a SIFI – Dodd-Frank Act, s 168 Fed can prescribe regulations establishing requirements to provide for the early remediation of financial distress of a nonbank financial company, excluding financial assistance – Dodd-Frank Act, s 166 In order to prevent or mitigate risks to the financial stability of the United States that could arise from the material financial distress or failure, or on-going activities, of large, interconnected financial institutions, the Board of Governors shall, on its own or pursuant to recommendations FSOC, establish prudential standards for SIFIs – Dodd-Frank Act, s 165(a)	National competent/designated authorities of Eurosystem Member States shall apply requirements for capital buffers and own funds to be held, including countercyclical buffer rates, and any other measures aimed at addressing systemic or macro-prudential risks set out of the CRR and CRD IV – SSM Regulation, art 5(1) ECB may apply higher requirements than those set by National competent/designated authorities of Eurosystem for capital buffers and own funds to be held, including countercyclical buffer rates, and any other measures aimed at addressing systemic or macro-prudential risks set out in the CRR and CRD IV – SSM Regulation, art 5(2) Policy instruments in CRR and CRD IV follow a hierarchy: CRR, arts 124/164, CCB, capital conservation buffer, G/O-SII, Pillar 2 and (2) SRB; CRR, arts 124/164, Pillar 2, SRB and CCB and (2) CRR, art 458, and lastly Pillar 2 measures

(continued)

(Continued)

	UK	US	EU
		Fed carries out consolidated supervision under enhanced prudential standards which address liquidity requirements, risk management processes, resolution plan reports, credit exposure reports, and limits on risk concentration, a contingent capital requirement; enhanced public disclosures; short-term debt limits; and such other prudential standards – Dodd-Frank Act, s 165(b) Fed can take action to mitigate threats to financial stability, including limiting mergers, acquisitions and certain financial products, terminating and imposing conditions on activities or force the sale and transfer of assets – Dodd-Frank Act, s 121 Fed has authority to write rules for, impose reporting obligations on, examine the activities and financial health of, and bring enforcement actions against subsidiaries, including entities regulated by the Securities and Exchange Commission (SEC) or the Commodity Futures Trading Commission (CFTC) and state-regulated entities – Dodd-Frank Act, s 604 Domestic and foreign non-Bank financial holding companies are subject to prudential standards and supervision by the Fed – Dodd-Frank Act, s 113	

(continued)

(Continued)

	UK	US	EU
		Fed shall have authority to issue regulations to implement standards for enhanced supervision of SIFIs subtitles A and C and the amendments made thereunder. Except as otherwise specified in subtitle A or C, not later than 18 months after the effective date of this Act, the Board of Governors shall issue final regulations to implement subtitles A and C, and the amendments made thereunder. If the Fed determines that a condition, practice, or activity of a depository institution subsidiary or functionally regulated subsidiary of a non-bank financial company supervised by the Board of Governors does not comply with the regulations or it may recommend, in writing, to the primary financial regulatory agency for the subsidiary that such agency initiate a supervisory action or enforcement proceeding. If, during the 60-day period from receiving the recommendation, the primary regulatory agency does not action against a subsidiary the Fed that is acceptable to the Board of Governors may take the recommended supervisory or enforcement action – Dodd-Frank Act, s 162 May initiate resolution process to shut down firms that pose a grave threat to financial stability (requires concurrence of two-thirds of the FSOC). The FDIC and the Treasury Secretary have similar powers.	

(continued)

(Continued)

	UK	US	EU
FINANCIAL AUTONOMY	Covered by monetary policy provisions	Any expenses of the Council shall be treated as expenses of, and paid by, the Office of Financial Research – Dodd-Frank Act, s 118 The OFR is funded by a specially set up Financial Research Fund, to which SIFI are required to contribute – Dodd-Frank Act, s 155.	The ECB shall provide sufficient human and financial resources for the fulfilment of its task of ensuring the Secretariat – SI No 1096/2010 Conferring Special Tasks, art 3(1)
DECISIONAL AUTONOMY	Before determining or revising the Bank's financial stability strategy, the court of directors must consult the Treasury – BoE Act 1998, s 9A(2) Where the Bank undertakes the Article 458 notification process, it must consult the Treasury about the assessment required by the Capital Requirements Regulation, Article 458(2)(f) – BoE Act 1998, s 2AA (7) & (8) Treasury may give a direction to the Bank of England relating to the provision by the Bank to one or more financial institutions or the exercise by the Bank of its administrative powers where it is necessary to resolve or reduce a serious threat to the stability of the financial system of the United Kingdom and to protect the public interest – Financial Services Act 2012, s 61(2)		When participating in the activities of the General Board and of the Steering Committee or when conducting any other activity relating to the ESRB, the members of the ESRB shall perform their duties impartially and solely in the interest of the Union as a whole. They shall neither seek nor take instructions from the Member States, the Union institutions or any other public or private body – Art 7(2) & (3)

(continued)

(Continued)

	UK	US	EU
	The Treasury may make recommendations to the Committee, on a 'comply or explain' basis, about (a) matters that the Committee should regard as relevant to the Committee's understanding of the Bank's Financial Stability Objective; (b) the responsibility of the Committee in relation to the achievement of that objective; (c) the responsibility of the Committee in relation to support for the economic policy of Government (d) matters to which the Committee should have regard in exercising its functions – BoE Act 1998, s 9E(1) and (3)		

ANNEXURE 3: LEGAL ARTICULATION OF INDEPENDENCE IN MONETARY POLICY

	UK	US	EU
Objective	Treasury may specify what price stability is to be taken to consist of and what the economic policy of Her Majesty's Government is to be taken to be – BoE Act 1998, s 12	Goal of the Board of Governors and the Federal Open Market Committee is to promote effectively the goals of maximum employment, stable prices, and moderate long-term interest rates – Federal Reserve Act, s 2A	The main objective of Eurosystem is to maintain price stability – TFEU, art 127(1)
Appointment	Appointments to the Court of the Bank of England, which serves as the board of directors, are made by the Queen on the advice of the Prime Minister and the Chancellor of the Exchequer – BoE Act 1998, s 1(2) Court consists of five executive members and nine non-executive directors – BoE Act 1998, s 1(2) Bank's policy making committees are also pluralistic – BoE Act 1998, ss 13 and 30A:	Board of Governors of the Federal Reserve System is composed of seven members, appointed by the President, by and with the advice and consent of the Senate – Federal Reserve Act, s 10(1)	Governing Council of the ECB comprises the governors of the NCBs of the Eurosystem and the six members of the Executive Board – ESCB Statute, art 10 Executive Board of the ECB is appointed by the European Council, after consulting the European Parliament and the Governing Council of the European Central Bank – TFEU, art 283(2).

(continued)

(Continued)

	UK	US	EU
	Monetary Policy Committee, (MPC), consists of the Governor and Deputy Governors, excluding the COO, the Bank's Chief Economist, appointed by the Governor after consultation with the Chancellor, and four external members appointed by the Chancellor. *Prudential Regulation Committee*, (PRC), consists of the Governor and Deputy Governors of the Bank, excluding the COO; the Chief Executive of the Financial Conduct Authority, one member appointed by the Governor of the Bank with the approval of the Chancellor, and at least six members appointed by the Chancellor of the Exchequer.	Twelve Federal Reserve Banks supervised by a Board of Directors made up of nine members, all chosen from outside the Reserve Bank and divided into three equal classes – Class A and B elected by the member commercial banks of the S and District, and Class C appointed by the Board of Governors – the Federal Reserve Act, s 4(9)	The TFEU and ESCB Statute are silent on the procedure of appointment of governors for National Central Banks, (NCBs); therefore, the process varies from state to state.
Term	Governor of the BoE is appointed for a period of eight years, five years for the Deputy Governors and four years for non-executive directors – BoE Act 1998, Sch 1, para 1(1)–(2) A person may not be appointed as Governor more than once or as Deputy Governor more than twice – BoE Act 1998, Sch 1, para 1(3) Appointment as a non-executive member of the MPC and the PRC is for a period of three years and not more than twice – BoE Act 1998, Sch 6A, para 3(1) & 2A(1) National elections are held at intervals of no more than five years.	Members of the Board of Governors serve for 14 years, although a member can only act as chairperson and or vice-chairperson for periods of four years at a time – Federal Reserve Act, s 10(1) Members of Federal Bank Boards hold office for three years – Federal Reserve Act, s 4(9) Election of the President of the United States occurs every four years, while elections to the House of Representatives and the Senate are held every two years.	ECB Executive Board members have non-renewable term of eight years – art 283(2) (see also ESCB Statute, art 11(2)) NCB governors minimum term is five years, upper limit, is decided by individual member states – ESCB Statute, art 14(2) first paragraph

(continued)

(Continued)

	UK	US	EU
Dismissal	The Court of Directors can remove a member, subject to the consent of the Chancellor if they are absent from meetings for more than three months without consent, bankruptcy and unable to discharge their functions as a member – BoE Act 1998, Sch 1, paras 7 and 8 Same grounds for dismissal apply to members of the MPC, PRC – BoE Act 1998, Sch 3, paras 7, 8 and 9 and Sch 6A, para 9(2)	Members of the Board of Governors can hold office, unless sooner removed for cause by the President – Federal Reserve Act, s 10(2)	Member of the ECB Executive Board can be dismissed if they no longer fulfil the conditions required for the performance of duties or has been guilty of serious misconduct – ESCB Statute, art 11(4) Only the Court of Justice may, on application by the Governing Council or the Executive Board, compulsorily retire a member. Other members of the Governing Council may be dismissed on the same grounds, by the executive or legislature of a member state although this may be appealed to the CJEU – ESCB Statute, art 14.2
Suitability & Salary	Appointment to MPC made based on the individual's knowledge or experience which are relevant to the Committee's functions – BoE Act 1998, s 13(4) Remuneration Committee of the Court of Directors determines the remuneration of the Governors and advises Court on the remuneration of other senior executives, and the external members of the MPC and the PRC – BoE Act 1998, Sch 1, para 14(A1)	President shall have due regard to a fair representation of the financial, agricultural, industrial, and commercial interests, and geographical divisions of the country, and at least one of the members appointed shall have demonstrated primary experience working in or supervising community banks – Federal Reserve Act, s 10(1) Class B and Class C directors for Federal Reserve Banks represent the public with due but not exclusive consideration to the interests of agriculture, commerce, industry, services, labour and consumers – Federal Reserve Act, s 4(11) & (12)	Members of the ECB Executive Board appointed 'from among persons of recognised standing and professional experience in monetary or banking matters' – TFEU, art 283 (also ESCB Statute, art 11(1)) Salaries, pensions and other social seurity benefits are the subject of contracts with the ECB and are fixed by the Governing Council. on a proposal from a committee comprising three members appointed by the Governing Council and three members appointed by the Council – ESCB Statute, art 11(3)

(continued)

(Continued)

	UK	US	EU
		US Congress sets the salaries of members of the Board of Governors. Directors of Federal Reserve Banks shall receive, in addition to any compensation otherwise provided, a reasonable allowance for necessary expenses in attending meetings – Federal Reserve Act, s 4(22)	Treaty is silent on the suitability and salaries of NCB governors, which are therefore determined by the member states.
Restrictions In Office and After	Governors are required to give their exclusive services to the Bank, while non-executive Directors may have other roles outside – BoE Act 1998, Sch 1, para 1(4) No restrictions placed on Directors and Committee members after they leave office.	Board of Governors shall devote their entire time to the business of the Board – Federal Reserve Act, s 10(2) Members of the Board of Governors cannot be officers or directors of any bank, banking institution, trust company, or Federal Reserve bank or hold stock in any bank, banking institution, or trust company. Class B and Class C directors of Federal Reserve Banks may not be officers, directors or employees of any private s tor bank or bank holding company. Additionally, Class C directors may not own shares in any bank or bank holding company – Federal Reserve Act, ss 10(2), 4(14) & 4(15) After leaving office Board of Governors ineligible for two years thereafter to hold any office, position, or employment in any member bank, unless they compete their full 14-year term – Federal Reserve Act, s 10(2)	The members of the ESCB perform their duties on a full-time basis, unless exemption is exceptionally granted by the Governing Council of the ECB – ESCB Statute, art 11(1) No mandatory cooling-off period or revolving-door-policy at EU level.

(continued)

(Continued)

	UK	US	EU
Liaisons with Treasury	Representative of the Treasury may attend, and speak at, any meeting of the MPC, but does not have a voting right – BoE Act 1998, Sch 3, para 13	No legal provisions. However, there is a tradition of weekly luncheons hosted for the Fed and Treasury senior staff	Council of the European Union is permitted to submit motions for deliberation at meetings of the ECB's General Council and attend the meetings, along with the European Commission, however neither exercise any voting rights – TFEU, arts 127(4) & 284(1) ECB is consulted on any proposed Union act in its fields of competence or can provide unsolicited opinions to European or Member State bodies – TFEU art 127(4) President of the ECB can be invited to Council meetings in which matters related to the ESCB's objectives are discussed, and meetings of the Eurogroup – TFEU, art 284(2) ECB is a statutory member of the Council's Economic and Financial Committee No specific provisions directing the relationships between NCBs and national Treasuries.
Limits on Lending	BoE is prohibited from monetary financing as part of ESCB – TFEU, art 123	The Federal Reserve Banks can lend to individuals, partnership or corporations on promissory notes insured by US treasuries for periods not exceeding 90 days and at interest rates fixed by the Federal reserve bank, subject to the review and determination of the Board of Governors of the Federal Reserve System –Federal Reserve Act, s 13(3)	ECB and NCBs prohibited from providing overdraft facilities or any other type of credit facility to and directly purchasing debt instruments from Union institutions, bodies, offices or agencies; central government, regional, local or other public authorities; other bodies governed by public law, or public undertakings of Member States – TFEU, art 123(1)

(continued)

(Continued)

	UK	US	EU
		Federal Reserve Banks can purchase Treasury securities held in the open market, under the direction and regulations of the Federal Open Market Committee – Federal Reserve Act, s 14(2)(b)	Prohibition does not extend to publicly owned credit institutions which, are given the same treatment as private credit institutions.
Conduct of Policy	MPC is required to meet at least eight times a year (and at least once in any 10-week period) to set interest rates and other monetary conditions to meet that target – BoE Act 1998, s 11	FOMC controls monetary policy using federal funds rate, discount rate, reserve requirements, and quantitative easing. FOMC, in its eight annual meetings, establishes the target federal funds rate, and reaches this target, by buying or selling securities on the open market.	ESCB formulates and implements monetary policy –ESCB Statute, art 3 Governing Council decides intermediate monetary objectives, key interest rates and the supply of reserves in the ESCB, and establishes the necessary guidelines for their implementation ESCB Statute, art 12(1) Executive Board of ECB and NCBs can engage in open market operation and lending activities – ESCB Statute, art 18 ECB may require credit institutions established in Member States to hold minimum reserve on accounts with the ECB and national central banks in pursuance of monetary policy objectives – ESCB Statutes, art 19(1) Governing Council may further decide on the use of other operational methods of monetary control as it sees fit – ESCB Statute, art 20

(continued)

(Continued)

	UK	US	EU
Regulatory Powers	Bank acts as a prudential regulator, the Prudential Regulation Authority, which is a subsidiary of the Bank – FSM, s 2A inserted by Bank of England and FMS Act 2016, s 2A Bank is responsible for supervising financial market infrastructure providers, ie payment systems, central securities depositories and central counterparties – Banking Act 2009 and FSMA 2000 Bank is the United Kingdom's Resolution Authority – Banking Act 2009, s 1(5)	The FOMC shall consider, adopt, and transmit to the several Federal Reserve banks, regulations relating to the open-market transactions of such banks – Federal Reserve Act, s 12A(b). The Board of Governors shall make and promulgate from time-to-time regulations governing the transfer of funds and charges therefor among Federal reserve banks and their branches – Federal Reserve Act, s 16(14)	ECB shall make regulations to the extent necessary to implement the tasks – TFEU, art 132 ECB shall make regulations on reserve requirements, clearing and payment systems, other monetary policy instruments and prudential supervision – TFEU, art 19(1), 22 & 25(2) In cases of non-compliance the ECB shall be entitled to levy penalty interest and to impose other sanctions with comparable effect – TFEU, art 132(3)
Financial Autonomy	The whole of the existing capital stock of the Bank is held by Treasury –BoE 1946 Act, s 1 The court of directors of the Bank shall manage the Bank's affairs, in particular determining the Bank's objectives including objectives for its financial management – BoE Act 1998, s 1	Stock of the 12 Federal Reserve Banks is privately held by the Federal Reserve member banks. Board of Governors has the power to levy upon the Federal reserve banks an assessment sufficient to pay its estimated expenses and the salaries of its members and employees. Funds derived from such assessments shall not be construed to be government funds or appropriated moneys – Federal Reserve Act, s 10(3)	The ECB shall be independent in the management of its finances – TFEU, art 282(3) National central banks shall be the sole subscribers to and holders of the capital of the ECB – ESCB Statute, art 28(2)

(continued)

(Continued)

	UK	US	EU
	Under Cash Ratio Deposit scheme banks and building societies are required to place an interest-free deposit at the Bank which is a set percentage of their deposit base – BoE Act 1998, Sch 2 In its capacity as the PRA, Bank may levy regulated firms to recover all costs incurred in the performance of the PRA's functions – FSMA 2000, Sch 1ZB, para 31 Bank's post-tax profit is shared 50:50 with HM Treasury unless otherwise agreed	Board determines and prescribes the manner in which its obligations shall be incurred and its disbursements and expenses allowed and paid, and may leave on deposit in the Federal Reserve banks the proceeds of assessments levied upon them to defray its estimated expenses – Federal Reserve Act, s 10(4)	The ECB shall be provided by the national central banks with foreign reserve assets, other than Member States' currencies, euro, IMF reserve positions and SDRs, up to an amount equivalent to €50,000 million – ESCB Statute, art 30(1) ECB can request the NCBs to make further contributions to increase its capital, to make further transfers of foreign reserves and to resort to monetary income to cover any losses – ESCB Statute, art 32 The income accruing to the national central banks in the performance of the ESCB's monetary policy function shall be allocated at the end of each financial year along with net profit – ESCB Statute, art 32(1) All other operations in foreign reserve assets remaining with the national central banks and transactions with their foreign exchange working balances shall be consistent with the framework designed by the governing council and subject to approval by the ECB – ESCB Statute, art 31(2) The TFEU does not prohibit the distribution of profits and it is up to the decision-making bodies of the NCBs to decide on this.

(continued)

(Continued)

	UK	US	EU
Decisional Autonomy	The Treasury may from time to time give directions to the Bank … except in relation to monetary policy – BoE 1946 Act, s 4. The Treasury, after consultation with the Governor of the Bank, may by order, approved by both Houses of Parliament, give the Bank directions with respect to monetary policy if they are satisfied that the directions are required in the public interest and by extreme economic circumstances – BoE Act 1998, s 19(1)	No officer or agency of the United States shall have any authority to require, among others, the Board of Governors to submit legislative recommendations, or testimony, or comments on legislation, for approval, comments, or review, prior to the submission of such recommendations, testimony, or comments to the Congress if such recommendations, testimony, or comments to the Congress include a statement indicating that the views expressed therein are those of the agency submitting them and do not necessarily represent the views of the President. Title 12 USC 250 In cases where the Board's powers conflict with powers of the Secretary of the Treasury, such powers shall be exercised subject to the supervision and control of the Secretary – Federal Reserve Act, s 10(6)	When exercising the powers and carrying out the tasks and duties conferred upon them neither the European Central Bank, nor a national central bank, nor any member of their decision-making bodies shall seek or take instructions from Union institutions, bodies, offices or agencies, from any government of a Member State or from any other body – TFEU, art 130 The Union institutions, bodies, offices or agencies and the governments of the Member States undertake to respect this principle and not to seek to influence the members of the decision-making bodies of the European Central Bank or of the national central banks in the performance of their tasks – TFEU, art 130

BIBLIOGRAPHY

Acharya, V, 'Financial Stability in The Broader Mandate for Central Banks: A Political Economy Perspective' (14 April 2015) Hutchins Center Working Paper #11.

Adler, M, 'Cost–Benefit Analysis and Distributional Weight: An Overview' (2013) Duke Environmental and Energy Economics Working Paper Series EE 13-04.

Adler, M and Posner E, *New Foundations of Cost–Benefit Analysis* (Harvard University Press, 2006).

Adrian, T, 'Macroprudential Responses to the COVID-19 Pandemic and Outlook' (Speech at IMF 5th European Systemic Risk Board Annual Conference, 'Strengthening the Financial System Post-COVID-19,' 8 December 2021).

Admati A and Hellwig M, *The Banker's New Clothes: What's Wrong with Banking and What to Do About It* (Princeton University Press, 2013).

Adolph, C, *Bankers, Bureaucrats and the Politics of Central Banks* (Cambridge University Press, 2013).

Ahnert, T, Forbes KJ, and Reinhardt, D, 'Macroprudential FX Regulations: Shifting the Snowbanks of FX Vulnerability?' (November 2018) Bank of Canada Staff Working Paper 2018-55.

Aiyar, S, Calomiris, CW and Wieladek, T, 'Does Macro-pru Leak? Evidence From a UK Policy Experiment' (2014) 46 *Journal of Money, Credit and Banking* 181.

Akerlof, G, 'The Market for "Lemons": Quality Uncertainty and the Market Mechanism' (1970) 84(3) *The Quarterly Journal of Economics* 488.

Albacete, N, Fessler, P and Lindner, P, 'One Policy to Rule Them All? On the Effectiveness of LTV, DTI and DSTI Ratio Limits as Macroprudential Policy Tools' (2018) 35 *Oesterreichische Nationalbank Financial Stability Report*.

Alesina, A and Tabellini, G, 'Bureaucrats or Politicians?' (2004) NBER Working Paper 10241.

Allen, F and Carletti, E, 'Systemic Risk from Real Estate and Macro-Prudential Regulation' (2013) 5(1/2) *International Journal of Banking, Accounting and Finance* 28–48.

Allen, F and Gale, D, 'Financial Contagion' (2000) 108(1) *Journal of Political Economy* 1.

Allen, HJ, 'What is "Financial Stability"? The Need for Some Common Language in International Financial Regulation' (2013–2014) 45 *Georgetown Journal of International Law* 929.

Allen, WA and Wood, G, 'Defining and Achieving Financial Stability' (2006) 2(2) *Journal of Financial Stability* 152.

Amtenbrink, F, 'The Three Pillars of Central Bank Governance – Towards a Model Central Bank Law or a Code of Good Governance?' in International Monetary Fund, *Current Developments in Monetary and Financial Law* (International Monetary Fund 2005) 101–32.

Amtenbrink, F and Lastra, RM, 'Securing Democratic Accountability of Financial Regulatory Agencies – A Theoretical Framework' in Richard Victor de Mulder (ed), *Mitigating Risk in the Context of Safety and Security. How Relevant is a Rational Approach?* (Erasmus School of Law and Research School for Safety and Security (OMV), 2008) 115–32.

Andenas, M and Chiu, IHY, *The Foundations and Future of Financial Regulation: Governance for Responsibility* (Routledge, 2013).

Archer, D, 'A Coming Crisis of Legitimacy' (2016) 3 *Sveriges Riksbank Economic Review* 86.

Armour J, Awrey D, Davies P, Enriques L, Gordon JN, Mayer C and Payne J, *Principles of Financial Regulation* (Oxford University Press, 2016).

Arner, D, *Financial Stability, Economic Growth, and the Role of Law* (Cambridge University Press, 2007).

Atkinson, T, Luttrell, D and Rosenblum, H, 'How Bad Was It? The Costs and Consequences of the 2007–09 Financial Crisis' (July 2013) *Dallas Fed Staff Papers No 20*.

Avgouleas, E, *Governance of Global Financial Markets: The Law the Economics the Politics* (Cambridge University Press, 2012).

Awrey, D, 'Law, Financial Instability and Institutional Structure of Financial Regulation' in Anita Anand (ed) *Systemic Risk, Institutional Design, and the Regulation of Financial Markets* (Oxford University Press, 2016).

Ayres, I and Braithwaite, J, *Responsive Regulation: Transcending the Deregulation Debate* (Oxford University Press, 1992).

Bade, R and Parkin, M, 'Central Bank Laws and Monetary Policy' (1987) *University of Ontario*, Department of Economics Discussion Paper.

Bagehot, W, *Lombard Street: A Description of the Money Market*, (Wiley, 1999).

Baker, A, 'The Banker's Paradox: The Political Economy of Macroprudential Regulation' (April 2015) *SRC Discussion Paper No 17.*

Baker, A, 'Political Economy and the Paradoxes of Macroprudential Policy' (September 2017) *SPERI Paper No 40.*

Baker, A, 'Macroprudential Regimes and the Politics of Social Purpose' (2018) 25(3) *Review of International Political Economy* 293.

Balls, E, Howat, J and Stansbury, A 'Central Bank Independence Revisited: After the Financial Crisis, What Should a Model Central Bank Look Like?' (April 2018) M-RCBG Associate Working Paper Series No. 87.

Baldwin, R, Cave, M and Lodge M, *Understanding Regulation: Theory, Strategy, and Practice* 2nd edn (Oxford University Press, 2011).

Bandt de, O and Hartmann, P, 'Systemic Risk: A Survey' (2000) European Central Bank Working Paper No 35.

Bank of England, 'Assessing the Impact of the FPC's Recommendations on the Mortgage Market' Financial Stability Report (2014) 60.

Bank of England, 'Financial Policy Committee Statement on Housing Market Powers of Direction from Its Policy Meeting, 26 September 2014' (2 October 2014).

Bank of England, 'The Bank of England's Approach to Resolution' (October 2017).

Bank of England, 'The Bank of England's Amendments to Financial Services Legislation Under The European Union (Withdrawal) Act 2018' (June 2019) Bank of England Policy Statement | PRA Policy Statement PS5/19.

Bank for International Settlements, *Recent Innovations in International Banking* (Cross Report) (BIS, 1986).

Bank for International Settlements, *Recent Developments in International Bank Relation* (Promisel Report) (BIS, 1992).

Bank for International Settlements, *Issues Related to The Measurement of Market Size and Macroprudential Risks in Derivatives Markets (Brockmeijer Report)* (BIS, 1995).

Bank for International Settlements, *Central Bank Governance and Financial Stability* (Ingves Report) (BIS, 2011).

Bank for International Settlements, *86th Annual Report 2015/16* (26 June 2016).

Bank for International Settlements, *Objective-setting and Communication of Macroprudential Policies* (November 2016) *CGFS Papers No 57.*

Barro, D and Gordon, DM, 'Rules, Discretion and Reputation in a Model of Monetary Policy' (1983) NBER Working Paper No 1079.

Basle Committee on Banking Supervision, *International Convergence of Capital Measurement and Capital Standards* (BIS July 1988).

Basle Committee on Banking Supervision, *Principles for the Management of Credit Risk* (BIS September 2002).

Basle Committee on Banking Supervision, *International Convergence of Capital Measures and Capital Standard: A Revised Framework (Basel II)* (BIS 2004).

Basle Committee on Banking Supervision, *Basel II: International Convergence on Capital Measurement and Capital Standards: A Revised Framework – Comprehensive Version* (BIS June 2006).

Basle Committee on Banking Supervision, *Principles for Sound Liquidity Risk Management and Supervision. Bank for International Settlements* (BIS 2008).

Basle Committee on Banking Supervision, *Basel III: A Global Regulatory Framework for More Resilient Banks and Banking Systems* (BIS 2010).
Basle Committee on Banking Supervision, *Guidance for National Authorities Operating the Countercyclical Capital Buffer* (BIS December 2010).
Basle Committee on Banking Supervision, A *Framework for Dealing with Domestic Systemically Important Banks* (BIS October 2012).
Basle Committee on Banking Supervision, *Core Principles for Effective Banking Supervision* (BIS September 2012).
Basle Committee on Banking Supervision, *Global Systemically Important Banks: Updated Assessment Methodology and the Higher Loss Absorbency Requirement* (BIS July 2013).
Basle Committee on Banking Supervision, *Basel III: Leverage Ratio Framework and Disclosure Requirements* (BIS January 2014).
Baxter, LG, 'Capture in Financial Regulation: Can We Channel It Toward the Common Good?' (2011) 21 *Cornell Journal of Law and Public Policy* 176.
Beaussier, A, Demeritt, D, Griffiths, A and Rothstein, H, 'Accounting for Failure: Risk-Based Regulation and The Problems of Ensuring Healthcare Quality in the NHS' (2016) 18(3–4) *Health, Risk and Society* 205.
Beetham, D, *Legitimation of Power* (Palgrave, 1991).
Beitz, CR, *Political Equality: Essay in Democratic Theory* (Princeton University Press, 1992).
Bekkers, V and Edwards, A, 'Legitimacy and Democracy: A conceptual framework for assessing governance practices' in Victor Bekker et al, eds *Governance and Democratic Deficit: Assessing the Democratic Legitimacy of Governance Practices* (Ashgate Publishing 2007) 35–60.
Bekkers V, Dijkstra G, Fenger M (eds), Governance and Democratic Deficit: Assessing the Democratic Legitimacy of Governance Practices (Ashgate Publishing, 2007).
Benediktsdóttir, S, Feldberg, G and Liang, N, 'What Macroprudential Policies Are Countries Using to Help Their Economies Through The COVID-19 Crisis?' (6 April 2020, Brookings Institute).
Bengtsson, E, 'Macroprudential Policy in the EU: A Political Economy Perspective' [2020] *Global Financial Journal* 100490.
Benston, G, *Regulating Financial Markets: A Critique and Some Proposals* (Institute of Economic Affairs, 1998).
Bentham, J, *An Introduction to the Principles of Morals and Legislation* (Clarendon Press, 1907).
Bernanke, B, *The Federal Reserve and The Financial Crisis* (Princeton University Press, 2012).
Bernanke, B, 'Stress Testing Banks: What Have We Learned?' (Speech at 'Maintaining Financial Stability: Holding a Tiger by the Tail', Financial Markets Conference Atlanta, 8 April 2013).
Bianchi, J and Bengui, J, 'Macroprudential Policy with Leakages' (September 2018) Federal Reserve Bank of Minneapolis Working Paper 754.
Bichsel, R and Blum, J, 'Capital Regulation of Banks: Where Do We Stand and Where Are We Going?' (2005) 4 *Swiss National Bank Quarterly Bulletin* 42.
Black J, 'Forms and Paradoxes of Principles-based Regulation' (2008) LSE Law, Society and Economy Working Papers No 13/2008.
Black, J, 'Legitimacy and the Competition for Regulatory Share' LSE Law, Society and Economy Working Papers 14/2009.
Blanchard, O, Dell'Ariccia, G and Mauro P, 'Rethinking Macroeconomic Policy' (12 February 2012) IMF SPN/10/03.
Blinder, AS, Ehrmann, M, Fratzscher, M, De Haan, J and Jansen, DJ, 'Central Bank Communication and Monetary Policy: A Survey of Theory and Evidence' (May 2008) ECB Working Paper Series No 898.
Bodenstein, M, Guerrieri, L and LaBriola, J, 'Macroeconomic Policy Games' (2014) Finance and Economics Discussion Paper No 2014-87.
Borio, C, 'Towards a Macroprudential Framework for Supervision and Regulation?' *BIS* (February 2003) Working Paper No 128.
Borio, C, 'Implementing a Macroprudential Framework: Blending Boldness and Realism' (2011) 6(1) *Article 1 Capitalism and Society* 1.

Borio, C, 'The Financial Cycle and Macroeconomics: What Have We Learnt?' (December 2012) BIS Working Papers No 395.
Borio, C, '"Helicopter Money" – Reality Bites' (Commentary in *Nikkei Asian Review* 4 September 2016).
Borio, C, and Van den Bergh P 'The Nature and Management of Payment System Risks: An International Perspective' (13 February 1993) BIS Economic Papers No 36.
Borio, C, and Zabai A 'Unconventional Monetary Policies: A Re-Appraisal' (2016) BIS Working Papers No 570.
Bovens, M, 'Analyzing and Assessing Public Accountability. A Conceptual Framework' (2006) European Governance Papers, No. C-06-01 14.
Brave, SA and Lopez, JA, 'Calibrating Macroprudential Policy to Forecasts of Financial Stability' Federal Reserve (2018) Bank of San Francisco Working Paper 2017-17.
Brotman, SN, 'Revisiting the Broadcast Public Interest Standard in Communications Law and Regulation' (2017) Brookings Institute.
Brown, AC, 'Regulators, Policy Makers, and the Making of Policy: Who Does What and When Do They Do It?' (2003) 3(1) *International Journal of Regulation and Governance* 1.
Brunnermeier, MK, Crocket, A, Goodhart, CAE, Persaud AD and Shi HS, *The Fundamental Principles of Financial Regulation* (International Centre for Monetary and Banking Studies/Centre for Economic Policy Research, 2009).
Brunnermeier, MK and Pedersen, LH, 'Market Liquidity and Funding Liquidity' (2009) 22(3) *The Review of Financial Studies* 2201.
Buiter, W, 'The Proposed European Systemic Risk Board is Overweight with Central Bankers', *Willem Buiter's Maverecon*, FT.com, 28 October 2009.
Buiter, W, 'Central Banks: Powerful, Political and Unaccountable?' (2014) Centre for Economic Policy Research Discussion Paper No 10223.
Búrca de, G, 'The Quest for Legitimacy in the European Union' (1996) 59(3) *Modern Law Review* 349.
Calomaris, C, 'Restoring the Rule of Law in Financial Regulation' (24 September 2018) *Cato Journal*.
Calomiris, CW and Mason, J, 'Contagion and Bank Failures during the Great Depression: The June 1932 Chicago Bank Panic' (1997) 87(5) *American Economic Review* 863.
Calomiris, CW and Haber, SH, *Fragile by Design: The Political Origins of Banking Crises and Scarce Credit* (Princeton University Press, 2014).
Caprio, B and Levine, R, *Rethinking Banking Regulation* (Cambridge University Press, 2006).
Cargill, TF, 'The Myth of Central Bank Independence' (October 2016) Mercatus Working Paper.
Carney, M, 'Inclusive Capitalism – Creating a Sense of the Systemic' (Speech at Conference on Inclusive Capitalism, London, 27 May 2014).
Carney, M, 'Introduction to the Open Forum' (London, 11 November 2015).
Carney, M, 'Enable, Empower, Ensure: A New Finance for the New Economy' (Speech at the Lord Mayor's Banquet for Bankers and Merchants of the City of London, London, 20 June 2019).
Carroll, L, *Through the Looking-Glass* (The Modern Library, 1934).
Caruana, J, 'Monetary Policy in a World with Macroprudential Policy' (Speech at the SAARCFINANCE Governors' Symposium, Kerala, 11 June 2011).
Caruana, J, 'Macroprudential Policy: What We Have Learned and Where We Are Going' (Keynote Speech at the Second Financial Stability Conference of the International Journal of Central Banking, Madrid, 17 June 2010).
Cecchetti, SG, Fender, I and McGuire, P, 'Toward a Global Risk Map' (May 2010) BIS Working Paper No 309.
Cerutti, E, Claessens S, and Laeven L, 'The Use and Effectiveness of Macroprudential Policies: New Evidence' (2015) IMF Working Paper WP/15/61.
Cerutti, E, Correa, R, Fiorentino, E and Segalla E, 'Changes in Prudential Policy Instruments – A New Cross-Country Database' (June 2016) IMF Working Paper WP/16/110.
Chiu, IHY, 'The Nature of a Financial Investment Intermediary's Duty to his Client' (2008) 28 *Legal Studies* 254.
Čihák, M, 'How Do Central Banks Write on Financial Stability?' (June 2006) IMF Working Paper WP/06/163.

Čihák, M, 'Price Stability, Financial Stability, and Central Bank Independence' [2010] *Oesterreichische Nationalbank* 38th Economic Conference 45.

Čihák, M, Muñoz, S, Sharifuddin ST and Tintchev, K, 'Financial Stability Reports: What Are They Good For?' (January 2012) IMF Working Paper WP/12/1.

Claessens, S and Kose, MA, 'Financial Crises: Explanations, Types, and Implications' (January 2013) IMF Working Paper WP/13/28.

Claessens, S and Kodres, L, 'The Regulatory Responses to the Global Financial Crisis: Some Uncomfortable Questions' (March 2014) IMF Working Paper WP/14/46.

Clement, P, 'The Term 'Macroprudential': Origins and Evolution' (March 2010) *BIS Quarterly Review* 59.

Coase, RH, 'The Problem of Social Cost' (1960) 3 *Journal of Law and Economics* 1.

Coates IV, JC, 'Cost–Benefit Analysis of Financial Regulation: Case Studies and Implications' (2015) 4(124) *Yale Law Journal.*

Coen, D and Thatcher, M, 'The New Governance of Markets and Non-Majoritarian Regulators" (2005) 18(3) *Governance – An International Journal of Policy and Administration* 329.

Cœuré, B, 'The implications of Bail-In Rules for Bank Activity and Stability' (Opening Speech at ECB Conference on 'Financing the recovery after the crisis – the roles of bank profitability, stability and regulation', Milan, 30 September 2013).

Coffee Jnr, JC, 'Market Failure and the Economic Case for a Mandatory Disclosure System' (1984) 70 *Virginia Law Review* 717.

Commission, 'Proposal for a Regulation of the European Parliament and of the Council on Community Macro Prudential Oversight of the Financial System and Establishing a European Systemic Risk Board' COM (2009) 499 final.

Conti-Brown, P, *The Power and Independence of the Federal Reserve* (Princeton University Press, 2016).

Cottrell, R, *Law's Community Legal Theory in Sociological Perspective* (Oxford University Press, 1997) 137.

Crockett, A, 'Marrying the Micro- and Macroprudential Dimensions of Financial Stability' (Remarks before the Eleventh International Conference of Banking Supervisors, Basel, 20–21 September 2000).

Crockett, A, 'International Standard Setting in Financial Supervision' (Lecture at Cass Business School, City University, London, 5 February 2003).

Crouch, C, della Porta, D and Streeck W, 'Democracy in Neoliberalism?' (2016) 16(4) *Anthropological Theory* 497.

Crowe, C and Meade, E, 'Central Bank Independence and Transparency: Evolution and Effectiveness' (May 2008) IMF Working Paper WP/08/119.

Cukierman, A, 'Regulatory Reforms and the Independence of Central Banks and Financial Supervisors' in EG Morten Balling, *States, Banks and the Financing of the Economy: Monetary Policy and Regulatory Regimes* (SUERF, 2013) 121.

Cukierman, A, and Webb SB, Neyapti B, 'The Measurement of Central Bank Independence and Its Effect on Policy Outcomes' (1992) 6 *The World Bank Economic Review* 353.

Cunningham, L, 'A Prescription to Retire the Rhetoric of Principles-Based Systems in Corporate Law, Securities Regulation and Accounting' (2007) 60 *Vanderbilt Law Review* 1411.

Dahger, J, 'Regulatory Cycles: Revisiting the Political Economy of Financial Crises' (15 January 2018) IMF Working Paper WP/18/8.

Dalhuisen JH, *Dalhuisen on Transnational Comparative, Commercial, Financial and Trade Law: Financial Products, Financial Services and Financial Regulation* Vol 3, 6th edn (Hart Publishing, 2016).

Dalhuisen JH, *Dalhuisen on Transnational Comparative, Commercial, Financial and Trade Law: Financial Products, Financial Services and Financial Regulation* Vol 3, 7th edn (Hart Publishing, 2019).

Dalhuisen JH, 'Management of Systemic Risk from a Legal Perspective' in Mads Andenas and Gudula Deipenbrock (eds), *Regulating and Supervising European Financial Markets* (Springer International Publishing, 2016) 365–92.

Danielson, J, 'The Emperor has No Clothes: Limits to Risk Modelling' (2002) 26 *Journal of Banking and Finance* 1252.

Das US and Quintyn M, 'Crisis Prevention and Crisis Management: The Role of Regulatory Governance' in RE Litan, M Pomerleano, and V Sundararajan (eds), *Financial Sector Governance: The Role of the Public and Private Sectors* (Brookings Institution, 2002).

Dassatti, C, Peydro, JL and Rodriguez-Tous, F, 'Macroprudential and Monetary Policy: Loan-Level Evidence from Reserve Requirements' (March 2019) Universitat of Pompeu Fabra Barcelona Working Paper No 1650.

De Larosière Group, *Report of the High-Level Group on Financial Supervision in the EU* (European Commission, 2009).

De Nederlandsche Bank, 'Towards a More Stable Financial System: Macroprudential Supervision at DNB' (7 May 2010).

Debelle, G and Fisher, S, 'How Independent Should a Central Bank Be?' (1994) Working Papers in Applied Economic Theory 94/05.

Diamond, D, 'Financial Intermediation and Delegated Monitoring' (1984) 51(3) *Review of Economic Studies* 393.

Diamond, D and Dybvig, PH, "Bank Runs, Deposit Insurance, and Liquidity" (1983) 93(1) *Journal of Political Economy* 401.

Draghi, M, 'Introductory Statement' (Press Conference, Barcelona, 3 May 2012).

Drehmann, M and Nikolaou, K, 'Funding Liquidity Risk: Definition and Measurement' (12 July 2010) BIS Working Papers No 316.

Duff, AWS, 'Central Bank Independence and Macroprudential Policy: A Critical Look at the U.S. Financial Stability Framework' (2014) 11(1) *Berkeley Business Law Journal* 183.

Dworkin R, *Sovereign Virtue: The Theory and Practice of Equality* (Harvard University Press, 2000).

Easterbrook, F and Fischel, DR, *The Economic Structure of Corporate Law* (Harvard University Press, 1991).

Edge, R and Liang, N, 'New Financial Stability Governance Structures and Central Banks' (10 August 2017) Hutchins Center Working Paper No 32.

Egawa, E, Otani, A and Sakiyama, T, 'What Drives Institutional Arrangements for Macroprudential Policy' (June 2015) Institute of Monetary and Economic Studies, Discussion Paper No 2015-E-3.

Ekins, E, 'Wall Street vs. The Regulators: Public Attitudes on Banks, Financial Regulation, Consumer Finance, and the Federal Reserve' (Cato Institute Survey Reports, Cato Institute 2017).

Ellis L, 'Macroprudential Policy: A Suite of Tools or a State of Mind?' (Speech delivered at Paul Woolley Centre for Capital Market Dysfunctionality Annual Conference, Sydney, 11 October 2012).

European Banking Authority, 'Draft Regulatory Technical Standards on the conditions that competent authorities shall take into account when determining higher risk-weights, in particular the term of "financial stability considerations" under Article 124(4)(b) CRR and the conditions that competent authorities shall take into account when determining higher minimum LGD values under Article 164(6) CRR' (6 July 2015) Consultation Paper EBA/CP/2015/12.

European Central Bank, 'Assessing Financial Stability: Conceptual Boundaries and Challenges' *Financial Stability Review* (June 2005).

European Central Bank, *Financial Stability Review* (December 2009).

European Central Bank, *Virtual Currency Schemes* (October 2012).

European Parliament Special Committee on the Financial, Economic and Social Crisis, *Documentation Relating to the Committee's Work from October 2009 to July 2011* (European Parliament, 2011).

European Systemic Risk Board, 'Allocating Macroprudential Powers' Reports of the Advisory Scientific Committee No 5, (November 2011).

ESRB Instruments Working Group, *The ESRB Handbook on Operationalizing Macroprudential Instruments* (ESRB 2018).

Feintuck M, 'Regulatory Rationales Beyond the Economic: In Search of the Public Interest' in Robert Baldwin, Martin Cave, and Martin Lodge (eds) *The Oxford Handbook of Regulation* (Oxford University Press, 2010) 39–63.

Ferran E, 'The Break-up of the Financial Services Authority' (2011) 31 *Oxford Journal of Legal Studies* 455.

Financial Policy Committee, 'Financial Policy Committee Statement on Housing Market Powers of Direction from Its Policy Meeting, 26 September 2014' (October 2014).

Financial Services Authority, 'Principles-based Regulation Focusing on the Outcomes That Matter' (April 2007).

Financial Services Authority, *The Turner Review: A Regulatory Response to the Global Banking Crisis* (FSA, 2009).

Financial Stability Board, 'Financial Stability Implications from FinTech: Supervisory and Regulatory Issues that Merit Authorities' Attention' (June 2017).

Financial Stability Forum, 'Guidance for Developing Effective Deposit Insurance Systems' (September 2001).

Financial Stability Oversight Council, 'Supplemental Procedures Relating to Nonbank Financial Company Determinations' (February 2015).

Financial Stability Oversight Council, 'Staff Guidance Methodologies Relating to Stage 1 Thresholds' (June 2015).

Fontan, C, Claveau F and Dietsch P, 'Central Banking and Inequalities: Taking off the Blinders' (2016) 15(4) *Politics, Philosophy & Economics* 319.

Ford, C, 'Principles-based Securities Regulation in the Wake of the Global Financial Crisis' (2010) 55(2) *McGill L.aw Journal* 257.

Ford J, *The Indebted Society* (Taylor and Francis 1988), 184.

Fouque, JP and Langham, JA (eds), *Handbook on Systemic Risk* (Cambridge University Press, 2013).

Fox, MB, 'Rethinking Disclosure Liability in the Modern Era' (1997) 75 *Washington University Law Quarterly* 903.

Franck, T, *The Power of Legitimacy Among Nations* (Oxford University Press, 1990).

Freixas, X, Parigi, BM and Rochet, J, 'Systemic Risk, Interbank Relations and Liquidity Provision by the Central Bank' (2000) 32(3) *Journal of Money, Credit & Banking* 611.

Freixas, X and Rochet, J, *Microeconomics of Banking* 2nd edn (MIT Press, 2008).

Freixas, X, Laeven, L and Peydró J, *Systemic Risk, Crises, and Macroprudential Regulation* (MIT Press, 2015).

Friedman, M, *Dollars and Deficits* (Prentice-Hall 1968), reprinted from Leland B Yeager (ed), *In Search of a Monetary Constitution* (Harvard University Press, 1962).

Frost J and van R Stralen, 'Macroprudential Policy and Income Inequality' (May 2018) DNB Working Paper No 598.

FSB-IMF-BIS, 'Macroprudential Policy Tools and Frameworks: Progress Report to G20' (27 October 2011).

Gadinis S, 'From Independence to Politics in Financial Regulation' (2013) 101 *California Law Review* 327.

Galati, G and Moessner, R, 'Macroprudential Policy – A Literature Review' (February 2011) Bank for International Settlements Working Papers No 337 13.

Gleeson S, *Gleeson on the International Regulation of Banking* 2nd edn (Oxford University Press, 2012).

Godwin, A, Kourabas S and Ramsay I 'Financial Stability Authorities and Macroprudential Regulation' (2017) 32 *Banking & Finance Law Review* 223.

Goetzmann, WN, Shiller, RJ, Mendillo, J, Swensen, DF and Chen Z, 'What Should Finance Do for Society?' (January 2014) *Yale Insights*.

Goldby, M and Keller, A, "The Commission's Proposal for a New Systemic Risk Board: An Evaluation" (2010) 4(1) *Law and Financial Markets Review* 48.

Goodhart CAE, 'Central Bank Independence' In: *The Central Bank and the Financial System*. (Palgrave Macmillan, London, 1991).

Goodhart CAE, 'Regulating the Regulators – A Lawyer's Perspective on Accountability and Control' Ellis Ferran and Charles AE Goodhart (eds) in *Regulating Financial Services and Markets in the 21st Century* (Hart Publishing, 2001) 127–50.

Goodhart CAE, *Financial Development and Economic Growth: Explaining the Links* (Palgrave, Macmillan 2004).

Goodhart CAE, 'A Framework for Assessing Financial Stability?' (2006) 30 *Journal of Banking and Finance* 3415.
Goodhart CAE, 'The Macro-Prudential Authority: Powers, Scope and Accountability' (2011) 2 *OECD Journal: Financial Market Trends* 5.
Goodhart CAE, 'The Changing Fortunes of Central Banking' Lecture delivered at Queen Mary, University of London LLM Seminar in Regulation of Financial Markets, 23 November 2016.
Goodhart CAE, and Hartmann P, Llewellyn DT, Rojas-Suarez L, Weisbrod S, *Financial Regulation: Why, How and Where Now?* (Routledge 1998).
Goodhart, CAE and Lastra RM, 'Populism and Central Bank Independence' (2018) 29(1) *Open Economies Review* 49.
Goodhart, CAE and Perotti, E, 'Preventive Macroprudential Policy' (2013) 1(1) *Journal of Financial Management, Markets and Institutions* 115.
Goodhart LM, 'Brave New World? Macro-prudential Policy and The New Political Economy of The Federal Reserve' (2015) 22(2) *Review of International Political Economy* 280.
Gordon, JN and Kornhauser, LA, 'Efficient Markets, Costly Information and Securities Research' (1985) 60 *New York University Law Review* 761.
Group of Ten, Report on Consolidation in the Financial Sector (BIS-IMF-OECD 2001).
Group of Twenty 'The Global Plan for Recovery and Reform' Final communiqué of meeting of G20 Leaders in London, 2 April (2009).
Group of Thirty (G30), *The Structure of Financial Regulation: Approaches and Challenges in a Global Market Place* (2008).
Haan de, J and & Kooi W, 'What Really Matters: Conservativeness or Independence?' (1997) 50 *Banca Nazionale del Lavoro Quarterly Review 23.*
Habermas, J, *Communication and the Evolution of Society* (Thomas McCarthy trs Beacon Press, 1979).
Habermas, J, 'Life Forms, Morality and the Task of the Philosopher' in Peter Dews (ed), *Autonomy and Solidarity: Interviews with Jurgen Habermas* (Verso, 1986) 187.
Haldane, AG, 'Macroprudential Policies: When and How to Use Them?' (Re-Thinking Macro Policy II: First Steps and Early Lessons Conference Washington DC, April 2013).
Haldane, AG, Saporta, V, Hall, SG and Tanaka, M, 'Financial Stability and Macroeconomic Models' (2004) 16 *Bank of England Financial Stability Review* 106–16.
Hanson SG, Kashyap AK, and Stein JC, 'A Macroprudential Approach to Financial Regulation' (2011) 25(1) *Journal of Economic Perspectives* 3.
Hardy, DC and Hochreiter, P, 'A Simple Macroprudential Liquidity Buffer' (2014) IMF Working Paper WP/14/235.
Hart, HLA, *The Concept of Law* 3rd edn (Oxford University Press, 2012).
Hausman, A and Johnston, WJ, 'Timeline of a Financial Crisis: Introduction to the Special Issue' (2014) 67 *Journal of Business Research* 2667.
Haynes R, McPhail L, Zhu H, Assessing the Impact of the Basel III Leverage Ratio on the Competitive Landscape of US Derivatives Markets: Evidence from Options' (June 2018) CFTC Policy Brief.
Hellwig, M, 'Capital Regulation after the Crisis: Business as Usual?' (2010) 2010/31 Preprints of the Max Planck Institute for Research on Collective Goods Bonn.
HM Treasury, *A New Approach to Financial Regulation: The Blueprint for Reform* (Cm 8083, 2011).
HM Treasury *Review of the Monetary Policy Framework*, (Cm 8588, 2012).
HM Treasury *Memorandum of Understanding on Resolution Planning and Financial Crisis Management* (2017).
HM Treasury, *The Green Book: Central Government Guidance on Appraisal and Evaluation* (2018).
Hoerova, M, Mendicino, C, Nikolov, K, Schepens G, Van den Heuvel, S, 'Benefits and Costs of Liquidity Regulation' ECB Working Paper Series No 2169 (July 2018).
Horton, M and El-Ganainy A, 'Fiscal Policy: Taking and Giving Away' *Finance & Development* (29 July 2017).
House of Commons Treasury Committee Inquiry into the Banking Crisis.

House of Representatives Committee on Banking, Finance and Urban Affairs, 'Inquiry into The Continental Illinois Corp. and Continental Illinois National Bank' (Hearings Before the Subcommittee on Financial Institutions Supervisors, Regulation and Insurance, Serial 98-111, 1984).

House of Representatives Committee on Oversight and Government Reform, 'The Financial Crisis and The Role of Federal Regulator' (Serial No. 110–209, 23 October 2008).

House of Representatives Committee on Financial Services, 'Oversight of The Financial Stability Oversight Council' (Serial 114-65, 8 December 2015).

Igan, D, Mirzaei, A and Moore, T, 'Does Macroprudential Policy Alleviate the Adverse Impact of COVID-19 on the Resilience of Banks?' (2023) 147 *Journal of Banking and Finance* 1–16.

IMF-BIS-FSB, 'Guidance to Assess the Systemic Importance of Financial Institutions, Markets and Instruments: Initial Considerations' Report to the G-20 Finance Ministers and Central Bank Governors (October 2009).

IMF-FSB-BIS, 'Elements of Effective Macroprudential Policies Lessons from International Experience' (31 August 2016).

Ingves, S, '"It takes all sorts …" – Macroprudential Oversight in the EU' (Keynote address First ESRB Annual Conference 22–23 September 2016).

International Monetary Fund 'Macroprudential Policy: An Organising Framework' IMF Policy Papers (March 2011).

International Monetary Fund, 'Key Aspects of Macroprudential Policy' IMF Policy Papers (June 2013).

International Monetary Fund, 'Implementing Macroprudential Policy – Selected Legal Issues' *IMF Policy Papers* (June 2013).

International Monetary Fund, 'The Role of The Fund in Governance Issues – Review of the Guidance Note – Preliminary Considerations – Background Notes' IMF Policy Papers (August 2017).

International Monetary Fund, 'Implementing Macroprudential Policy – Selected Legal Issues' IMF Board Paper (June 2013).

International Monetary Fund, 'Macroprudential Policy Survey' (April 2018).

Israel, J, Sandars, P, Schubert, A and Fischer, B, 'Statistics and Indicators for Financial Stability Analysis and Policy' ECB Occasional Policy Paper No 145 (April 2013).

Issing, O, 'Monetary and Financial Stability: Is There a Trade-Off?' (Paper Delivered to Conference on 'Monetary Stability, Financial Stability and the Business Cycle', Basel, 28–29 March 2003).

Joint Committee on the Draft Financial Services Bill, *Draft Financial Services Bill* (2010–12, HL 236, HC 1447).

Jorda, O, Schularick, M and Taylor, AM, 'Financial Crises, Credit Booms and External Imbalances: 140 Years of Lessons' (2011) 59(2) *IMF Economic Review* 340.

Jorda, O, Schularick, M and Taylor, AM, 'When Credit Bites Back: Leverage, Business Cycles, And Crises' (2013) 45(2) *Journal of Money, Credit and Banking* 3.

Jorda, O, Schularick, M and Taylor, AM, 'Leveraged Bubbles' (August 2015) Federal Reserve Bank of San Francisco Working Paper Series Working Paper 2015-10.

Jorda, O, Schularick, M and Taylor, AM, 'Macrofinancial History and the New Business Cycle Facts' in M Eichenbaum and JA Parker (eds), *NBER Macroeconomics Annual 2016* Vol 31 (NBER, 2017) 213.

Joyce, M, Miles, D, Scott A and Vayanos, D, 'Quantitative Easing and Unconventional Monetary Policy – An Introduction' (2012) 122(564) *The Economic Journal* 271.

Kahan, M, 'Securities Law and the Social Costs of "Inaccurate" Stock Prices' (1992) 41 *Duke Law Journal* 977.

Kaplow, L, 'Rules Versus Standards: An Economic Analysis' (1992) 42 *Duke Law Journal* 557.

Kashyap AK, 'My Reflections on the FPC's Strategy' (Speech given at the 50th Anniversary of the Journal of Money, Credit and Banking, Frankfurt, 28 March 2019).

Kashyap AK, Berner, R and Goodhart, CAE, 'The Macroprudential Toolkit' (2011) 59(2) *IMF Economic Review* 145.

Kastner, L, *Civil Society and Financial Regulation* (Routledge, 2017).

Kaufmann D, Kraay A, and Zoido-Lobaton P, 'Governance Matters' (October 1999) World Bank, Policy Research Working Paper, No 2196.

Keller A, 'Independence, Accountability and Transparency: Are Conventional Mechanisms Suitable for the European Systemic Risk Board?' (2017) 5 *International Company and Commercial Law Review* 176.
Kelman, M, 'Legal Economists and Normative Social Theory', in Avery Wiener Katz (ed), *Foundations of the Economic Approach to Law* (Oxford University Press, 1998).
Khan, A, 'Central Bank Legal Frameworks in the Aftermath of the Global Financial Crisis' (2017) IMF Working Paper WP/17/101.
Khan, A, Khan, H and Dewan, H, 'Central Bank Autonomy, Legal Institutions and Banking Crisis Incidence' (2013 18(1) *International Journal of Finance and Economics* 51.
Kindleberger, C and Aliber, R, *Manias, Panics and Crashes: A History of Financial Crises* 6th edn (Palgrave McMillan, 2011).
King, M, 'Changes in UK Monetary Policy: Rules and Discretion in Practice' (1997) 39 *Journal of Monetary Economics* 81.
King, RG and Levine, R, 'Finance, Entrepreneurship, and Growth' (1993) 32 *Journal of Monetary Economics* 513.
Klomp, J and de Haan, J, 'Central Bank Independence and Financial Instability' (2005) 5 *Journal of Financial Stability* 321.
Knight, MD, 'Marrying the Micro- and Macroprudential Dimensions of Financial Stability: Six Years On' (Address at the 14th International Conference of Banking Supervisors, Mérida, 4–5 October 2006).
Knot, K, 'Governance of Macroprudential Policy' (2014) 18 *Banque de France Financial Stability Review* 25.
Kohn, D, 'Institutions for Macroprudential Regulation: The UK and the U.S.' (April 2014) Brookings Institute.
Kohn, D, 'Macroprudential Policy: Implementation and Effectiveness' (Speech, Frankfurt, 27 April 2016).
Korniyenko, Y and Loukoianova, E, 'The Impact of Unconventional Monetary Policy Measures by the Systemic Four on Global Liquidity and Monetary Conditions' (2015) IMF Working Paper WP/15/287, 7.
Kriesi, H, 'Democratic Legitimacy: Is There a Legitimacy Crisis in Contemporary Politics?' (2013) 54(4) *Politische Vierteljahresschrift* 609.
Krugman, P, 'How Did Economists Get It So Wrong?' *New York Times* (6 September 2009).
Kydland, FE and Prescott, EC, 'Rules Rather than Discretion: The Inconsistency of Optimal Plans' (1977) 85 *Journal of Political Economy* 473.
Lamfalussy, A, (1979) 'The Use of Prudential Measures in the International Banking Markets' (24 October 1979) BISA 7.18(15) – Papers Lamfalussy, LAM25/F67.
Landau, JP, 'A Liquidity-Based Approach to Macroprudential Policy' (September 2016) BIS Papers No 86.
Langley, P, 'Toxic Assets, Turbulence and Biopolitical Security: Governing the Crisis of Global Financial Circulation' (2013) 44 (2) *Security Dialogue* 111.
Lastra, RM, 'The Independence of the European System of Central Banks' (1992) 33(2) *Harvard International Law Journal* 475.
Lastra, RM, *Central Banking and Bank Regulation* (LSE Financial Markets Group, 1996).
Lastra, RM, 'The Governance Structure for Financial Regulation and Supervision in Europe' (2003) 10 *Columbia Journal of European Law* 50.
Lastra, RM, *International Financial Law* (Oxford University Press, 2015).
Lastra, RM, 'Systemic Risk and Macro-prudential Supervision' in N Moloney, E Ferran, and J Payne (eds), Oxford Handbook of Financial Regulation (Oxford University Press, 2015).
Lastra, RM, and Miller G, 'Central Bank Independence in Ordinary and Extraordinary Times' in Jan Kleineman (ed), *Central Bank Independence. The Economic Foundations, the Constitutional Implications and Democratic Accountability* (Kluwer Law International 2001) 31–50.
Lee, M, Gaspar, R and Villaruel, ML, 'Macroprudential Policy Frameworks in Developing Asian Economies' (March 2017) ADB Economics Working Paper No 510.

Leff, AA, 'Economic Analysis of Law: Some Realism About Nominalism' in Avery Wiener Katz (ed), *Foundations of the Economic Approach to Law* (Oxford University Press, 1998).
Levine, R, 'The Governance of Financial Regulation: Reform Lessons from the Recent Crisis' (2012) 12(1) *International Review of Finance* 39.
Lim, CH, Columba, F, Costa, A, Kongsamut, P, Otani, A, Saiyid, M, Wezel, T and Wu X 'Macroprudential Policy: What Instruments and How to Use Them? Lessons from Country Experiences' (2011) IMF Working Paper 11/238.
Lim, CH, Krznar, I, Lipinsky, F, Otani, A and Wu, X 'The Macroprudential Framework; Policy Responsiveness, and Institutional Arrangements' (2013) IMF Working Papers 13/166.
Lindgren CJ and Folkerts-Landau D, *Toward a Framework for a Sound Financial System* (International Monetary Fund 1998).
Lipset, SM, 'Some Social Requisites of Democracy: Economic Development and Political Legitimacy' (1959) 53(1) *The American Political Science Review* 69.
Lleywellyn, DT, 'Institutional Structure of Financial Regulation and Supervision: The Basic Issues' (Aligning Supervisory Structures with Country Needs Seminar Washington DC, June 2006).
Lombardia, D and Moschellaa, M, 'The Symbolic Politics of Delegation: Macroprudential Policy and Independent Regulatory Authorities' (2017) 22(1) *New Political Economy* 92–108.
Luhmann, N, *Risk: A Sociological Theory* (Walter de Gruyter, 1993).
Maggetti, M, 'Legitimacy and Accountability of Independent Regulatory Agencies: A Critical Review' (2010) 2 *Living Reviews in Democracy* 1.
Maguze, TC, 'EU Bank Recapitalisation and the Bail-in Option: An Analysis of the Effects of Mandatory Bail-in on Creditors' Property Rights' (2016) 5(2) *UCL Journal of Law and Jurisprudence* 1.
Majone G, 'Independence v Accountability: European Non-Majoritarian Institutions and Democratic Government in Europe' (1994) EUI Working Papers (SPS) 1993/09.
Majone G (ed.), *Regulating Europe*, (Routledge, 1996).
Mallaby, S, *The Man Who Knew: The Life and Times of Alan Greenspan* (Bloomsbury Publishing, 2015).
Masciandero, D and Tabellini,GE, 'Monetary Regimes and Fiscal Deficits: A Comparative Analysis' in Hang-Sheng Cheng, *Monetary Policy in Pacific Basin Countries* (Kluwer Academic Publishers 1988).
Masciandaro, D and Volpicella, A 'Macro Prudential Governance and Central Banks: Facts and Drivers' (2016) 61 *Journal of International Money and Finance* 101.
Mathai, K, 'Monetary Policy: Stabilizing Prices and Output' *Finance & Development* (29 July 2017).
Weber, M, *Economy and Society: An Outline of Interpretive Sociology* (University of California Press, 1979).
Melsheimer RE and Laurence W, *The Law and Customs of the London Stock Exchange: With an Appendix Containing the Rules and Regulations Authorised by the Committee for the Conduct of Business* (Henry Sweet 1879).
Meltzer, AH, 'Financial Failures and Financial Policies' in G C Kaufman and R C Kormendi (eds), *Deregulation of Financial Services: Public Policy in Flux* (Ballinger, 1986).
Memorandum of Understanding Between the Minister of Finance and the Governor of the Reserve Bank of New Zealand, 13 May 2013.
Merrouche, O and Nier, E (2010) 'What Caused the Global Financial Crisis: Evidence on the Drivers of Financial Imbalances 1999–2007' (2010) IMF Working Paper WP/10/265.
Mill, JS, *Considerations on Representative Government* (first published 1861, Prometheus Books 1991).
Miller, D, *Principles of Social Justice* (Harvard University Press, 2001).
Minsky, HP, 'The Financial Instability Hypothesis' (May 1992) Levy Economics Institute Working Paper No 74.
Minsky HP, *Stabilizing an Unstable Economy* (Yale University Press, 1986).
Mishkin, FS, 'Anatomy of Financial Crisis' (1991) NBER Working Paper No 3934.
Mishkin, FS, *The Economics of Money, Banking and Financial Markets* 7th edn (Pearson, 2004).
Modigliani F and Miller MH, 'The Cost of Capital, Corporation Finance and the Theory of Investment' (1958) 48(3) *American Economic Review* 261.
Moe, TM, 'Interests, Institutions, and Positive Theory: The Politics of NLBR' (1987) 2 *Studies in American Political Development* 236.

Moravcsik, A, 'Reassessing Legitimacy in the European Union' (2002) 40(4) *Journal of Common Market Studies* 603.

Nier, EW, 'Financial Stability Frameworks and the Role of Central Banks: Lessons from the Crisis' (2009) IMF Working Paper 09/70.

Nier, EW, 'On the Governance of Macroprudential Policies' in Stijn Classens (ed) *Macroprudential Regulatory Policies: The New Road to Financial Stability?* (World Scientific Publishing, 2012) 183.

Nier, EW, Osiński, J, Jácome, LI and Madrid P 'Institutional Models for Macroprudential Policy' (November 2011) IMF Staff Discussion Note SDN/11/18.

Nozick, R, *Anarchy, State and Utopia* (Basic Books, 1974).

Office of Financial Research, 'Financial Stability Assessment' Financial Stability Report (2016) 7.

Omarova, S, 'Bankers, Bureaucrats, and Guardians: Toward Tripartism in Financial Services Regulation' (2012) *Cornell Law Faculty Publications Paper 1010.*

Organisation for Economic Co-operation and Development, *Reducing the Risk of Policy Failure: Challenges for Regulatory Compliance* (OECD, 2000).

Organisation for Economic Co-operation and Development, *Risk and Regulatory Policy: Improving the Governance of Risk* (OECD 2010).

Osiński, J, Seal, K and Hoogduin, L, 'Macroprudential and Microprudential Policies: Toward Cohabitation' (June 2013) IMF Staff Discussion Note SDN 13/05.

Padoa-Schioppa, T, 'Central Banks and Financial Stability: Exploring a Land in Between' (Paper Delivered at the Second ECB Central Banking Conference 'The Transformation of the European Financial System', Frankfurt, October 2002).

Passmore, W and Hafften von, AH, 'Are Basel's Capital Surcharges for Global Systemically Important Banks Too Small?' (2019) 15(1) *International Journal of Central Banking* 107.

Persaud, A, 'The Locus of Financial Regulation: Home Versus Host' (2010) 86(3) *International Affairs* 637.

Pigou, AC, *The Economics of Welfare* 4th edn (Macmillan, 1932).

Poghosyan, T, 'How Effective is Macroprudential Policy? Evidence from Lending Restriction Measures in EU Countries' (2019) IMF Working Paper WP/19/45.

Powell J, 'Financial Stability and Central Bank Transparency' Speech at '350 years of central banking: the Past, The Present and The Future', Sveriges Riksbank Anniversary Conference, Stockholm, 25 May 2018.

Power, M, 'The Invention of Operational Risk' (June 2003) ESRC Centre for Analysis of Risk and Regulation Discussion Paper No 16.

Prates, MM, 'Why Prudential Regulation Will Fail to Prevent Financial Crises. A Legal Approach' (November 2013) Banco Central do Brasil Working Paper 335.

Prudential Regulation Authority, 'Q&A on the use of Liquidity and Capital Buffers' 20 April 2020 (updated 6 July 2020).

Prudential Regulation Authority, 'Covid-19: IFRS 9, Capital Requirements and Loan Covenants' (March 2020).

Quintyn, M and Taylor, MW, 'Regulatory and Supervisory Independence and Financial Stability' (2002) IMF Working Paper WP02/46.

Rajan RG, 'The Credit Crisis and Cycle-Proof Regulation' (2009) 91(September) *Federal Reserve Bank of St. Louis Review* 397.

Rajan, RG, *Fault Lines* (Princeton University Press, 2010).

Ramsay I, 'Consumer Credit Law, Distributive Justice and the Welfare State' 1995 (15)2 *Oxford Journal of Legal Studies* 177.

Rawls, J, *A Theory of Justice* (Harvard University Press, 1971).

Rawls, J, *Justice as Fairness: A Restatement* (Harvard University Press, 2001).

Raz, J, *The Authority of Law: Essays on Law and Morality* 2nd edn (Oxford University Press, 2009).

Reinhart, C and Rogoff, K, *This Time Is Different: Eight Century of Financial Folly* (Princeton University Press, 2009).

Rogoff, KS, "The Optimal Degree of Commitment to an Intermediate" (1985) 100 *Quarterly Journal of Economics* 1169.

Rossi J, 'Participation Run Amok: The Costs of Mass Participation for Deliberative Agency Decision-making' (1997) 92 *Northwestern University Law Review* 173.

Roth, F, 'The Effects of the Financial Crisis on Systemic Trust' CEPS Working Document No 316 (July 2009).

Rousseau JJ, *The Social Contract* (first published 1762, Penguin 1968).

Saad-Filho, A and Johnston, D (eds), *Neoliberalism: A Critical Reader* (Pluto Press, 2005).

Scalia, A, 'The Rule of Law as a Law of Rules' (1989) 56 *University of Chicago Law Review* 1175.

Scharpf, F, *Governing in Europe: Effective and Democratic?* (Oxford University Press, 1999).

Schauer, F, 'The Tyranny of Choice and the Rulification of Standards' (2005) 14 *Journal of Contemporary Legal Issues* 803.

Schinasi, GJ, 'Defining Financial Stability' (October 2004) IMF Working Paper WP/04/187.

Schinasi, GJ, 'Responsibility of Central Banks for Stability in Financial Markets' (2003) IMF Working Paper WP/03/121.

Schinasi, GJ, *Safeguarding Financial Stability: Theory and Practice* (International Monetary Fund, 2006).

Schlag, P, 'Rules and Standards' (1985) 33 *UCLA Law Review* 379.

Schmidt, VA, 'Democracy and Legitimacy in the European Union Revisited: Input, Output and 'Throughput'' (2013) 61(1) *Political Studies* 2.

Schoenmaker D and Wierts P, 'Macroprudential Policy: The Need for a Coherent Policy Framework' *Duisenburg School of Finance Policy Paper No 13* (July 2011).

Schoenmaker, D, *Contagion Risk in Banking* (LSE Financial Markets Group, 1996).

Schooner, HM and Taylor, MW, *Global Bank Regulation: Principles and Policies* (Elsevier, 2010).

Schularick M and Taylor AM, 'Credit Booms Gone Bust: Monetary Policy, Leverage Cycles, And Financial Crises' (2012) 102(2) *American Economic Review* 102.

Schwarcz, SL, 'Systemic Risk', (2008–2009) 97 *Georgetown Law Journal* 193.

Schwarcz, SL, 'The "Principles" Paradox' (2009) 10 *European Business Organization Law Review* 175.

Schwarcz, SL, 'Systematic Regulation of Systemic Risk' (2019) 1 *Wisconsin Law Review* 1.

Schwartz, AJ, 'Real and Pseudo Financial Crises' in Forest Capie & Geoffrey Wood (eds), *Financial Crises and the World Banking System* (Macmillan, 1986).

Scott E, *Capital Adequacy Beyond Basel* (Oxford University Press, 2005).

Scott, HS, *Connectedness and Contagion: Protecting the Financial System from Panics* (MIT Press, 2016).

Seabrooke, L, 'What Do I Get? The Everyday Politics of Expectations and the Subprime Crisis' (2010) 15(1) *New Political Economy* 51.

Shapiro, S, 'Authority' in Jules L. Coleman et al (eds), *The Oxford Handbook of Jurisprudence and Philosophy of Law* (Oxford University Press, 2004) 391.

Shiller R, *The New Financial Order. Risk in the 21st Century* (Princeton University Press, 2003).

Shiller R, *Finance and the Good Society* (Princeton University Press, 2012).

Smith, JA, Grill, M and Lang, JH 'The Leverage Ratio, Risk-Taking and Bank Stability' ECB Working Paper Series No 2079 (June 2017).

Smith RC and Walter I, *Governing the Modern Corporation* (Oxford University Press, 2006).

Soros G, 'The Worst Market Crisis In 60 Years' *Financial Times* (23 January 2008).

Springer, S, Birch, K and MacLeavy J, *Handbook of Neoliberalism* (Routledge, 2016).

Stapelbroek, K, 'The Idea of Democracy and the Eighteenth Century' in Victor Bekker et al (eds), *Governance and Democratic Deficit: Assessing the Democratic Legitimacy of Governance Practices* (Ashgate Publishing, 2007) 61–79.

Suchman, MC, 'Managing Legitimacy: Strategic and Institutional Approaches' (1995) 20(3) *Academy of Management Review* 571.

Sullivan, KM, 'The Justices of Rules and Standards: Foreword, The Supreme Court, 1991 Term' (1992) 106 *Harvard Law Review* 22.

Sunstein, CR, 'Problems with Rules' (1995) 83 *California Law Review* 953.

Tarullo D, *Banking on Basel* (Patersen Institute, 2008).

Taylor JB, 'Discretion versus Policy Rules in Practice' (1991) 39 *Carnegie Rochester Conference Series on Public Policy* 195.

Taylor MW, Quintyn, MG and Ramirez S, 'The Fear of Freedom: Politicians and the Independence and Accountability of Financial Sector Supervisors' (February 2007) IMF Working Paper WP 07/05.

Thatcher M and Sweet AS, 'Theory and Practice of Delegation to Non- Majoritarian Institutions' (2002) 25(1) *Western European Politics* 1, 2.

Thirkell-White, B, 'Dealing with The Banks: Populism and The Public Interest in the Global Financial Crisis' (2009) 85(4) *International Affairs* 689.

Thornton, H, *An Enquiry into the Nature and Effects of the Paper Credit of Great Britain 1802.*

Thorsen, DE and Lie, A, 'What is Neo-Liberalism' (2006) Department of Political Science University of Oslo.

United Kingdom Treasury Committee, *Banking Crisis:* Regulation and Supervision (HC 2007-08, 144–I).

United Kingdom Treasury Committee, *Banking Crisis: Regulation and Supervision* (HC 2008-09, 767).

Tripartite Group of Bank, Securities and Insurance Regulators, 'Supervision of Financial Conglomerates' (July 1995).

Tucker, P, 'The Debate on Financial System Resilience: Macroprudential Instruments' (Speech at Barclays Annual Lecture, London, 22 October 2009).

Tucker, P, *Unelected Power: The Quest for Legitimacy in Central Banking and the Regulatory State* (Princeton University Press, 2018).

Tyler TR, 'The Psychology of Legitimacy: A Relational Perspective on Voluntary Deference to Authorities' (1997) 1 *Personality and Social Psychology Review* 323.

Tyler, TR, *Why People Obey the Law: Procedural Justice, Legitimacy and Compliance* (Yale University Press, 1990).

Ueda K and Valencia F, 'Central Bank Independence and Macro-Prudential Regulation' (April 2012) IMF Working Paper, IMF WP/12/101.

United States Financial Crisis Inquiry Commission, *The Financial Crisis Inquiry Report* (US Government Printing Office, 2011).

Valentini, L, 'Justice and Democracy' (November 2010) CSSJ Working Paper SJ012.

Van den End, JW and Kruidhof, M, 'Modelling the Liquidity Ratio as Macroprudential Instrument' (2012) DNB Working Paper 342.

Waldron, J, 'Legislation, Authority and Voting' (1996) 84 *Georgetown Law Journal* 2185.

Wallach, PA, *To the Edge: Legality, Legitimacy, and the Responses to the 2008 Financial Crisis* (Brookings Institution Press, 2015).

Watson, M, 'Headlong in the Polanyian Dilemma: The Impact of Middle-Class Moral Panic on the British Government's Response to the Sub-prime Crisis' (2009) 11(3) *The British Journal of Politics and International Relations* 422.

Wellman C, 'Liberalism, Samaritanism, and Political Legitimacy' (1996) 25(3) *Philosophy and Public Affairs* 211.

Wolf M, 'Basel III: The Mouse that Did Not Roar' *The Financial Times* (14 September 2010).

Wolff, RP, 'The Conflict Between Authority and Autonomy', in Joseph Raz (ed), *Authority* (New York University Press, 1990) 20.

Wong, E, Fong, T, Ka-fai L, and Choi H, 'Loan-To-Value Ratio as a Macroprudential Tool: Hong Kong's Experience and Cross-Country Evidence' (2011) Hong Kong Monetary Authority Working Paper 01/2011.

Woodford, M, *Interest and Prices: Foundations of a Theory of Monetary Policy* (Princeton University Press, 2013).

World Economic Forum, 'The Role of Financial Services in Society: A Multistakeholder Compact' (August 2013).

Wurgler, J, 'Financial Markets and the Allocation of Capital' (2000) 58 *Journal of Financial Economics* 187.

Yellen, JL, 'A Painfully Slow Recovery for America's Workers: Causes, Implications, and the Federal Reserve's Response' (Address at the 'A Trans-Atlantic Agenda for Shared Prosperity' Conference, Washington, DC, 11 February 2013).

Yellen JL, 'Perspectives on Inequality and Opportunity from the Survey of Consumer Finances' (Speech at the Conference on Economic Opportunity and Inequality, Boston, 17 October 2014).

Zhou C, 'Why the Micro-Prudential Regulation Fails? The Impact on Systemic Risk by Imposing a Capital Requirement' DNB Working Paper No 256 (July 2010).

Zhou, J, Rutledge, V, Bossu, W, Dobler M, Jassaud, N and Moore, M, 'From Bail-out to Bail-in: Mandatory Debt Restructuring of Systemic Financial Institutions' (2012) IMF Staff Discussion Note SDN/12/03.

Zilioli, C, 'Accountability and Independence: Irreconcilable Values or Complementary Instruments for Democracy? The Specific Case of the European Central Bank' in Georges Vandersandern (ed) *Melanges en homage a Jean-Victor Louis* Vol 2 (ULB 2003) 400.

Zucker, LG, 'Institutional Theory of Organizations' (1987) 13 *Annual Review of Sociology* 443.

INDEX

www.ingramcontent.com/pod-product-compliance
Ingram Content Group UK Ltd.
Pitfield, Milton Keynes, MK11 3LW, UK
UKHW020801290926
15470UKWH00003B/888

9 781509 968398